MSBuild Trickery

99 Ways to Bend the Build Engine to Your Will

Brian Kretzler

PUBLISHED BY
K CROSS SEVEN RANCH COMPANY
Kerrville, TX

Copyright © 2011 by Brian Kretzler

All rights reserved. No part of the contents of this book may be reproduced or transmitted in any form or by any means without the hand-written permission of the author. Copyright infringement is a crime.

Library of Congress Control Number: 2011911627

ISBN-13   978-0-615-50907-5
ISBN-10   0-615-50907-X

Printed and bound in the United States of America.

This book was published using the print and other services for making published works available on various Internet hosted commercial book merchants. These companies are in no way responsible for any of the content of the book. How could they be, they've never even read it.

Microsoft, Constantia, Candera, Gabriola, Lucida Sans, Segoe, Visual C#, Visual C++, Visual Studio, Win32, Windows are either registered trademarks or trademarks of Microsoft Corporation in the United States and/or other countries. Other product and company names mentioned in this book may be the trademarks of their owners.

Any content in this book was intended to be fictitious and no association with any real entity is intended, and none should be inferred.

This book expresses the author's views and opinions. The information presented in this book is provided without any express, statutory or implied warranties. No person or organization connected to this book will be held liable for any damages caused or alleged to be caused either directly or indirectly by any of the content contained herein. Use at your own risk. If you break the build, you can't blame anyone but yourself.

Editor: Amy Blew
Photographs: Trisha Kretzler, Cody Kretzler, Ty Kretzler
Technical Review: Dan Moseley and Cullen Waters

The cover and title page photographs are of the first days of the metal raising for our barn in the Texas Hill Country. The main center beam was lifted by what may have been the world's largest sawhorse, seen on the left of the title page photo and affectionately known as "the trebuchet" which is now a part of my sons' fort.

Along the way

On ordering a hamburger:
Waitress: "Do you want cheese with that?"
Ty: "No, just the ham."

On opening birthday presents:
"Duct tape. Yessss!"
Cody

On, well...anything:
"Really?"
Mitch

On pronunciation:
"The speficic security occifer was mad at his emeny because he lost the certicafate for the cimmanon roll tourmanent"
Vanessa

On Parenting:
"Tag, you're it."
Trisha

On parenting:
"Keep it up and I'll take away your duct tape."
Brian

On California:
"If I had to drive on the L.A. freeway every day I'd put a bullet in my skull."
Amy

On arriving after a long journey:
"Who wants a BLT?"
Mom

On patience:
"..."
Dad

On good police work:
"I'm playing with matches and gasoline...so if you see or hear a boom it's just me."
The Jono

On life:
"I wiped a booger on your back while you weren't looking"
Uncle Matt

i

Table of Contents

Foreword

When four of us sat together in a room to write MSBuild 4.0, someone wrote this on the wall:

"Coding, the boring bit between builds"

It may not really be true, but certainly, build doesn't get the respect it deserves. If you create or maintain a build process, you're making developers lives easier and faster, but you probably don't get much credit.

From the start, MSBuild was developed while converting real build processes—the work that happens when you hit "Build" inside Visual Studio—and the huge build of Visual Studio itself. Finding something difficult or messy to express, we tried to improve MSBuild to make it easier. Hitting a crash or hang overnight in the Developer Division "build lab" was strong motivation to make it as robust and reliable as we could.

Our goal was to get Visual Studio out of the business of running the build, so it could be easily customized, and work just the same with or without Visual Studio installed. We did that. We based the syntax on XML, believing that great tools would quickly appear so that nobody would have to type it. They haven't appeared yet. Sorry about that. Meanwhile this book will help you get the job done.

I originally worked on MSBuild as a tester. I tapped away in Notepad. I did sensible things, and I did insane things. When I crashed it, I banged on the wall to annoy the developer. Later, I was that developer. I probably know more about MSBuild than anyone, but I learnt a lot from this ingenious book.

Dan Moseley
Senior Development Lead, Visual Studio Project & Build

Preface

Your Background

I'd hope that you are interested in large project design, but it doesn't really matter if you prefer C# or C++. It would be helpful if you had some familiarity with a prior version of MSBuild, if only to the extent of having deciphered C# project files in their native XML format, but that is not a requirement, as you'll be led through the experience step-by-step.

My Background

A couple years ago[1], frustrated with the malbehavior of Visual Studio solution files and their inability to help build the several hundred C++ projects that made up the product I was working on, I created from scratch a C# command line application that drove our build. It did everything, including generating VS solution files so that we didn't have to maintain them. Five years later, at a new company and starting a new project, I made a decision to try as hard as I could to make MSBuild work. This project was a mix of C#, C++/CLI and native C++ projects, which introduced a fair amount of complexity to the build.

It turns out that MSBuild was up to the task, but only after putting in a huge investment in learning MSBuild. After a conversation with some of the guys on the MSBuild team at Microsoft, I was enlisted as the Technical Reviewer for the one-and-only other MSBuild book currently on the market, from Microsoft Press.

On a subsequent trip to Redmond, again talking to the MSBuild team, it became evident that some of the tricks I had worked out—all in an effort to make our complex build easier to maintain—were novel enough that they asked me to provide them as test cases. Some of the tricks I'd discovered were unknown to the group that wrote MSBuild, or at least unexpected. Seemed at the time to convince me there could be another book on the topic. I never actually supplied them with the test cases— they're really tough to whittle down from a real life build—hopefully the pages that follow will suffice.

---

[1] Okay, full disclosure, we're talking circa Visual Studio .NET 2002

This Book

Working on that book project providing technical review was interesting in several ways, including how it introduced me to the process of getting a technical book published. While "that other book" is a useful reference for MSBuild, like any language, the real power of this particular technology lies not in knowing what the features are, but in knowing how to put them together in novel ways to do useful things. This book, by comparison, attempts to be light on the reference material and weighs in more heavily with "cookbook" material and "tips and tricks."

Now the purpose of this book is twofold: to help you gain a richer understanding of the potential of MSBuild, but also to help give practical advice on how to use it. Sometimes those two things get mixed up. For example, in the section on version numbers I use an XML file to record each build increment. This was done intentionally to highlight the XmlPeek and XmlPoke tasks in MSBuild. It would have been easier for this particular example simply to write a single digit to a file using the WriteLinesToFile task. But[2] the WriteLinesToFile task had already been covered elsewhere, and the likelihood of needing persistence for additional build options beside a single digit seems probable, so I chose this particular trick to bloviate about on the XmlPeek and XmlPoke tasks. So if you reach a section like this and think, "Wouldn't it be easier..." then congratulations, you've matriculated.

The original subtitle for this book was "50 ways...," which quickly jumped to "65 ways...," and finally "99 ways..." There ended up being a total of 105, but I liked the "99" subtitle[3], so just discard any of the extra six you wish and we can call it even.

Acknowledgements

I am deeply indebted to Dan Moseley from Microsoft. Dan's team—on which he is a Senior Development Lead—owns project systems and build. He's the guy behind much of what is in MSBuild and has provided me with great guidance in completing this book, and has given me a great head start on the next one. Throughout this book you'll see mention of some odd or unexpected behavior, or discussion of simple workarounds

---

[2] Ever since watching the excellent movie "Finding Forrester" I can't stop myself from occasionally starting sentences with a preposition.

[3] That, and it turns out that subtitles are difficult to change once the publication process is well underway.

for things that aren't so obvious. Be glad to know that while reviewing this book, Dan appeared to have the source code to the next version of MSBuild open, as many of his comments were along the lines of "Just fixed this in the next version."

Another great guy at Microsoft who helped out tremendously is Cullen Waters. Cullen Waters has the official title of Software Development Engineer II at Microsoft Studios, and the unofficial one of "resident MSBuild power user." His work there has included converting to MSBuild the legacy build systems for multiple games. His real-world experience with large MSBuild systems provided just the right perspective to balance out many of the topics covered in this book, and for that I'm indebted.

Thanks to my editor, Amy Blew, for her keen eye and for her ability to handle my peculiar sense of humor, and to my wife Trisha for letting this project occupy our dining room table for far too long. Jason Cohen, a former coworker of mine, deserves some credit too, as it was his prodding of "dude, you should write a book" that pushed me to finally hit the keyboard on this book.

Requirements

While some of the content of this book will work perfectly well with MSBuild 3.5—the version shipped with Visual Studio 2008—there are many techniques specific to MSBuild 4.0—the version shipped with Microsoft .NET Framework version 4.0 and Visual Studio 2010.

You have to be familiar with Visual Studio of course, and should have a version of Visual Studio 2010, though previous versions will often work with a little tweaking.

Typography

In an effort to make code listings easier on the eyes, there are a few typographical conventions used throughout,

```
<Project ...>
```

really means,

```
<Project
    xmlns="http://schemas.microsoft.com/developer/msbuild/2003">
```

And if you're trying to be precise about which tools version is used, it means,

```
<Project
    xmlns="http://schemas.microsoft.com/developer/msbuild/2003"
    ToolsVersion="4.0">
```

For VS 2008, the ToolsVersion needs to be 3.5 instead.

Likewise, I've used ellipses to make code listings more readable when the details are irrelevant, as in the following, where I've omitted the value of the property and the closing tag,

```
<PropertyGroup>
    <SomeProperty>...
```

For the project files created to demonstrate various tricks the file extension ".trkproj" (short for "trickery project") is used. This is to help distinguish it from C# or C++ project files. MSBuild recognizes files with a ".*proj" file extension in a special way, so any project file you intend to pass as the project to MSBuild on a command line should have a file extension that ends with "proj" to be sure. I had to put "to be sure" at the end of the last sentence, because punctuation rules would have required the period to be inside the quotes, and "proj." would have made it appear as though I didn't know what a file extension looked like.

Sometimes the code listings are too wide to fit the printed page. I've used a couple different conventions to accommodate this. If possible, the XML is line-wrapped, but always in a manner that is still valid XML and valid MSBuild. Where this becomes important is when string values would take on an extra carriage return due to the format wrapping that in some cases causes the MSBuild execution to behave badly. So instead of wrapping inside the xml element like this,

```
    <ItemGroup>
        <AssemblyAttributes Include="Guid">
            <_Parameter1>
0ca6105a-7f2d-4314-91b7-6439b3e83724</_Parameter1>
        </AssemblyAttributes>
    </ItemGroup>
```

instead, you will see long lines wrapped like this,

```
    <ItemGroup>
        <AssemblyAttributes Include="Guid">
            <_Parameter1
                >0ca6105a-7f2d-4314-91b7-6439b3e83724</_Parameter1>
        </AssemblyAttributes>
```

```
    </ItemGroup>
```

The difference can be significant, in the first case the carriage return is part of the value of $(Parameter₁), while in the second case, it is just ignored white space within the <Parameter₁> element tag; not within the tag's value.

You will soon be introduced to other syntax, such as the "property function" shown below, and rest assured that the wrapping is very intentional, in this case, the opening "$(" of the property is wrapped because what follows is evaluated properly when wrapped at that point. What is important is what happens after the closing ")" which in this case results in a property without any embedded carriage returns.

```
<Message Text="Count of Item is: $(
    [MSBuild]::Divide(
        $([MSBuild]::Add(
            1,
            $(_Item.Length))),
        2))"
    />
```

It turns out you can't wrap a property function just after the literal "[MSBuild]" because the exact string "]::" is searched for by the internal parser, so if you had wrapped the code like this, it wouldn't work:

```
<Message Text="Count of Item is: $([MSBuild]
    ::Divide($([MSBuild]
        ::Add(
            1,
            $(_Item.Length))),
        2))"
    />
```

When the line is just too long and neither of those techniques gets the job done, and I can't reasonably shorten any of the identifiers to get within the limits of the page, you will see a wrap indicator on the right hand margin. When you see this, be careful about reproducing the carriage returns, they are unintentional and unavoidable, and possibly dangerously wrong, for example,

```
xmlns="clr-namespace:
    Microsoft.Build.Framework.XamlTypes;
    assembly=Microsoft.Build.Framework"
```

Finally, I've placed numeric comment decorations on the code listings to refer to corresponding locations in the commentary surrounding the code. I've taken care to ensure that the comments don't invalidate the XML, and since you can't put an XML comment in an attribute listing, the numbers are always attached to the beginning or end of the enclosing element.

```
<ItemGroup>
  <Groups
    Include="@(BuildItem->Metadata('Group'))"
    />                                          <!-- 6 -->
  <DistinctGroups
    Include="@(Groups->Distinct())"
    />                                          <!-- 7 -->
```

These references match up with parenthesized clues inline, for example when discussing Groups (6) or DistinctGroups (7) in the listing above.

Downloads

The sources containing the examples in the book can be downloaded in a single zip file from http://www.k7ranch.net/Trickery/Supplemental[4]. The Ms-PL license under which the sources are delivered enables you to use them freely in your own builds. That license does not extend to the contents of this book used to describe those sources though, which means you can't recreate the discussions within this book on your MSBuild blog. Don't be surprised if you notice that some of the content of this book bears a striking resemblance to something you've seen on StackOverflow with the [msbuild] tag, I'm frequently the top monthly contributor for that tag and have been flirting with the top-5 all-time users list. I've only included my own contributions, many of which I copied right out of the text that follows, while the book was being readied for publication.

---

[4] Also available as http://bit.ly/trkproj

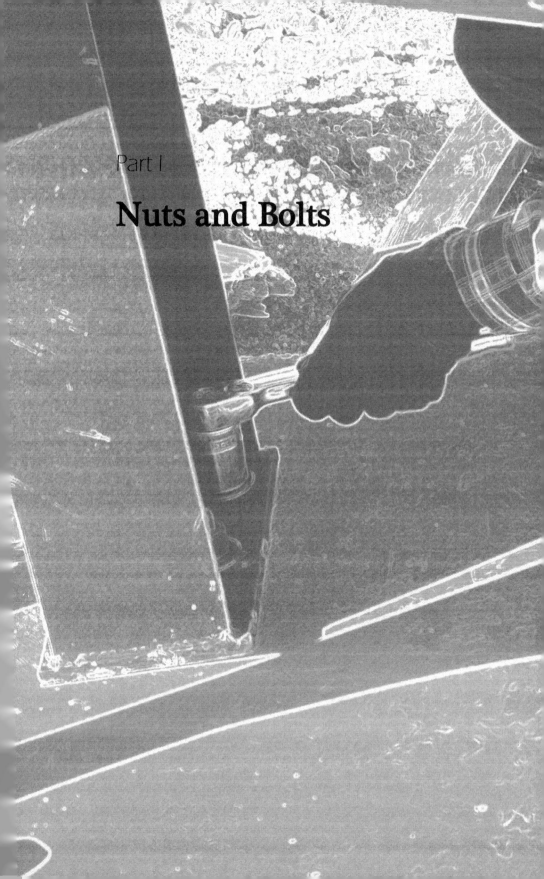

Part I

Nuts and Bolts

Chapter 1
The Basics, Quickly

MSBuild has very little to it, in terms of what you actually put in a project file. To wit; Properties, Items, Item Metadata, Targets and Tasks—that's pretty much it—so this chapter will be short and sweet. Or just short.

Constructs

Properties

Properties are scalar values declared in a PropertyGroup or created as output from a task. They are referenced using the $(*PropertyName*) syntax.

```
<PropertyGroup>
    <Path>c:/trk/folder</Path>
    <File>file.txt</File>
    <FullPath>$(Path)/$(File)</FullPath>
    <Escaped>%24(Prop)</Escaped>
</PropertyGroup>
```

The code above would declare these properties:

```
Path = c:/trk/folder
File = file.txt
FullPath = c:/trk/foo/file.txt
Escaped = $(Prop)
```

By the way, the above printout was achieved with a simple target:

```
<Target Name="SimpleProperties">
    <Message Text="Path = $(Path)" />
    <Message Text="File = $(File)" />
    <Message Text="FullPath = $(FullPath)" />
    <Message Text="Escaped = $(Escaped)" />
</Target>
```

A value can be set to an empty string using either of these:

```
<Value></Value>
<Value />
```

Any time a property value is set, it will override the value previously encountered, if any. The critical exception to this rule is that values supplied to MSBuild on the command line will not be overwritten by static values detected in the project files. *See trick #27, Understand the property precedence rules.*

Any environment variable visible to the MSBuild process is automatically a property, so for example $(WinDir) is likely to have the value "C:\Windows" on most machines. These property values can be overridden by any property in an MSBuild file or supplied on the command line. If an environment variable name happens to contain characters that would be invalid as an XML token, they will be ignored.

Properties can also be passed into the MSBuild process on the command line, using the syntax:

```
/p:Property1=PropertyValue /p:Property2="Value with spaces"
/p:Property3=FirstValue;Property4="Second Value"
```

There are more sophisticated ways to inject properties into MSBuild executions that are described in the chapter on Mechanics.

There are also a set of pre-defined properties, known as "reserved properties," available in any build script. The names of all of these start with "MSBuild," as in $(MSBuildThisFile). For a comprehensive list perform a Bing search on "MSBuild reserved" and be sure to look at the comments section, which lists some additional ones.

Items

Items are essentially named arrays of structures. While the most common use for items is for lists of files, and there is significant support built into the *Item* data type to manipulate lists of file and folder names, there is no restriction against using items to store lists of arbitrary data and metadata—in fact that ability is the source of many of the tricks described herein.

Individual items always contain an *Identity* value. If the identity value is a file or folder, there are built-in "meta" properties also available. These built-in meta values are named "well-known metadata" and for the most part represent the different parts of a file name, when the item can be construed as a path to a file. For example, there are well known meta values named %(FullPath) and %(Extension). There is also a well-known meta value named %(Identity) that retrieves the evaluated item specification derived from the Include attribute, and a couple others that supply the various file times such as %(ModifiedTime).

It is always possible to add any number of your own arbitrary meta values to each item; these are referred to as custom metadata. When metadata is being retrieved from an item, the syntax and usage is the same regardless of whether it is a well-known value or a custom one, which is the %( ) syntax.

There is a separation between the declaration of an item and the list of values available once the item is processed. This is not always one-to-one. If an item identity contains wildcards, the item may evaluate to zero or more item values.

Some item declarations:

```
<ItemGroup>
    <SomeItem Include="*.txt" />          <!-- 1 -->
    <SomeItem Include="**\*.txt" />        <!-- 2 -->
    <SomeItem Include="ArbitraryName" />   <!-- 3 -->
    <SomeItem Include="WithMeta">
        <Meta01>one</Meta01>               <!-- 4 -->
        <Meta02>two</Meta02>
    </SomeItem>
</ItemGroup>
```

In the listing above (1) declares an item that will expand to one item value for each file in the current folder matching the wildcard. The variation in (2) uses the "globbing" wildcard "**" which indicates a recursive folder search for the wildcard file pattern. The declaration in (3) simply adds another item to the array named "SomeItem" which may or may not match a file in the current folder that happens to be named "ArbitraryName" and just adds an item to the array whether or not such a file exists. Variation (4) is similar to (3) except that it adds two pieces of custom metadata to the item. In addition to custom metadata defined for items, there is a set of "well known" item metadata that is always available. With the exception of the %(Identity) well-known metadata, all the other values are meaningful for items that refer to files, for things like the paths, partial paths, file names and extensions, and file dates.

Printing the item array SomeItem defined above with a Message task,

```
<Message Text="SomeItem = '@(SomeItem)'" />
```

Results in the following output:

```
SomeItem = 'one.txt;two.txt;one.txt;two.txt;ArbitraryName;WithMeta'
```

Note: the single quotes surrounding @(SomeItem) in the message above are not required. You could just as easily have written <Message Task="@(SomeItem)" />, they are used to provide a visual delimiter to the output message, in case @(SomeItem) is empty. *See trick #49, Ensure Messages always print something.*

This will be fully explored in the chapter on Mechanics.

The *Include* attribute describes a pattern that is used to discover one or more items. The expanded list of items, once the wildcards have been used for the search in the case of files and folders, each contain a unique value derived from the Include pattern. This value is named "Identity" and appears as a metadata value on the item. For example, if the wildcard pattern "c:\Code*.txt" discovers two files, one.txt and two.txt, the Identity values for each of these items would be "c:\Code\one.txt" and "c:\Code\two.txt" respectively. If however, the wildcard did not include a path, as "*.txt" and the current path happened to be c:\Code, the identity values would not contain the path. Well-known metadata on the item could be used to extract the full path if it is needed.

I've often thought that the name "Include" should have just been "Identity" to avoid the confusion, and also to indicate that the value isn't just for file paths, which seems implied by the "Include" name.

There are several forms of syntax used to reference items, which are described below.

@(ItemName) refers to the entire item array as a collection. If used in a location that expects a scalar string, the item array will be expanded to a semicolon-delimited string containing the Identity value for each item. Note that even though a string is composed of just the Identity values, the @() syntax actually carries with it each of the item meta values as well, for example when passed as a parameter to a task, or used to deduce target dependencies. See the mechanics of *trick #71, Forming delimited lists for repeated arguments* for more detail.

%(MetaDataName) can be used within the scope of an @(ItemName) within the same task, to identify a particular named value in the item's metadata.

%(ItemName.MetaDataName) is used to denote an iteration on each of the items, using the named meta value to determine uniqueness. If more than one item share the same named meta value, even if they have unique identities, this form will present this shared meta value only once. It also is the form used to disambiguate between the meta on two items that have the same name, in essence a fully qualified meta value name. This can be done for targets using the Outputs attribute, which is called "target batching," or for tasks in any value, which is called "task batching."

Other meta values with different names can be referred to in the same target or task, and they will be correlated with the value of the current iteration. Batching is further explained below in the sections on Targets and Tasks, but for now just understand that it is a technique used to iterate over items, either individually or in chunks, which are called "batches."

@(ItemName->'%(MetaDataName)') is a rather odd syntax that is used to refer to a particular meta value of an item, mainly for the purpose of transforming it to another form. In general, the @(->'%') form will refer to the entire item collection at once, while the "bare metadata" form %() refers to each item separately, as part of a sequencing or batching operation. Take the following example, which is shown with the resulting print out of the item array using the two forms:

```
<ItemGroup>
    <Value Include="one"><Meta>1</Meta></Value>
    <Value Include="two"><Meta>2</Meta></Value>
</ItemGroup>

<Message Text="@(Value->'%(Meta)')" />
1;2

<Message Text="%(Value.Meta)" />
1
2
```

The primary use for this form is not as an alias for a single piece of metadata, but to concatenate various pieces of metadata along with other properties or strings to form new values. For example, if an item array contained file names from one folder and you wished to duplicate the file names, but not the paths, in another folder, you could use this form to transform the paths. This is accomplished by adding additional text to the contents of the single quoted part of the construct:

```
@(ItemName->'d:\newpath\%(FileName)%(Extension)')
```

However, when the item array contains a single item, as when a target is batched using an item array—which causes one target invocation for each unique batching value—and the same item is referenced within the target, there are times when the `@(->'%')` form can be used interchangeably with `%(ItemName.MetaDataName)`. At other times it cannot be interchanged, adding to the confusion of this particular syntax. This is because in the case of target batching, the synthesized semicolon delimited list will result in a single item and no delimiter.

For example, in a target that is being batched with `%(ItemName.Identity)`, you can use the `%()` syntax on a Condition in a Message task, but you cannot use it in a Condition on a PropertyGroup within the same target; the `@(->'%')` form will work where the other fails with an error message, as shown below.

Conditions.trkproj[5]

```
<ItemGroup>
    <Item Include="A" />
    <Item Include="B" />
</ItemGroup>

<Target Name="ConditionsWithItems"
    Outputs="%(Item.Identity)">

    <Message Text="Item batch: @(Item)" />

    <Message
        Condition="'@(Item->'%(Identity)')' == 'A'"
        Text="Found 'A' using @"
        />

    <Message
        Condition="'%(Item.Identity)' == 'A'"
        Text="Found 'A' using %"
        />

    <PropertyGroup
        Condition="'%(Item.Identity)' == 'A'">
        <FoundOne>this will cause an error</FoundOne>
    </PropertyGroup>
</Target>
```

Output

```
ConditionsWithItems:
  Item batch: A
  Found 'A' using @
  Found 'A' using %
  ...\Conditions.trkproj(85,7): error MSB4190: The reference to the
built-in metadata "Identity" at position 1 is not allowed in this
condition "'%(Item.Identity)' != 'A'".
```

---

[5] These source listings show the filename from the downloadable supplemental sources, see the Preface for the link.

Generally the %(ItemName.MetaDataName) form is preferable because it is a bit more readable, but if you get an error like the one above stating that reference to the metadata is not allowed in a particular construct, just switch to the other form.

Semicolons, as stated above, are used as the default delimiter when multiple items are combined into a string. They can also be used when declaring the Include value, to combine the declaration of multiple individual items or wildcards in a single item definition. The following two are equivalent:

```
<ItemName Include="c:\trk\one.txt" />
<ItemName Include="c:\trk\two.txt" />

<ItemName Include="c:\trk\one.txt;c:\trk\two.txt" />
```

Finally, particularly for items containing large numbers of meta values, or where the default values of the meta values are important, there exists a top-level construct named ItemDefinitionGroup. This is used exclusively to provide default values for custom meta values on items.

```
<ItemDefinitionGroup>
   <SomeItem>
      <Meta>DefaultValue</Meta>
      <EmptyMeta />
   </SomeItem>
</ItemDefinitionGroup>
```

Notice that there is no Include attribute, since this does not refer to a specific item, but rather to all items. Any specific item can override this value when it is declared, or alter it dynamically, including setting it back to an empty value. It may seem odd to provide an empty default for a meta value, as shown above with %(SomeItem.EmptyMeta). It turns out that some operations on meta values require that a value actually exist, and declaring an ItemDefinitionGroup with this empty value is necessary.

Static & Dynamic Properties

Static properties are properties whose values are determined as soon as the project file and all imported files are parsed prior to any targets being run. Typically, they are declared globally as a child of the top-level Project element in a PropertyGroup. Properties derived from environment variables or those passed into the MSBuild execution are also static.

In addition to static properties, you can create dynamic properties as well, as shown here:

```
<Target Name="...">
   <PropertyGroup>
     <MyDynamicProperty>Value</MyDynamicProperty>
   </PropertyGroup>
</Target>
```

There is an older form of this from previous versions of MSBuild that required a task named CreateProperty from which you pulled the property value into an output parameter, which is described in *trick #48, Prefer inline syntax to CreateProperty/CreateItem.*

Although an ItemGroup can be declared inside a target, an ItemDefinitionGroup must be declared statically at the top level in a project.

What about an attempt to have the name of a property be determined at runtime based on the value of another property, as follows?

```
<Term>Foo</Term>
<Value$(Term)>Really?</Value$(Term)>
```

Well, since MSBuild files are XML, that doesn't work, because the dollar sign can't be part of a token in an XML file, even though the MSBuild engine could conceivably replace it, it requires the file to load first as valid XML.

You could use the CreateProperty task within a target to create a property with the name Value$(Term), which would properly be expanded to ValueFoo in this case. The problem is, you wouldn't really be able to reference the property, since MSBuild would later reject the $(Value$(Term)) syntax you'd need to use to extract the value. One rather ambitious workaround is demonstrated in *trick #67, An alternative to $($(NestedProperty)).*

Static & Dynamic Items

Like Static Properties, Static Items are declared globally in a child of the top-level Project element in an ItemGroup. Unlike properties, the values of items cannot be passed to MSBuild on the command line (excepting the technique in *trick #30, How to convert properties into items.*

Dynamic items have the same history as dynamic properties; originally available only as the output of a CreateItem task, but now available by declaring an ItemGroup directly within a target body. There are no restrictions on the use of items within a target.

A very important consideration though, is to understand the timing of when the item is being discovered, evaluated and prepared as a list of values in an item array. Whereas static items—specifically those where the Include value refers to files on disk and contains a wildcard—are discovered when the project file is loaded, prior to any targets being run, if a file does not exist at that moment, the item array will not contain an entry for it in the list. If the file is later created by the operations in a target, the static item array will not be reevaluated to include the item.

On the other hand, dynamic item arrays are prepared and evaluated at the specific time of execution of their placement within a target body. Depending on the order in which tasks and targets execute, the item may or may not be included in the item array solely depending on whether or not the file exists at that moment. More important discussion on this important feature and its sometimes subtle behavior can be found in *trick #31, Understand how dynamic values are published*.

Dynamic Meta

If you consider that the ItemDefinitionGroup provides a mechanism for supplying default meta values for all items, even prior to any individual item being declared, there is a corollary in terms of providing dynamic meta values for all items. Typically, this form is used to calculate some new meta value from existing meta values. Here's a quick example:

```
<Target Name="...">
   <ItemGroup>
      <SomeItem>
         <MyMeta>%(Extension).extra</MyMeta>
      </SomeItem>
   </ItemGroup>
</Target>
```

Notable are a couple things; first of all this form can only be used within the body of a target, think of it as being executed on the items in the item array at the point of execution. Second, notice that there is no "Include" attribute specified, which implies that you are operating on all items and manipulating the metadata. It is possible of course to only operate on a subset of items by using a condition, either on the entire item array or on a particular meta declaration. This pattern will be seen throughout the book, just remember, if an item is declared in a target and there is no Include attribute, pay attention to the meta value manipulation.

Targets

A target is a procedural unit, similar in some respects to a global function. Understanding the various forms of target execution is critical. Targets can be executed by inclusion in the MSBuild command line, as one of the InitialTargets specified in a project, as the DefaultTargets specified in a project for the case where no target is explicitly invoked, or as specified in the Targets attribute on a CallTarget task. One MSBuild file can invoke targets in another or recursively in itself using the Targets attribute on the MSBuild task. Targets can also be indirectly invoked via the DependsOnTargets, or using the BeforeTargets and AfterTargets attributes on another target.

Targets have a Name attribute that uniquely identifies them. If a subsequent target is discovered with the same name as an existing target, it fully replaces the original, essentially leaving no way to execute the original target once it is overridden by a new definition. This ability to hide an existing target implementation by defining a new one with the same name is a powerful and heavily used extensibility technique.

Significantly, MSBuild keeps track of executions of a target within the scope of a project and will invoke it one time only, no matter how many of these various invocation forms exist. A target run as a result of its inclusion in InitialTargets will not also execute again when the DefaultTargets execute, or as the result of a CallTargets task later on. To achieve the effect of multiple separate invocations, you must rely on the various batching techniques discussed in many of the Tips, including *trick #85, How to drive targets as if in a loop*, or you must fall back on the MSBuild task and execute the target directly through multiple calls to MSBuild on a separate project. This does have some limitations though and they are discussed in *trick #32, Understand the limitations of the MSBuild task*.

For many common targets the execution is controlled through the Inputs and Outputs attributes on the target, which in the traditional usage denote the input files used as sources and the output files generated by the actions of the target, typically through compilation of some sort. See the following Tricks for more detail:

Trick #35, Understand batched target execution

Trick #36, Use target inputs and outputs

Trick #39, Understand CallTarget target execution

Trick #41, Understand target execution sequencing

Trick #84, How to force target execution with fake outputs

The body of the target is composed exclusively of tasks, with syntactical support for declaring property and item definitions.

Tasks

Targets are composed of various task declarations, analogous to a single statement in a function. A standard set of built-in tasks exists for most common build operations, such as file operations (Copy, MakeDir, Move, Touch), informative or error control (Message, Warning, Error), procedural (CallTarget, FindInList, and the inline group declaration syntax for dynamic properties and items, which operate as if they were tasks) or functional (WriteLinesToFile, XmlPoke).

For custom actions, you can often use the Exec task to execute arbitrary programs, or define your own custom tasks. The Microsoft supplied languages each have their own set of custom tasks (e.g. ClCompile, Link, Csc) and a set of shared custom tasks (e.g. ResolveAssemblyReferences, GetFrameworkPath) that are shipped, along with .targets files defining MSBuild wrappers for them. They are not part of the MSBuild engine itself, but rather are custom extensions to it for a particular project flavor. These extensions have been designed in most cases to permit further extension by end users.

Tasks can have input parameters, which are supplied as attributes on the task declaration, and output parameters, which are gathered using an Output child element of the task.

Find Under Path.trkproj

```
<ItemGroup>
    <Item Include="c:\trk\one.txt" />
    <Item Include="c:\trk\subfolder\three.txt" />
    <Item Include="d:\temp\a.file" />
    <Item Include="d:\temp\b.file" />
</ItemGroup>
```

```
<Target Name="FindUnderPath">
  <FindUnderPath
     Files="@(Item)"
     Path="c:\trk">
     <!-- first output parameter -->
     <Output
        TaskParameter="InPath"
        ItemName="IncludedFiles"
        />
     <!-- second output parameter -->
     <Output
        TaskParameter="OutOfPath"
        ItemName="ExcludedFiles"
        />
  </FindUnderPath>
  <Message Text="IncludedFiles = '@(IncludedFiles)'" />
  <Message Text="ExcludedFiles = '@(ExcludedFiles)'" />
</Target>
```

Output

```
IncludedFiles = 'c:\trk\one.txt;c:\trk\subfolder\three.txt'
ExcludedFiles = 'd:\temp\a.file;d:\temp\b.file'
```

The Path specified in the FindUnderPath[6] task doesn't actually have to exist, nor do the files in the item array. The task doesn't access the file system in any way; it is simply determining whether or not the individual files in the item array would be located under the Path, if they happened to be actual paths and files. The project listing from above actually produced the output shown, even though none of the paths or files in the example existed in the given locations.

Tasks that cause an error generally terminate the build, a result that can be controlled specifically to some degree with attributes on certain tasks, as the StopOnFirstFailure attribute on the MSBuild task, though use of this attribute will serialize the build operations (because otherwise "First" would not be deterministic). For other cases, all tasks, whether custom or built-in, accept an attribute named ContinueOnError that can be set to true to alter this behavior at task granularity.

Following is a quick list of the most commonly used standard tasks, shown in valid MSBuild usage in a target,

---

[6] The FindUnderPath task was originally implemented by the MSBuild team in order to make the Clean operation work in projects, with the restriction that only files under the output directories would be deleted by the Clean target, to prevent possible catastrophic data loss. It is still a useful task for risky, destructive operations you may want to restrict to only certain folders.

Simple Tasks.trkproj

```
<Target Name="Test">
  <Message
    Text="This text will be written to the log"
    Importance="High"
    />                                              <!-- 1 -->
  <MakeDir
    Directories="PathTo\test-a;PathTo\test-b"
    />                                              <!-- 2 -->
  <Copy
    SourceFiles="$(MSBuildThisFile)"
    DestinationFolder="PathTo\test-a"
    />                                              <!-- 3 -->
  <ItemGroup>
    <SourceFiles Include="$(MSBuildThisFile)" />    <!-- 4 -->
  </ItemGroup>
  <Copy
    SourceFiles="@(SourceFiles)"
    DestinationFiles="@(SourceFiles->
      'PathTo\test-b\%(Filename)%(Extension)')"
    />                                              <!-- 5 -->
  <Exec
    Command="dir"
    WorkingDirectory="PathTo\test-a"
    />                                              <!-- 6 -->
</Target>
```

This starts off with a Message task (1). The verbosity level of the message is set with the Importance attribute. Generally, you will only specify "High" if you always want to see the message, and "Low" if you only want to see it in logs with heightened verbosity. Throughout the examples in this book, the Message task will serve as a proxy for almost every other possible task, because the Text parameter can be used to mimic attributes of other tasks, and because when used in a simple sample, the output can easily be seen. You'll also likely make copious use of Message tasks for diagnostics, and during development, to serve as placeholders for potentially destructive tasks while you're getting the form of the parameters just right.

Next, a directory is created (2), actually a pair of them, with a semicolon delimited list. The "PathTo" folder is also used throughout the book. When you download the sources, there is actually a PathTo folder with various files in it, also used repeatedly throughout the samples. Into the first of these newly created folders the current project file is copied (3) with a Copy task. In this form of the Copy task, the destination is specified as a single folder. To show the second form, an item array is first created (4) which in a rather non-creative way is an item array that contains the current project. This item array is specified as the source for the next Copy task (5) as well as for the destination, using an item transformation. Finally, the ever-useful Exec task (6) is called. The Exec task allows you to provide any command line you want, in this case just a simple command shell command[7] to get a directory listing.

The output this little target produces is,

Output

```
Test:
  This text will be written to the log
  Creating directory "PathTo\test-a".
  Creating directory "PathTo\test-b".
  Copying file from "Simple Tasks.trkproj" to "PathTo\test-a\     ↱
Simple Tasks.trkproj".
  Copying file from "Simple Tasks.trkproj" to "PathTo\test-b\     ↱
Simple Tasks.trkproj".
  dir
   Volume in drive F is Phoenix Feather
   Volume Serial Number is BEEF-7AC0

   Directory of F:\Code\...\PathTo\test-a

06/05/2011  12:19 AM    <DIR>          .
06/05/2011  12:19 AM    <DIR>          ..
06/05/2011  12:19 AM                 873 Simple Tasks.trkproj
               1 File(s)            873 bytes
               2 Dir(s)  430,195,879,936 bytes free
```

A couple of the lines in the output were provided by the Copy tasks, which will sometimes emit other text depending on the options specified with other parameters. The Exec task shows both the command—the lone "dir" on one line—and also the output of the command. If the verbosity level is adjusted to minimal, the Copy task output will be omitted, as will the echo of the "dir," but the Exec task output—the actual directory listing—will still be emitted.

Conditions

The Condition attribute can be placed on anything in your build project file, other than the top-level Project element itself. Generally, it will be in the form of a string comparison, often based on the value of a property, though some other forms are available. Some examples are shown here:

---

[7] Does anyone else still call these DOS commands? Is that wrong?

See Conditions.trkproj

```
Condition="'$(PropOne)|$(PropTwo)' == 'One|Two'"          <!-- 1 -->
Condition="'$(SomeProperty)' == 'true'"                   <!-- 2 -->
                                                          <!-- 3 -->
Condition="$(PropertyDoesNotExist)|$(PropertyExists) != '''"
Condition="'ONE+TWO' == 'One+Two'"                        <!-- 4 -->
Condition="Exists('c:\trk\file.txt')"                     <!-- 5 -->
```

The use of single quotes, as in (1) and (2), is optional when the operand does not have a value, but they are required for cases when the operand contains a literal, since the parser is expecting to find a delimiter. In (3) above, the vertical bar breaks the condition since it is not enclosed in quotes. For this reason, since it is often difficult to know whether or not a property has been set to a value, it is a good practice to always use single quotes in all conditional expressions. The use of the vertical bar character in (1) is insignificant except that it is another character that must be present in both string operands to the comparison. The string comparisons in Conditions are case insensitive, so the equality in (4) will evaluate to "true." The *Exists* condition in (5) tests for the existence of the named file or folder in the file system. There is no way to use this condition to distinguish between files and folders, you'll need property functions for that, see *trick #57, Know how to enable more property functions.*

Conditions.trkproj

```
<PropertyGroup>
  <Ten>10</Ten>
  <BooleanTrue>true</BooleanTrue>
  <BooleanFalse>false</BooleanFalse>
</PropertyGroup>

<Target Name="ConditionalOperators">
  <Message
    Condition="$(Ten) &lt; 20"
    Text="10 &lt; 20"
    />
  <Message
    Condition="$(BooleanTrue)"
    Text="True is true"
    />
  <Message
    Condition="!$(BooleanFalse)"
    Text="False is false"
    />
</Target>
```

Output

```
ConditionalOperators:
```

```
10 < 20
True is true
False is false
```

Conditions can be arbitrarily complex, using parenthesis to set precedence and the AND, OR and NOT operators to build expressions, as well as comparison operators like ==, < and >, properly escaped as < and >[8] of course.

Condition HasTrailingSlash

There is an additional conditional test, HasTrailingSlash, which is used in the Microsoft supplied build files, but for which I've never found a compelling reason to use. The Microsoft files seem to use this exclusively to force properties containing a directory path to have a trailing slash, so that they can be appended to a filename to form a full file path, as:

`$(ProjectDir)$(FileName)`

This seems completely unnecessary, since you could just as easily use these:

`$(ProjectDir)\$(FileName)`
`$(ProjectDir)/$(FileName)`

Perhaps this is legacy from the old VC project system, which had built-in macros where the values for directories always contained a trailing slash.

Even in the case where the property $(ProjectDir) already contained a trailing slash, the value of $(ProjectDir)\$(FileName) would evaluate to something like `c:\trk\\FileName.txt`, which works in nearly every conceivable usage. Even using a forward slash to produce a path of `c:\trk\/FileName.txt` will only rarely cause any issue, and then only with tasks written with assumptions about how paths are formed.

Throughout the samples in this book, you may notice that I often use forward slashes, as in,

```
<Import Project="../Common.props" />
```

There is no difference in these cases to the same line composed with backslashes. This habit was formed when working on a Mono-saturated cross-platform project some time ago and has stuck, I hope it isn't too

---

[8] Actually, in XML content, such as the string value of a Condition attribute, only the < needs to be escaped typically, you can usually get away with leaving > in place.

distracting or off-putting, but rest assured in all cases where shown it is functionally equivalent.

Multiple slashes are, as far as I can tell, always properly resolved, the only exception being when performing a string comparison of paths in a conditional, as in the following example:

ComparingPaths.trkproj

```
<Project ...>
   <PropertyGroup>
      <Path01>c:\trk\foo</Path01>                            <!-- 1 -->
      <Path02>c:\trk\foo\</Path02>
      <Path03>c:/trk/foo</Path03>
      <TestA>false</TestA>                                   <!-- 2 -->
      <TestB>false</TestB>
      <TestC>false</TestC>
      <TestD>false</TestD>
   </PropertyGroup>
   <ItemGroup>                                               <!-- 3 -->
      <Item01 Include="$(Path01)\bar.txt" />
      <Item02 Include="$(Path02)\bar.txt" />
      <Item03 Include="$(Path03)\bar.txt" />
   </ItemGroup>
   <PropertyGroup>                                           <!-- 4 -->
      <TestA Condition="'$(Path01)\bar.txt' ==
            'c:\trk\foo\bar.txt'">true</TestA>
      <TestB Condition="'$(Path01)\bar.txt' ==
         '$(Path02)\bar.txt'">true</TestB>
      <TestC Condition="'@(Item01)' == '@(Item02)'">true<TestC>
      <TestD Condition="'@(Item02)' == '@(Item03)'">true<TestD>
   </PropertyGroup>
   <Target Name="Test">                                      <!-- 5 -->
      <Message Text="TestA is '$(TestA)'" />
      <Message Text="TestB is '$(TestB)'" />
      <Message Text="TestC is '$(TestC)'" />
      <Message Text="TestD is '$(TestD)'" />
   </Target>
</Project>
```

Granted, comparing paths is not something that you should ever be doing in a Conditional expression. If you need that sort of discrimination, use an inline task that makes use of System.Path to perform the comparison. See *trick #50, Use System.IO.Path for path comparisons*.

One other thing to be careful with is the use of forward slashes in an Exclude attribute of an item declaration. The following won't work as expected,

```
<ItemGroup>
   <Item Include="**\*" Exclude="PathTo/Folder" />
</ItemGroup>
```

There is a glitch present in the evaluation. Although the path for the Include attribute are normalized, they aren't for the Exclude attribute, so if the "PathTo\Folder" exists, it won't be excluded unless you specify it with a back slash. When doing tricky compositions in Exclude attributes, always test them in a little scratch project to be sure it is working as you expect.

One of the real problems with trailing slashes is readability. When you see the form `$(Value)$(AnotherValue)` how do you know if that represents a path or just a string concatenation? If instead you saw `$(Value)/$(AnotherValue)` the intent would be perfectly clear.

Imports

Simply stated, an import forces the inclusion of another file, allowing your build to be defined in a modular manner. Imports, like any other element in an MSBuild file, can contain a Condition that enables or disables the import.

A file may only be imported into an MSBuild project, directly or indirectly through another imported file, a single time. If a second import of the same file is detected, it is ignored and a warning is issued. The same is true if a project directly or indirectly attempts to import itself. See *trick #81, How to avoid the circular import warning* for a workaround.

You can also import more than one file at a time with a single import statement by using a wildcard pattern in the Project attribute.

Other Constructs

There are some other rarely used constructs such as Choose/When/Otherwise, which are pretty self-explanatory. They are really just a syntactic nicety, as it is always possible to create identical behavior with strategically placed Conditions, though at times some confusion can be avoided by the use of them as the complexity of the conditions and operations increases.

The OnError construct is declared in the same manner as a task, within a target and declares targets to execute when an error occurs, similar to an exception handling declaration. All OnError constructs must appear at the end of the target, after any other task. If more than one handler is declared, they are all executed sequentially. If the target being executed was a dependent target of another, or executed with the CallTarget task, any additional OnError constructs all the way up the target call chain will also be executed. Although this construct is quite useful for providing rich diagnostic information when there is a build failure, it was originally intended to allow the target containing the post build step of a project to execute even in the case that the build had failed.

The UsingTask construct is used to associate a custom task name with the assembly in which it is defined, and with 4.0, it can even include the source code inline within the MSBuild project. See the chapter on Customization for all the details on custom tasks.

Quotes

Finally, a quick note on how strings are composed when quotes are involved. Recall that XML doesn't care what kind of quote character you use. Both of these are equivalent:

```
<Target Name="MyTarget" />
<Target Name='MyTarget' />
```

Likewise, when calling MSBuild tasks, the following are equivalent:

```
<Message Text="My message" />
<Message Text='My message' />
```

By convention, I'm using double quotes exclusively for XML attributes, and single quotes for the primary quote character used when nesting quotes, as is the case with Conditions, described above. Sometimes though, two sets of quotes aren't enough. Some of the constructions presented in this book can nest more than two levels, and for this, MSBuild allows a third quote delimiter, the back tick character '`', which is typically found to the left of the '1' key, below the tilde '~' on US keyboards. It doesn't come up often, but when you see it, you'll know what it is.

Basic Command Line Usage

Project Files

MSBuild recognizes files whose extensions end in "proj" in a special way. Similar to how *make* recognizes the filename "makefile" or NAnt recognizes the ".build" extension; if only a single file with a "proj" extension (or any extension that ends with "proj") is detected, it does not need to be specified on the command line; MSBuild will use it. If there is more than one file then you need to be explicit. Unfortunately, MSBuild also detects files ending in .sln as well, so even if there is only a single file with a "proj" extension, a single .sln file in the same folder will force you to be explicit. There is a command line option, /ignoreprojectextensions, which can be used to control this behavior.

This seems like a cool feature, except that in order to support multiple versions of Visual Studio I always have more than one project file in a folder, so it never works out. There is no way to supply MSBuild with default options of this sort except for on the command line, except with the use of a response file, as is covered in *trick #44, Use a response file named @*.

A project file is an XML file with a root element named Project. There are two significant attributes that can be placed on the Project element. One is the DefaultTargets attribute, which specifies the target to be run in the case that none is specified on the command line. The other is the InitialTargets attribute, which specifies targets—typically validation targets—that should always be run prior to whatever targets would normally be executed, either the ones specified on the command line or those specified in DefaultTargets.

Common Command Lines

Running "msbuild /?" will display the options available. For what it's worth, MSBuild also accepts options with a hyphen instead of a slash. Each command line option also has a shorthand notation.

`/t[arget]:targetname[;targetname]...`

More than one target can be specified, they will be run in the order declared, unless of course target dependencies force an out of order execution. As with the other command line options that accept multiple values separated by semicolons, you can instead specify the option multiple times. The following two invocations are equivalent:

```
msbuild myproj.trkproj /t:firsttarget;secondtarget
msbuild myproj.trkproj /t:firsttarget /t:secondtarget
```

To provide values for properties, use /p[roperty], as follows:

```
msbuild myproj.trkproj /p:someproperty=value;skipproperty=true
```

Aside from specifying the target to run and supplying property values, the most frequently used will be for verbosity and logging. To specify the verbosity of the output logged to the console, use:

```
/v[erbosity]:level
```

Where *level* is one of:

```
q[uiet]
m[inimal]
n[ormal]
d[etailed]
diag[nostic]
```

The default if unspecified is *normal*, which works well in most situations. When trying to figure out what is going on with the build, crank it up in steps, first to *detailed* then to *diagnostic*, but don't expect to get much out of the command line at the higher levels as you may have to scroll for thousands of lines. The build will also be noticeably slower when logging causes the console window to output so much text. Instead, switch on file loggers and search the resulting log file.

```
/filelogger[n] or /fl[n]
/fileloggerparameters[n]:parameters or /flp[n]:parameters
```

Where parameters, among other options, are:

```
v[erbosity]=level
logfile=logfilename
```

If not specified, the default logfile name is msbuild[n].log. You can attach multiple file loggers, each with a unique value of *n* up to 9. In summary, a typical command line when you need diagnostic logging and minimal noise on the command line would be specified as:

```
msbuild myproj.trkproj /v:m /fl /flp:v=diag;logfile=foo.log
```

The verbosity can also be controlled from within Visual Studio. Go to Tools | Options | Projects and Solutions | Build and Run and locate the two verbosity settings, one for the console output which appears in the

Output tool window for all project types and another for the log file output which will appear in the BuildLog.htm file for C++ projects.

Another useful option new to 4.0 is /preprocess. Using this option will create a single build file from the preprocessed contents of all imported build files, which is useful for debugging complex build scenarios.

The "console logger" is a special built-in logger that formats the build results for display on the command line. It has its own controlling parameter, /ConsoleLoggerParameters:*value*, or /clp for short. The most important ones to know are:

For diagnosing build performance,

```
/clp:PerformanceSummary
/clp:ShowTimestamp
```

For filtering out various messages, typically when examining another aspect of the build,

```
/clp:ErrorsOnly
/clp:WarningsOnly
/clp:NoItemAndPropertyList
```

Multiple console logger parameters can be specified, separated by a command line, if desired.

Lastly in the list of commonly used options is the response file option @filename. See *trick #44, Use a response file named @* for more discussion.

Chapter 2
Simple Programmability

While MSBuild is flexible and expressive enough to handle many fairly common build related actions, there is a limit to what you can do with the standard tasks operating on properties and items. Even in cases where it is possible to do something rather complex within the constraints of the MSBuild language, sometimes the complexity introduced is better expressed in a richer language like C#. MSBuild has this flexibility expressed in several forms.

You can create a custom task assembly and add pretty much any behavior you want to add to the built-in tasks. You can also use inline task scripts to code anything as simple as a single line mathematical expression or as complex as a compiler and include the code right in the XML of your project file. You can describe in XAML how to not only drive a separate command line tool, but how to generate UI for it that will appear as if it is part of the Visual Studio IDE.

1. Use custom tasks in an assembly

Custom MSBuild tasks are so trivial to implement that they can easily replace much of the tedious scripting in builds. For this discussion, let's examine the creation of a custom task that takes a text file with a string table and generates a C# source file. You could just as easily generate any target source using the same task since the file format is specified as a template using properties and is supplied as arguments to the task. First, the string table file is of the form,

```
Token,String
```

where Token can be any token name valid as an identifier in the target language being generated, followed by a single comma, and the remainder of the line.

Execution of the task will provide the input file, the name of the file to be generated, and three separate strings to be used as the generated file template. These three template strings are: a prolog containing the beginning of the file, an epilog containing the end of the file, and a line template to be used to generate the contents of the file, emitting one instance of the template for each string definition in the input file. The task execution syntax will be:

Custom Tasks/Build Files/GenerateFileFromTokens.trkproj

```
<?xml version="1.0" encoding="utf-8"?>
<Project ...>
  <UsingTask
     TaskName="GenerateFileFromTokens"
     AssemblyFile="./<Path>/MyCustomTasks.dll"
     />

  <PropertyGroup>
    <Prolog>using System;

struct StringTable
{
// begin generated lines
</Prolog>
    <Content><![CDATA[    const string {0} = "{1}";]]></Content>
    <Epilog>// end generated lines
}
    </Epilog>
  </PropertyGroup>

  <Target Name="GenerateFileFromTokens">
    <GenerateFileFromTokens
       InputFile="Tokens.txt"
       OutputFile="Tokens.cs"
       Prolog="$(Prolog)"
       Content="$(Content)"
       Epilog="$(Epilog)"
       />
    <Exec Command="type Tokens.cs" />          <!-- Output-2 -->
  </Target>
</Project>
```

The use of the CDATA section for the Content ensures that the leading spaces are preserved in the generated output file. As it is not always possible in this type of construction to get the leading and trailing spaces and interleaved indentation and carriage returns to look correct in a generated file, I often include the begin and end comments starting in column zero to mask what would otherwise be unaligned text, though in this particular example it isn't needed. The resulting output for the given input would be:

Input file Custom Tasks/Build Files/Tokens.txt

```
String1,First String
String2,Second, with commas,
String3,
```

Generated Output file Tokens.cs

```csharp
using System;

struct StringTable
{
// begin generated lines
   const string String1 = "First String";
   const string String2 = "Second, with commas,";
   const string String3 = "";
// end generated lines
}
```

The source code for this task is surprisingly trivial. First, create a new C# Class Library project and add a reference to the MSBuild framework by choosing the Microsoft.Build.Framework assembly and the Microsoft.Build.Utilities.v4.o assembly. These two assemblies are located in the C:\Windows\Microsoft.NET\Frameworks\v4.o.# folder. If the assemblies do not appear on the .NET tab of the Add References view, make sure the project is configured for the full framework version 4.0 and not the client profile subset. This assembly contains base classes for task implementation. The rest of the source is easy:

Custom Tasks/GenerateFileFromTokens.cs

```csharp
using System;
using System.IO;
using Microsoft.Build.Framework;
using Microsoft.Build.Utilities;

namespace Trickery
{
   public class GenerateFileFromTokens : Task
   {
      public override bool Execute()
      {
         var contents = new StringBuilder();
         using (TextReader tr = new StreamReader(InputFile))
         {
            string line;
            int ct = 0;
            while ((line = tr.ReadLine()) != null)
            {
               var tokens = line.Split(
                  new[] { ',' },
                  2,
                  StringSplitOptions.RemoveEmptyEntries);
```

```
            if (tokens.Length < 1)
                continue;
            var output = string.Format(
                Content,
                tokens[0],
                tokens.Length > 1 ? tokens[1] : "");
            contents.AppendLine(output);
            ++ct;
        }
    }
    Log.LogMessage(
        MessageImportance.Normal,
        "GenerateFileFromTokens wrote {0} lines.",   // Output-1
        ct);

    using (TextWriter tw = new StreamWriter(OutputFile))
    {
        tw.Write(Prolog);
        tw.Write(contents);
        tw.Write(Epilog);
    }

    return !Log.HasLoggedErrors;
}

[Required]
public string InputFile { get; set; }

[Required]
public string OutputFile { get; set; }

[Required]
public string Prolog { get; set; }

[Required]
public string Content { get; set; }

[Required]
public string Epilog { get; set; }
    }
}
```

Of note is the base class Task which is from the Microsoft.Build.Utilities, and the use of Required attributes to indicate that MSBuild should report an error if the task is used without a value for the attribute. The Execute method is an override of a method in the ITask interface inherited from the task base class.

The base Task class provides a Log member that can be used to emit messages, errors and warnings to the console or attached loggers. It is used above to display the number of content lines written to the output file.

Command

```
Custom Tasks\Build Files> msbuild GenerateFilesFromTokens.trkproj
```

Output

```
Build:
  GenerateFileFromTokens wrote 3 lines.
  type Tokens.cs
  using System;

  struct StringTable
  {
  // begin generated lines
     const string String1 = "First String";
     const string String2 = "Second, with commas,";
     const string String3 = "";
  // end generated lines
  }
```

When executed with MSBuild, the output first shows the Log message output from the source listing of the custom task (Output-1) followed by the execution of the "type" command using an Exec task from the target file (Output-2), which displays the generated file.

2. Always return !Log.HasLoggedErrors from Execute

The ITask.Execute method in a custom task must return a Boolean indicating success or failure. MSBuild does not enforce the notions that a successful task execution must not have logged any errors, or that an unsuccessful task execution must have logged at least one error. This can be confusing, leading to build diagnostics that indicate either that the build has failed but which provide no clue as to why, or that no tasks failed even though errors have been logged.

So, when authoring the C# code for your custom tasks, don't ever return anything from the ITask.Execute method other than the following, which in hindsight is how MSBuild should be behaving by default:

```
return !Log.HasLoggedErrors;
```

Doing this consistently will enforce a proper correlation between your error output and build success and failure.

3. Understand task outputs and FileWrites

If the custom GenerateFilesFromTokens task extension from the previous trick is being used within a standard Visual Studio project type (e.g.

csproj, fsproj, vbproj or vcxproj) then there are additional customizations needed. First, since you are generating a new file in the build, the file needs to be added to the list of known generated files so that it can be cleaned up automatically. The convention used in the Microsoft supplied build projects is to add these files to an item array named FileWrites.

The FileWrites item array exists in support of a feature named "incremental clean." If the project is changed between builds in a manner that incremental files will be removed, the incremental clean feature can remove them, even though in the subsequent build there is no mention of them. This is because a temporary file with the contents of the FileWrites item array is persisted between builds. Similarly, if the assembly name is changed and the project is rebuilt, the old assembly will be cleaned from the output directory.

Be sure to place all output files into the FileWrites item array, even if you don't actually write them during a particular build execution because they are already up-to-date. Perhaps the name is a bit misleading; think of it as "FilesThatWouldHaveBeenWrittenIfEverythingWereOutOfDate."

Then after the end of a build that's not a clean build the common targets cache this list. They compare the new list with the list from the last build. Missing lines indicate files that are then deleted.

The use of FileWrites comes with a few caveats; all files in FileWrites must be under the intermediate object folder specified in the project— typically somewhere under the ./obj folder—and you need to be sure that you are adding files to the project at the proper point in the processing. The default project mechanics takes the contents of the FileWrites item array and writes it out to a file named *ProjectFileName*.FileList-Absolute.txt which is written to the intermediate output folder. Your entries into the FileWrites item array need to be in place prior to that file being written by the main project build. Ensure your target executes prior to completion of the *Build* target in the Visual Studio project.

There are two approaches to wiring up the FileWrites item array with your customization. The simplest is to presume the task succeeds and add the file directly in the target, noticing that the output path passed into the custom task has been changed to place the file in the intermediate files folder, so that it can be removed during a project clean operation:

```
<Target Name="GenerateFileFromTokens">
  <GenerateFileFromTokens
     InputFile="Tokens.txt"
     OutputFile="$(IntermediateOutputPath)/Tokens.cs"
```

```
    Prolog="$(Prolog)"
    Content="$(Content)"
    Epilog="$(Epilog)"
    />
  <ItemGroup>
    <FileWrites Include="Tokens.cs" />
  </ItemGroup>
  ...
```

This isn't quite right though. To be more exacting, follow the pattern used by other standard tasks and provide an output parameter you can populate the FileWrites with:

```
<Target Name="GenerateFileFromTokens">
  <GenerateFileFromTokens
    InputFile="Tokens.txt"
    OutputFile="$(IntermediateOutputPath)/Tokens.cs"
    Prolog="$(Prolog)"
    Content="$(Content)"
    Epilog="$(Epilog)"
    >
    <Output
      TaskParameter="GeneratedFiles"
      ItemName="FileWrites"
      />
  </GenerateFileFromTokens>
  ...
```

For even more control, consider first storing the outputs in a unique item set which is then copied into the FileWrites item.

```
<GenerateFileFromTokens ... >
  <Output
    TaskParameter="GeneratedFiles"
    ItemName="GeneratedTokenFileWrites"
    />
</GenerateFileFromTokens>
<ItemGroup>
  <FileWrites Include="@(GeneratedTokenFileWrites)" />
</ItemGroup>
```

Now alter the source for the task to provide this output parameter:

Add to class

```
private ArrayList _generatedFiles = new ArrayList();

[Output]
public ITaskItem[] GeneratedFiles
{
    get
    {
        return (ITaskItem[])
            _generatedFiles.ToArray(typeof(ITaskItem));
    }
```

```
        }
```

Add to the Execute method

```
using (TextWriter tw = new StreamWriter(OutputFile))
{
    _generatedFiles.Add(
        new TaskItem { ItemSpec = OutputFile });
```

This demonstrates a new attribute from the MSBuild framework, Output, used to designate output properties. It can be used on any data type with a default conversion to the System.String type in the case of output properties, which correlate to the PropertyName attribute of the <Output> element, or as in this case, use type ITaskItem or ITaskItem[] to correlate to the ItemName attribute for the requested output. Since in this case the output is of type ITaskItem[], notice that a new TaskItem was created and added to the ArrayList. The ItemSpec property of the TaskItem class correlates to the value of the Include attribute for items, which as you recall is the value of the item's %(Identity) metadata.

4. Understand file-based task inputs

In addition to basic types for task inputs, tasks can be passed items, which you recall are essentially arrays of structures, often files. A task input of type ITaskItem will accept any string and create a single item from it. A common usage is to pass a property containing a path, or an item array in which there is known to be only a single item. More common is to specify inputs of type ITaskItem[ ], note the array syntax this time, to accept an entire collection of items in an item array.

In the source code for the custom task you have access to all of the built-in and custom meta-data on each item in the item array, as shown below:

From Custom Tasks/ItemGroupTask.cs, in MyCustomTasks.dll

```
public class ItemGroupTask : Task
{
    public ITaskItem[] InputFiles { get; set; }
    public override bool Execute()
    {
        foreach (ITaskItem item in InputFiles)
        {
            if (item.ItemSpec.Length > 0)
            {
                // instead of using item.GetMetadata("FullPath"),
                // let's construct it piecemeal from various other
                // well-known metadata, just for grins
                //
```

```
            string fullpath = Path.Combine(
                item.GetMetadata("RootDir"),
                item.GetMetadata("Directory"),
                item.GetMetadata("RecursiveDir"),
                item.GetMetadata("Filename"));
            fullpath = Path.ChangeExtension(
                fullpath,
                item.GetMetadata("Extension"));
            Log.LogMessage(
                "Path is '{0}'",
                fullpath);
            Log.LogMessage(
                "  Modified {0}",
                item.GetMetadata("ModifiedTime"));
        }
    }
    return !Log.HasLoggedErrors;
    }
}
```

From project file CustomItemGroupTask.trkproj

```
<Project ...>
  <UsingTask
    TaskName="ItemGroupTask"
    AssemblyFile="./Path/MyCustomTasks.dll"
    />

  <ItemGroup>
    <ItemGroupTask Include="*.trkproj" />
  </ItemGroup>

  <Target Name="Build">
    <ItemGroupTask
      InputFiles="@(ItemGroupTask)"
      />
  </Target>
</Project>
```

Output

```
Build:
  Path is 'C:\Trickery\AutoBootstrap.trkproj'
    Modified 2010-12-19 12:17:41.0224609
  Path is 'C:\Trickery\Custom Inline Task.trkproj'
    Modified 2010-12-19 12:21:33.9755859
  Path is 'C:\Trickery\CustomTask.trkproj'
    Modified 2010-12-19 18:47:20.5546875
  Path is 'C:\Trickery\CustomTaskItemTask.trkproj'
    Modified 2010-12-19 18:47:44.6484375
```

The ITaskItem type declared as an array allows access to all of the contents of an item array. The original string used for the Include attribute is available from the ITaskItem.ItemSpec property, and all of the well-known metadata and custom metadata can be retrieved using the GetMetadata method, passing in the case-insensitive name of the metadata being retrieved. You can also create new entries of type TaskItem, provided by the MSBuild Utilities assembly, or any custom type you define that implements ITaskItem, and modify or add metadata using the SetMetadata method.

5. Consider complex items for task parameters

In some cases you may wish to define items that refer to files, but that may not all exist at the start of the build. Because of the limitations on target execution, it may not be convenient to always have these declared in a dynamic item array executed from within a target, and besides, having them declared statically in a property file is often more convenient. To get around the load time evaluation that determines if an item exists in the file system, you can declare the path and the file name as item metadata and perform the evaluation later on in a target as needed.

Consider the following listing, where the path and file name are each declared separately. In this example, declaring them both as a single meta value containing the full path would also work. The declarations also provide a custom meta item named Tag that is examined by a fictional custom task. In typical usage, the target file will be provided along with the assembly containing the task. In the listing below, along with the primary target matching the task, an ItemDefinitionGroup (3) is declared, in order to provide default values to any item metadata for which a default value is meaningful.

From your project file

```
<ItemGroup>
  <MyTask Include="Item01">
    <Path>./PathTo</Path>                        <!-- 1 -->
    <File>Item01.txt</File>                       <!-- 2 -->
    <Tag>alpha</Tag>
  </MyTask>
  <MyTask Include="Item02">
    <Path>./PathTo</Path>
    <File>Item02.txt</File>
    <Tag>bravo</Tag>
  </MyTask>
</ItemGroup>
```

From MyTask.targets

```
<ItemDefinitionGroup>
```

```
    <MyTask>
        <Tag>default-tag</Tag>                              <!-- 3 -->
    </MyTask>
</ItemDefinitionGroup>

<Target Name="MyTask">
                                                            <!-- 4 -->
    <MyTask
        Inputs="@(MyTask)"
        ProcessItemsWithTag="alpha"
        />
                                                            <!-- 5 -->
    <Message
        Text="Composed path is '%(MyTask.Path)/%(File)'"
        />
</Target>
```

It is significant when using this technique that the value used for the
Include attribute on each individual item in an item array is globally
unique. Failure to use a globally unique item specification will work in
many instances, but may cause issues where items are referenced via the
item specification as distinct items, in such a manner that the metadata
of a repeated item may appear to merge with the former values from the
previous item encountered with the same item specification. To get the
correct conceptual model, it is important to understand that an item
array is not associative with respect to the Include (or "Identity" or
"ItemSpec") value. It is just an array, not a dictionary. There is no
restriction that identity values need to be unique. As such, it is possible
for items in the array with the same identity to have multiple entries in
the array, and even unique metadata associated with them.

The items in the listing are numbered (1) with item specifications
"Item01" etc. that happen to match the root file name (2) encoded in the
item metadata, though any unique naming scheme can be used. A
default value for the Tag metadata value (3) is provided with the item
definition.

Presumably the imaginary custom task (4) builds the path to the file
using the Path and File custom meta values, and performs some
processing only on those items also having a Tag value matching that
passed into the task. A second usage of the metadata is shown (5) which
composes a path from the individual meta values. Notice the shorthand
notation for %(File) instead of the fully qualified %(MyTask.File). In this
case, the "MyTask" is inferred, because it is already mentioned elsewhere
in the task body. To be precise, there is only one item referenced in the
task that has a metadata value named "File" which makes it possible for
MSBuild to deduce to which item the inference is being made.

This type of processing on items and metadata will be covered extensively throughout the book, since items are the predominant construct used for most customizations in MSBuild.

6. Use inline custom tasks coded in the project file

The shining new feature of MSBuild in version 4.0 in my opinion is the introduction of inline custom task code right in the project files. Many of the headaches associated with building custom assemblies can be worked around more easily when the code is in the MSBuild file and doesn't need to be compiled to an assembly prior to executing the build.

If you've ever had to deal with this sort of thing, these headaches will sound familiar. The tasks have to be built, and in order to get a repeatable build, you need to have the task sources checked in to source control. If they are built in the same build, you'll probably run into chicken-and-egg problems for clean builds, even if you try hard to avoid them, or if you get past that, you'll hit file locking problems, if not from your command line build then certainly from the IDE, which is a bit more aggressive at locking assemblies referenced in the build. Since this is build tooling and not part of your shipping application, you really probably just want to be able to tweak a script file and check it in, without having to worry about all the other mechanics of the build, which is probably already complex enough, right? Inline tasks alleviate much of these issues.

Shown below is an example inline task that calculates the number of processors on the machine minus one. This is a somewhat contrived example chosen because it involves a simple arithmetic calculation. It could potentially be useful in a rather obscure customization when using the BuildInParallel attribute on the MSBuild task, in conjunction with the ProcessorNumber item metadata on the ClCompile task. By default, running a multiprocessor build using the /m parameter to MSBuild.exe will use all of the processors available on your machine. While desirable for build machines it will bog down your development machine. Of course, this is how I configure my own multiprocessor builds, leaving one processor available to serve my impatience, but then again, I tend to enjoy the obscurity of it.

Custom Inline Task.trktasks, imported into a C++ project file

```
<Project ...>

  <!-- 1 -->
  <UsingTask
```

```xml
      TaskName="CalculateProcessorCount"
      TaskFactory="CodeTaskFactory"
    AssemblyFile=
      "$(MSBuildToolsPath)\Microsoft.Build.Tasks.v4.0.dll">
    <ParameterGroup>
      <!-- 2 -->
      <NumberOfProcessors
        ParameterType="System.Int32"
        Required="true"
        />
      <!-- 3 -->
      <ProcessorCountMinusOne
        ParameterType="System.Int32"
        Output="true"
        />
    </ParameterGroup>
    <!-- 4 -->
    <Task>
      <Using Namespace="System" />
      <Code Type="Fragment" Language="cs">
        <![CDATA[
          ProcessorCountMinusOne = NumberOfProcessors - 1;
        ]]>
      </Code>
    </Task>
  </UsingTask>

  <Target Name="CalculateProcessorCount">
    <!-- 5 -->
    <CalculateProcessorCount
      NumberofProcessors="$(NUMBER_OF_PROCESSORS)">
      <!-- 6 -->
      <Output
        TaskParameter="ProcessorCountMinusOne"
        PropertyName="ProcessorCountMinusOne"
        />
    </CalculateProcessorCount>
  </Target>

  <Target Name="Build"
    DependsOnTargets="CalculateProcessorCount">
    <!-- 7 -->
    <Message
      Text="ProcessorCount - 1 = '$(ProcessorCountMinusOne)'"
      />
    <MSBuild
      Projects="SomeProject.vcxproj"
      Properties=
        "ProcessorCountMinusOne=$(ProcessorCountMinusOne)"
      />
  </Target>
</Project>
```

In the C++ project file being built

```xml
<!-- 8 -->
```

```
<ItemDefinitionGroup>
  <ClCompile>
    <ProcessorNumber>$(ProcessorCountMinusOne)</ProcessorNumber>
  </ClCompile>
</ItemDefinitionGroup>
```

Output, on a quad core machine

```
Build:
  ProcessorCount - 1 = '3'
```

The UsingTask at (1) is different from the typical usage that specifies a TaskName within the custom AssemblyFile specified. All inline tasks use the same AssemblyFile, Microsoft.Build.Tasks.v4.0.dll, the key difference is in the attribute named TaskFactory. By specifying a TaskFactory of type CodeTaskFactory, the MSBuild engine will look in the specified AssemblyFile not for a class implementing ITask, but rather for a class implementing ITaskFactory. The CodeTaskFactory implementation expects additional UsingTask child elements named ParameterGroup and Task. Although I've seen the Task child element documented in MSDN with the name TaskBody, using TaskBody causes an error.

If you wish to have fixed MSBuild properties and items referenced directly in the code body rather than passing them in as arguments, add an Evaluate="true" attribute to the Body element. When this attribute is specified, MSBuild will essentially perform a "macro replacement" on your code body, using currently available values of properties and items, prior to passing the code source along to the task factory for compilation.

The two parameters at (2) and (3) declare a single input and a single output parameter. The Task at (4) declares any references needed and the inline Code of the task, also specifying the language the code is written in with the Language attribute and what type of code structure the code represents using the Type attribute. Since source code will very often contain characters that would otherwise be reserved, it is good practice to contain the code within a CDATA section.

Valid values for the Types attribute are:

```
Fragment  Code element contains the body of an ITask.Execute
Method    Code element implements the entire ITask.Execute method
Class     Code element contains an entire class implementing ITask
```

Valid values for the Languages are:

```
cs, Code element is written in Visual C#
vb, Code element is written in Visual Basic
js, Code element is written in JScript
```

When the CalculateProcessorCount target executes, it calls (5) the CalculateProcessorCount task. In this example, the target and task share the same name but that is just a convention not a requirement of any sort. Just as with any other task, the task arguments are specified as attributes, in this case the single input parameter named NumberOfProcessors is given a value from the standard system environment variable named $(NUMBER_OF_PROCESSORS). Also just as with any other task, the output property is at (6) collected using an Output child element of the task. It takes the value of the task output parameter named ProcessorCountMinusOne and assigns it to a property, which in this case is a new property not declared elsewhere that just happens to have the same name as the output parameter, ProcessorCountMinusOne. Again, there is no requirement that the name of the task parameter Output value match the name of the property to which it is assigned.

By (7) the CalculateProcessorCount target has already been run as a dependency of the Build target, and the $(ProcessorCountMinusOne) property has been set.

The next two tasks following (6) display the calculated property, and then pass it along to the build of the C++ project named SomeProject.vcxproj. Within the C++ project, a modification (7) is needed in order to use this new property properly. Since the C++ build system will attempt to locate the ProcessorNumber value as metadata on each file being built, you can set it globally using an item definition group as shown. It is also possible to set this metadata only for individual files. In the C++ project, this would look like:

```
<ItemGroup>
   <ClCompile Include="SomeFile.cs">
     <ProcessorNumber>$(ProcessorCountMinusOne)</ProcessorNumber>
   </ClCompile>
</ItemGroup>
```

Taking this introduction one step further, it is possible to examine how the Code Task Factory functions, by introducing an artificial error in the code. Alter the Code definition so it reads:

```
<![CDATA[
   ProcessorCountMinusOne = UndeclaredValue - 1;
]]>
```

When the project is built, you should see an error of the following form.

```
...\Custom Inline Task.trktasks(33,7): error : The source file for
this compilation can be found at:
"$(TEMP)\MSBUILDCodeTaskFactoryGeneratedFile_GUID_.txt"
```

```
...\Custom Inline Task.trktasks(33,7): error MSB3758: An error has
occurred during compliation. $(TEMP)\0lg4x4ws.0.cs(59,41) : error
CS0103: The name 'UndeclaredValue' does not exist in the current
context
```

That isn't a typo; the error message in the 4.0 version states an error occurred during 'compliation' (sic).

Decomposing this error, the Code Task Factory synthesizes a text file in the temporary folder containing the full, generated source for the task created by the factory. That is the first named file with the GUID in the name and a .txt extension. The second named file, with the .cs extension, is the file actually compiled, but it is transient and no longer exists. The error given for it however, in this case the file olg4x4ws.0.cs at line and column (59, 41) will indicate the proper line number and position in the text file that remains.

The contents of the generated source file are shown below.

$(TEMP)\MSBUILDCodeTaskFactoryGeneratedFile_GUID_.txt

```
//------------------------------------------------------------------
// <auto-generated>
//     This code was generated by a tool.
//     Runtime Version:4.0.30319.1
//
//     Changes to this file may cause incorrect behavior and will
//     be lost if the code is regenerated.
// </auto-generated>
//------------------------------------------------------------------
namespace InlineCode {
    using System;
    using System.Collections;
    using System.Collections.Generic;
    using System.Text;
    using System.Linq;
    using System.IO;
    using Microsoft.Build.Framework;
    using Microsoft.Build.Utilities;

    public class CalculateProcessorCount :
      Microsoft.Build.Utilities.Task
        {
            private bool _Success = true;
            public virtual bool Success
            {
                get { return _Success; }
                set { _Success = value; }
            }

            private int _NumberOfProcessors;
            public virtual int NumberOfProcessors
            {
```

```
        get { return _NumberOfProcessors; }
        set { _NumberOfProcessors = value; }
    }

    private int _ProcessorCountMinusOne;
    public virtual int ProcessorCountMinusOne
    {
        get { return _ProcessorCountMinusOne; }
        set { _ProcessorCountMinusOne = value; }
    }

    public override bool Execute()
    {
        ProcessorCountMinusOne = UndeclaredValue - 1;
        return _Success;
    }
  }
}
```

The drawback to the inline task approach is the still immature support for authoring and debugging inline tasks. For that reason, you might want to adopt a development workflow where the body of a task is initially authored in a temporary C# command line project, giving you debugging and IntelliSense, then pasted into the CDATA code section of a UsingTask in the MSBuild file. You can use a C# project file just for authoring support and compilation, or you can initially compile to an assembly that is tested with MSBuild, it all depends on the complexity of the task.

7. Put tasks in .tasks files

The previous example had the inline task body and the build definition co-located in a single project file. That is an artifact of making simple samples for the book. Generally, you will want to remove all of your <UsingTask> statements to separate project files with a .tasks extension. This is true not just for inline tasks which are declared in the body of a <UsingTask> element, but also for any <UsingTask> that is referencing a compiled task in a task assembly.

There are several reasons for this. The most obvious for inline tasks is that you keep a separation between the implementation of tasks and their usage in the build. It is likely on larger teams that the folks writing tasks may be a different group of people than those consuming them in project files, so keeping this separation is important and aids in the reusability across multiple projects.

The less obvious reason is that it provides an optimization in large builds. Consider an approach where multiple project files reference tasks with their own <UsingTask> elements.

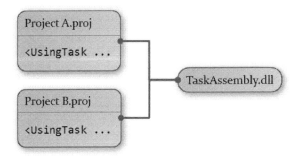

When MSBuild is processing these separate projects, even within the same outer build, it will search for and identify the task assembly reference by the UsingTask twice; once for each UsingTask element that is encountered. Because MSBuild is forgiving about how you reference the task by name, it will need to find and load the assembly, then search for an appropriately named class, which can be time consuming in large builds where this may happen hundreds or even thousands of times. Next consider the arrangement below, where these same two projects reference the same task indirectly, through the import of a .tasks MSBuild file, which in turn reference the task with a UsingTask element.

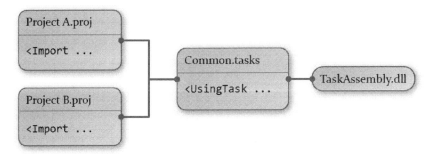

In this arrangement, the task assembly is only going to be searched for and loaded once, when MSBuild first encounters the Common.tasks file in an import. This is because MSBuild will cache the import of a project file, and indirectly will not reevaluate the task referenced in the task assembly.

A couple of other speed improvements can be deduced by looking at the Microsoft.Common.Tasks file in the Microsoft .NET Framework folder, the first couple lines of which are shown here:

```
<UsingTask TaskName="Microsoft.Build.Tasks.AL"
  AssemblyName="Microsoft.Build.Tasks.v4.0, Version=4.0.0.0,
  Culture=neutral, PublicKeyToken=b03f5f7f11d50a3a"/>
<UsingTask TaskName="Microsoft.Build.Tasks.AspNetCompiler"
  AssemblyName="Microsoft.Build.Tasks.v4.0, Version=4.0.0.0,
  Culture=neutral, PublicKeyToken=b03f5f7f11d50a3a"/>
<UsingTask TaskName="Microsoft.Build.Tasks.AssignCulture"
  AssemblyName="Microsoft.Build.Tasks.v4.0, Version=4.0.0.0,
  Culture=neutral, PublicKeyToken=b03f5f7f11d50a3a"/>
...
```

The file also contains the following comment:

```
NOTE: Using the fully qualified class name in a <UsingTask> tag is
faster than using a partially qualified name.
```

By being precise about the name of the task class, specifying the full namespace instead of just the class name, and by including a fully qualified assembly name, MSBuild is able to discover the task more quickly, and as it reflects upon the task assembly is able to discard from evaluation entire namespaces.

Now if you've ever traversed deep into the standard Microsoft supplied MSBuild files, most of which are in the .NET Framework folder, or possibly in the Program Files\MSBuild folder, you will have seen a complex conglomeration of imported files. You won't however find any reference to the Microsoft.Common.Tasks file.

It turns out that MSBuild treats this particular pattern in a special way. Any files named *.tasks that are found in the folder denoted by the reserved property $(MSBuildToolsPath) are always imported into every project as it is being built. To be precise, the first time any task is executed in the build, part of the internal initialization will seek out these files located in $(MSBuildToolsPath)*.tasks and effectively import them into the project. When this import is performed, it appears as though MSBuild only processes the UsingTask statements and ignores any other declarations that may appear, which makes sense because all of the property and item processing and target discovery and overloading will have already occurred, now that the build is executing. This first execution will typically be in an InitialTargets, whichever one happens to execute first. This is the mechanism by which MSBuild bootstraps all of the "built-in" tasks that are considered part of the language.

There is one additional customization point on this process. In addition to loading all files named $(MSBuildToolsPath)*.tasks, MSBuild also performs a second pass and finds and loads files named $(MSBuildToolsPath)*.overridetasks. If you look in the .NET Framework folder, you'll see a single file named Microsoft.Common.OverrideTasks, which (in the current version on my machine) contains UsingTask overloads for the following tasks:

- Microsoft.Build.Tasks.ResolveComReference

- Microsoft.BuildTaasks.GenerateResource

- ResolveComReference

- GenerateResource

- ReadLinesFromFile

- FindUnderPath

- ConvertToAbsolutePath

- MSBuild

What is interesting about these overrides is that they each contain a Condition activating them only for specific versions of MSBuild. Examine the conditions on the following two UsingTask statements pulled from the list above,

```
<UsingTask TaskName="GenerateResource"
  AssemblyName="Microsoft.Build.Tasks.v4.0, Version=4.0.0.0,
  Culture=neutral, PublicKeyToken=b03f5f7f11d50a3a"
  Condition="'$(MSBuildToolsVersion)' == '2.0'" />
<UsingTask TaskName="ReadLinesFromFile"
  AssemblyName="Microsoft.Build.Tasks.v4.0,Version=4.0.0.0,
  Culture=neutral, PublicKeyToken=b03f5f7f11d50a3a"
  Condition="'$(MSBuildToolsVersion)' == '3.5' or
    '$(MSBuildToolsVersion)' == '2.0'" />
```

During the CTP period for Visual Studio 2010, this .OverrideTasks file was used to determine at the last minute which new tasks were available by default. As backward compatibility issues were discovered, or as backward compatibility was broken by fixing bugs or otherwise altering the behavior of standard tasks, build support for older projects was maintained by carefully curating this list and specifying the exact versions of the previous toolsets that needed updated tasks. This allows MSBuild, when multi-targeting the v3.5 framework, to first import the Microsoft.Common.tasks file located in the v3.5 Framework folder, then selectively overloading specific tasks that are not compatible with the 4.0 engine driving the multi-targeting build by switching to the newer 4.0 version in the case that a specific task is both referenced in the Microsoft.Common.OverloadTasks file in the v4.0 folder, and also has the Condition that the target $(MSBuildToolsVersion) is '3.5.'

Because MSBuild uses a wildcard to find these files, you are able to add your own .tasks to this automated discovery mechanism simply by dropping a .tasks file with appropriate UsingTask statements right alongside the Microsoft.Common.Tasks file. Doing this however has a bad smell about it, since that is a special OS location and shouldn't require customization just to get your local build to work. There are better techniques, specifically *trick #19, Consider using the standard extensions path*.

8. Understand task factories

Inline tasks are possible because MSBuild ships with a task factory implementation that supports them, in this case the CodeTaskFactory that ships with MSBuild, the one described above in *trick #6, Use inline custom tasks coded in the project file*. It turns out that this is just one possible implementation of a task factory; there are others, and you can create your own as well. For example, you could provide support for task authoring using languages other than those supported by inline tasks, but task factories can be used for more than just inline task support.

One example of this is in another provided task factory—the XAML Task factory—which is described in detail in the companion book to this one, *More MSBuild Trickery*[9].

One other example is the PowerShell task factory available on the MSDN Code Gallery. If you are a PowerShell guru, perform a Bing search for "MSBuild factory" to find more information.

9. Use property functions

It turns out that the trivial inline task defined above has an even easier implementation. A small subset of the .NET Framework is available for use within the specification of property values. The following is a complete replacement of the inline task defined above, and can be coded directly in the C++ project:

```
<ItemGroupDefinition>
   <ClCompile>
      <ProcessorNumber>$([MSBuild]::Subtract(
         $(NUMBER_OF_PROCESSORS),
         1))</ProcessorNumber>
   </ClCompile>
</ItemGroupDefinition>
```

---

[9] Available Fall 2011 on Amazon.com

There are currently several basic forms available for property functions:

```
$(AnyProperty.AnyPublicStringMethod())
e.g.  $(WINDIR.Substring(0, 3))
```

Any public method on the System.String class can be called directly using the C# calling syntax as shown above. In the example above, the environment variable property $(WINDIR) is treated as if it were a string, and the first three characters containing the drive letter, colon and initial backslash will be returned. If you need a specific assembly version you can fully qualify it within the square brackets, for example:

```
$([Microsoft.VisualBasic.FileIO.FileSystem, Microsoft.        ⏎
VisualBasic,Version=10.0.0.0, Culture=neutral,                ⏎
PublicKeyToken=b03f5f7f11d50a3a]::
  CurrentDirectory)
```

Property functions are fairly forgiving in how parameters are passed. Take for example the following property functions using the string syntax...

```
<Message
  Text="$([System.String]::Empty.PadLeft(10, -).PadRight(20, +))"
  />
```

...which will produce the following output:

```
----------++++++++++
```

Notice that the character arguments to PadLeft and PadRight are not quoted characters, as would be required in equivalent C# code.

The special syntax [MSBuild]:: in a property gives access to a variety of built-in functions. There are three categories of these available: the math property functions Add, Subtract, Multiply, Divide and Modulo; character escaping with Escape and Unescape; and bit manipulation using BitwiseOr, BitwiseAnd, BitwiseXor and BitwiseNot.

```
[MSBuild]::BuiltInPropertyFunction
e.g. $([MSBuild]::Escape($(PropertyWithSpecialCharacters)))
```

Static class property functions allow the specification of a limited subset of available basic types as the ClassName using the syntax above, including static methods on the basic System types (e.g. System.String, System.Guid), System.Convert, System.Math, System.IO.Path, System.Text.RegularExpressions.Regex, and a special class in the Build Framework named Microsoft.Build.Utilities.ToolLocationHelper. Additionally, some selected static methods on specific classes are available for System.Environment, System.IO.Directory and System.IO.File.

```
$([ClassName]::PublicStaticProperty)
e.g.  $([System.DateTime]::Now)

$([ClassName]::PublicMember(Arguments)
e.g.  $([System.Guid]::NewGuid())
```

There is an additional special property function named
GetDirectoryOfFileAbove that is described in more detail in *trick #16, Use
GetDirectoryNameOfFileAbove to discover shared properties*, and another
one named MakeRelative, covered in *trick #50, Use System.IO.Path for
path comparisons*.

Eliminating a lame trailing slash with property functions

```
<PropertyGroup>
  <RootDir>$(MSBuildThisFileDirectory)</RootDir>
  <RootDir Condition="$(RootDir.EndsWith('\'))"
    >$(RootDir.SubString(
      0,
      $([MSBuild]::Add(
        $(RootDir.Length),
        -1))))</RootDir>
  <DeploymentRoot>$(RootDir)\Deployed</DeploymentRoot>
</PropertyGroup>
```

This new ability seems essentially to make obsolete the specialized
HasTrailingSlash Condition.

There are so many property functions available; in order to demonstrate
them all I've broken them down into a series of targets. The main target
and the enclosing project file skeleton are shown below, with each of the
dependent targets listed separately in order in the sections that follow.

Use Property Functions.trkproj

```
<Project ...
  ToolsVersion="4.0"
  DefaultTargets="UsePropertyFunctions">

  <!-- See individual targets in listings below -->

  <Target Name="UsePropertyFunctions"
    DependsOnTargets="
      BitwisePropertyFunctions;
      DateTimePropertyFunctions;
      GuidPropertyFunctions;
      ConvertPropertyFunctions;
      NumericConstantPropertyFunctions;
      CharacterPropertyFunctions;
      IoPropertyFunctions;
      DoublePropertyFunctions;
      EscapePropertyFunctions;
```

```
      MathPropertyFunctions;
      RegexPropertyFunctions;
      EnumPropertyFunctions;
      EnvironmentPropertyFunctions;"
      />
</Project>
```

Bitwise Property Functions

For the first set of property functions dealing with bitwise operations, an inline task is shown that converts the numeric decimal results to a binary representation, so that the results of the bit twiddling can be sensibly seen in the output.

BitwisePropertyFunctions target

```
<UsingTask
  TaskName="AsBinary"
  TaskFactory="CodeTaskFactory"
  AssemblyFile="$(MSBuildToolsPath)\Microsoft.Build.Tasks.v4.0 ⤸
.dll">
  <ParameterGroup>
    <Value
      ParameterType="System.Int32"
      Required="true"
      />
    <Result
      ParameterType="System.String"
      Output="true"
      />
  </ParameterGroup>

  <Task>
    <Code Type="Fragment" Language="cs">
      <![CDATA[                                          // -- 1 --
        Result = System.Convert.ToString(
          (byte) Value, 2)                               // -- 2 --
          .PadLeft(8, '0');
      ]]>
    </Code>
  </Task>
</UsingTask>

<Target Name="BitwisePropertyFunctions">
  <PropertyGroup>
    <!-- 00001111 -->                                    <!-- 3 -->
    <Bitwise15>15</Bitwise15>
    <!-- 01010101 -->
    <Bitwise85>85</Bitwise85>
                                                         <!-- 4 -->
    <BitwiseOr>$([MSBuild]::BitwiseOr(
      $(Bitwise15),
```

```
      $(Bitwise85)))</BitwiseOr>
    <BitwiseNot15>$([MSBuild]::BitwiseNot(
      $(Bitwise15)))</BitwiseNot15>
  </PropertyGroup>
  <AsBinary Value="$(Bitwise85)">                        <!-- 5 -->
    <Output TaskParameter="Result" PropertyName="Bitwise85" />
  </AsBinary>
  <AsBinary Value="$(Bitwise15)">
    <Output TaskParameter="Result" PropertyName="Bitwise15" />
  </AsBinary>
  <AsBinary Value="$(BitwiseOr)">
    <Output TaskParameter="Result" PropertyName="BitwiseOr" />
  </AsBinary>
  <AsBinary Value="$(BitwiseNot15)">
    <Output TaskParameter="Result" PropertyName="BitwiseNot15" />
  </AsBinary>

  <Message Text="Bitwise15 =    '$(Bitwise15)'" />
  <Message Text="Bitwise85 =    '$(Bitwise85)'" />
  <Message Text="BitwiseOr =    '$(BitwiseOr)'" />
  <Message Text="BitwiseNot15 = '$(BitwiseNot15)'" />
</Target>
```

Output

```
BitwisePropertyFunctions:
  Bitwise15 =    '00001111'
  Bitwise85 =    '01010101'
  BitwiseOr =    '01011111'
  BitwiseNot15 = '11110000'
```

The inline task (1) named "AsBinary" takes an integer input named Value and returns a string representation of that integer using the base 2 conversion (2) with left padding of zeroes so that the bits align. The numbers 15 and 85 are chosen (3) because they have interesting bit patterns. A series of properties (4) are created using the built-in bitwise operators available from the implicit $([MSBuild]::*Function*) syntax. Both Or and Not are shown but functions are available for other bitwise operations And and Xor.

As these functions return integer values, it is difficult to diagnose their success, which is where the inline function comes in. Each of the Bitwise properties (5) is run through the AsBinary task, replacing the original value with the resulting formatted string, which is then printed out with a Message task. Notice that properties are always strings, even though in the case of the inline function the Value property is coerced to an integer type, the input property is then overwritten with the string output Result, which contains the binary representation.

DateTime Property Functions

DateTime functions can come into play when dealing with custom build dependencies that need to examine file times, as well as in various automated build numbering schemes, some of which are discussed in more detail in *trick #100, How to manipulate version numbers* and *trick #101, How to auto-increment the daily build revision.* Those tricks rely on some of these general date related functions.

DateTimePropertyFunctions target

```
<Target Name="DateTimePropertyFunctions">
  <PropertyGroup>
    <DateTimeNow>$([System.DateTime]::Now)</DateTimeNow>
    <DateTimeUtcNow>$([System.DateTime]::UtcNow)</DateTimeUtcNow>
    <DateTimeToday>$([System.DateTime]::Today)</DateTimeToday>
    <DateTimeIsLeapYear>$([System.DateTime]::
      IsLeapYear(2011))</DateTimeIsLeapYear>
    <DateTimeDaysInFeb>$([System.DateTime]::
      DaysInMonth(2011, 2))</DateTimeDaysInFeb>
                                                  <!-- 1 -->
    <DateTimeFormatted>$([System.DateTime]::
      Now.ToString("dddd, MMMM dd, yyyy"))</DateTimeFormatted>
    <TimeTicksPerDay>$([System.TimeSpan]::
      TicksPerDay)</TimeTicksPerDay>
  </PropertyGroup>

  <Message Text="DateTimeNow       = '$(DateTimeNow)'" />
  <Message Text="DateTimeUtcNow = '$(DateTimeUtcNow)'" />
  <Message Text="DateTimeToday   = '$(DateTimeToday)'" />
  <Message Text="DateTimeIsLeapYear = '$(DateTimeIsLeapYear)'" />
  <Message Text="DateTimeDaysInFeb  = '$(DateTimeDaysInFeb)'" />
  <Message Text="DateTimeFormatted  = '$(DateTimeFormatted)'" />
                                                  <!-- 2 -->
  <Message Text="TimeSpanTicksPerDay = '$(TimeTicksPerDay)'" />
</Target>
```

Output

```
DateTimePropertyFunctions:
  DateTimeNow     = '4/2/2011 2:39:56 PM'
  DateTimeUtcNow = '4/2/2011 7:39:56 PM'
  DateTimeToday   = '4/2/2011 12:00:00 AM'
  DateTimeIsLeapYear = 'False'
  DateTimeDaysInFeb  = '28'
  DateTimeFormatted  = 'Saturday, April 02, 2011'
  TimeSpanTicksPerDay = '864000000000'
```

Of particular interest is the formatted DateTime (1) which allows for any of the available DateTime formatting options. In addition to the DateType system type, one function (2) for System.TimeSpan is also shown.

Guid Property Functions

Property functions for Guids, which for the most part are self-explanatory, are shown below.

```xml
<Target Name="GuidPropertyFunctions">
  <PropertyGroup>
    <GuidNewGuid>$([System.Guid]::NewGuid())</GuidNewGuid>
    <GuidEmpty>$([System.Guid]::Empty)</GuidEmpty>
    <ParseThis>AA37A30E-2362-4351-9575-EEA0B2EB41A7</ParseThis>
    <GuidParse>$([System.Guid]::Parse($(ParseThis)))</GuidParse>
    <ParseExact>D526087E106648E4A956AE711F7EC81A</ParseExact>
    <GuidParseExact>$([System.Guid]::
      ParseExact($(ParseExact), "N"))</GuidParseExact>
                                                   <!-- 1 -->
    <Guid1>BE916F3F-6764-4B3E-A791-835B9A84E79D</Guid1>
    <Guid2>be916f3f-6764-4b3e-a791-835b9a84e79d</Guid2>
    <GuidsMatch
      Condition="'$(Guid1)' == '$(Guid2)'"
      >true</GuidsMatch>
    <GuidsEquality
      Condition="$([System.Guid]::
        op_Equality(
          $([System.Guid]::new('$(Guid1)')),
          $([System.Guid]::new('$(Guid2)'))))"
        >true</GuidsEquality>
  </PropertyGroup>

  <Message Text="GuidNewGuid     = '$(GuidNewGuid)'" />
  <Message Text="GuidEmpty       = '$(GuidEmpty)'" />
  <Message Text="GuidParse       = '$(GuidParse)'" />
  <Message Text="GuidParseExact  = '$(GuidParseExact)'" />
  <Message Text="GuidsMatch      = '$(GuidsMatch)'" />
  <Message Text="GuidsEquality   = '$(GuidsEquality)'" />
</Target>
```

Output

```
GuidPropertyFunctions:
  GuidNewGuid    = '4fecb628-70e0-4be4-be56-7805dfcf2589'
  GuidEmpty      = '00000000-0000-0000-0000-000000000000'
  GuidParse      = 'aa37a30e-2362-4351-9575-eea0b2eb41a7'
  GuidParseExact = 'd526087e-1066-48e4-a956-ae711f7ec81a'
  GuidsMatch     = 'true'
  GuidsEquality  = 'true'
```

Of these, the most likely to be used is in a build is Guid.NewGuid. If you are planning on passing Guids as parameters to tasks, realize that the parameter type must be declared as a string as there is no way currently to coerce MSBuild to create one.

In the documentation for the Guid type, Equality and Inequality are shown as static functions for Guid as well as other types available in

MSBuild property functions, but there is no obvious way to access these directly in a property function since the syntax requires the use of those operators, which is not supported in MSBuild. To compare Guids, as the two identical values at (1) each with different casing, two different techniques are used, the first using the string equivalents recalling that condition comparisons are case insensitive, or use an inline function. The second comparison exercises the Equality operator using the syntax ::op_Equality. This isn't quite obvious at first; to familiarize yourself with these syntactical patterns take a look at PowerShell or IL syntax documentation.

Convert Property Functions

The System.Convert class has too-may-to-show methods named To*Type*, a few of which get an assist on some of the other property functions in other targets in this tip, but only ToChar is shown below, even then in an assisting role in a demonstration of the more interesting Base64 conversion functions in the System.Convert class.

ConvertPropertyFunctions target

```
<Target Name="ConvertPropertyFunctions">
  <PropertyGroup>                                    <!-- 1 -->
    <ConvertBase64>$([System.Convert]::
      FromBase64String("SGVsbG8gV29ybGQgNjQ="))</ConvertBase64>
  </PropertyGroup>
  <Message
    Text="%24(ConvertBase64) = '$(ConvertBase64)'"
    />                                               <!-- 2 -->

  <ItemGroup>                                        <!-- 3 -->
    <ConvertBase64
      Include="$([System.Convert]::
        FromBase64String('SGVsbG8gV29ybGQgNjQ='))"
      />
  </ItemGroup>
  <Message
    Text="%40(ConvertBase64) = '@(ConvertBase64)'"
    />                                               <!-- 4 -->

  <ItemGroup>
    <ConvertBase64>                                  <!-- 5 -->
      <Character>$([System.Convert]::ToChar(
        $([System.Convert]::ToUInt32(%(Identity)))))</Character>
    </ConvertBase64>
  </ItemGroup>

  <PropertyGroup>                                    <!-- 6 -->
```

```
      <ConvertBase64>@(ConvertBase64->'%(Character)',
        '')</ConvertBase64>
    </PropertyGroup>
    <Message
      Text="%24(ConvertBase64) = '$(ConvertBase64)'"
      />
  </Target>
```

Output

```
ConvertPropertyFunctions:
  $(ConvertBase64) = '72;101;108;108;111;32;87;111;114;108;100;   ↵
32;54;52'
  @(ConvertBase64) = '72;101;108;108;111;32;87;111;114;108;100;   ↵
32; 54;52'
  $(ConvertBase64) = 'Hello World 64'
```

A property $(ConvertBase64) is created by passing a Base64 encoded
string (1) with the value "SGVsbG8gV29ybGQgNjQ=" as the input
parameter to the System.Convert.FromBase64String method. It is
immediately printed out (2) with a Message task, which from the Output
can be seen to be an array of numbers. Looking at the signature for the
FromBase64String methods it can be seen the return value of byte[] type
has been coerced into a string using the MSBuild default behavior of
making a semicolon delimited list. With a property in this form, you
could feed it directly into an item with this code:

```
<ItemGroup>
  <ConvertBase64 Include="$(ConvertBase64)" />
</ItemGroup>
```

Instead, let's see how the item array declaration fares being passed an
array of byte (3) directly in the identity attribute repeating the call to
FromBase64String made above for the property assignment. The second
line of output from the message (4) that follows shows that MSBuild
completes the conversion from an array to an item list just fine on its
own. But an array of integers isn't interesting if the desired result is a
string. To complete the conversion, each item in the list is given (5) a
meta value named <Character> by calling System.Convert.ToChar on
the identity value, which is the byte value integer in string form, by using
a dynamic meta value calculation. Remember that MSBuild deals in
strings, so even though the ConvertBase64 returned an array of byte
values, MSBuild converted each to the string form of the number, for
example "72," to be used as the identity of the item. System.Convert
contains eighteen overloads of ToChar, and since the value passed as
%(Identity) is a string, that overload would be incorrectly chosen by
default. To coerce the selection of ToChar(Int32), the identity is first
passed through System.Convert.ToUInt32, ensuring that the proper

overload is selected. Failure to convert first to a UInt32 would result in the following error:

```
...\Use Property Functions.trkproj(148,9): error MSB4184: The
expression "[System.Convert]::ToChar(72)" cannot be evaluated. String
must be exactly one character long.
```

Now that each item in the item list contains a meta value which is the character value of the identity number, an item transform (6) is performed to pull these meta values together as a single string. Since default item transforms generate a semicolon-delimited list, the syntax supplying a custom delimiter—in this case an empty string—is used. The transformed property is printed and the result can be seen to be the string "Hello World 64" in the output listing.

Numeric Constant Property Functions

Once again, there are a large number of numeric conversion functions for both integral and floating-point values. The emphasis in this next target is to show the various constants and IsCondition static methods on the various System.Type numeric types.

Although these are not all that interesting in and of themselves since floating point math seldom comes up in a build, these examples demonstrate a few interesting behaviors with respect to coerced values and comparisons, and how MSBuild retains values of any type within a property function, and then converts result types using ToString when the type is finally assigned to a property.

NumericConstanPropertyFunctions target

```
<Target Name="NumericConstantPropertyFunctions">          <!-- 1 -->
  <Message Text="ByteMin  = '$([System.Byte]::MinValue)'" />
  <Message Text="ByteMax  = '$([System.Byte]::MaxValue)'" />
  <Message Text="Int32Min = '$([System.Int32]::MinValue)'" />
  <Message Text="Int32Max = '$([System.Int32]::MaxValue)'" />

  <Message Text="%0d" />                                    <!-- 2 -->
  <PropertyGroup>
    <DoubleNaN>$([System.Double]::NaN)</DoubleNaN>          <!-- 3 -->
    <DoubleIsNaN1>$([System.Double]::
      IsNaN($(DoubleNaN)))</DoubleIsNaN1>                   <!-- 4 -->
    <DoubleCalcNaN>$([MSBuild]::Divide(0, 0))</DoubleCalcNaN>
    <DoubleIsNaN2>$([System.Double]::
      IsNaN($(DoubleCalcNaN)))</DoubleIsNaN2>

    <DoublePosInfinity>$([System.Double]::
      PositiveInfinity)</DoublePosInfinity>
```

```
        <DoubleNegInfinity>$([System.Double]::
          NegativeInfinity)</DoubleNegInfinity>
                                                            <!-- 5 -->
        <DoubleIsInfinity1>$([System.Double]::
          IsInfinity($(DoublePosInfinity)))</DoubleIsInfinity1>
        <DoubleIsInfinity2>$([System.Double]::
          IsInfinity($(DoubleNegInfinity)))</DoubleIsInfinity2>
                                                            <!-- 6 -->
        <DoubleCalcInfinity>$([MSBuild]::
          Divide(1.0, 0.0))</DoubleCalcInfinity>
        <DoubleIsInfinity3>$([System.Double]::
          IsInfinity($(DoubleCalcInfinity)))</DoubleIsInfinity3>
      </PropertyGroup>
      <Message Text="DoubleMin = '$([System.Double]::MinValue)'" />
      <Message Text="DoubleMax = '$([System.Double]::MaxValue)'" />
      <Message Text="DoubleEpsilon = '$([System.Double]::Epsilon)'"
/>
      <Message Text="DoubleNaN     = '$(DoubleNaN)'" />
      <Message Text="DoublePosInfinity  = '$(DoublePosInfinity)'" />
      <Message Text="DoubleNegInfinity  = '$(DoubleNegInfinity)'" />
      <Message Text="DoubleIsInfinity1  = '$(DoubleIsInfinity1)'" />
      <Message Text="DoubleIsInfinity2  = '$(DoubleIsInfinity2)'" />
      <Message Text="DoubleCalcInfinity = '$(DoubleCalcInfinity)'" />
      <Message Text="DoubleIsInfinity3  = '$(DoubleIsInfinity3)'" />
      <Message Text="DoubleIsNaN1 = '$(DoubleIsNaN1)'" />
      <Message Text="DoubleCalcNaN = '$(DoubleCalcNaN)'" />
      <Message Text="DoubleIsNaN2 = '$(DoubleIsNaN2)'" />
    </Target>
```

Output

```
NumericConstantPropertyFunctions:
  ByteMin  = '0'
  ByteMax  = '255'
  Int32Min = '-2147483648'
  Int32Max = '2147483647'

  DoubleMin = '-1.79769313486232E+308'
  DoubleMax = '1.79769313486232E+308'
  DoubleEpsilon = '4.94065645841247E-324'
  DoubleNaN     = 'NaN'
  DoublePosInfinity  = 'Infinity'
  DoubleNegInfinity  = '-Infinity'
  DoubleIsInfinity1  = 'True'
  DoubleIsInfinity2  = 'True'
  DoubleCalcInfinity = 'Infinity'
  DoubleIsInfinity3  = 'True'
  DoubleIsNaN1 = 'True'
  DoubleCalcNaN = 'NaN'
  DoubleIsNaN2 = 'True'
```

The minimum and maximum Byte and Int32 values (1) are printed directly in Message tasks, followed by (2) a newline for clarity in the Output listing. Next, a series of properties are defined from System.Double constants, including NaN (3) which is the floating point

"Not a Number" value, a property (4) testing the NaN value using System.Double.IsNan, which is shown to be the value 'True' near the bottom of the Output listing. The same type of property constant definition and testing is shown for Infinity and NegativeInfinity. To generate these constants, they are either pulled from static constants (5) declared on the numeric types, as with System.Double.Infinity, or calculated directly (6) using math, as with $(DoubleCalcInfinity) which is the result of a divide by zero calculation.

Character Property Functions

Since MSBuild deals primarily in string values, character manipulation functions can often come in handy. The next target runs through the various character testing functions available on the System.Char type.

CharacterPropertyFunctions target

```
<Target Name="CharacterPropertyFunctions">
  <PropertyGroup>
    <ABC_123>ABC 123</ABC_123>                          <!-- 1 -->
    <DEF_def>DEF!def</DEF_def>                           <!-- 2 -->
  </PropertyGroup>
                                                         <!-- 3 -->
  <Message Text="IsDigitX = '$([System.Char]::IsDigit('X'))'" />
  <Message Text="IsDigit9 = '$([System.Char]::IsDigit('9'))'" />
                                                         <!-- 4 -->
  <Message Text="IsDigit Abc 123[0] = '$([System.Char]::
    IsDigit($(ABC_123), 0))'"
    />
  <Message Text="IsDigit Abc 123[4] = '$([System.Char]::
    IsDigit($(ABC_123), 4))'"
    />
  <Message Text="IsPunctuation       = '$([System.Char]::
    IsPunctuation('?'))'"
    />
  <Message Text="IsPunctuation DEF!def[3] = '$([System.Char]::
    IsPunctuation($(DEF_def), 3))'"
    />
                                                         <!-- 5 -->
  <Message Text="ToLower    = '$([System.Char]::ToLower('Z'))'" />
  <Message Text="IsLower DEF!def[2] = '$([System.Char]::
    IsLower($(DEF_def), 2))'"
    />
  <Message Text="IsLower DEF!def[5] = '$([System.Char]::
    IsLower($(DEF_def), 5))'"
    />
  <Message Text="IsWhiteSpace ABC 123[3] = '$([System.Char]::
    IsWhiteSpace($(ABC_123), 3))'"
    />
```

```
      </Target>
```

Output

```
CharacterPropertyFunctions:
  IsDigitX = 'False'
  IsDigit9 = 'True'
  IsDigit Abc 123[0] = 'False'
  IsDigit Abc 123[4] = 'True'
  IsPunctuation      = 'True'
  IsPunctuation DEF!def[3] = 'True'
  ToLower    = 'z'
  IsLower DEF!def[2] = 'False'
  IsLower DEF!def[5] = 'True'
  IsWhiteSpace ABC 123[3] = 'True'
```

A couple characters are tested directly (3) using System.Char.IsDigit, then
(4) the overloads for IsDigit that accept a string and a character position
within the string are used with two different strings (1) declared in
properties. Tests for IsDigit and IsPunctuation are performed showing
both true and false results. Finally, a similar pattern (5) is used for the
ToLower and IsWhiteSpace methods.

IO Property Functions

There are many static functions available in System.IO.Path that already
have built-in representation in MSBuild, for example, the well-known
metadata for file based items, which mirror the static functions that allow
you to extract base file names, folders and extensions. The target below
focuses on other methods that quite often come into play in complex
builds, specifically where generated files need to have paths or file names
constructed at build time.

IoPropertyFunctions

```
<Target Name="IoPropertyFunctions">
  <PropertyGroup>
    <IoPathRandom>$([System.IO.Path]::
      GetRandomFileName())</IoPathRandom>              <!-- 1 -->
    <BasePath>C:\ImaginaryPath</BasePath>              <!-- 2 -->
    <IoPathCombine>$([System.IO.Path]::
      Combine($(BasePath), $(IoPathRandom)))</IoPathCombine>
    <IoPathTemp>$([System.IO.Path]::
      GetTempFileName())</IoPathTemp>                  <!-- 3 -->
    <IoPathChangeExt>$([System.IO.Path]::
      ChangeExtension(
        $(MSBuildThisFile),
        ".txt"))</IoPathChangeExt>                     <!-- 4 -->
```

```
        <IoPathDirSeparator>$([System.IO.Path]::
            DirectorySeparatorChar)</IoPathDirSeparator>      <!-- 5 -->
        <IoPathAltSeparator>$([System.IO.Path]::
            AltDirectorySeparatorChar)</IoPathAltSeparator>
        <IoPathInvalidName>$([System.IO.Path]::
            GetInvalidFileNameChars())</IoPathInvalidName>
        <IoPathInvalidPath>$([System.IO.Path]::
            GetInvalidPathChars())</IoPathInvalidPath>
    </PropertyGroup>
    <Message Text="IoPathRandom = '$(IoPathRandom)'" />
    <Message Text="IoPathTemp    = '$(IoPathTemp)'" />
    <Message Text="IoPathChangeExtension = '$(IoPathChangeExt)'" />
    <Message Text="IoPathDirSeparator = '$(IoPathDirSeparator)'" />
    <Message Text="IoPathAltSeparator = '$(IoPathAltSeparator)'" />
    <Message Text="IoPathInvalidName = '$(IoPathInvalidName)'" />
    <Message Text="IoPathInvalidPath = '$(IoPathInvalidPath)'" />
</Target>
```

Output

```
IoPropertyFunctions:
  IoPathRandom  = '1x1npzks.ka3'
  IoPathCombine = 'C:\ImaginaryPath\1x1npzks.ka3'
  IoPathTemp    = 'C:\Users\Trickery\AppData\Local\Temp\tmpC661.tmp'
  IoPathChangeExtension = 'Use Property Functions.txt'
  IoPathDirSeparator = '\'
  IoPathAltSeparator = '/'
  IoPathInvalidName = '";<;>;|; ;0;0;♥;♦;♣;♠;    ;
;♫;○;►;◄;↕;‼;¶;§;▬;↨;↑;↓;→;←;∟;↔;▲;▼;;;*;?;\;/'
  IoPathInvalidPath = '";<;>;|; ;0;0;♥;♦;♣;♠;    ;
;♫;○;►;◄;↕;‼;¶;§;▬;↨;↑;↓;→;←;∟;↔;▲;▼'
```

The System.IO.Path.GetRandomFileName() static method (1) returns a statistically "cryptographically strong" string that can be used as a file or folder name without a path, in this case the file "1x1npzks.ka3" is returned, as seen in the output. A contrived path (2) is then combined with this file name using System.IO.Path.Combine. This is similar to the behavior of System.IO.Path.GetTempFileName (3) which returns a file name in the Temp folder that is guaranteed to be unique, but which also has the side effect of creating a file with the returned file name. In builds the use of GetTempFileName is not advised due to several limitations, including a limit of 64K different values which would easily be hit in larger builds, and race conditions in some versions of Windows.

The call to System.IO.Path.ChangeExtension is a clean alternative to the somewhat wordy alternative built into MSBuild, which requires the creation of an item, and then the recreation of the entire path with the commonly seen item transform below:

```
@(SomeItem->'%(RootDir)%(Directory)%(FileName).txt')
```

The remaining properties (5) show various static methods that relate to separator characters and valid path characters.

Double & Long Property Functions

Previously in the NumericConstantPropertyFunctions target various constants and constant tests were shown. This target focuses on the built-in math routines on the $([MSBuild]::*Function*) methods. These exist for all the numeric types; this target focuses on the distinction between the Double and Long types, which serve as proxies for the other numeric types available.

DoublePropertyFunctions target

```
<Target Name="DoublePropertyFunctions">
  <PropertyGroup>
    <DoubleVal7>7.0</DoubleVal7>                          <!-- 1 -->
    <DoubleVal2>2.0</DoubleVal2>
    <LongVal7>7</LongVal7>
    <LongVal2>2</LongVal2>
                                                          <!-- 2 -->
    <AddDoubles>$([MSBuild]::Add(
      $(DoubleVal7),
      $(DoubleVal2)))</AddDoubles>

    <AddLongs>$([MSBuild]::Add(
      $(LongVal7),
      $(LongVal2)))</AddLongs>

    <SubtractDoubles>$([MSBuild]::Subtract(
      $(DoubleVal7),
      $(DoubleVal2)))</SubtractDoubles>

    <SubtractLongs>$([MSBuild]::Subtract(
      $(LongVal7),
      $(LongVal2)))</SubtractLongs>

    <MultiplyDoubles>$([MSBuild]::Multiply(
      $(DoubleVal7),
      $(DoubleVal2)))</MultiplyDoubles>

    <MultiplyLongs>$([MSBuild]::Multiply(
      $(LongVal7),
      $(LongVal2)))</MultiplyLongs>

    <DivideDoubles>$([MSBuild]::Divide(
      $(DoubleVal7),
      $(DoubleVal2)))</DivideDoubles>
                                                          <!-- 3 -->
    <DivideLongs>$([MSBuild]::Divide(
```

```
        $(LongVal7),
        $(LongVal2)))</DivideLongs>
                                                            <!-- 4 -->

    <DivideLongsCoerced>$([MSBuild]::Divide(
        $([System.Convert]::ToInt32($(LongVal7))),
        $([System.Convert]::ToInt32($(LongVal2)))
        ))</DivideLongsCoerced>

    <ModuloDoubles>$([MSBuild]::Modulo(
        $(DoubleVal7),
        $(DoubleVal2)))</ModuloDoubles>

    <ModuloLongs>$([MSBuild]::Modulo(
        $(LongVal7),
        $(LongVal2)))</ModuloLongs>

</PropertyGroup>

<Message Text="AddDoubles      = '$(AddDoubles)'" />
<Message Text="AddLongs        = '$(AddLongs)'" />
<Message Text="SubtractDoubles = '$(SubtractDoubles)'" />
<Message Text="SubtractLongs   = '$(SubtractLongs)'" />
<Message Text="MultiplyDoubles = '$(MultiplyDoubles)'" />
<Message Text="MultiplyLongs   = '$(MultiplyLongs)'" />
<Message Text="DivideLongsCoerced = '$(DivideLongsCoerced)'" />
<Message Text="DivideDoubles   = '$(DivideDoubles)'" />
<Message Text="DivideLongs     = '$(DivideLongs)'" />
<Message Text="ModuloDoubles   = '$(ModuloDoubles)'" />
<Message Text="ModuloLongs     = '$(ModuloLongs)'" />
</Target>
```

Output

```
DoublePropertyFunctions:
  AddDoubles      = '9'
  AddLongs        = '9'
  SubtractDoubles = '5'
  SubtractLongs   = '5'
  MultiplyDoubles = '14'
  MultiplyLongs   = '14'
  DivideDoubles   = '3.5'
  DivideLongs     = '3.5'
  DivideLongsCoerced = '3'
  ModuloDoubles   = '1'
  ModuloLongs     = '1'
```

To start out, two doubles and two longs are declared (1) as properties. These are then passed (2) to various built-in math functions, Add, Subtract etc., producing expected outputs. When the two long values are divided (3) though, it can be seen that the output is not expected. The $([MSBuild]::Divide(long) is documented to return a long, but the output shows the value "3.5" which is clearly not an integral value. Once again, realize that MSBuild is using strings, and has selected the floating point form of the Divide function using default conversions. To coerce the desired function (4), the properties are first passed through System.Convert.ToInt32, which produces the expected result of "3" properly truncated as an integer.

Escape Property Functions

The built-in character escaping functions are intended to allow the proper escaping of strings with respect to MSBuild escaping rules. Unfortunately, they fall short as will be shown below.

EscapePropertyFunctions target

```
<Target Name="ReadEscapedFromFile">
  <ReadLinesFromFile
    File="Use Property Functions Escaped.txt">        <!-- 1 -->
    <Output
      TaskParameter="Lines"
      ItemName="HasUnescapedFromFile"
      />
    <Output
      TaskParameter="Lines"
      PropertyName="HasUnescapedFromFile"
      />
  </ReadLinesFromFile>                                <!-- 2 -->
  <Message
    Text="HasUnescapedFromFile = '@(HasUnescapedFromFile)'"
    />
  <Message
    Text="HasUnescapedFromFile = '$(HasUnescapedFromFile)'"
    />
</Target>

<Target Name="EscapePropertyFunctions"
  DependsOnTargets="ReadEscapedFromFile">

  <PropertyGroup>                                     <!-- 3 -->
    <HasEscaped>%24 %40 %25 %27 %3b %3f %2a</HasEscaped>
    <HasSpecial>$ @ % ' ; ? *</HasSpecial>
    <UnescapedString>$([MSBuild]::Unescape(
      $(HasEscaped)))</UnescapedString>
    <EscapedString>$([MSBuild]::Escape(
      $(HasSpecial)))</EscapedString>
  </PropertyGroup>

  <!-- 4 -->
  <Message Text="HasEscaped = '$(HasEscaped)'" />
  <Message Text="HasSpecial = '$(HasSpecial)'" />
  <Message Text="UnescapedString = '$(UnescapedString)'" />
  <Message Text="%0d" />
```

```
    <Message Text="EscapedString..." />
    <!-- 5 -->
    <Message Text="  Fail: '$(EscapedString)'" />
    <!-- 6 -->
    <Message Text="  Fail: $([MSBuild]::Escape($ @ % ' ; ? *))" />
    <!-- 7 -->
    <Message Text="  Fail: $([MSBuild]::Escape($ @ % ; ? *))" />
    <!-- 8 -->
    <Message Text="  Fail: $([MSBuild]::Escape(`$ @ % ' ; ? *`))"
      />

    <PropertyGroup>                                       <!-- 9 -->
      <EscapedFromFileItem>$([MSBuild]::Escape(
        @(HasUnescapedFromFile)))</EscapedFromFileItem>
      <EscapedFromFileProp>$([MSBuild]::Escape(
        $(HasUnescapedFromFile)))</EscapedFromFileProp>
    </PropertyGroup>
    <Message
      Text="  Fail: EscapedFromFileItem = '$(EscapedFromFileItem)'"
      />
    <Message
      Text="  Fail: EscapedFromFileProp = '$(EscapedFromFileProp)'"
      />
  </Target>
```

Output

```
ReadEscapedFromFile:
  HasUnescapedFromFile = '$ @ % ' ; ? *'
  HasUnescapedFromFile = '$ @ % ' ; ? *'
EscapePropertyFunctions:
  HasEscaped = '$ @ % ' ; ? *'
  HasSpecial = '$ @ % ' ; ? *'
  UnescapedString = '$ @ % ' ; ? *'

  EscapedString...
    Fail: '$ @ % ' ; ? *'
    Fail: $([MSBuild]::Escape($ @ % ' ; ? *))
    Fail: $ @ % ; ? *
    Fail: $ @ % ' ; ? *
    Fail: EscapedFromFileItem = '@(HasUnescapedFromFile)'
    Fail: EscapedFromFileProp = '$ @ % ' ; ? *'
```

The first complexity when dealing with demonstrating escaping behavior in MSBuild is that any escaped characters in the MSBuild file will be transformed when the file is read. To work around that, this target reads escaped values from a text file using the dependent target ReadEscapedFromFile. The contents of the file "Use Property Functions Escaped.txt" is a single line with the following characters:

```
$ @ % ' ; ? *
```

These are read into both an item and a property of the same name (1) using the Output parameter "Lines" twice. Both the item and property are printed (2) using Message tasks, to show the values were properly read.

Next, a series of properties (3) are defined, first $(HasEscaped) composed of escaped special characters, then $(HasSpecial) which has the same characters in their un-escaped form. The $(HasEscaped) is passed through the [MSBuild]::Unescape method, and the un-escaped string is passed through the [MSBuild]::Escape method, creating two new properties. The original strings are displayed (4) followed by the un-escaped version of the escaped string, which from the output can be seen to have been properly formed.

It starts to break down when the escaped version of the un-escaped string is displayed (5). The string prints the same value as was passed in, $(HasSpecial), when converted to $(UnescapedString) is unchanged by the call to [MSBuild]::Unescape(). What follows is a series of experiments to try to get the un-escaping to work, using the values directly (6), which fails due to the quote character, showing a commonly seen error where the original property expression is displayed when parsing fails. The next attempt removes the quote character (7) but still doesn't produce unescaped results. Next, an attempt to use the tertiary string delimiter backquote character (8) is used, again with a failed result.

Finally the values pulled from the text file are used (9), which not only fails to work again, but shows a limitation of the property function when an item is passed to the method, it is not even processed and the resulting output just shows the raw item name, @(HasUnescapedFromFile). In this case, you need to actually use the %(.) syntax, passing instead %(HasUnescapedFromFile.Identity), but alas, even the proper syntax would also fail to escape the string passed that it is passed.

Math Property Functions

As many of the static methods in System.Math are used elsewhere, this target focuses on some additional methods not yet seen.

MathPropertyFunctions target

```
<Target Name="MathPropertyFunctions">
  <Message Text="&#960; = $([System.Math]::Pi)" />
  <Message Text="E = $([System.Math]::E)" />
  <Message Text="DecimalAdd ='$([System.Decimal]::
```

```
    Add(3.0, 0.14))'"
    />
  <Message Text="DecimalCeiling  ='$([System.Decimal]::
    Ceiling($([System.Math]::Pi)))'"
    />
  <Message Text="DecimalFloor    ='$([System.Decimal]::
    Floor($([System.Math]::Pi)))'"
    />
</Target>
```

Output

```
MathPropertyFunctions:
  π = 3.14159265358979
  E = 2.71828182845905
  DecimalAdd  ='3.14'
  DecimalCeiling  ='4'
  DecimalFloor    ='3'
```

The built-in constants for Pi and the natural log constant *e* are shown, demonstrating that not just static methods that are available, but also static fields. These floating-point values are passed to System.Decimal.Ceiling and Floor, showing two forms of integer truncation.

Regex Property Functions

Most of the static methods on the System.Text.RegularExpressions.Regex class have direct application in MSBuild and can be easily integrated into your build. The following target shows some simple pattern matching and escaping.

RegexPropertyFunctions target

```
<Target Name="RegexPropertyFunctions">
                                                        <!-- 1 -->
  <PropertyGroup>
    <RegexString>"Quoted" [Bracketed] ^${Other}\</RegexString>
    <RegexEscape>$([System.Text.RegularExpressions.Regex]::
      Escape($(RegexString)))</RegexEscape>
    <RegexUnescape>$([System.Text.RegularExpressions.Regex]::
      Unescape($(RegexEscape)))</RegexUnescape>
                                                        <!-- 2 -->
    <GuidRegex>^([\w]{8}-[\w]{4}-[\w]{4}-[\w]{4}-[\w]{12})    ↵
</GuidRegex>
  </PropertyGroup>
  <Message Text="RegexEscape    = '$(RegexEscape)'" />
  <Message Text="RegexUnescape = '$(RegexUnescape)'" />
  <Message Text="RegexIsMatch  = '$(
    [System.Text.RegularExpressions.Regex]::
```

```
      IsMatch($(GuidNewGuid), $(GuidRegex)))'"
    />
                                                    <!-- 3 -->
    <PropertyGroup>
      <RegexSentence>The quick brown fox</RegexSentence>
      <WordRegex>\b\w+</WordRegex>
      <RegexReplace>$([System.Text.RegularExpressions.Regex]::
        Replace(
          $(RegexSentence), $(WordRegex), trick))</RegexReplace>
    </PropertyGroup>
                                                    <!-- 4 -->
    <ItemGroup>
      <RegexMatches
        Include="$([System.Text.RegularExpressions.Regex]::
        Matches($(RegexSentence), $(WordRegex)))"
        />
    </ItemGroup>
    <Message Text="RegexReplace  = '$(RegexReplace)'" />
    <Message Text="RegexMatches  = '@(RegexMatches)'" />
  </Target>
```

Output

```
RegexPropertyFunctions:
  RegexEscape   = '"Quoted"\ \[Bracketed]\ \^\$\{Other}\\'
  RegexUnescape = '"Quoted" [Bracketed] ^${Other}\'
  RegexIsMatch  = 'True'
  RegexReplace  = 'trick trick trick trick'
  RegexMatches  = 'The;quick;brown;fox'
```

A string containing characters with special meaning in regular
expressions (1) is declared in the $(RegexString) property. It is then
escaped, and the resulting escaped string is then un-escaped, with those
values printed in a Message task, showing how the special characters are
escaped with back slashes.

Next a Guid Regex (2) is declared, and a regex match is performed for the
value of $(GuidNewGuid), which if you recall was previously declared in
the GuidPropertyFunctionsTarget from a property function call to
System.Guid.NewGuid. This pattern match prints 'True' in the output.

Finally, a "word matching" regular expression, "\b\w" is used to replace
the words in the $(RegexSentence) property with the string "trick" with
a call to Regex.Replace (3). The result shows that the four words in "The
quick brown fox" have become "trick trick trick trick" with the word
replacement.

Finally, Regex.Matches is called (4) passing in the same sentence and the
word matching regular expression. The result is passed as the identity of
a new item named @(RegexMatches), which accepts the result of this
static method invocation; somehow managing to transform the result to

the proper type. The call to Regex.Matches returns the type System.Text.RegularExpressions.MatchCollection, which is not intrinsically known to MSBuild, but since it is a type that implements the IEnumerable interface, and since each of the enumerated Match objects, when converted to a string, returns the match, then MSBuild is able to coerce the result into an item list. The item list is printed out with a Message task, showing the semicolon-delimited list synthesized by MSBuild, which is pretty cool.

Environment Property Functions

The System.Environment property functions provide access to some useful functionality, as well as access to extended information and usage of environment variables.

Since the use of environment variables can make builds indeterminate from one machine to another or even from one command prompt configuration to another, I generally recommend against their use. For many of the commonly seen environment variables, an equivalent call in the .NET Framework will provide the same value when called from a custom or inline task, achieving the desired result in a somewhat more repeatable manner. However, there are a few times where environment variables can add value. One time in particular deals with installed third-party SDK material, or to be more specific, tools and libraries you want to make use of in your build that are installed and that leave traces of their installation in environment variables. For a discussion of this, see trick #25, Don't use custom environment variables for paths.

The following listing shows a single target that accesses several static properties and functions on the System.Environment class.

EnvironmentPropertyFunctions target

```
<Target Name="EnvironmentPropertyFunctions">
  <PropertyGroup>
    <!-- 1 -->
    <CommandLine>$([System.Environment]::
      CommandLine)</CommandLine>
    <!-- 2 -->
    <ExpandString>Computer is %COMPUTERNAME%</ExpandString>
    <EnvVarExpand>$([System.Environment]::
      ExpandEnvironmentVariables($(ExpandString)))</EnvVarExpand>
    <!-- 3 -->
    <EnvVar>$([System.Environment]::
      GetEnvironmentVariable('WINDIR'))</EnvVar>
```

```
      <!-- 4 -->
      <EnvVarFolder>$([System.Environment]::
        GetFolderPath(SpecialFolder.System))</EnvVarFolder>
      <!-- 5 -->
      <EnvVarDrive>$([System.Environment]::
        GetLogicalDrives())</EnvVarDrive>
      <EnvVars>$([System.Environment]::
        GetEnvironmentVariables())</EnvVars>
    </PropertyGroup>
    <ItemGroup>
      <!-- 6 -->
      <EnvVarDrive Include="$([System.Environment]::
        GetLogicalDrives())"
        />
      <EnvVars Include="$([System.Environment]::
        GetEnvironmentVariables())"
        />
    </ItemGroup>
    <Message Text="CommandLine  = $(CommandLine)" />
    <Message Text="EnvVarExpand = $(EnvVarExpand)" />
    <Message Text="EnvVar       = $(EnvVar)" />
    <Message Text="EnvVarFolder = $(EnvVarFolder)" />

    <Message Text="%0d" />
    <Message Text="EnvVarDrive = $(EnvVarDrive)" />
    <Message Text="EnvVarDrive = %(EnvVarDrive.Identity)" />

    <Message Text="%0d" />
    <Message Text="EnvVars = $(EnvVars)" />
    <Message Text="EnvVars = %(EnvVars.Identity)" />
  </Target>
```

Output

```
EnvironmentPropertyFunctions:
  CommandLine  = msbuild  "Use Property Functions.trkproj"      ↵
/t:EnvironmentPropertyFunctions
  EnvVarExpand = Computer is LEAKYCAULDRON
  EnvVar       = C:\Windows
  EnvVarFolder = C:\Windows\system32

  EnvVarDrive = C:\;D:\;E:\;F:\;G:\;H:\
  EnvVarDrive = C:\
  EnvVarDrive = D:\
  EnvVarDrive = E:\
  EnvVarDrive = F:\
  EnvVarDrive = G:\
  EnvVarDrive = H:\

  EnvVars = ProgramData=C:\ProgramData;COMPUTERNAME=LEAKYCAULDRON↵
;CommonProgramFiles(x86)=C:\Program Files (x86)\... (many removed)
  EnvVars = ProgramData=C:\ProgramData
  EnvVars = COMPUTERNAME=LEAKYCAULDRON
  EnvVars = CommonProgramFiles(x86)=C:\Program Files (x86)\...
(many removed)
```

The System.Environment class has several useful static properties available from MSBuild. The command line used to run the current MSBuild process is placed in a property (1) and later printed with a message, as are all the other examples. Next a property is declared (2) containing a reference to the COMPUTERNAME environment variable escaped using the syntax of the command shell; delimited with percent signs. This property is then expanded using the System.Environment. ExpandEnvironmentVariables property function. From the output, it can be seen that the embedded %COMPUTERNAME% has been replaced by "LEAKYCAULDRON" which is the name of the computer on which this example was executed.

What follows is an extraction of the environment variable "WINDIR," which in this case is of course no different than just using $(WINDIR) in your MSBuild file, but which could be useful in situations where the name of the environment variable needs to be determined at build time through other means. The use of an enumeration is shown next in the call to System.Environment.GetFolderPath (4) where SpecialFolder.System is provided, producing in the output the path to the System32 folder. Of special note is that SpecialFolder.System does not contain a full namespace. If instead, either of the following forms were used...

```
<EnvVarFolder>$([System.Environment]::
  GetFolderPath(
    System.Environment.SpecialFolder.System))</EnvVarFolder>
<EnvVarFolder>$([System.Environment]::
  GetFolderPath(
    Environment.SpecialFolder.System))</EnvVarFolder>
```

...the following strange error would have been displayed by MSBuild in both cases:

```
Requested value 'System.Environment.System' was not found.
```

This appears to be a bug specific to this particular enumeration.

Next, a pair of functions that return an array or enumerable result are shown, first when the value is captured in a property (5) and then when captured in an item (6). The properties become a semicolon-delimited list, while the item retains each member individually. The output shows an abbreviated listing of all environment variables.

In the introductory section on Properties, it was explained that environment variables named with invalid XML tokens are skipped by MSBuild when determining property values derived from environment variables. It turns out that you can still get those values using a property function, as shown below.

```
<Target Name="InvalidXmlToken">
    <Message Text="Invalid: '$(A:B)'" />
    <Message Text="Invalid: '$([System.Environment]::
        GetEnvironmentVariable('A:B'))'" />
</Target>

> set A:B=InvalidTokenName
> msbuild /t:InvalidXmlToken

InvalidXmlToken:
  Invalid: ''
  Invalid: 'InvalidTokenName'
```

The environment variable named "A:B" contains a colon which is invalid in XML tokens, so it can't be retrieved using the $(A:B) property syntax and is skipped, but is available when accessed directly using the property function.

Enum Property Functions

The documentation for PropertyFunctions list the System.Enum type as one of the types supported by default. It turns out that there are no static functions in System.Enum that are usable in the default case. Usage of System.Enum is limited to the types being supported as arguments passed to other property functions, as shown below.

```
$([System.Text.RegularExpressions.Regex]::Replace(
    $(LibraryPath),
    '$(DXSDK_DIR)\\lib\\x86',
    '',
    System.Text.RegularExpressions.RegexOptions.IgnoreCase))
```

The real reason is that manipulation of System.Enum types requires the use of System.Type, which is not available by default. However, there is a simple, recommended workaround to make other types available beyond the set of types and functions discussed here.

These additional property functions will be shown later on, in the following sections

Trick #57, Know how to enable more property functions

Trick #58, Know how to alter environment variables

Trick #59, Know even more property functions

Throughout the book there is extensive use of property functions, which play a starring role in the following tricks,

Trick #63, How to count items in an item array – Math

Trick #92, How to generate assembly attributes – DateTime

Trick #100, How to manipulate version numbers – DateTime, Math, String.Format, System.Convert

Trick #101, How to auto-increment the daily build revision – DateTime, Math

That concludes an almost exhaustive tour of the available item functions. Perform a Bing search on "MSBuild Functions" for a comprehensive list, keeping in mind that not all static methods on the indicated types are callable from MSBuild directly. In those cases, your best option is probably a simple inline task.

10. Know how to diagnose property function issues

The syntax for property functions is subject to a easily malformed arguments, missing or mismatched parenthesis and quotes, even requiring nested quotes of all three forms (double quote, single quote and back ticks) at times. On top of that, the need for explicit type coercion and the inability to use ReSharper to check your work can lend a bit of uncertainty. There is another environment variable available to help get property functions just right.

```
> set MSBuildDebugExpansion=1
```

Setting this variable causes MSBuild to emit diagnostics each time it expands a property function.

Diagnosing Property Functions.trkproj

```
<Target Name="Diagnose">
  <Message
    Text="$([System.Environment]::
      SetEnvironmentVariable(
        'MSBuildDebugExpansion',
        '1'))"
    />

  <PropertyGroup>
    <A>A</A>
    <B>B</B>
    <C>C</C>
  </PropertyGroup>
  <Message
    Text="$([System.String]::
      Compare(
        `$([System.String]::
```

```
                    Concat($(A), $(B), $(C)).SubString(1, 1))`,
            `B`))"
    />
</Target>
```

Output

```
Expanding: [System.String]::
            Compare(
                `$([System.String]::
                    Concat($(A), $(B), $(C)).SubString(1, 1))`,
                `B`)
Expanding: [System.String]::
                    Concat($(A), $(B), $(C)).SubString(1, 1)
Expanding: .SubString(1, 1)
Diagnose:
  0
```

It is interesting to see how MSBuild is recursively emitting these values. The first "Expanding" message contains the entire body of the outermost System.String.Compare property function, which in turn contains an explicit call to System.String.Concat, shown in the subsequent "Expanding" message, followed again by the final property function, in this case the trailing .SubString() string property function applied to the return value of the call to Concat.

11. Use item functions

Prior to the introduction of item functions, transforming one item into another was possible in many cases using dynamic item arrays decorated with conditions, or multiple successive transformations, but often really required custom tasks to perform complex custom transformations.

The introduction of item functions in MSBuild 4.0 makes many common transformations much easier to write as well as easier to follow when reading the project file as XML. The project file below demonstrates the use of item functions that are likely to be used commonly.

To introduce item functions, the listing below (1) contains an array of @(BuildItem) composed with unique identity values and a single meta value named "Group." In some cases, there is more than one item with the same value for the Group meta; for example Item2 and Item5 both have a Group meta with the value "B." This item array is then operated on using various item functions, in some cases creating new item arrays that are then further processed by a subsequent item function.

Use Item Functions.trkproj

```
<Project ...
  DefaultTargets="UseItemFunctions">

  <!-- 1 -->
  <ItemGroup>
    <BuildItem Include="Item1">
      <Group>A</Group>                                    <!-- 2 -->
    </BuildItem>
    <BuildItem Include="Item2">
      <Group>B</Group>
    </BuildItem>
    <BuildItem Include="Item3">
      <Group>C</Group>
    </BuildItem>
    <BuildItem Include="Item4">
      <Group>A</Group>
    </BuildItem>
    <BuildItem Include="Item5">
      <Group>B</Group>
    </BuildItem>
    <BuildItem Include="Item6;Item7;Item8">               <!-- 3 -->
      <Group>A</Group>
    </BuildItem>
    <BuildItem Include="Item9" />                          <!-- 4 -->
    <BuildItem Include="Item10">                           <!-- 5 -->
      <Group></Group>
    </BuildItem>
  </ItemGroup>

  <ItemGroup>
    <Group
      Include="@(BuildItem->Metadata('Group'))"
      />                                                   <!-- 6 -->
    <DistinctGroup
      Include="@(Group->Distinct())"
      />                                                   <!-- 7 -->
    <None
      Include="@(BuildItem->WithMetadataValue('Group', ''))"
      />                                                   <!-- 8 -->
    <Aye
      Include="@(BuildItem->WithMetadataValue('Group', 'A'))"
      />                                                   <!-- 9 -->
    <ReverseAye
      Include="@(Aye->Reverse())"
      />                                                   <!-- 10 -->
  </ItemGroup>

  <Target Name="UseItemFunctions">                         <!-- 11 -->
    <Message Text="Group='@(Group)'" />
    <Message Text="DistinctGroup='@(DistinctGroup)'" />
    <Message Text="None='@(None)'" />
    <Message Text="Aye='@(Aye)'" />
    <Message Text="ReverseAye='@(ReverseAye)'" />
                                                           <!-- 12 -->
    <Message
```

```
   Condition="'%(Group)' == 'A'"
   Text="Aye.Group='@(Aye->'%(Group)')'"
  />
 </Target>

</Project>
```

Output

```
UseItemFunctions:
  Group='A;B;C;A;B;A;A;A'
  DistinctGroup='A;B;C'
  None='Item9;Item10'
  Aye='Item1;Item4;Item6;Item7;Item8'
  ReverseAye='Item8;Item7;Item6;Item4;Item1'
  Aye.Group='A;A;A;A;A'
```

An item array (1) is defined for @(BuildItem), each with a unique non-file identity and an optional meta (2) for a "Group" value. This is a simplified contrived example of something you may actually want to do to drive a multiple project build with more sophistication and less frustration than trying to muscle a solution file into performing with similar behavior. Notice that at (3) there are three separate items declared, with the use of a semicolon delimited list of identities, but where all three share the value of "A" for their "Group" meta. Also note that Item9 (4) does not declare the "Group" meta, and Item10 (5) declares an empty value.

The second ItemGroup section declares five new item arrays; each a transformation via an item function of either the original @(BuildItem) item array, or of one of the new item arrays created from a previous item function. The target (11) simply prints out the resulting item arrays.

The item array (6) named "Groups" uses the "Metadata" item function. This creates a new item array, the identities of which are derived from the specified meta values from the original array. In this case, the meta value named "Group" is used, and as can be seen in the output, the new @(Groups) group contains one item for each item in the original @(BuildItem) that actually declared a value for the Group meta. There are eight members in @(Groups), since Item9 and Item10 from @(BuildItem), having not declared a value for the Group meta, were excluded from the item function transformation. The original identity values from @(BuildItem), the "Item1" through "Item#" values, are lost in the transformed @(Group) item array, since it is composed using the meta value alone.

The item array (7) named @(Distinct) is derived from the @(Groups) item array just created in (6). This removes any items containing a duplicated identity value. In this case, since the first three items in @(Groups) provide the three distinct identity values of "A," "B," and "C," the remaining items are stripped from the new item array.

The next item array (8) named @(None) demonstrates the WithMetadataValue item function, which tests that the named meta value contains a specific value, in this case, an empty value. As would be expected, the @(None) item array ends up with only two items from the original @(BuildItems) array, "Item9" and "Item10," which each declared an empty value for the meta, in one case implicitly by omission and in the other case explicitly with an empty value. Note the distinction of this with the behavior of the Metadata item function, which required that the named meta value passed to it actually contained a non-empty value.

The @(Aye) group (9) is similar to @(None) except that it requires a value of "A" for the "Group" meta. Note that Item6 through Item8, all declared in the same item are all included in the @(Aye) group. Finally, the @(ReverseAye) group (10) demonstrates an undocumented item function, reversing the order of the items in the @(Aye) group that was just created.

The last message in this example (12) demonstrates that the transformed "copies" of the item arrays created with item functions contain the meta values as well as the identity values. The @(Aye) group was a transformation built from the items in the @(BuildItems) group that contained a meta value named "Group" with "A" as the value. The resulting transformed group @(Aye) is shown in (12) to contain items that also contain a "Group" meta value with "A" as the value as well, since they were copied over when the transformation occurred.

This next example demonstrates a side effect of the Distinct item function as it relates to the item meta values.

Use Item Functions Distinct Meta Test

```
<Project ...>
  <ItemGroup>
    <BuildItem Include="Item1">
      <Group>A</Group>
    </BuildItem>
    <BuildItem Include="Item2">
      <Group>B</Group>
    </BuildItem>
    <BuildItem Include="Item3;Item4;Item5">          <!-- 1 -->
      <Group>C</Group>
    </BuildItem>
    <BuildItem Include="Item6" />
    <BuildItem Include="Item3;Item4;Item5">          <!-- 2 -->
```

```
      <Group>D</Group>
    </BuildItem>
  </ItemGroup>

  <Target Name="UseItemFunctionsDistinctMetaTest">
    <ItemGroup>
      <DistinctBuildItem
        Include="@(BuildItem->Distinct())"
        />                                              <!-- 3 -->
    </ItemGroup>
    <Message
      Text="BuildItem='@(BuildItem)'"
      />                                                <!-- 4 -->
    <Message
      Text="DistinctBuildItem='@(DistinctBuildItem)'"
      />                                                <!-- 5 -->
    <Message
      Text=
        "DistinctBuildItemGroup='@(DistinctBuildItem->'%(Group)')'"
      />                                                <!-- 6 -->
  </Target>
</Project>
```

Output

```
UseItemFunctionsDistinctMetaTest:
  BuildItem='Item1;Item2;Item3;Item4;Item5;Item6;Item3;Item4;Item5'
  DistinctBuildItem='Item1;Item2;Item3;Item4;Item5;Item6'
  DistinctBuildItemGroup='A;B;C;C;C;'
```

This example is quite similar to the previous with a minor alteration. Note that Item3 through Item5 (1) are declared with a Group meta value of "C." Later at (2) three new items are added to the @(BuildItems) item array that duplicate the identities of Item3 through Item5, but declare instead a Group meta value of "D." The target (3) creates a single new item array @(DistinctBuildItems) from the result of calling the Distinct item function on the original item array. The first message (4) shows that the original @(BuildItem) group contained duplicated entries for items with the identity names "Item3," "Item4," and "Item5." The second message (5) shows that the @(DistinctBuildItems) group eliminates the duplication, removing the second entry of each of these three identity names. The third message (6) prints out the Group meta value of the items that remained in @(DistinctBuildItems) after the Distinct transformation. Notice that there are no values of "D" which indicates that the Distinct item function keeps the first item it finds for each unique identity name, as well as whatever meta values were copied over with it, and drops any subsequent items using an already discovered identity name, regardless of what the meta values were.

For a comprehensive list of all item functions, do a Bing search on "MSBuild item functions" to find the MSDN reference.

12. Know how to debug MSBuild

There is an unsupported and undocumented capability built into Visual Studio 2010 for debugging MSBuild execution using the Visual Studio debugger. The feature is disabled by default, but can be activated by enabling the "Just My Code" debugger option and setting a registry key— being sure to get the correct registry hive for the bitness you require:

```
HKLM\SOFTWARE\Microsoft\MSBuild\4.0@debuggerenabled = string 'true'
```

This activates a new command line option to MSBuild.exe:

```
> msbuild /debug
```

Running a command line build on any project passing this option will cause a debug exception, allowing you to connect to the process using the debugger. Manually select the Managed debugger when prompted and you will be debugging your project at the first line of the MSBuild project file in the Visual Studio Editor.

You can set breakpoints, step through targets and examine properties and items in the Variables view. There is some curious behavior related to how MSBuild processes the project file in multiple passes, first evaluating properties, then items, and then finally running targets. In the debugger, this multi-pass program flow can be discovered by carefully stepping or "stepping in" with F10 and F11, and by "stepping out" of the current evaluations using "Shift+F11."

A member of the MSBuild team at Microsoft, Dan Moseley, has produced an excellent walkthrough of this feature on the Visual Studio Team blog on MSDN. It also explains the technology behind the implementation and the approach used to map the build engine to standard debugger semantics. It is so comprehensive there is little point repeating it all here. Do a Bing search on "Debugging MSBuild" and be sure to locate all three parts of the blog posting.

13. Know how to bootstrap build custom tasks

For any situation where an MSBuild project file depends on a custom task in an assembly, the assembly must exist prior to the MSBuild file being loaded and resolved by the build engine. If the targets being executed do not cause the execution of the particular task, you can build without the assembly file existing. But, at the moment a task from an assembly is first executed, if the assembly does not exist, an error will occur. For a one-step build though, there is a bootstrapping issue, when you would like for your custom tasks to be built as part of your build, and then consumed later on.

There are two approaches to this dilemma. One approach is to introduce a configuration step to the build. The configuration step can be manual, or can be one that auto-detects that the custom task assembly doesn't exist, or that it is out of date, and builds it, issuing an error or warning indicating that the build has gone through a configuration bootstrap and requesting that you build again. For build servers, the configuration can be explicitly executed first, followed by a second invocation for the remainder of the build.

Don't be fooled into trying to use the Exec task to execute MSBuild.exe, since doing so will completely disrupt the ability of the console logger to properly colorize and format the build output, making it all but unusable, and making it difficult to get a proper build log from multiple sequential builds loosely coupled together from subsequent usages of the Exec task.

There are some concerns generally about bootstrap building tasks as part of a single build. The most obvious is that when a task is executed, the assembly in which the task is located will be locked by MSBuild. This is particularly noticeable when builds are performed from the IDE. By default, this lock will not be released when the build completes, but rather is held for an additional fifteen minutes. This is done as an optimization, since typically some tasks can be executed thousands of times in a build and the constant unloading and reloading is undesirable in the general case. This behavior can be modified in two ways. One is to supply the /nodereuse:false command line switch, which it turns out really has a negligible effect on build times, less than a second in most cases. Another is to set the MSBuildNodeCounnectionTimeout environment variable to a value in milliseconds.

Knowing these limitations, the following demonstrates a two step build utilizing a configuration step.

Bootstrap.trkproj

```
<Project DefaultTargets="Build" ...
    <UsingTask
        Condition="Exists('./Path/MyCustomTasks.dll')"
        TaskName="MyTask"
        AssemblyFile="./Path/MyCustomTasks.dll"
        />
```

```
    <Target Name="Configure">
      <MSBuild Projects="MyCustomTasks.csproj" />
    </Target>
    <Target Name="Build">
      <MyTask ... />
    </Target>
</Project>
```

```
> msbuild Bootstrap.trkproj /t:Configure
> msbuild Bootstrap.trkproj
```

AutoBootstrap.trkproj

```
<Project DefaultTargets="Build" ...
    <UsingTask
       Condition="Exists('./Path/MyCustomTasks.dll')"
       TaskName="MyTask"
       AssemblyFile="./Path/MyCustomTasks.dll"
       />
    <ItemGroup>                                      <!-- 1 -->
       <MyCustomTaskSources Include="./Path/MyCustomTasks.csproj" />
       <MyCustomTaskSources Include="./Path/MyCustomTasks.cs" />
    </ItemGroup>
    <Target Name="Configure"
       Condition="!Exists('./Path/MyCustomTasks.dll')"
       Inputs="@(MyCustomTaskSources)"
       Outputs="./Path/MyCustomTasks.dll">          <!-- 2 -->
       <Message Text="Bootstrap build..." />
       <MSBuild Projects="./Path/MyCustomTasks.csproj" />
       <Error Text="Detected boostrap, build again" />    <!-- 3 -->
    </Target>
    <Target Name="Build"
       DependsOnTargets="Configure">                <!-- 4 -->
       <MyTask ... />
    </Target>
</Project>
```

The resulting build output of this project when the task assembly is out of date would be, with paths abbreviated for clarity:

```
> msbuild Bootstrap.trkproj

Configure:
  Bootstrap build...
Project ".\AutoBootstrap.trkproj" is building \
  ".\Path\MyCustomTasks.csproj"
\AutoBootstrap.trkproj(24,7): error : Detected boostrap, build again
```

The item group at (1) would need to contain all the sources used to create the custom task specified as the output (2), but this creates two points of maintenance for the source list. It could make sense to factor this file list to a separate .props file in MSBuild format and share it between the Compile item array in the C# project containing the MSBuild task being built and the dependency detection in the Configure target Inputs and Outputs. It also is possible to create a custom target within the task project that emits the contents of the Compile item array to a text file using WriteLinesToFile, and to have the bootstrap project reconstitute the list using ReadLinesFromFile. Finally, you can create a custom target in the task project that uses the Returns attribute to fetch the value of the @(Compile) item array as shown in *trick #37, Understand target Returns*.

After building the out of date assembly, the build terminates with an error (3). Note that the Configure step (4) is always attempted as a dependency but that it only executes when the assembly doesn't exist, via the Exists Condition defined at (2).

A better approach, if it fits with your build, is possible when there is an outer build project that serves as a type of solution, which uses the MSBuild task to build multiple projects. As long as the outer build does not require custom tasks in an assembly, it can ensure the building of the custom task assembly early in the build, prior to calling out to the MSBuild task on the remaining projects that contain dependencies. Because the remaining projects are not loaded until the point in the outer build where the MSBuild task is executed with the project as a parameter, there is no bootstrapping issue, since by that time the task assembly would have been built during a prior call to the MSBuild task.

For a quick example, an "outer build" project is shown below, which first builds a custom task assembly, and then uses it.

Outer Build Bootstrap.trkproj

```
<Project ...
   InitialTargets="BootstrapBuild"
   DefaultTargets="Build">                              <!-- 5 -->

                                                        <!-- 4 -->
   <UsingTask
      TaskName="ItemGroupTask"
      AssemblyFile="./Custom Tasks/bin/Debug/MyCustomTasks.dll"
      />

   <Target Name="BootstrapBuild">                       <!-- 2 -->
      <MsBuild
         Projects="./Custom Tasks/MyCustomTasks.csproj"
         />
   </Target>

   <ItemGroup>
      <Empty Include="." />
   </ItemGroup>
   <Target Name="Build">                                <!-- 1 -->
```

```
    <ItemGroupTask
        InputFiles="@(Empty)"
        />                                          <!-- 5 -->
    </Target>
</Project>
```

The default target "Build" (1) will executes after the target
"BootstrapBuild" (2) which is declared as an initial target for the project
file (3). In the dependent target, the task assembly referenced in the
UsingTask statement (4) is actually built. There is no error, because up
until this point in the execution of the "BootstrapBuild" target, the task in
the task assembly is not used. However, when the BootstrapBuild
completes and execution control returns to the "Build" target, the call to
the custom task (5) can succeed.

Now, with the knowledge of basic functionality, and some general advise
on how to start structuring MSBuild project files, we'll move on to the
next chapter, titled Organizing Projects, which goes a great deal further
regarding how projects should be structured in a well-architected build
system.

Chapter 3
Organizing Projects

In a small build, one with just a couple projects, the overall organization isn't much of a concern. A small build implies a small team, and if you can keep all the complexity in your head, you can avoid thinking about where every single file and project is placed, if that is your style.

In a big build, one with multiple people working on multiple projects, probably different project types even, a well-organized project and source code structure can become part of the "common language" used by the team to reduce developer pain.

A well-organized code base will help answer two important questions that will come up nearly every day, when a developer is about to write some new code. The first question is, "if someone has already written something like this, where in the code base would it be?" The second question, a corollary to the first is, "where should this new code be placed?"

If you come up with a flexible strategy for answering these questions close to the beginning of a project, you should end up with consistent patterns that lend themselves to repetition, reuse, automation, and, to the point of this book, a well-defined structure in which to organize your build intelligence. To that point, since a well-organized code repository lends itself to more efficient, understandable and maintainable builds, a brief conversation about project organization is warranted.

Typically, in larger projects, we tend to see one of a few patterns emerge over time, as shown below. The simplest scheme is one separate project per folder:

```
One subfolder per project

Root/
   Project A/
   Project B/
```

For some strange historical reason, you occasionally see a similar organization with the exception of the project files being removed from the sources and placed in their own folder, all together. Avoid this at all costs, as some of the built-in functionality for various standard project types expects unique intermediate folders per project, and you're better off not getting mired in that tough to diagnose set of issues:

One subfolder per project, project files together

```
Root/
    Project A/
    Project B/
    Projects/
```

Most commonly seen is a random collection of folders at varying depths of hierarchy. Often this isn't random at all to one or two folks who've been along for the ride, but seldom do the arguments make sense. Typically, this type of organization applies not only to the projects alone, but also to the files within the projects:

Folder anarchy

```
Root/
    Feature A/
        Project A/
        Organizing Folder B/
            Project B1/
            Project B2/
            Another Subfolder C/
                Project C/
    Feature X/
        Anything Goes.../
```

When I see this, I like to calculate a quick metric. Count how many files there are and divide by how many folders there are. For any tree or sub-tree of folders where the result approaches one, or even as I've seen many times, less than one, you have a problem. Even the small—small by today's typical developer monitor resolution—window below easily shows about 30 items. Placing 30 files into a dozen or more organizing folders, adds more complexity to your repository than dumping them all together in one place—as shown in the screenshot below—would, since it would increase the number of places someone has to look for a file by an order of magnitude.

Collections of projects

```
Root/
    Collection A/
        Project A1/
        Project A2/
    Collection B/
        Project B1/
        Project B2/
```

By using the "Collection of Projects" approach from the listing above, considering 30 top-level organizing folders, each with around 30 projects, you can archive tens of thousands of files with each one no more than a couple folders from the top.

Eventually—or even a couple days into—a big project though, any attempts to organize folders will typically break down. This breakdown occurs when code in support of some feature, originally housed with the feature code, grows into something that spans multiple features, or perhaps even becomes a bit generic. It is neither one nor the other, and a code-base organized by feature doesn't have a single place for it to belong.

The other breakdown occurs when code is organized by abstraction layers. In this style, code is grouped naturally by how the dependencies flow from one module to another. When this is the driving concern, code that is truly feature specific doesn't have a single "home" when it cuts across abstraction layers.

These concerns arise in old school monolithic C++ code and in modern C# MVC apps. A good guiding principle is to always be considerate of both of these as cross-cutting dimensions that make up the true taxonomy of your code base. These two dimensions are often at odds with each other, as they are essentially two competing lenses by which the code of a project can be organized. But the file system only allows us to use one at a time, since a file can't reasonably be in two places at once.

Collections of projects, both Feature and Dependency

```
Root/
    Imports/
        Build/
        Resources/
    Vendors/
        3rd Party Sdk 1/
        3rd Party Sdk 2/
    Collection A/
        ...as above
```

In a nutshell, when organizing complex repositories into "Collections of Projects" as shown above, make some of the collections primarily about specific features, and make some of them focused entirely on pure abstraction layers, typically the lower levels of abstraction. Taking it a step further, establish policies about what kind of code may be placed in certain locations, which will help guide the implementation in a structured manner.

The intent is to avoid spaghetti, which implies a web of inter-dependencies, and interdependencies can become complex or even circular and those things are tough to build with a build script.

So, if you are defining "Common" or "Core" code, establish a guiding principle for the code collection in which it resides that states, "nothing goes here that won't be useful on the next project, no matter what kind of project it is." In C# projects, I call this "Framework" code, as in "stuff I wish were already in the .NET Framework." It is hard to convince yourself that code with this guiding principle should break the abstraction for any reason that wouldn't pass muster if you were trying to add the same behavior to System.IO.File, right?

14. Use shared imported properties

As your solution grows, the consistent maintenance of project files can become cumbersome. You will want to establish patterns to use in every project, but manually changing these settings using the property editor in the IDE can be a burden, not to mention that the modifications the IDE makes to your project files are nowhere near optimal and can cause the readability of the XML to suffer. For example, in a project with just two configurations, altering a single setting for "all configurations" may introduce two separate entries in the project file, when one would suffice.

IDE generated settings

```xml
<PropertyGroup Condition=" '$(Configuration)|$(Platform)' ==
  'Debug|x86' ">
  <PlatformTarget>x86</PlatformTarget>
  <DebugSymbols>true</DebugSymbols>
  <DebugType>full</DebugType>
  <Optimize>false</Optimize>
  <OutputPath>bin\Debug\</OutputPath>
  <DefineConstants>DEBUG;TRACE</DefineConstants>
  <ErrorReport>prompt</ErrorReport>
  <WarningLevel>4</WarningLevel>
</PropertyGroup>
<PropertyGroup Condition=" '$(Configuration)|$(Platform)' ==
  'Release|x86' ">
  <PlatformTarget>x86</PlatformTarget>
  <DebugType>pdbonly</DebugType>
  <Optimize>true</Optimize>
  <OutputPath>bin\Release\</OutputPath>
  <DefineConstants>TRACE</DefineConstants>
  <ErrorReport>prompt</ErrorReport>
  <WarningLevel>4</WarningLevel>
</PropertyGroup>
```

Manually configured settings

```xml
<PropertyGroup>                                          <!-- 1 -->
  <PlatformTarget>x86</PlatformTarget>
  <OutputPath>bin\$(Configuration)\</OutputPath>         <!-- 2 -->
  <DefineConstants>TRACE</DefineConstants>
  <ErrorReport>prompt</ErrorReport>
  <WarningLevel>4</WarningLevel>
</PropertyGroup>
<PropertyGroup Condition="'$(Configuration)' == 'Debug' ">
```

```
    <DebugSymbols>true</DebugSymbols>
    <DebugType>full</DebugType>
    <Optimize>false</Optimize>
    <!-- 3 -->
    <DefineConstants>$(DefineConstants);TRACE</DefineConstants>
  </PropertyGroup>
  <PropertyGroup Condition="'$(Configuration)' == 'Release' ">
    <DebugType>pdbonly</DebugType>
    <Optimize>true</Optimize>
  </PropertyGroup>
```

Notice that several of the properties (1) were identical and were pulled to a common property group, including the Output Path, which though distinct for each configuration, was defined using the $(Configuration) property. Because the remaining properties were identical for any value of $(Platform), the "|$(Platform)" part of the Condition expression was removed. If there were platform-specific properties not affected by the configuration, a similar Condition with only the value of $(Platform) could be used. The value for $(DefineConstants), though different for each configuration, has a shared part that is defined globally, only the debug-specific constants are added in the debug-specific property group.

This gets considerably messier for per-file settings or pretty much anything in a C++ project.

Furthermore, you may want to alter conventions globally, for example those used to determine how the output of references is handled. A Reference (for assemblies) or ProjectReference (for other project files) uses item metadata to specify whether or not a specific version is required, whether the assemblies are copied locally when the project is built, which can cause excessive copying of files when your program launch is configured to run from a secondary location, not from the output file directory.

As you add your own customizations to the build, these will also need to be managed with global default values.

If you were to view a diff of all of your project files, essentially everything that is common among them can be pulled out to a shared property file. In the example above, none of the properties are likely to be specific to any one project and could all be moved to a shared, imported file. One exception to this is the ItemGroup labeled "ProjectConfigurations" in a C++ project file, which a bug in the C++ project system loading requires in the actual project file itself and not imported (as of VS 2010). By the way, labels such as this one are put on item and property groups in the default project types to help the IDE locate the contents for display in the user interface.

To facilitate this type of project file refactoring, define a common, shared property file to import into every project. If your source code organization is highly structured, you can use a relative path to locate this file. The following two tips describe some alternate approaches for locating these files, so that they can be properly imported with a configurable or searchable path.

As a final note on the use of imported properties, please be sure to check out *trick #75, How to customize developer builds with My.props* and *trick #81, How to avoid the circular import warning.*

15. Use hierarchical property files

Imagine a contrived source tree containing separate locations for common build files (Imports/Build), a folder hierarchy for custom framework assemblies and a separate folder hierarchy for service assemblies.

```
Directory structure
Root/
    Imports/
        Build/
            Common.props
            ExtraCustomization.props
    Frameworks/
        Data/
            Data.csproj
        .../
    Services/
        Logging/
            Logging.csproj
        .../
```

A first approach to getting the shared property file Common.props imported into each of the two C# project files will be considered, one that uses relative paths. In this case, each of the two project files would contain—preferably right at the top of the project file—the following import.

```
<Project ...>
    <Import Project="../../Imports/Build/Common.props" />
```

This is pretty cut-and-dried simple. But as your codebase grows and projects are rearranged, it may be necessary to edit these imports. If intervening folders are introduced or a particular project is moved elsewhere, the relative depth may change and the import will break.

Instead, the imports could be altered to expect that a property file of a particular name always reside in the immediate parent folder.

```
<Project ...>
   <Import Project="../Common.props" />
```

This won't work just yet, as the file does not exist where it is expected. Next, a file of this name with the trivial implementation below is placed in each of the two parent folders named Frameworks and Services.

Hierarchy Search Common.props

```
<Project ...>
   <Import Project="../Common.props" />
</Project>
```

Both of these files expect to import a property file of the same name in the Root folder, so another file is created there, this one containing the final import of the shared property file.

Root Redirecting Common.props

```
<Project ...>
   <Import Project="./Imports/Build/Common.props" />
</Project>
```

It is now possible to provide customizations of the common property file for particular folder trees in your hierarchy, by redefining properties and items after the redirection imports.

Furthermore, this relative searching only needs to happen one time for the main common property file. Inside that file, you can define a property to be used elsewhere.

./Imports/Build/Common.props

```
<Project ...>
   <PropertyGroup>
      <ImportsFolder>$(MSBuildThisFileDirectory)</ImportsFolder>
   </PropertyGroup>
   ...
</Project>
```

Any project file

```
<Project ...>
   <Import Project="../Common.props" />
```

```
...
<Import Project="$(ImportsFolder)/ExtraCustomization.props" />
...
```

Using this technique, only a single file in the whole codebase knows the exact location of the eventual imported common property file. The drawback is that you need to scatter redirecting Common.props files in all of the folders between the root and the eventual parent folder of projects, or something similar to match how your repository is structured.

A more flexible technique requiring fewer files is discussed in the next tip.

16. Use GetDirectoryNameOfFileAbove to discover shared properties

New to MSBuild 4.0 is a property function that can be used to search for any file up a folder hierarchy, and return the fully qualified path. Instead of a series of redirecting imports leading up to a root folder that has the final redirection defined, this function can be used to achieve a similar result with a bit less scaffolding.

Any project file

```
<Project ...>
  <PropertyGroup>                                         <!-- 1 -->
    <RootFolder>$([MSBuild]::GetDirectoryNameOfFileAbove(
      $(MSBuildThisFileDirectory),
      Common.props)
    )</RootFolder>
  </PropertyGroup>
  <Import
    Condition="Exists('$(RootFolder)/Common.props')"
    Project="$(RootFolder)/Common.props" />              <!-- 2 -->
  ...
  <!-- 3 -->
  <Import Project="$(ImportsFolder)/Common.targets" />
</Project>
```

Root Redirecting Common.props

```
<Project ...>
  <Import Project="./Imports/Build/Common.props" />      <!-- 4 -->
</Project>
```

./Imports/Build/Common.props

```
<Project ...>
  <PropertyGroup>                                         <!-- 5 -->
    <ImportsFolder>$(MSBuildThisFileDirectory)</ImportsFolder>
  </PropertyGroup>
```

```
    ...
</Project>
```

This is very similar to the previous example. The first line of the project (1) declares a property named $(RootFolder). This property is evaluated by MSBuild by searching the tree from the specified folder, in this case since $(MSBuildThisFileDirectory) is used so the search starts with the folder containing the project itself. The search continues up the directory structure, skipping the Frameworks or Services folders shown in the directory structure of the previous trick, since they do not contain a file of the name being searched, finally discovering the file in the root folder. The absolute path of the folder in which the first file of that name is found is returned as the value of the property function, which in this case becomes the value of the $(ImportProperty) being defined.

Protected by a condition, the property file just discovered by the property function is imported (2) using the property value just declared for both the condition and the import path. Whether or not to include this condition on this particular import should be a matter of serious consideration for you. Only use it if there is a meaningful condition in which the build will exist and must succeed in the absence of the import file. If the file is created by a bootstrap target, and the project importing it is involved in creating the file, then a condition would be required. If, on the other hand, the build requires the file to exist, then you are better off letting the import fail, which will indicate a build failure early in the build. You can also create some more detailed diagnostic support, for example keeping the condition on the import but creating an initial target that forces an error if the file doesn't exist, and displays a meaningful error message that explains how to get the build properly configured. In other words, make the build fail hard at the exact moment the behavior becomes undefined, rather than encouraging it to continue, delaying the error until the context of it won't help the user fix the root problem.

Because the root common property file redirects (4) to the eventual property file in ./Imports/Build, which declares a property for the import folder (5), that property can be used (3) in subsequent imports. Adhering to the soon to be seen guidance in *trick #18, Import properties first, targets last*, this example shows importing properties at the beginning of the project and target customizations at the very end.

Of note in (1) is how carriage returns are used. Any carriage returns or whitespace within the property function parenthesis will not be part of the returned string. If instead, the following definition were used, the property would contain both a leading and a trailing carriage return which in some cases would be undesirable.

```
<PropertyGroup>
  <RootFolder>
    $([MSBuild]::GetDirectoryNameOfFileAbove(
    $(MSBuildThisFileDirectory),
    Common.props))
  </RootFolder>
</PropertyGroup>
```

Of course, if any project file modifications are made in the IDE, it will wipe out any carriage returns within a property and replace them with XML escaped characters, so in most cases you'll settle on a property definition on a single long line anyway, something like this:

```
<PropertyGroup>
  <RootFolder>$([MSBuild]::GetDirectoryNameOfFileAbove($(MSBu...
</PropertyGroup>
```

Combining this trick with the previous one, it is still possible to customize properties for entire folder hierarchies merely by adding a redirecting property file anywhere in the GetDirectoryNameOfFileAbove search path, and redefining the RootFolder property along the way.

Intervening Hierarchy Search Common.props

```
<Project ...>
  <PropertyGroup>                                              <!-- 6 -->
    <RootFolder>$([MSBuild]::GetDirectoryNameOfFileAbove(
      $(MSBuildThisFileDirectory),
      Common.props)
    )</RootFolder>
  </PropertyGroup>
  <Import
    Condition="Exists('$(RootFolder)/Common.props')"
    Project="$(RootFolder)/Common.props" />                    <!-- 7 -->
  ...
  <!-- local customizations -->
```

In the intervening property file, the $(RootFolder) property is redefined (6) with a continued search, and the next discovered property file is imported (7) using the exact same declarations as the original file. By the time the import resolves the eventual common property file, the value of $(RootFolder) will be properly set, irrespective of how many different values it had along the way.

By using this technique you gain a useful side effect. Often you may want to create a "spike" or "scratch" project dissociated from your main codebase, perhaps in a separate "user" area of your repository. You may however wish to take advantage of the various build customizations that exist in your primary source tree. This is very easy to accomplish. Consider the following source tree:

```
Root/
    MainProject/
        Source/
            Common.props
            ...remainder of project sources...
    Users/
        Your.Name/
            Scratch/
                Temp/
                    Temp.csproj
                    Temp.cs
```

To gain access to the Common.props file from the main project's source tree, simply drop a redirecting common import property file into the Users/Your.Name folder, with the following definition,

```
<Project ...>
    <Import Project="../../MainProject/Source/Common.props" />
</Project>
```

then import this redirecting Common.props folder into your scratch Temp.csproj project file using GetDirectoryNameOfFileAbove. This single Common.props file can service every project file created under the Users/Your.Name location in your repository or file system.

17. Understand DefaultTargets and InitialTargets

While we're on the topic of imports, there is a bit you'll need to understand about the behavior of the default and initial targets, specifically with respect to how they behave with regard to imported files.

There are some straightforward rules regarding how DefaultTargets and InitialTargets are processed. The following demonstrates DefaultTargets processing.

ImportsDefault.trkproj

```
<Project ...>
  <Import Project="Imports/Imported.targets" />

  <Target Name="FirstTarget">
    <Message Text="First target" />
  </Target>
  <Target Name="Default">
    <Message Text="Default" />
  </Target>
  <Target Name="ImportDefault">
```

```
    <Message Text="ImportDefault target" />
  </Target>
</Project>
```

Imports/ImportedDefault.targets

```
<Project ...
  DefaultTarget="ImportDefault">
  <Target Name="FirstImportedTarget">
    <Message Text="First imported target" />
  </Target>
</Project>
```

Output when executed without specifying a target

```
ImportDefault:
  ImportDefault target
```

From the above, the main project file does not declare a DefaultTargets. The imported file references one named "ImportDefault" but does not define a target named "ImportDefault." Even though the main file does declare any DefaultTargets, since the imported file does reference a DefaultTargets that exists in the main file, it will be used. Control flows to the "ImportDefault" target in the main project file.

If, in the example above, a DefaultTargets declaration is created in the primary ImportsDefault.trkproj file, control would flow to whatever target or targets are declared there. For example, if the following were added to the main ImportsDefault.trkproj,

```
    DefaultTargets="Default"
```

The resulting output would instead become,

```
Default:
  Default target
```

Notice that in this case, the DefaultTargets declared in the imported file is ignored, the declaration from the main project file takes precedence. In the case where there are potentially many imports, it is the very first DefaultTargets declaration encountered that takes precedence. Once one is found, any additional declarations encountered are ignored.

The InitialTargets declaration is a bit different.

ImportsInitial.trkproj

```
<Project ...
  InitialTargets="InitialImported">
  <Target Name="FirstTarget">
    <Message Text="First target" />
```

```
    </Target>
    <Target Name="Initial">
      <Message Text="Initial" />
    </Target>

    <Import Project="Imports/ImportedInitial.targets" />

    <Target Name="Build">
      <Message Text="Build" />
    </Target>
</Project>
```

Imports/ImportedInitial.trkpoj

```
<Project ...
  InitialTargets="Initial">
  <Target Name="FirstImportedTarget">
    <Message Text="First imported target" />
  </Target>
  <Target Name="InitialImported">
    <Message Text="Initial Imported" />
  </Target>
</Project>
```

Output when executed, specifying /t:Build

```
InitialImported:
  Initial Imported
Initial:
  Initial
Build:
  Build
```

In this example, the main project specifies an InitialTargets that names a target that will be provided by the target file that it imports. The imported target file likewise specifies an InitialTargets declared in the main project. From the output, it can be seen that both were executed. The Import statement was moved until after the declaration of the "Initial" target to prove that the order the targets were executed in is the order they were declared by the InitialTargets attributes on the Project elements, and not the order in which the targets themselves were discovered. Only after all of the InitialTargets are executed is the build target specified on the command line is executed.

So, to summarize the behavior of these two declarations:

- If a target declared in DefaultTargets or InitialTargets does not exist anywhere, an error is shown.

- The target or targets declared in DefaultTargets or InitialTargets can exist in any project file in the chain of imported files, as long as it is defined when the file parsing and importing is complete.

- If there are no valid DefaultTargets declarations, the first target discovered will be executed. This first target may not be the first in the main project file, just the first one encountered as imports are processed, so it could be from an imported targets file.

- Only the very first DefaultTargets declaration is processed, any additional ones encountered will be skipped.

- For DefaultTargets, if there are more than one target declared in the first encountered declaration, they will all be processed in the order they are declared.

- For InitialTargets, all discovered declarations will have their targets aggregated, and all targets in the resulting list will be processed in the order they are declared.

The primary difference between the two is that InitialTargets are aggregated, while there will only be one DefaultTargets used, and that is the first one encountered.

18. Import properties first, targets last

As you begin to organize your projects with shared property, target and tasks files, some common patterns typically arise. These patterns, which are also present in the Microsoft supplied MSBuild files, allow for shared MSBuild code even among different project types, like C++ and C# projects built together.

In this scenario, the file "Main Project.proj" referenced in the diagram below can represent two distinct types of projects in your build; the pattern is the same for both. It can either be what I've referred to as the "outer build" project file—one that serves the same purpose as a solution file in the IDE—to accumulate a set of projects and build them together in one step. It can also serve as a proxy for one of the individual projects referenced by the outer build, for example a C# .csproj or a C++ .vcxproj. Now in each of these two distinct cases, the nature of the Common.props file that is used may be different. You may choose to comingle and share custom properties and targets from the build activity of both types of project in a single Common.props file, or you may factor items specific to only one build into a separate file. Regardless, there will always be properties shared among both. For example, if your build can generate documentation automatically, a property named $(SkipDocumentation) might be shared, but serve a different purpose in each build. In the "inner build" of a single project, it may determine what documentation is built from comments in the sources. It may also be used to conditionally determine whether or not documentation items are deployed for later aggregation in the outer build. That same property, in the outer build, would determine if your full product documentation sources are compiled, perhaps using a third party documentation compiler. In either case, the general best practice being discussed here, properties first, targets last, still maintains the same basic structure in your build.

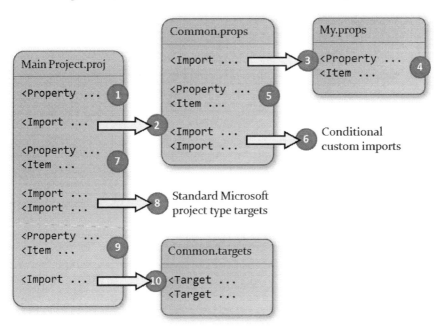

Consider the diagram above. The main project file starts out with an opportunity (1) to declare important properties that will alter the behavior of anything that follows. We'll return to this notion a bit further on in the discussion. There is then an immediate Import (2) of a Common.props file. This file immediately follows with a conditional import (3) of a local My.props file, if it exists, following the guidance of *trick #75, How to customize developer builds with My.props.* The My.props file give an opportunity for a developer to modify the behavior of their local build by getting the first shot at declaring Properties and Items (4) that will guide the remaining build.

Returning to the Common.props file, the shared Properties and Items (5) are declared. These may likely be declared in one or more separately maintained .props files that are imported at this point in the project file processing (6), and some of these imports may be conditioned upon custom metadata from the Main Project.proj file. For example, you can import common items depending on what type of project, as follows,

```
<ImportGroup>
  <Import
    Condition="'$(MSBuildProjectExtension)' == '.csproj'"
    Project="./Common.C#.props"
    />
  <Import
    Condition="'$(MSBuildProjectExtension)' == '.vcxproj'"
    Project="./Common.C++.props"
    />
<ImportGroup>
```

Useful at this point are some of the properties that can be declared early in the project, at (1). Consider setting up default properties that can be used for all of your C# projects. For some properties, it is important to know what the main project type is, for example whether or not you are compiling a command line executable or a class library. Inside the imported files for a C++ project at (6), you might see something like this:

```
<PropertyGroup>
  <ConfigurationType
    Condition="'$(ConfigurationType)' == ''"
    >DynamicLibrary</ConfigurationType>
  <TargetName
    Condition="'$(TargetName)' == ''"
    >Trickery.$(ProjectName)</TargetName>
</PropertyGroup>
<ItemDefinitionGroup>
  <Link>
    <SubSystem
      Condition="'$(ConfigurationType)' == 'Application'"
      >Console</SubSystem>
    <SubSystem
      Condition="'$(ConfigurationType)' == 'DynamicLibrary'"
      >Windows</SubSystem>
  </Link>
</ItemDefinitionGroup>
```

For the default case, if $(ConfigurationType) isn't specified at (1), a default value of DynamicLibrary is picked up. Later, the %(SubSystem) meta value on the @(Link) item array can be set, based on the value of $(ConfigurationType). For application projects, all that needs to be set at (1) to alter the default behavior would be,

```
<PropertyGroup>
  <ConfigurationType>Application</ConfigurationType>
</PropertyGroup>
```

Processing returns to the Main Project file (7) giving the first chance to declare the general project contents. These usually consist of ItemGroups containing items that will be compiled or used to drive other build steps, and properties unique to the project, such as the ProjectGuid, default namespace etc. These definitions are often conditional based on the values of other properties, typically the $(Platform) and $(Configuration) being built.

Typically at this point (8), everything that is needed for the standard build has already been declared. It is now time to import the standard Microsoft supplied project type targets typically seen in new projects created from a template,

```
<Import Project="$(MSBuildToolsPath)\Microsoft.CSharp.targets" />
```

or,

```
<Import Project="$(VCTargetsPath)\Microsoft.Cpp.props" />
<Import Project="$(VCTargetsPath)\Microsoft.Cpp.targets" />
```

These will declare the primary targets used to control the build, and have their own import customization points, which will be discussed in the next trick. Recalling that targets are customized by implementing a target of the same name that will be discovered at a later point in the file processing, you have one more chance to customize the build. These customizations can be additions to existing targets, either by adding your new target to the "DependsOn" property consumed by a standard target, or by carefully wiring a target into the execution sequence using BeforeTargets and AfterTargets. You can also supply wholesale replacements of existing targets that don't have other extension points, which typically involves a cut-and-paste-and-modify. For my own custom targets that are extending the build, I like to segregate the definition of properties and items used to drive them at (9) rather than (7). This spot is the place in a project file where you will see the default customization point, commented out as,

```
<!-- To modify your build process, add your task inside one of the
targets below and uncomment it.
     Other similar extension points exist, see
Microsoft.Common.targets.
  <Target Name="BeforeBuild">
  </Target>
  <Target Name="AfterBuild">
  </Target>
  -->
```

I typically yank these out when replacing them with my own extension points. See *trick #23, Use BeforeBuild and AfterBuild only for local customizations*. After declaring your own custom properties and items, the final target import (10) can occur. This final import, shown as an import of a file named Common.props, can also follow the My.props pattern used in Common.props and conditionally import a file named My.targets, if your development team has enough MSBuild savvy to handle localized customizations in this manner. On a typical team however, these types of customizations would likely be provided by the resident MSBuild expert, and wired into the shared Common.targets file, defined in a manner that they can be controlled by tweaking properties in the developers My.props file as needed.

19. Consider using the standard extensions path

As was mentioned in the previous section, MSBuild has a built-in mechanism for locating imports. It defines three reserved properties:

```
$(MSBuildExtensionsPath32)
$(MSBuildExtensionsPath64)
$(MSBuildExtensionsPath)
```

Generally, these properties will point to a folder named "MSBuild" under the "Program Files" folder. Problem is, there isn't just one such folder on increasingly common 64-bit OS machines.

The MSDN documentation for these reserved properties indicates that the unadorned $(MSBuildExtensionsPath) would point to either one or the other, depending on the bitness of the command window it is run from. The Community Content at the bottom of the page in MSDN online however indicates that the behavior was changed late in the development cycle; presumably, the change didn't get noted in the documentation. In cases where you need to pull extensions from whichever path matches the bitness of your build process, you can't rely on this unadorned property as documented. It seems to exist primarily in support of legacy build operations. If you need to get the documented behavior, where the property refers to either one or the other, you need to set the following environment variable:

```
> set MSBuildLegacyExtensionsPath=1
```

Doing so alters the behavior of MSBuild with respect to that reserved property in a 64-bit command window, and has it point to the 64-bit version of the Program Files folder, as shown in the output below.

Standard Extensions Paths.trkproj

```
<Target Name="StandardExtensionsPaths">
  <Message Text="$(MSBuildExtensionsPath)" />
  <Message Text="$(MSBuildExtensionsPath32)" />
```

```
    <Message Text="$(MSBuildExtensionsPath64)" />
</Target>
```

Output (any platform)

```
StandardExtensionsPaths:
  C:\Program Files (x86)\MSBuild
  C:\Program Files (x86)\MSBuild
  C:\Program Files\MSBuild
```

Output, 64-bit, with MSBuildLegacyExtensionsPath set

```
  C:\Program Files\MSBuild
  C:\Program Files (x86)\MSBuild
  C:\Program Files\MSBuild
```

The reason for this bit of backward compatible functionality is that in the transition to MSBuild 4.0 and Visual Studio 2010, it was discovered that many builds that relied on the $(MSBuildExtensionsPath) property had assumed that there was only a 32-bit configuration to deal with. Not surprising, since Visual Studio was and remains 32-bit only. Late in the cycle, when Team Build started using the 64-bit version of MSBuild by default, the build breakages experienced made this legacy support environment variable an important workaround to this breaking change. If you are savvy enough to use the 64-bit version of MSBuild and have worked through the potential compatibility pitfalls, you should use the $(MSBuildExtensionsPath64) property explicitly.

Alternatively you can rely on property functions, an example for this very scenario is discussed in *trick #59, Know even more property functions, 32 and 64 Bitness.*

There is some crazy environment variable detection needed to determine if the OS on which the build is running is 32 or 64-bit, and then if the build process is 32 or 64-bit. Both of these are important, particularly in developer builds, where you want the result of the build to mimic as closely as possible what the product would look like installed on an end users machine, which can be either 32 or 64 bit. On a build machine these issues are less important, in fact are counter indicated, since on a build machine the results should be deterministic regardless of the bitness of the OS or process in which the build is performed.

The target below shows one technique for OS bitness detection using the various standard "PROCESSOR" environment variables, in various scenarios.

AvoidTheseEnvironmentVariables target

```
<Target Name="AvoidTheseEnvironmentVariables">
   <Message
      Text="Hopefully not set is Platform = '$(Platform)'"
      />
   <Message
      Text="PROCESSOR_ARCHITECTURE is '$(PROCESSOR_ARCHITECTURE)'"
      />
   <Message
      Text="PROCESSOR_ARCHITEW6432 is '$(PROCESSOR_ARCHITEW6432)'"
      />
</Target>
```

Output, 32-bit command shell, 32-bit machine[10]

```
AvoidTheseEnvironmentVariables:
  Hopefully not set is Platform = ''
  PROCESSOR_ARCHITECTURE is 'x86'
  PROCESSOR_ARCHITEW6432 is ''
```

Output, 32-bit command shell, 64-bit machine

```
AvoidTheseEnvironmentVariables:
  Hopefully not set is Platform = ''
  PROCESSOR_ARCHITECTURE is 'x86'
  PROCESSOR_ARCHITEW6432 is 'AMD64'
```

Output, 64-bit command shell

```
AvoidTheseEnvironmentVariables:
  Hopefully not set is Platform = 'X64'
  PROCESSOR_ARCHITECTURE is 'AMD64'
  PROCESSOR_ARCHITEW6432 is ''
```

From this output, the following logic is evident. It isn't enough to just check PROCESSOR_ARCHITECTURE for the value "x86," because it ignores the case where you are on a 64-bit machine running under SYSWOW64.

You are on a 32-bit OS only when PROCESSOR_ARCHITECTURE is "x86" and the value of PROCESSOR_ARCHITEW6432 is undefined. If the value of the PROCESSOR_ARCHITECURE environment variable is "AMD64" or the less common "IA64" then you are on a 64-bit machine.

These properties are used in the standard Microsoft.Cpp.targets file, which is shown below.

---

[10] If you happen to have a computer from by Hewlett Packard, with their default OS image, you'll likely run into a problem where the value of $(Platform) is set to "MCD." Be sure to permanently remove this, or if you like, rename it to PlatformHP, it does not appear to affect any HP supplied software, and will definitely screw up your builds.

From Microsoft.Cpp.targets

```
<PropertyGroup>
  <_IsNativeEnvironment
    Condition="'$(PROCESSOR_ARCHITECTURE)' == 'AMD64' and
    '$(Platform)' == 'X64'">true</_IsNativeEnvironment>

  <_IsNativeEnvironment
    Condition="'$(PROCESSOR_ARCHITECTURE)' == 'IA64' and
    '$(Platform)' == 'Itanium'">true</_IsNativeEnvironment>

  <DefaultToolArchitecture
    Condition="'$(DefaultToolArchitecture)' == '' and
    '$(_IsNativeEnvironment)' !=
    'true'">Native32Bit</DefaultToolArchitecture>

  <DefaultToolArchitecture
    Condition="'$(DefaultToolArchitecture)' == '' and
    '$(_IsNativeEnvironment)' ==
    'true'">Native64Bit</DefaultToolArchitecture>
</PropertyGroup>
```

One interesting use of this type of detection is in dealing with a build in which there is a mix of C# and C++ projects. Because these two project systems have their own default Platform names, and since C# projects can be compiled to an agnostic "AnyCPU" platform, you need to rely on some system of matching the platform values between these two project types. If you've ever looked inside a solution file you would have been exposed to some of this mess. Rather than rely on the build configuration system of a solution file, it is easy to represent this in your own MSBuild project that drives the build of many projects, as shown below.

FakeBitnessBuild target

```
<ItemGroup>                                             <!-- 1 -->
   <Project Include="Project.csproj" />
   <Project Include="Project.vcxproj" />
</ItemGroup>
<Target Name="FakeBitnessBuild">
   <ItemGroup>
      <Project>
        <ConfigToBuild
           Condition="'%(Extension)' == '.csproj'"
           >AnyCPU</ConfigToBuild>                       <!-- 2 -->
        <ConfigToBuild
           Condition="'%(Extension)' == '.vcxproj'
              AND '$(Is64BitOperatingSystem)' == 'true'"
           >x64</ConfigToBuild>
        <ConfigToBuild
           Condition="'%(Extension)' == '.vcxproj'
              AND '$(Is64BitOperatingSystem)' != 'true'"
           >Win32</ConfigToBuild>
      </Project>
```

```
    </ItemGroup>
    <Message
      Text="Building %(Project.Identity) with %(ConfigToBuild)"
      />
</Target>
```

Command

```
> msbuild "Standard Extensions Path.trkproj" /t:FakeBitnessBuild ↵
 /p:Is64BitOperatingSystem=false
```

Output

```
for now
FakeBitnessBuild:
  Building Project.csproj with AnyCPU
  Building Project.vcxproj with Win32
```

This project takes as a parameter a property that indicates whether or not you are building on a 64-bit OS, and selects the proper Platform value for C++ projects. Two projects are added to an item array (1) named "Project" the first being a C# and the second a C++ project. Inside the target, a metadata value named "ConfigToBuild" is added to every member of this item array, using a condition that checks the file extension. For C# projects (2) the "ConfigToBuild" is set to "AnyCPU." For C++ projects, this metadata value is set to either "x64" or "Win32" depending on the value passed in on the command line. Finally, a Message task is used to mimic a call to the MSBuild task, showing how the "ConfigToBuild" meta value can be extracted. To use with the MSBuild task, use a similar syntax:

```
<MSBuild
    Projects="%(Project.Identity)"
    Properties="Platform=%(ConfigToBuild)"
    />
```

Alternatively, you can rely on support for supplying properties to items passed to the MSBuild task via the AdditionalProperties metadata value.

```
...
<ItemGroup>
    <Project>
        <AdditionalProperties
            Condition="'%(Extension)' == '.csproj'"
            >Platform=AnyCPU</ConfigToBuild>
        ...
    </Project>
</ItemGroup>
    <MSBuild Projects="@(Project)" />
```

The MSBuild task looks for this specially named metadata value and extracts from it a semicolon delimited list of property name and value assignments. By using %(AdditionalProperties), these values will be aggregated with any other property values passed into the MSBuild task that will build the projects via the MSBuild task's Properties attribute. If you want to completely override the properties passed into the MSBuild task, you would use the %(Properties) metadata in the example above, not %(AdditionalProperties).

Later on, in *trick #59, Know even more property functions, 32 and 64 Bitness*, you will see how to detect automatically the bitness of the build in a more reliable manner. Using System.Environment, either in an inline task or in a property function that refers directly to System.Environment static properties.

As a final note, there is a strangely named environment variable on 64-bit systems, "ProgramFiles(x86)." You'd think that this value could be used to compose the path to the 32-bit MSBuild extensions path folder, but it is a bit trickier than you might imagine as shown below.

ProgramFilesX86 target

```
<Target Name="ProgramFilesX86">
  <Message Text="1. '$(ProgramFiles)'" />
  <Message Text="2. '$(ProgramFiles%28x86%29)'" />
  <Message Text="3. '$([System.Environment]::
    GetEnvironmentVariable(
      'ProgramFiles(x86)'))"
    />
</Target>
```

Output, Visual Studio Command Prompt (2010)

```
ProgramFilesX86:
1. 'C:\Program Files (x86)'
2. ''
3. 'C:\Program Files (x86)
```

Output, Visual Studio x64 Win64 Command Prompt (2010)

```
ProgramFilesX86:
1. 'C:\Program Files'
2. ''
3. 'C:\Program Files (x86)
```

The standard PROGRAMFILES environment variable, used as an MSBuild property, will report one or the other path depending on the bitness of the command shell in which it is used. Trying to compose the environment variable name using escaped characters for the parenthesis doesn't work. The only way to extract properties that don't have valid XML token names is to go directly to System.Environment.

20. Consider the supported import patterns

A quick examination of the Microsoft.Common.targets file, found in the .NET Framework folder alongside MSBuild.exe, reveals a flurry of property file imports at the top of the file and likewise for targets files at the bottom. A very simplified version of the imports at the top of the file is shown below,

From Microsoft.Common.targets, simplified

```xml
<!-- 1 -->
<Import
    Project="$(MSBuildExtensionsPath)\$(MSBuildToolsVersion)\
        $(MSBuildThisFile)\ImportBefore\*"
    Condition="..."
    />

<!-- 2 -->
<Import
    Project="$(MSBuildProjectFullPath).user"
    Condition="Exists('$(MSBuildProjectFullPath).user')"
    />

<PropertyGroup>
    <!-- 3 -->
    <CustomBeforeMicrosoftCommonTargets
        Condition="..."
        >$(MSBuildExtensionsPath)\v4.0\
            Custom.Before.$(MSBuildThisFile)
    </CustomBeforeMicrosoftCommonTargets>
    ...
</PropertyGroup>

<!-- 4 -->
<Import
    Project="$(CustomBeforeMicrosoftCommonTargets)"
    Condition="Exists('$(CustomBeforeMicrosoftCommonTargets)')"
    />
```

These imports provide a few interesting built-in extension points for adding in your own customizations. The first import (1) uses a wildcard to pull in any number of import files based on their location in the file system. Specifically, the path,

```
$(MSBuildExtensionsPath)\
  $(MSBuildToolsVersion)\
    $(MSBuildThisFile)\
      ImportBefore\*
```

A peek at the very last line of the file reveals a corresponding ImportAfter, which looks in a sibling to the ImportBefore folder above. Thes paths will typically resolve to the following locations,

```
C:\Program Files (x86)\
  MSBuild\
    4.0\
      Microsoft.Common.targets\
        ImportAfter\*
        ImportBefore\*
```

Any and all files you place in this folder will be imported into every project that imports Microsoft.Common.targets, providing a pretty dramatic extension point. Not shown in the listing above is the condition that controls the import, which can be controlled by setting the property $(ImportByWildcardBeforeMicrosoftCommonTargets) to "false" or likewise for the "After" variation of the property. Of course, you would have to ensure that this property is set prior to the import of the Microsoft.Common.targets file.

Also note how the name of the file is composed into the path to be searched, localizing these imports to this particular point only in this file. The same pattern is used in the Microsoft.CSharp.targets file, with the corresponding paths,

```
C:\Program Files (x86)\
  MSBuild\
    4.0\
      Microsoft.CSharp.targets\
        ImportAfter\*
        ImportBefore\*
```

The second customization point at (2) looks for a file that sits beside the main project file, with the .user extension, for example,

```
./MyProject.csproj
./MyProject.csproj.user
```

Typically these projects contain arbitrary XML contained within a top-level <ProjectExtensions> element, which is allowed by MSBuild but ignored by it. However, there is nothing that would prevent you from putting additional MSBuild declarations into this file. Because this file is created and maintained by the IDE, and is intended to hold user-specific information and is thus typically not checked into source control, I would avoid using it for MSBuild customizations, and strongly recommend using regular MSBuild properties, using the technique described below.

The remaining import, shown with the overrideable property defined at (3) and the import of the file named by the property at (5) is similar to the import at (1) but using a subtly different path. This import appears to be legacy from a prior version, before MSBuild supported wildcard imports. Although I would recommend against using this extension point, it is worth showing the path that this import resolves to, which is,

```
C:\Program Files (x86)\
  MSBuild\
    v4.0\
      Custom.Before.Microsoft.Common.targets
```

What is particularly disturbing about this is the subtle difference between the hardcoded "v4.0" folder in the path, and the "4.0" folder in the previous import path which is derived from the $(MSBuildToolsVersion) reserved property.

Now previously it has been recommended to provide customizations in your build by supplying a common import that will be imported by every project in your build. For existing builds with a large number of projects—and in my experience, until you hit the 300 to 400 project mark you aren't really too large yet—but large numbers of project that would each have to be modified just to add an import can cause too much disruption for some to even consider it. This customization point—the first import that is—provides an alternative that can give the customization without having to modify every file.

The biggest sticky point though, is that in a reproducible build, having to install files to a particular location under the Program Files folder has a bad smell to it. The technique described here alleviates to some extent that concern, using the extension point only to point back to the place on your file system where the code from source control is maintained, and providing a trick to have your build configure itself.

Examine the following targets file definition,

CustomExtension.Microsoft.Common.targets

```
<Project ...
  InitialTargets="VerifyCommonProps">

  <PropertyGroup>
    <CommonPropsImportStatus>skipped</CommonPropsImportStatus>
    <RedirectedImport>$([MSBuild]::GetDirectoryNameOfFileAbove(
      $(MSBuildProjectDirectory),
      Common.props))</RedirectedImport>
  </PropertyGroup>
  <Import
    Condition="Exists('$(RedirectedImport)/Common.props')"
    Project="$(RedirectedImport)/Common.props"
    />
```

```
<Target Name="VerifyCommonProps">
  <Message
    Text="Common.props has been '$(CommonPropsImportStatus)'"
    />
</Target>
</Project>
```

This small targets file can be the entire expression of this extension point customization. The significant line is the Import statement, which would suffice to implement the pattern. Using the GetDirectoryOfFileAbove property function, it looks for a file named Common.props in any folder above the folder containing the project file being built. If the file exists it is imported, bringing all further MSBuild customizations back to the source folders under source code control and out of the uncontrolled badlands of the developer's file system. The remaining code is just for sanity checking. An InitialTarget named VerifyCommonProps is declared, which prints out a message saying whether or not the Common.props file was imported. The property in the message is supplied with a default value of "skipped" so in the case where there is no customization to be found, the project will harmlessly print out,

```
Common.props has been 'skipped'
```

The rest of the story relies on the contents of Common.props, which is shown below,

Common.props, boilerplate

```
<Project ...
  InitialTargets="TellCommonImport">
  <PropertyGroup>
    <ImportsFolder>$(MSBuildThisFileDirectory)</ImportsFolder>
    <CommonPropsImportStatus>imported</CommonPropsImportStatus>
  </PropertyGroup>

  <Target Name="TellCommonImport">
    <Message
      Text="Imported Common.props from $(MSBuildThisFileDirectory)"
      />
  </Target>

  ...additional customizations
```

In this file, the $(CommonPropsImportStatus) property referenced in the verification message is reassigned the value "imported." A second property declaring the location where the Common.props file was found—to be used presumably later on for additional file discovery—is also declared. For added sanity an additional InitialTarget is declared, this one printing out the location of the Common.props file, which can be a useful message in the build log for diagnosing issues that may arise when you make extensive use of customization points. The output for the two possible cases is shown below.

Output, for any project file below a Common.props file

```
> msbuild SomeProject.csproj /t:VerifyCommonProps

TellCommonImport:
  Imported Common.props from C:\...
VerifyCommonProps:
  Common.props has been 'imported'
```

Output for all other files,

```
> msbuild SomeProject.csproj /t:VerifyCommonProps

VerifyCommonProps:
  Common.props has been 'skipped'
```

Now for one final customization to finish it all off. The extension file shown above, CustomExtension.Microsoft.Common.targets, would certainly need to be checked into your source control system somewhere, but not in the location it needs to sit in order to be useful. You can add another target to this file so that it is able to deploy itself.

CustomBefore.Microsoft.Common.targets, continuted

```
<Target Name="Configure">
  <PropertyGroup>
    <_ExtensionPoint>$(MSBuildExtensionsPath)\
      $(MSBuildToolsVersion)\Microsoft.Common.targets\
      ImportBefore</_ExtensionPoint>
  </PropertyGroup>
  <Copy
    SourceFiles="$(MSBuildThisFile)"
    DestinationFolder="$(_ExtensionPoint)"
    />
</Target>
```

Just wire this target into your build bootstrapping, as described in *trick #13, Know how to bootstrap build custom tasks*, and you've gotten some extreme extensibility with very little risk of disruption to other projects that may reside on the same machine.

21. Consider using wildcard imports

In addition to importing a single file in a known location with a known file name, it is possible to use wildcards in import elements. When importing with wildcards, all of the files matching the wildcard are accumulated, then sorted by the full path name—in support reproducibility and consistent behavior between runs—then processed one at a time.

The target below examines this process, noting that when a property is redefined in a subsequent imported file, the value is replaced. Each of the four imported files, two at the top-level folder and two in a subfolder, define two properties. One property is redefined in each file, and one is unique.

Imports/AC/A.imp

```
<PropertyGroup>
  <ImportedA>$(Imported)</ImportedA>
  <Imported>A</Imported>
</PropertyGroup>
```

Imports/B.imp

```
<PropertyGroup>
  <ImportedB>$(Imported)</ImportedB>
  <Imported>B</Imported>
</PropertyGroup>
```

Imports/AC/C.imp

```
<PropertyGroup>
  <ImportedB>$(Imported)</ImportedB>
  <Imported>B</Imported>
</PropertyGroup>
```

Imports/D.imp

```
<PropertyGroup>
  <ImportedD>$(Imported)</ImportedD>
  <Imported>D</Imported>
</PropertyGroup>
```

Imports With Wildcards.trkproj

```
<Import Project="Imports/*.imp" />
<Target Name="Tell">
  <Message Text="Imported = '$(Imported)'" />
  <Message Text="ImportedA = '$(ImportedA)'" />
  <Message Text="ImportedB = '$(ImportedB)'" />
  <Message Text="ImportedC = '$(ImportedC)'" />
  <Message Text="ImportedD = '$(ImportedD)'" />
```

```
    </Target>
```

Output

```
    Imported = 'D'
    ImportedA = ''
    ImportedB = 'C'
    ImportedC = 'A'
    ImportedD = 'B'
```

These four files sorted by their path would be

```
Imports/AC/A.imp
Imports/AC/C.imp
Imports/B.imp
Imports/D.imp
```

From the output, it see that in fact the files are sorted by their full path names. When AC/A.imp is imported first, there is no value for $(Imported) when $(ImportedA) is defined, and it ends up with no value in the output. On the next line, $(Imported) takes the value "A" which is then used to initialize $(ImportedC) and so on, finally importing "D.imp" and leaving $(Imported) with the value "D" declared in that file.

22. Keep the build files together

MSBuild tends to keep all of its files together, though using two separate locations. The .NET Framework folder, which is the home for the framework, MSBuild.exe, most of the standard .targets files, and the task assemblies referenced by them is the first such location. The next location, newly populated with C++ build content in Visual Studio 2010 is the Program Files\MSBuild folder, the same one that can be referenced with the $(MSBuildExtensionsPath32) property, the 64-bit path is generally not used, except for by Windows Workflow, which installs a duplicate of the same files found in the 32-bit path.

Building on the recommendation from *trick #19, Consider using the standard extensions path*, try to organize your own build in a similar manner.

You may over time develop fairly specialized MSBuild content for a variety of purposes. The names of some that I've used recently are shown in this list, to give an idea of the kind of customizations a mature build system may have.

- Max.Documentation.targets

- Max.BuildItems.props

- Max.InstallItems.props

- Max.UnitTests.targets

- Max.CustomWebDeploy.targets

- Max.CustomAzureCloud.targets

Each of these provides customizations for source code or other content—as in the case of the Documentation—that may be somewhat widely dispersed in your code base. As such, it may be enticing to place these build customizations alongside the source material on which they will operate. Consider however the complexity this will add to your project files. Within individual project files, you will need to import one or more, or perhaps all of these customizations. In good MSBuild fashion, these import statements should be expressed with paths composed of MSBuild properties, as in,

```
<Import
  Project="$(SourceRoot)\$(DocsFolder)\Max.Documentation.targets"
  />
```

If each of these files is in a separate location, you've just created a bunch of properties to maintain somewhere, without much benefit. Instead, put all of these files together in a single location where all your build files are maintained. Through adherence to a simple naming convention, the purpose of each file is completely clear, and the imports become easier to maintain.

23. Use BeforeBuild and AfterBuild only for local customizations

The standard project systems, through their import of Microsoft.Common.targets, establish a standard extension point for project files through empty targets named BeforeBuild and AfterBuild. These targets can be seen in most project files, tucked away at the bottom, commented out, with the note:

```
<!-- To modify your build process, add your task inside one of the
targets below and uncomment it.
Other similar extension points exist, see Microsoft.Common.targets. -->
```

The mechanism by which they are executed is target overloading. These targets are listed in the BuildDependsOn property used by the main Build target.

```
<PropertyGroup>
    <BuildDependsOn>
        BeforeBuild;
```

```
        CoreBuild;
        AfterBuild
    </BuildDependsOn>
</PropertyGroup>
```

Typically, the empty default versions of these targets are called. They are defined in Microsoft.Common.targets as:

```
<Target Name="BeforeBuild"/>
<Target Name="AfterBuild"/>
```

These empty targets are important, without them, MSBuild would issue a missing target error when it evaluated the $(BuildDependsOn) target prior to running the Build target; if the listed target isn't implemented, it is an error, so the empty implementations are required. Because the commented out overloads provided by default in most project files appear after the import of the Microsoft.Common.targets file containing the empty declarations, when they are uncommented they will override the empty defaults.

In the general case though, you do not want to use these targets. For most multi-project builds, if there is something that you need to wire into the build, it is more likely than not that you will need to do so in more than one place. Also, since any sophisticated build will likely have a common import property file shared by all projects, or by all projects of a certain type, you already have your own nearly unlimited set of extension points available. Consider what would happen if you relied on these stock targets. Eventually someone would modify the target, putting their own customization either before or after the "standard" modification already in place. How do you establish a repeatable pattern for per-project modifications?

From a different perspective, consider the BeforeBuild and AfterBuild targets as extensions points for use in situations that are truly unique only to the one project in which they are coded. There will never be any question about their location with respect to other more standard customizations.

Your standard customizations can establish their own extension point, perhaps using one of the following conventions:

```
<Target Name="BeforeCoreBuild"
    BeforeTargets="CoreBuild"
    AfterTargets="BeforeBuild">
```

Using both BeforeTargets and AfterTargets, you can precisely set the point in the sequence where your target will execute.

```
<Target Name="BeforeBuildAny"
    BeforeTargets="BeforeBuild">
```

If you don't rely on processing that needs to be performed in a previously executing target, for example the transformation of an item array, you may only need to specify a single target that your target needs to run before. This usually isn't the case when you need to run after a particular target, because generally that target will be creating content that will be deployed or at least copied by a subsequent target, so the first approach of specifying both a before and after target would be used in that case.

```
<PropertyGroup>
    <BuildDependsOn>
        BeforeBuildAny;
        BeforeBuild;
        CoreBuild;
        AfterBuild;
    </BuildDependsOn>
</PropertyGroup>
<Target Name="Build" DependsOnTargets="$(BuildDependsOn)" ...
```

Many targets declare a property that contains all the targets that must be executed prior, using the DependsOnTargets attribute of the target. You can extend this, typically in one of two ways,

```
<PropertyGroup>
    <BuildDependsOn>
        $(BuildDependsOn);
        MyTarget;
    </BuildDependsOn>
</PropertyGroup>
```

or,

```
<PropertyGroup>
    <BuildDependsOn>
        MyTarget;
        $(BuildDependsOn);
    </BuildDependsOn>
</PropertyGroup>
```

Basically, you retain all targets defined previously, and add your own target to either the beginning or the end of the list gathered up to that point. Realize of course that other targets from subsequent imports may continue to extend either the beginning or end of the list, or perhaps, as shown below, both ends of the sequence.

```
<PropertyGroup>
    <BuildDependsOn>
        MyBeforeTarget;
        $(BuildDependsOn);
        MyAfterTarget;
    </BuildDependsOn>
```

```
</PropertyGroup>
```

24. How to launch a command prompt for building

At some point, as builds mature and provide functionality useful for developers that can't easily be accessed from within the IDE, building from the command line may become commonplace. I've seen otherwise experienced developers struggle with setting up a command prompt that is useful with MSBuild. Here's how I do it.

First of all, the use of MSBuild from the command line requires that the .NET Framework folder is set in the PATH environment variable. Typically this is done in a batch file that is executed when the command prompt is opened. The vcvarsall.bat file is all set up when Visual Studio is installed, and can be found under the Start menu at:

Start | All Programs | Microsoft Visual Studio 2010 | Visual Studio Tools | Visual Studio Command Prompt (2010)

I'm starting to think of this as legacy though, as it does far more than is required by MSBuild, and as it has caused all sorts of trouble in the past, since there are a few tools that when installed actually modify the contents of this batch file or one of the other batch files it executes. It is a simple matter to create your own path-setting batch file and check it into source control, the one below will work just fine,

buildvars.bat

```
set PATH=%SYSTEMROOT%\Microsoft.NET\Framework\v4.0.30319;%PATH%
set PATH=%VS100COMNTOOLS%..\IDE;%PATH%
```

The second line, which adds the Common7\IDE folder of the Visual Studio installation to the path is useful because it exposes the MSTest.exe program location, along with other useful tools, such as TF.exe for control of Team System from the command line, or from an Exec task.

I like to have the command prompt available from the task bar, so to configure it, do the following.

1. Click the Start menu and type "cmd" in the search box, which should find cmd.exe
2. Right click on the discovered "cmd.exe" and select "Pin to Taskbar"
3. Right click on the new cmd shell icon in the task bar, right click again on "Windows Command Processor" and select "Properties"

4. Click on the General tab and select a name for this shortcut, I typically use "(2010)" to distinguish it from command shells set up for other purposes or with different versions of Visual Studio.

5. Click on the Shortcut tab and enter the following value for in the "Target" field:

```
%comspec% /k "...\buildvars.bat" & title Code & F: & cd \Code & cls
```

6. Click "Advanced" and check "Run as Administrator"

The setup above points to F:\Code, which is the root of all the sources on my machine, adjust yours as needed, likewise with the path to where your buildvars.bat file is located. If you elect to use the Microsoft supplied file, use the following instead:

```
%comspec% /k "C:\Program Files (x86)\Microsoft Visual Studio
10.0\VC\vcvarsall.bat" x86 & title Code & F: & cd \Code & cls
```

This differs from the Visual Studio supplied shortcut by adding additional commands after the call to vcvarsall.bat, which requires carefully fixing the enclosing quotes, which are doubled in the Visual Studio supplied shortcut. Such doubling doesn't work if you wish to add additional commands.

7. Click on "Options" and check "Quick Edit mode"
8. Click on "Font" and select the Consolas font.
9. Click on layout and set a screen buffer of ~120 by 3000, and a Window size of ~120 by 60 or 70, whatever fits on your screen.

You can take this to extremes if it suits you, and define different prompts that declare different "properties" as environment variables, or shortcuts aliases for common build command lines, even pre-defining important properties such as $(OutDir) or $(Configuration). There are other techniques we'll soon get to that can provide similar behavior—primarily with shared import property files—that don't require so much customization for each developer, so consider that when deciding which techniques to use.

25. Don't use custom environment variables for paths

In the previous tip, I recommended setting up a command prompt by adding to the PATH environment variable a folder relative to the one defined by the VS100COMNTOOLS environment variable, that is configured by the installation of Visual Studio. Other program's installers often define additional environment variables which provide similar breadcrumbs to follow to find where various tools are installed.

In general, it is best to keep all tools required in the build in your version control. It is really the only way to keep a build repeatable, especially if an older, long forgotten build needs to be recreated to trace down some problem, often when doing a binary search to detect when a previously undetected problem was first introduced. If you were relying on installed tools, there is no way to recreate which combination of specific versions of tools was installed if it isn't known by the version control history.

Sometimes, however, you come across a tool that just won't cooperate with this approach. Some tools rely on their installer for configuration, and are not functional otherwise. If such a tool doesn't create an environment variable, it will likely put an entry in the registry, which can be pulled out using a special MSBuild property syntax, for example,

```
<BuildToolsRoot
  Condition="'$(BuildToolsRoot)' == ''"
  >$(Registry:HKEY_LOCAL_MACHINE\Software\Microsoft\
  .NETFramework@InstallRoot)</BuildToolsRoot>
<MSDeployToolsRoot
  Condition="'$(MSDeployToolsRoot)' == ''"
  >$(Registry:HKEY_LOCAL_MACHINE\SOFTWARE\Microsoft\
  .NETFramework\AssemblyFolders\MSDeploy)</MSDeployToolsRoot>
<BuildToolsPath
  Condition="'$(BuildToolsPath)' == ''"
  >$(Registry:HKEY_LOCAL_MACHINE\SOFTWARE\Microsoft\MSBuild\
  ToolsVersions\4.0\MSBuildToolsPath)</BuildToolsPath>
```

Often this technique is more reliable than trying to compose a folder path based on the default installation location, which can become more difficult if your environment needs to support both 32 and 64-bit installations. If you find these important, check out the other values that can be found in the registry at,

```
HKLM\SOFTWARE\Microsoft\MSBuild\ToolsVersions\4.0
```

In support of a repeatable build, relying on an environment variable that may or may not have been properly set up by a tool that may or may not need to be installed can cause issues. The same sort of issues discussed in the next *trick #26, Don't rely on the GAC.*

Now just because MSBuild is able to use environment variables as properties doesn't mean that it is a particularly good idea. One option for third party tools that set up environment variables, and for your own build items for which you might think you wanted to repeat this bad pattern, is to use instead a shared .props file that points to paths under source control.

26. Don't rely on the GAC

Many third party development tools or libraries, particularly open source libraries, are available with a Windows installer. Once installed, the assemblies they provide typically end up in the GAC. In a well-mannered continuous integration environment, the pieces of these tools needed for the build and execution are also checked into source control.

Consider the popular NUnit unit and Rhino Mocks testing frameworks. If both are installed, even if checked into source control, and you use the IDE's Add Reference dialog to add a reference, your C# project file will end up looking something like this,

```
<Reference Include="nunit.framework, Version=2.5.0.8333,
  Culture=neutral, PublicKeyToken=96d09a1eb7f44a77,
  processorArchitecture=MSIL">
  <SpecificVersion>False</SpecificVersion>
  <HintPath>..\ThirdParty\Nunit.2.5\nunit.framework.dll</HintPath>
</Reference>

<Reference Include="Rhino.Mocks, Version=3.5.0.1337,
  Culture=neutral, PublicKeyToken=0b3305902db7183f,
  processorArchitecture=MSIL">
  <SpecificVersion>False</SpecificVersion>
  <HintPath>..\ThirdParty\Rhino.3.5\Rhino.Mocks.dll</HintPath>
</Reference>
```

Worse, if the developer adding the references didn't browse to the assembly under version control, you won't even have the HintPath, but instead may have this,

```
<Reference Include="nunit.framework, Version=2.5.0.8333,
  Culture=neutral, PublicKeyToken=96d09a1eb7f44a77,
  processorArchitecture=MSIL" />

<Reference Include="Rhino.Mocks, Version=3.5.0.1337,
  Culture=neutral, PublicKeyToken=0b3305902db7183f,
  processorArchitecture=MSIL" />
```

A bit of a nightmare has just been created. Even though there is nothing about either of these libraries that requires installation in order to be functional, when built on a machine on which these tools weren't installed you will get a build error. When built on a machine on which different versions other than those specified in the strong assembly name in the reference, you can get version incompatibility warnings.

Instead, ensure that assembly references are always explicit, and always of the simplified form shown below, without strong assembly names and with properly formed hint paths.

```
<Reference Include="nunit.framework>
  <HintPath>$(CommonRoot)\ThirdParty\Nunit.2.5\
    nunit.framework.dll</HintPath>
</Reference>

<Reference Include="Rhino.Mocks>
  <HintPath>$(CommonRoot)\ThirdParty\Rhino.3.5\
    Rhino.Mocks.dll</HintPath>
</Reference>
```

In the example above, the $(CommonRoot) property or a similar property would have been declared in the Common.props file, using the technique discussed in *trick #14, Use shared imported properties* and *trick #18, Import properties first, targets last.*

Part II

Trickery

Chapter 4
Mechanics

Basic Mechanics

Properties and Items are expressed simply, with values and metadata. For items, some of the metadata is pre-defined, and they have rules governing the calculation of these predefined values. There are also some things you might expect you could do that you can't, and some things you might expect you can't do that you can. The set of tricks that follows covers some of the basic tricks you need to master before moving on to the more expressive ones.

27. Understand the property precedence rules

Properties are scalar values that can change in the course of project file evaluation and execution. This simple project explains the precedence rules for them,

```
Property Precedence.trkproj

<PropertyGroup>
  <Value>FromStaticProperty</Value>                    <!-- 1 -->
</PropertyGroup>
<Target Name="PropertyPrecedence">
  <Message Text="Value = '$(Value)'" />                <!-- 2 -->
  <PropertyGroup>
    <Value>FromDynamicProperty</Value>                 <!-- 3 -->
  </PropertyGroup>
  <Message Text="Value = '$(Value)'" />                <!-- 4 -->
</Target>
```

Initially, when the project is loaded, the property $(Value) is assigned (1) the value "FromStaticProperty." In the "PropertyPrecedence" target, the value of the property is displayed (2). Next, a dynamic property assignment occurs (3) and the value is again displayed (4). When executed on a command line, the following output results,

Output without property on command line

```
> msbuild "Property Precedence'.trkproj"

PropertyPrecedence:
  Value = 'FromStaticProperty'
  Value = 'FromDynamicProperty'
```

When a value for the property is specified on the command line, as shown below, there is a different result,

Output with property on command line

```
> msbuild "Property Precedence'.trkproj" /p:Value=FromCommandLine

PropertyPrecedence:
  Value = 'FromCommandLine'
  Value = 'FromDynamicProperty'
```

In this case, the value at (1) is ignored. This is because properties passed on the command line take precedence over any statically defined property values. However, the assignment at (3) is a dynamic property assignment, which is able to override the assignment from the command line.

28. Understand well-known item meta

Items can be thought of as a type declaration of sorts. The fields of the type fall into two categories, well-known and custom. Custom metadata can be any named value, provided the name is not reserved for use by well-known metadata. The well-known or built-in metadata names are discussed below,

Built-in Item Metadata.trkproj, WellKnownIdentity target

```
<Target Name="WellKnownIdentity">
  <ItemGroup>
    <File Include="$(MSBuildThisFile)" />
    <File Include="PathTo\*.txt" />
    <File Include="NonPath\*.txt" />
  </ItemGroup>
  <Message Text="Identity = '%(NonFile.Identity)'" />
</Target>
```

Output

```
WellKnownIdentity:
  Identity = 'Built-in Item Metadata.trkproj'
  Identity = 'PathTo\One.txt'
  Identity = 'PathTo\Two.txt'
```

In this first listing, the primary metadata value "Identity" is used. In the sample sources there are actually two files that match the wildcard under "PathTo" and none under the "NonPath" path. Although the first uses a built-in property and the second two use a wildcard, the Identity values are shown to be the evaluated value, not the original string. Because the third item specification has a wildcard and does not evaluate to any actual files, there are no items added to the item array.

WellKnownFileParts target

```
<Target Name="WellKnownFileParts">
  <ItemGroup>
    <NonFile Include="NonPath\NonFile.txt" />
    <NonFile Include="X" />
    <NonFile Include="Y.Z" />
    <NonFile Include="1.2.3" />
  </ItemGroup>
  <Message Text="Extension = '%(NonFile.Extension)'" />
  <Message Text="Directory = '%(NonFile.Directory)'" />
</Target>
```

Output

```
WellKnownExtension:
  Extension = '.txt'
  Extension = ''
  Extension = '.Z'
  Extension = '.3'
  Directory = 'Code\Trickery\Source Code\NonPath\'
  Directory = 'Code\Trickery\Source Code\'
```

In this listing, an item array with four entries is declared. In this example, none of these refers to an actual file on in the file system. The first Message task uses task batching to display the well-known "Extension" metadata for each item. Note that whatever portion of the identity string occurs after a dot is presumed to be the file extension, without regard to whether or not the file exists. The second Message task also uses task batching to display the well-known "Directory" metadata.

Note in the output above that because task batching is used on the Message task, there are four distinct "extensions" reported but only two distinct "Directory" values. Since the same current folder value is used for three of them, only two batches are formed.

The other file based well-known metadata works in a similar manner,

1. FullPath
2. RootDir
3. Filename
4. RelativeDir
5. Directory

All of these will report either the actual file path values for cases where the item specification represents an actual file, or they will report the values of the individual parts of the path if a file existed in the location specified, using the folder containing the project file as the current folder if the path is not absolute.

However, MSBuild internally does do some evaluation on items which may become important. First, if the item specification contains a wildcard, either the * or ? character, MSBuild will call System.IO.Directory.GetFiles to attempt to expand the list of files. If for some reason the item specification contains both a wildcard character and a character that is illegal in a file name, an exception might be thrown. So, if in addition to the four in the listing above a fifth were added,

```
<NonFile Include-":*" />
```

the following error would be displayed, showing the MSBuild escaped form of ":*" as ":%2a" in the message.

```
F:\...\Built-in Item Metadata.trkproj(14,5): error MSB4023: Cannot
evaluate the item metadata "%(Extension)". The item metadata
"%(Extension)" cannot be applied to the path ":%2a". The path is not
of a legal form.
```

If on the other hand, the item specification were slightly different, with the wildcard first,

```
<NonFile Include="*:" />
```

MSBuild would throw an internal exception and the build would terminate. So care must be taken with non-file items that contain item specifications in a form that causes MSBuild to attempt file system operations.

There are a couple of other file related well-known metadata values that behave a little differently,

6. ModifiedTime
7. CreatedTime
8. AccessTime

Because these require an actual file system representation to report any meaningful value, in the case where an item is not represented by an actual file system element these pieces of item metadata will be empty.

```
<Target Name="WellKnownTime">
  <Message Text="CreatedTime = '%(File.CreatedTime)'" />
</Target>
```

Reusing the item array declared in the WellKnownIdentity target, this target will report something like the following:

```
WellKnownTime:
  CreatedTime = '2011-04-09 20:54:45.2239994'
  CreatedTime = '2011-03-05 01:34:34.7346800'
  CreatedTime = '2011-03-05 01:34:40.0698893'
```

The final well-known metadata value is RecursiveDir, which is only relevant when the item specification contains the recursive "globbing" double asterisk "**" wildcard. This metadata is discussed next in *trick #29, How to use RecursiveDir.*

29. How to use RecursiveDir

Given the following source tree,

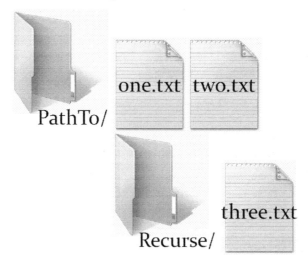

Examine the item array declaration that follows, noting the use of the double asterisk in the pattern matching item specification.

```
<ItemGroup>
  <RecursiveItem
```

```
          Include="PathTo\**\*.txt"
        />                                                    <!-- 1 -->
    <TransformedItem
      Include="@(RecursiveItem->
         'AnotherPath\%(RecursiveDir)%(FileName)%(Extension)')"
        />                                                    <!-- 2 -->
</ItemGroup>

<Target Name="RecursiveDir">
    <!-- 3 -->
    <Message
      Text="Items='%(RecursiveItem.Identity)'"
        />
    <!-- 4 -->
    <Message
      Text="RecursiveDir='@(RecursiveItem->'%(RecursiveDir)')'"
        />
    <!-- 5 -->
    <Message
      Text="Transformed='%(TransformedItem.Identity)'"
        />
</Target>
```

Output

```
RecursiveDir:
  Items='PathTo\One.txt'
  Items='PathTo\Recurse\Three.txt'
  Items='PathTo\Two.txt'
  RecursiveDir=';Recurse\;'
  Transformed='AnotherPath\One.txt'
  Transformed='AnotherPath\Recurse\Three.txt'
  Transformed='AnotherPath\Two.txt'
```

Above, an item array is formed (1) by searching the specified path recursively. Three files are discovered. This item array is then transformed, using an item transformation (2) with three pieces of item metadata, one of which is the %(RecursiveDir). The messages that follow first enumerate the identity (3) which in the output is shown to list all three files. Notice that the files have been sorted alphabetically using the entire path; the "R" in "Recurse" falls between "One" and "Two" in the paths. The next message (4) emits the RecursiveDir item metadata, showing a semicolon delimited list of three values that associate with the three identities listed previously. The first and third values are empty. This is because when the files were discovered using the wildcard pattern, no recursion from the root "PathTo" folder was needed, so the RecursiveDir metadata for these two files is empty. The second file in the sorted list was discovered in the recursive search in the folder "Recurse" and in this case the RecursiveDir metadata takes that part of the path for its value. The final message (5) shows how the RecursiveDir metadata is used when constructing a path with an item transformation.

The most common use of this is when performing a deep copy of files from one place to another while keeping the directory tree intact, as in,

```
<ItemGroup>
  <FilesToCopy Include="SourcePath\**\*.*" />
</ItemGroup>
<Copy
  SourceFiles="@(FilesToCopy)"
  DestinationFiles="@(FilesToCopy->
    'DestPath/%(RecursiveDir)/%(FileName)%(Extension)')"
  />
```

If you happen to use a pattern with multiple recursion wildcards, MSBuild is smart about reconstructing the value of %(RecursiveDir). For example, if the item specification is,

```
PathTo\**\IntermediateDir\**\*.*
```

The value of %(RecursiveDir) will include whatever folders (if any) are represented by the first instance of "**" in the specification, plus the Required "IntermediateDir" folder, plus whatever folders (if any) are represented by the second instance of "**" concatenated together.

30. How to convert properties into items

It is possible to convert a semicolon-delimited list of things defined in a single property into a list of individual things in an item, which is a technique that will be relied on repeatedly in the tricks that follow.

Properties As Items.trkproj

```
<PropertyGroup>
  <ItemProperty>One;Two</ItemProperty>
</PropertyGroup>
<Target Name="PropertiesAsItems">
  <ItemGroup>
    <FromProperty Include="$(ItemProperty)" />
  </ItemGroup>
  <Message Text="%(FromProperty.Identity)" />
</Target>
```

Output

```
PropertiesAsItems:
  One
  Two
```

Simply stated, a property containing a semicolon delimited list of values, $(ItemsProperty), is used as the item specification for the creation of an item array. The individual values are separated, resulting in two separate items seen in the output.

To pass these values on the command line, you need to be careful with the syntax used. Recalling that a property passed from the command line will override any value from a static property declaration, a first attempt,

```
> msbuild "Properties As Items.trkproj" /p:ItemProperty=Three;Four
```

will fail because MSBuild expects the semicolon to start a new property definition of the form Name=value. Escaping the semicolon,

```
> msbuild "Properties As Items.trkproj" /p:ItemProperty=Three%3bFour
```

Produces a subtly undesirable result,

```
PropertiesAsItems:
  Three;Four
```

Notice that this is a single item whose identity actually contains the escaped semicolon. Because it was escaped, MSBuild doesn't separate it as it would a normal semi-colon delimited list. The proper form is to quote the property,

```
> msbuild "Properties As Items.trkproj" /p:ItemProperty="Three;Four"
```

which will evaluate properly as,

```
PropertiesAsItems:
  Three
  Four
```

One caveat that applies to this type of conversion is that the rules that apply to the creation of items, specifically the rules that determine if the item is a file based item or an identity string based item, will also apply to the creation of items from a list of properties. If the individual elements of your property contain wildcards, at the first moment MSBuild first evaluates each individual tuple as the delimited property is being evaluated, the value with the wildcard must be a valid path that resolves to a file or folder on disk. In other words, given,

```
<ItemGroup>
  <SomeItem Include="$(SomeProperty)" />
</ItemGroup>
```

@(SomeItem) will only contain entries if $(SomeProperty) contains a delimited list of either things with either no wildcards, or qualified paths that actually exist. This may be okay in some circumstances, but if you want to manipulate the individual tuples of the property string, for instance composing a path from a fixed root declared in a separate property, some careful construction needs to be undertaken.

This is because MSBuild can't compose a path with a wildcard inside the Include attribute using a transform and evaluate the path to expand the wildcards at the same time. Instead, you need to first compose the full path separately, then feed it into the Include attribute.

The following demonstrates this technique.

Properties As Items.trkproj, ComposePropertiesAsItems target

```xml
<Project
  DefaultTargets="PropertiesAsItems">

  <PropertyGroup>                                      <!-- 1 -->
    <FullPathsWithWildcards>
      .\PathTo\One.*;
      .\PathTo\Two.*
    </FullPathsWithWildcards>
    <PathTo>.\PathTo</PathTo>
  </PropertyGroup>

  <ItemGroup>                                          <!-- 2 -->
    <FilePattern Include="FilePattern">
      <Pattern>One.*</Pattern>
    </FilePattern>
    <FilePattern Include="FilePattern">
      <Pattern>Two.*</Pattern>
    </FilePattern>
    <FilePattern Include="FilePattern">
      <Pattern>Three</Pattern>
    </FilePattern>
  </ItemGroup>

  <Target Name="Compose">
    <ItemGroup>
      <FilePattern Include="FilePattern">              <!-- 3 -->
        <ComposedPath>$(PathTo)\%(Pattern)</ComposedPath><!-- 4 -->
      </FilePattern>
    </ItemGroup>
  </Target>

  <Target Name="ComposePropertiesAsItems"
    DependsOnTargets="Compose">                        <!-- 5 -->
    <ItemGroup>
      <FullPathsWithWildcards
        Include="$(FullPathsWithWildcards)"
        />
      <NonComposedFiles
        Include="%(FilePattern.Pattern)"
        />
      <ComposedFiles
        Include="%(FilePattern.ComposedPath)"
```

```
        />
    </ItemGroup>
    <Message
      Text="From Full Path: @(FullPathsWithWildcards)"
      />
    <Message
      Text="Non-Composed: @(NonComposedFiles)"
      />
    <Message
      Text="Composed: @(ComposedFiles)"
      />
  </Target>
</Project>
```

Files

```
.\PathTo\One.txt
.\PathTo\Two.txt
```

Output

```
PropertiesAsItems:
  From Full Path: .\PathTo\One.txt;.\PathTo\Two.txt
  Non-Composed: Three
  Composed: .\PathTo\One.txt;.\PathTo\Two.txt;.\PathTo\Three
```

This listing, which reuses the same file and folder hierarchy shown in *trick #29, How to use RecursiveDir* previously, starts with two property declarations, $(FullPathsWithWildcards) which contains two distinct paths separated by semicolons, and $(PathTo) which contains the name of the folder that will be used when composing paths. Next an item array is constructed (2) for an item named @(FilePattern) containing three entries, distinguished by the %(Pattern) metadata values, which has no duplicated values in this example. Because the wildcard patterns are declared in item metadata they are not evaluated for file matches by MSBuild, which only performs wildcard evaluation for item specifications—which are the same as the Include attribute of an item declaration.

Control starts in the target "ComposePropertiesAsItems" which then executes the DependentTarget "Compose" which at (3) can be seen to add an additional metadata value to @(FilePattern), composing a path using the $(PathTo) property and the previously declared %(Pattern) metadata.

Returning to (5) there are three item arrays created, each of which is in turn displayed with a Message task. The first, FullPathsWithWildcards, is a typical item array created by expanding the wildcard item specification (1) declared in $(FullPathsWithWildcards). Each individual item specification pattern—there are two separated by semicolons—matches a single file, which can be seen in the first line of the output, finding the files One.txt and Two.txt. The second item array uses the bare %(Pattern) metadata as the item specification. Because it will be looking in the current folder, the two %(Pattern) values that contain wildcards are evaluated and found to be empty. The third value, "Three" does not have a wildcard and remains as the only entry in the @(NonComposedFiles) item when it is displayed. The final item array uses the %(ComposedPath) item metadata. When these are evaluated, the composed metadata containing a wildcard are evaluated during the execution of the target, finding the two files, but also retaining the third composed path even though it does not refer to an actual file.

The useful part of this technique is that although the initial item array was declared statically, the evaluation did not occur then. The paths were able to be composed using a property which could have had its value altered during processing prior to the Compose target being executed, and finally, the actual wildcard expansion, even though the wildcard patterns were declared statically, does not occur until the dynamic item array is created within the ComposePropertiesAsItems target. This is significant because it would include files that did not exist when the original @(FilePattern) item array was declared.

31. Understand how dynamic values are published

Static values, whether items or properties, are available as soon as the first target starts to execute. Dynamic values have some subtle behavior, necessary in the case of target batching iterations, but in other cases perhaps because of an implementation oversight or even a bug that probably is baked in, that affects when they become visible to tasks executing in targets.

The first example below shows the publishing sequence when CallTarget is involved.

Publishing Dynamic Values.trkproj

```
<Target Name="TellValue">
  <Message Text="Value is '$(Value)'" />
</Target>
```

Target PublishDynamicFail

```
<Target Name="PublishDynamicFail">
  <PropertyGroup>
    <Value>Ok</Value>                              <!-- 1 -->
  </PropertyGroup>
```

```
    <Message Text="Value is '$(Value)'" />              <!-- 2 -->
    <CallTarget Targets="TellValue" />                  <!-- 3 -->
  </Target>
```

Output of target PublishDynamicFail

```
PublishDynamicFail:
  Value is 'Ok'
TellValue:
  Value is ''
```

In the PublishDynamicFail target, a property (1) named $(Value) is given the value "Ok" which is then displayed (2) with the newly assigned value property shown in the output. Immediately after that, CallTarget is called (3) to execute the TellValue target. The TellValue target prints out what it believes to be the value of that property. From the output, it can be seen that the called target is unaware of the actual value of the property. It turns out that even though the property was immediately available in the scope of the target in which it was dynamically created, it is not yet available in other targets. In this case, the $(Value) property becomes available in other targets only when the "PublishDynamicFail" target completes its execution.

To get the desired results, the CallTarget execution needs to be converted to a DependentTargets execution. Dependent targets complete their execution prior to when the target creating the dependency is executed, satisfying the publication limitation.

Publishing Dynamic Values.trkproj, PublishDynamic target

```
  <Target Name="SetValueInDependent">
    <PropertyGroup>
      <Value>Ok</Value>                                 <!-- 2 -->
    </PropertyGroup>
    <Message Text="Value is '$(Value)'" />
  </Target>

  <Target Name="PublishDynamic"
    DependsOnTargets="SetValueInDependent">             <!-- 1 -->
    <CallTarget Targets="TellValue" />
    <Message Text="Value is '$(Value)'" />              <!-- 3 -->
  </Target>
```

Output of target PublishDynamic

```
PublishDynamic:
  Value is 'Ok'
TellValue:
  Value is 'Ok'
PublishDynamic:
  Value is 'Ok'
```

In this restructured example, the PublishDynamic target declares a new target (1) as a dependent. The dynamic property creation (2) and the message printing the value have been moved into this dependent target. The rest of the target remains the same, with CallTarget being executed to display the property once again, using the value known to another target. In this case the TellValue target properly sees the correct value, as does the main target (3), because the target in which the value was set has completed, and upon completion of that target the property value was "published" for visibility in lower scopes.

These publication rules and the workaround above apply to items in exactly the same manner.

Mechanics of MSBuild Execution and the MSBuild task

The MSBuild executable, being the centerpiece of MSBuild, deserves some special attention. Properly used, it can help make daily life inside the IDE approach the flexibility of the command line. Being the engine behind the C# and C++ project systems (not to forget Visual Basic .NET, F# and more), there is quite a bit of flexibility and complexity already wired in. Some of this is hidden from view, and in the mechanics tricks that follow we'll take a peek at on what is going on under the hood. The built-in task associated with the execution of MSBuild is interesting in ways that the other stock tasks are not. It provides the possibility of recursion, and when your back is up against the wall, it can release you from some of the inherent limitations in how targets are executed. It has some limitations of its own though, which also deserve some special attention with the mechanics tricks that follow.

32. Understand the limitations of the MSBuild task

The MSBuild task is the single-most important task when designing large builds of numerous projects. It has quite a bit of built-in flexibility discussed elsewhere; property overrides, usage of AdditionalProperties, multi-processor builds, target outputs. It does have some limitations to be aware of though.

The first limitation to understand is that not all properties available in the parent project will be available in the child project being executed by the

MSBuild task. This next example discusses which properties are available and which are not.

MSBuild task.trkproj

```
<PropertyGroup>
    <FromParent>true</FromParent>                        <!-- 1 -->
</PropertyGroup>
<Target Name="MSBuildTask">
    <PropertyGroup>
        <FromTarget>true</FromTarget>                    <!-- 2 -->
    </PropertyGroup>
                                                         <!-- 3 -->
    <MSBuild
        Projects="MSBuild task child.trkproj"
        Targets="Child"
        Properties="FromTask=true"
        />
</Target>
```

MSBuild task child.trkproj

```
<Target Name="Child">                                    <!-- 4 -->
    <Message Text="FromParent: '$(FromParent)'" />
    <Message Text="FromTask: '$(FromTask)'" />
    <Message Text="FromCommandLine: '$(FromCommandLine)'" />
</Target>
```

Command

```
> msbuild "MSBuild task.trkproj" /p:FromCommandLine=true
```

Output

```
Child:
  FromParent: ''
  FromTarget: ''
  FromTask: 'true'
  FromCommandLine: 'true'
```

The listing above shows the limitations with regard to property "inheritance" by a child MSBuild execution. A static property is declared (1) in the parent project file, and a dynamic property is declared in the target (2). Next, the child project file is executed (3). In this task execution, the "FromTask" property is passed explicitly. In the child project file, the target prints out four possible properties (4); the three already referenced, one declared statically, one declared dynamically, and one passed explicitly, and a fourth named FromCommandLine, which is passed using the command line as shown. In the output, see that the property passed explicitly is available in the child as would be expected. The property passed on the command line is also "inherited" by the child project. Both the statically declared and dynamically declared properties, however, are absent.

Passing properties to an MSBuild task target

There are two ways around this limitation. One would be to have both project files import the same .props file to make the same set of static properties available in the scope of both project executions. Another is to be aware of which properties from the parent scope are used or otherwise required in the child scope, and come up with an easy way to gather them and get them passed using the Properties attribute. The listing below shows one such technique.

MSBuild task.trkproj, MSBuildTaskPassingProperties target

```xml
<ItemGroup>
  <Param Include="FromParent" />                        <!-- 1 -->
  <Param Include="FromTarget" />
</ItemGroup>
<Target Name="MSBuildTaskPassingProperties">
  <PropertyGroup>
    <FromTarget>true</FromTarget>
  </PropertyGroup>
  <ItemGroup>
    <Param>
      <Value>$(%(Identity))</Value>                      <!-- 2 -->
    </Param>
  </ItemGroup>
  <PropertyGroup>                                        <!-- 3 -->
    <Params>@(Param->'%(Identity)=%(Value)', ';')</Params>
  </PropertyGroup>
  <Message Text="Params: '$(Params)'" />                 <!-- 4 -->
                                                         <!-- 5 -->
  <MSBuild
      Projects="MSBuild task child.trkproj"
      Targets="Child"
      Properties="FromTask=true;$(Params)"
      />
</Target>
```

Output

```
MSBuildTaskPassingProperties:
  Params: 'FromParent=true;FromTarget=true'
...
Child:
  FromParent: 'true'
  FromTarget: 'true'
  FromTask: 'true'
  FromCommandLine: 'true'
```

In this listing, an item array named @(Param) is constructed (1) that contains items whose item specification is simply the name of a property that needs to be passed to the child project executed with the MSBuild task. At some point prior to calling the task—in this example it is in the same target that makes the call, but it could have been done in a separate dependent target—at the point when the properties contain the values to be passed, a globally applied item metadata value (2) named %(Value) is added to all items in the item array. The %(Value) metadata gets its value from the creation of a property around the %(Identity) metadata. So for instance, the $(%(Identity)) expression for the first item in the @(Param) array, the item with the "FromParent" item specification, will resolve first to $(FromParent), which then is resolved to the value of the property whose property expression was just formed, and this property value expression is placed into the item metadata.

Next, a property named $(Params) is created (3) using an item transformation of the @(Param) item array, composing a semicolon delimited list of Name=Value declarations using the Identity and newly composed Value metadata. This new property is displayed (4) prior to calling the MSBuild task, and can be seen in the output. Finally, the $(Params) properety just created is appended (5) to the Properties attribute on the MSBuild task. In the output—presuming the same command line as the previous example—it can be seen that all of the expected properties are now available in the child.

An interesting extension to this technique could be to parse the command line options passed into the MSBuild task and contribute them to the list of predetermined values Added via the @(Param) item array. You can retrieve the command line using System.Environment.CommandLine, see *trick #9, Use property functions, Environment Property Functions*, but then you would also need to parse any response files, see *trick #44, Use a response file named @*, which can be recursive. Instead, I'd rely on the convention that any additional properties needed could be added to the @(Param) item array in the user's My.props file, which would need to be maintained alongside the response file.

Passing items to an MSBuild task target

While properties have specific rules about which are available, items are not. If the items from the parent project are not imported through a shared import file and evaluated identically, you are limited to the items passed to the MSBuild task's Projects attribute, which of course simply indicates which projects are supposed to be loaded and executed with the specified targets. Other than that, there is only a little bit you can do to pass items, as shown below, where a simple set of items without any custom metadata is bundled into a property, passed into a new project, then unbundled on the other side and reformed as an item array.

MSBuild task.trkproj, MSBuildTaskPassingItems target

```
<ItemGroup>
    <FromParent Include="One" />                    <!-- 1 -->
    <FromParent Include="Two" />
</ItemGroup>
<Target Name="MSBuildTaskPassingItems">
    <PropertyGroup>
        <Params>ArrayFromParent=@(FromParent)</Params>  <!-- 2 -->
    </PropertyGroup>
    <Message Text="Params: '$(Params)'" />
    <MSBuild
        Projects="MSBuild task child.trkproj"
        Targets="ChildWithItems"
        Properties="$(Params)"
        />                                          <!-- 3 -->
</Target>
```

MSBuild task child.trkproj

```
<ItemGroup>
    <FromParent Include="$(ArrayFromParent)" />     <!-- 4 -->
</ItemGroup>
<Target Name="ChildWithItems">
    <Message Text="ArrayFromParent: '$(ArrayFromParent)'" />
    <Message Text="FromParent: '%(FromParent.Identity)'" />
</Target>
```

Output

```
MSBuildTaskPassingItems:
  Params: 'ArrayFromParent=One;Two'
...
ChildWithItems:
  ArrayFromParent: 'One;Two'
  FromParent: 'One'
  FromParent: 'Two'
```

To start with, a static item with two entries (1) is declared. In the main target, this item is converted (2) to a property expression and given the name $(ArrayFromParent). This property is then passed to the child project using the Properties attribute (3) of the MSBuild task.

Once inside the child project, the property is converted back to an item array (4) and given the original item name @(FromParent), though any other name could have been used as well, since the original @(FromParent) item array is unknown in the child otherwise. The called target in the child project simply prints out the property and reconstituted item array.

Of course, the lack of any item metadata, and the inability to package and then reconstruct items with corresponding metadata using the built-in functionality of MSBuild is a big limitation. To do a similar sort of thing with metadata requires a pair of custom tasks.

To construct these tasks, you would first need to come up with a way of encoding the item specification as well as all of the custom metadata into a string, so that it could be passed as a single property. One custom task could perform this encoding, taking the item array as input and returning the encoded string as output. Once on the other side, a second custom task could decode this property, and return the reconstituted item array as output.

EncodeDecodeItemsTask.cs, class EncodeItemsTask

```
public class EncodeItemsTask : Task
{
    [Required]
    public ITaskItem[] InputItems { get; set; }

    [Output]
    public string EncodedItems { get; set; }

    public override bool Execute()
    {
        var encodedItems = new StringBuilder();
        foreach (ITaskItem item in InputItems)
        {
            if (item.ItemSpec.Length > 0)
            {
                var encoded = new StringBuilder(item.ItemSpec); // 2
                foreach (var meta in item.MetadataNames)
                {
                    if (!SkipWellKnown(meta.ToString()))            // 5
                    {
                        Log.LogMessage(
                            " Encoding '{0}:{1}'",
                            item.ItemSpec,
                            meta);
                        encoded.AppendFormat(
                            "|{0}={1}",                             // 3, 4
                            meta,
                            item.GetMetadata(meta.ToString()));
                    }
            }
```

```
                }
                encodedItems.AppendFormat(
                    encodedItems.Length == 0 ? "{0}" : ";{0}",    // 1
                    encoded);
            }
        }

        EncodedItems = encodedItems.ToString();
        return !Log.HasLoggedErrors;
    }

    internal static bool SkipWellKnown(string name)
    {
        switch (name)
        {
            // 5
            case "AccessedTime":
            case "CreatedTime":
            case "Directory":
            case "Extension":
            case "Filename":
            case "FullPath":
            case "Identity":
            case "ModifiedTime":
            case "RecursiveDir":
            case "RelativeDir":
            case "RootDir":
                return true;
        }
        return false;
    }
}
```

The simple task above uses a straightforward encoding scheme.
Individual items in the array are separated by semicolons (1). The item is
encoded as the item specification (2), followed by a vertical bar delimited
list of custom metadata (3). Each custom metadata value is encoded as
the name separated from the value by an equal sign (4).

The ITaskItem interface makes no distinction between custom metadata
values and well-known metadata. Since the well-known metadata will all
be calculated from the item specification, and can't be altered, it is
excluded from the encoding by checking against the list of well-known
metadata names (5), which are skipped.

EncodeDecodeItemsTask.cs, class DecodeItemsTask

```
public class DecodeItemsTask : Task
{
    [Required]
    public string EncodedItems { get; set; }

    private readonly ArrayList _decodedItems = new ArrayList();
```

```csharp
[Output]
public ITaskItem[] DecodedItems
{
    get
    {
        return (ITaskItem[])
            _decodedItems.ToArray(typeof(ITaskItem));
    }
}

public override bool Execute()
{
    var items = EncodedItems.Split(new [] { ';' });
    foreach (var item in items)
    {
        var metas = item.Split(new[] { '|' });
        TaskItem taskItem = null;
        foreach (var metaDef in metas)
        {
            if (taskItem == null)
            {
                taskItem = new TaskItem(metaDef);
                _decodedItems.Add(taskItem);
            }
            else
            {
                Log.LogMessage(
                    "  Decoding '{0}:{1}'",
                    taskItem.ItemSpec,
                    metaDef);
                var meta = metaDef.Split(new[] { '=' });
                taskItem.SetMetadata(meta[0], meta[1]);
            }
        }
    }

    return !Log.HasLoggedErrors;
}
}
```

The decoding task picks apart the encoded string in a rather simplistic way, the listing above doesn't contain any error checking to keep it simple; as written it requires a properly formed encoded input string.

Encode-Decode items task.trkproj

```xml
<ItemGroup>                                    <!-- 6 -->
    <FromParent Include="One">
        <A>A1</A>
        <B>B1</B>
    </FromParent>
    <FromParent Include="Two">
        <A>A2</A>
        <B>B2</B>
    </FromParent>
```

```
    </ItemGroup>

  <Target Name="Build">
                                                    <!-- 7 -->
    <EncodeItemsTask
      InputItems="@(FromParent)">
      <Output
        TaskParameter="EncodedItems"
        PropertyName="EncodedItems"
        />
    </EncodeItemsTask>
    <Message Text="EncodedItems: '$(EncodedItems)'" />
                                                    <!-- 8 -->
    <DecodeItemsTask
      EncodedItems="$(EncodedItems)">
      <Output
        TaskParameter="DecodedItems"
        ItemName="DecodedItems"
        />
    </DecodeItemsTask>
    <Message Text="DecodedItems: '@(DecodedItems)'" />
    <Message Text="  DecodedItems.A: '%(DecodedItems.A)'" />
    <Message Text="  DecodedItems.B: '%(DecodedItems.B)'" />
  </Target>
```

Output

```
Build:
    Encoding 'One:A'
    Encoding 'One:B'
    Encoding 'Two:A'
    Encoding 'Two:B'
  EncodedItems: 'One|A=A1|B=B1;Two|A=A2|B=B2'
    Decoding 'One:A:A1'
    Decoding 'One:B:B1'
    Decoding 'Two:A:A2'
    Decoding 'Two:B:B2'
  DecodedItems: 'One;Two'
    DecodedItems.A: 'A1'
    DecodedItems.A: 'A2'
    DecodedItems.B: 'B1'
    DecodedItems.B: 'B2'
```

The sample usage declares an item array (6) with two items, each with
two pieces of custom metadata. It performs the encoding (7) and
decoding (8) in the same target, but would work in the same manner as
the examples already discussed in this section if the property that is
formed by the encoding were to be passed as a property in an MSBuild
task. The output shows the Logging that comes from the custom tasks, as
well as the Message tasks in the target, which verify that all of the custom
metadata was successfully encoded into a string, then decoded and used
to reconstitute an item array.

As an enhancement, consider passing the delimiters used for the encoding as input parameters to both tasks, to more easily handle items with values that may be composed of the chosen delimiters, or to add escaping and un-escaping of the item specification and meta values.

Using an Exec task to run MSBuild

There are some rare edge cases where running MSBuild with the task of the same name won't quite cut it.

These situations have occurred for me most often in continuous integration scenarios, where you are setting up a complex series of builds on a build machine, when you want to drive multiple build configurations and provide different command line options to MSBuild for each. One reason would be to allow each build to have a separate logfile. Another would be to specify an alternate *toolsversion*, or perhaps to finely tune multi-processor builds with the /maxcpucount option, or perhaps to tune other performance optimizations, such as disabling node reuse. While it is possible to just set this up in whatever continuous integration system you are using, placing the various configuration options in an MSBuild property file and using MSBuild to drive it has a certain uniformity about it and provides a useful measure of separation of concerns. Since the build is already MSBuild based, I prefer to keep it MSBuild based and not rely on the peculiarities of other technologies to do essentially the same thing.

To run MSBuild using the Exec task, you may need to provide a path to the MSBuild executable, in order to ensure the correct one is being picked up. If you are using a Visual Studio command prompt, you can compose the path to MSBuild as,

```
$(FrameworkDir)$(FrameworkVersion)\MSBuild.exe
```

If not, pull the path from the registry, which is the preferred method since it can be used from any command environment,

```
$(Registry:HKEY_LOCAL_MACHINE\SOFTWARE\Microsoft\MSBuild\
    ToolsVersions\4.0\MSBuildToolsPath)\MSBuild.exe
```

At this point, the command line options provided can be gathered using a variation of *trick #71, Forming delimited lists for repeated arguments*.

There are some limitations to be aware of when running MSBuild in this manner. The most obvious is that you won't get any properties inherited by the child build, not even those supplied on the command line as you would with the MSBuild task. Another is that when it is being run through the Exec task, all of the MSBuild output is treated as raw text. The console logger will lose all colorization. For a build machine, this may not be an issue, but since it should be expected that the same build used by the build machine is used by developers, and at least one of them will be the person maintaining any build machine specific parts of the build, losing colorization can make command line builds mostly unreadable. Finally, there are some features of MSBuild that will be lost, or at least reduced, such as getting a meaningful build performance summary. Each individual log file will be able to maintain its own, but getting meaningful information across the whole build becomes more cumbersome.

33. Know how to control MSBuild from the IDE

As you begin to experiment with MSBuild, it is a good idea to become comfortable with driving your experiments from the command line, due to a couple Visual Studio limitations.

The Visual Studio project systems utilize an instance of the MSBuild engine for building from within the IDE. The project systems also load and manipulate projects (naturally) but remember that the projects are merely MSBuild files destined to be fed to the build engine. As project files are loaded, imports are discovered and loaded as well, so that a fully formed "object model" of the project can be interrogated and manipulated. An implication of this is that there is some disconnection between the state of the project file on disk and the one in memory, specifically when it comes to the import files. The project system is smart enough to detect when the solution or a project file changes, but it ignores changes to any imported property or target files within the projects.

As will be seen a bit further along in *trick #82, How to force Visual Studio to build properly when using imports*, when modifying project imports— an everyday occurrence for someone schooled in the build—you'll need to unload and reload project files, or often the solution file, to pick up any changes.

The primary feedback you receive about the build in the IDE appears in the Build pane of the Output Window. This output by default is set to the "minimal" verbosity from the MSBuild engine. As you add Message tasks to your experiments, you'll want to crank up this level to at least "Normal" so that your messages appear. To do so, navigate to Tools |

Options | Projects and Solutions | Build and Run. The bottom two settings are MSBuild related.

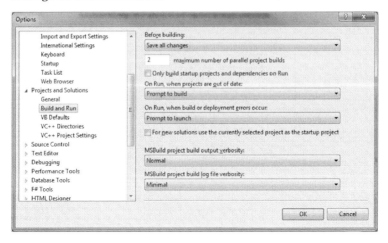

The first of these two settings affects the verbosity of the build output as it appears in the Output Window. The second option allows for a separate verbosity for the build log file, but this is only used by the C++ project system, and then only if build logging is enabled in the Tools | Options | Projects and Solutions | VC++ Project Settings page.

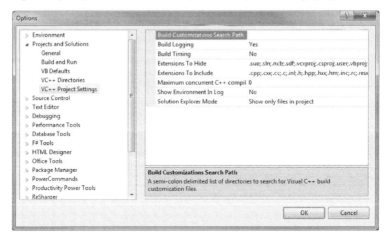

Also on this page is a setting to provide additional paths for MSBuild to search when looking for build customizations. As with anything build related in a production environment, it is best to leave this blank. Doing otherwise would result in inconsistencies between machines that could lead to hard to diagnose issues. In *trick #19, Consider using the standard extensions path* and elsewhere this is covered in detail.

If you are getting different behavior between command line builds and solution file builds, aside from avoiding solution builds altogether, you might get some help by examining how MSBuild builds a solution file. A .sln file is not an MSBuild file, yet MSBuild is able to build it. It does this by converting the solution file to a valid MSBuild file. This converted file is transient and deleted when the build completes, but you can see it by setting a special environment variable. As an experiment, find a solution file with multiple projects, then run the following in a VS Command Line.

```
> set MSBuildEmitSolution=1
> msbuild MySolution.sln
> dir *.metaproj
    ... MySolution.sln.metaproj
```

After running a build, look for a file alongside the solution file with the same name and a .metaproj extension. The key diagnostic thing to understand about this generated MSBuild file is the CurrentSolutionConfigurationContents property, which is an XML representation of the solution file contents, specifically all the configuration options that have been set using the Configuration Manager in the IDE. Notice that when the MSBuild task is called in the Build target within this generated file—which builds the item array containing the project files—this entire XML property is passed in to the task in the Properties attribute.

34. Know some other secret environment variables

The behavior of MSBuild can be altered when it detects certain environment variables during execution. Several of these are presented briefly below, categorized by usage. As you work with these environment variables, keep in mind that as with any other undocumented or unofficial behavior, these flags may silently disappear or have their meaning modified in future updates. Also, since these are unsupported, they are likely not completely tested, so you may experience crashes or other bugs. If you find any, go ahead and report them on the Microsoft Connect site, you might just gain some favor from the folks who are working on the next version.

In all cases except where noted, setting the environment variable to the value "1" will trigger the alternate behavior. In some cases, any value will work, but using "1" as the sentinel value is the best practice.

Debugger control

In *trick #12, Know how to debug MSBuild,* the basic steps for debugging an MSBuild script were discussed. This first set of environment variables gives an opportunity to make the debugging experience a bit more streamlined and informative.

MSBuildDebugging
This is similar to the /debug command line option for MSBuild.exe, except that if enabled in the environment from which Visual Studio is launched, it will enable debugging of the build for projects built within the IDE.

MSBuildDebugOnStart
Will trigger Just-in-Time (JIT) debugging upon the first execution of a child node in the build.

MSBuildDebugPath
Set to a path where you want MSBuild to place some of the debug-related trace dumps.

MSBuildDebugScheduler
Will write out verbose tracing from the build scheduler to a temporary file. This will emit detailed diagnostics about the various configurations in the build about to be processed.

MSBuildDoNotBreakOnStartup
When /debug is passed on the command line, or when the MsBuildDebugging environment variable is set, the initial initial JIT break on startup will not occur.

MSBuildDebugComm
Enables the creation of a file in the %TEMP% folder named MSBuild_CommsTrace_{SOME-GUID}.txt, which contains diagnostic information related to the communication between the IDE and the MSBuild process it uses for building. Probably only useful for reporting bugs or other issues to Microsoft.

MSBuildLaunchDebugger
Launch the debugger when there is an internal error in MSBuild itself. Otherwise, MSBuild will report the exception and terminate.

I've been told there will also be a new environment variable in the 4.5 version of MSBuild, named MSBuildDebugEvaluation, which will write debug output to the debug stream available using dbgview.exe. We'll

have to wait and see, but hopefully this means that the debugger features
will become more officially supported to some degree.

Output

MSBuildDebugExpansion

As previously discussed in *trick #10, Know how to diagnose property
function issues*, this tells MSBuild to output to the command line
diagnostics about how it is recursively expanding property function
values during property evaluation.

MSBuildDetailedSummary

It is supposed to function similar to the /detailedSummary (/ds)
command line option, but it doesn't appear to actually work in my
experience.

MSBuildDiagnostics

Will output additional information when a task exception occurs.

MSBuildEnableBuildPlan

This will write out even more scheduler tracing. MSBuild will read and
write a file named ProjectName.proj.buildplan. This allows you to cause
MSBuild to emit a build plan, which is a listing of projects and numbers
that detail how it will attack the build dependency hierarchy. You can
then alter the plan, and in a subsequent build have MSBuild work on the
altered plan when it is discovered. This works for solution files as well as
individual project files, and gains complexity based on how many projects
are being built. While this does give some insight into the inner workings
of the algorithms used by MSBuild, it isn't all that useful as a practical
matter.

MSBuildForwardAllPropertiesFromChild

When combined with diagnostic level verbosity, this will force the
property listings to be forwarded from child build node processes. This is
quite slow due to the volume of information that needs to be passed
between processes, which is why it is disabled by default.

MSBuildTargetOutputLogging

Will add additional output to the target logging. This requires at least
detailed level diagnostics before it comes into play. See the listing below
for an example of its usage,

Target Output Logging.trkproj

```
<Target Name="CheckOutputLogging">
  <Error
    Condition="'$(MSBuildTargetOutputLogging)' != '1'"
    Text="Meaningless without MSBuildTargetOutputLogging"
    />
</Target>

<Target Name="TargetOutputLogging"
   DependsOnTargets="CheckOutputLogging"
   Outputs="@(OutputItem);$(OutputProperty)">
   <ItemGroup>
      <OutputItem Include="Item1" />
      <OutputItem Include="Item2" />
         <MetaA>MetaA</MetaA>
         <MetaB>MetaB</MetaB>
      </OutputItem>
   </ItemGroup>

   <PropertyGroup>
      <OutputProperty>OutputProp</OutputProperty>
   </PropertyGroup>
</Target>
```

Output, partial, when run with verbosity at least "detailed"

```
...
Target "TargetOutputLogging" in project "F:\...\Target Output
Logging.proj" (entry point):
Target output items:
    Item1
    Item2
        MetaA = MetaA
        MetaB = MetaB
    OutputProp
```

Also with this setting, one useful bit of additional information is output for the ResolveAssemblyReference target, showing what mechanism was used to resolve a particular reference, and what the path to the assembly is. A very abbreviated version is shown below; notice the items listed as "ResolvedFrom" below:

```
Done executing task "ResolveAssemblyReference". (TaskId:11)
Target output items:
    C:\Program Files (x86)\Reference Assemblies\Microsoft\      ↳
Framework\.NETFramework\v4.0\Microsoft.CSharp.dll
        ResolvedFrom = {TargetFrameworkDirectory}
        CopyLocal = false
        FusionName = Microsoft.CSharp, Version=4.0.0.0,         ↳
Culture=neutral, PublicKeyToken=b03f5f7f11d50a3a
        Redist = Microsoft-Windows-CLRCoreComp.4.0
        OriginalItemSpec = Microsoft.CSharp
        Version = 4.0.0.0
```

```
     C:\Program Files (x86)\Reference Assemblies\Microsoft\       ↳
Framework\.NETFramework\v4.0\mscorlib.dll
        ResolvedFrom = C:\Program Files (x86)\Reference           ↳
Assemblies\Microsoft\Framework\.NETFramework\v4.0\mscorlib.dll
        CopyLocal = false
        FusionName = mscorlib, Version=4.0.0.0, Culture=neutral,  ↳
PublicKeyToken=b77a5c561934e089
        OriginalItemSpec = C:\Program Files (x86)\Reference        ↳
Assemblies\Microsoft\Framework\.NETFramework\v4.0\mscorlib.dll
        Version = 4.0.0.0
     C:\Program Files (x86)\Reference Assemblies\Microsoft\        ↳
Framework\.NETFramework\v4.0\System.Data.dll
        ResolvedFrom = {TargetFrameworkDirectory}
        CopyLocal = false
        FusionName = System.Data, Version=4.0.0.0,                ↳
Culture=neutral, PublicKeyToken=b77a5c561934e089
        Redist = Microsoft-Windows-CLRCoreComp.4.0
        OriginalItemSpec = System.Data
        Version = 4.0.0.0
```

MSBuildWarnOnUninitializedProperty

Will log if a static property is used in another static property before it obtains a value. Recall that uninitialized properties are evaluated as empty strings normally. Given the following static property declaration,

```
<PropertyGroup>
  <UseUninitialized>$(OriginallyUninitialized)</UseUninitialized>
  <OriginallyUninitialized>Init Here</OriginallyUninitialized>
</PropertyGroup>
```

The following warning would be emitted if this environment variable is defined,

```
F:\...\Proj.proj(8,5): warning MSB4211: The property
"OriginallyUninitialized" is being set to a value for the first
time, but it was already consumed at "F:\...\Proj.proj (7,5)".
```

MSBuildLogCodeTaskFactoryOutput

When set to "1" will force the creation of the generated task factory source file, even if there isn't an error during compilation, which is typically the only time the file will be created. The file will be located in your %TEMP% folder, and will have a name of the form,

```
MSBUILDCodeTaskFactoryGeneratedFile{SOME-GUID}.txt
```

MSBuildDumpFrameworkSubsetList

Causes the output of additional information from the ResolveAssembly-References task, e.g.

```
TargetFramework Profile List Information:
Redist List File Paths:
```

```
        Path: "C:\Program Files (x86)\Reference
Assemblies\Microsoft\Framework\.NETFramework\v4.0\RedistList\Framewor
kList.xml"
        Path: "C:\Program Files (x86)\Reference
Assemblies\Microsoft\Framework\.NETFramework\v4.0\RedistList\FSharpLi
st.xml"
  TargetFramework Profile List Paths:
  Computed TargetFramework profile exclusion list assembly full
names:
```

MSBuildWriteXamlTask

Emits a *TaskName*_XamlTask.cs file when the Xaml Task Factory is used.
This is similar to the behavior of the MSBuildLogCodeTaskFactoryOutput
environment variable, except that it will write the file to the current
folder, not to the Temp folder.

Runtime execution behavior

MSBuildCustomScheduler

Can be set to any one of the following values to adjust the project
scheduling algorithm.

- ByTraversalsFirst

- FIFO

- WithConfigurationCountLevelling

- WithLargestFileSize

- WithMaxWaitingRequests

- WithMaxWaitingRequests2

- WithPlanByGreatestPlanTime

- WithPlanByMostImmediateReferences

- WithSmallestFileSize

By default it uses a combination that seems to be fastest in some
performance tests performed by the MSBuild team.

MSBuildDisableNodeReuse

The environment variable equivalent of the /nodeReuse:false command
line switch.

MSBuildDoNotCatchTaskExceptions, MSBuildDoNotThrowInternal

Fairly self-explanitory, these alter the behavior of exception handling
within the MSBuild engine.

MSBuildNodeWindow

Causes the creation of a console window to which child nodes will write their debugging output. The use of this variable is related to the unsupported internal-use-only /nodemode:1 command line option. The node reuse switch, /nr is propagated to child nodes, and when child nodes are executed in a separate process, the process will be created with the CREATE_NEW_CONSOLE window flag. This allows each child node process to have a separate console to which debugging information is written, which can make debugging multi-processor builds easier.

MSBuildNoInProcNode

This will force all build requests onto child nodes. By default the parent node is available for builds. There will certainly be performance issues, and who knows what other kinds of issues were you to run Visual Studio solution builds with this enabled.

MSBuildLoadBalance

Alters the behavior of the load balancing in the build engine scheduling routines.

MSBuildProjectRootElementCacheSize

MSBuild maintains a cache of all the project files it has processed. This and the next environment variable control the cache creation and logging. The default cache size is 50. I'd consider that this is possibly useful only for huge project files, perhaps generated ones with thousands of children from the root element.

MSBuildDebugXmlCache,

MSBuild maintains a cache of all the project files it has processed. Enabling this environment variable will cause cache activity to be traced.

MSBuild_Exe_Name

Provides an alternate executable name, the default obviously being "MSBuild"

MSBuild_Exe_Path

Specifies the location where MSBuild will find the MSBuild.exe it should execute when launching a child node process. Otherwise will use the version of MSBuild found with the currently executing MSBuild assembly, or if that can't be found, the version in the .NET Framework 4.0 folder.

One somewhat odd use for this particular variable could be to make a local copy of the MSBuild stack. Simply copy "msbuild.*" from the framework folder to your own source code repository location. This allows you to add your own source-local .tasks files, use the automatic

MSBuild.rsp response file, and even edit the MSBuild.exe.config file if needed, and do so in a manner that isn't quite so global.

MSBuildThreadStackSize

The default is 256K. I've never encountered a situation where MSBuild ran out of stack, but if it did, this environment variable would seem to be handy for massive, deeply structured builds.

Performance Tuning

MSBuildConfigCacheSweepThreshhold

There are several caches maintained internally by MSBuild. This value, which defaults to 500, governs how many configurations this internal cache can grow to hold before several caches are reset. If you have huge numbers of projects and configurations in your build, adjusting this value may favorably (or not) alter build performance.

MSBuildDumpOpportunisticInternStats,

Enables gathering of additional statistics related to the internal string cache maintained by MSBuild. This behavior itself is controlled by more environment variables, shown with their default values,

- MSBuildSmallInternSize, 5

- MSBuildLargeInternSize, 10

- MSBuildHugeInternThreshold, 5

- MSBuildSmallInternThreshold, 100

- MSBuildLargeInternThreshold, 200

- MSBuildHugeInternThreshold, 2000

- MSBuildGinormousInternThreshold, 8000

This will print out a big chart showing the various sized buckets, and how many cache hits and misses there were for each bucket. Doubtful this is of much use unless you are trying really hard to optimize a seriously large build. Or should I say a "Ginormous" one. Works for all verbosity levels.

Hidden features

MSBuildEmitSolution

When MSBuild is processing a solution file (and when previous versions processed .vcproj file conversions), setting this environment variable causes the temporary MSBuild-compatible project file created from the solution—which is written to the same folder as the solution file—to be preserved upon completion of the build.

MSBuildEnableAllPropertyFunctions

Discussed in *trick #57, Know how to enable more property functions*, makes the entire framework available for property function usage.

MSBuildProfile

This environment variable, which worked in prior versions, has been disabled in VS 2010. Use /ds and /clp:PerformanceSummary instead to get the same results.

MSBuildCacheCheckFileContent

Causes the file cache to perform a check of the file contents before pulling the previously parsed file from the cache. This would only be useful if project file contents change but the file dates remains the same.

MSBuildClearXmlCacheOnBuildManager

Forces the clearing of the file cache after every build completes.

Target behavior modification

MSBuildForwardPropertiesFromChild

Provides an opportunity to supply a specific property list to forward to child nodes, rather than forwarding all of them.

MSBuildKeepDuplicateOutputs

Similar to the KeepDuplicateOutputs attribute on individual Target elements, instructs MSBuild to not coalesce duplicated items returned by a target into a single item in the output item array.

MSBuildSortInputsOutputs

When target Input and Output dependency analysis is being performed, the item arrays for reporting them during logging will be maintained in a sorted container prior to being evaluated, which may be useful when diagnosing the log for targets with many dependencies. Related to the use of MSBuildTargetOutputLogging.

MSBuild version spoofing

MSBuildLegacyExtensionsPath

Reverts to the behavior of prior versions of MSBuild with respect to the $(MSBuildExtensionsPath) reserved property.

MSBuildTreatHigherToolsVersionAsCurrent

Allows a project to specify a Project element ToolsVersion attribute of 4.5 or 5.1 (but not 5.0, probably due to a logic bug) and will still treat it as if it were 4.0. Presumes a future version of a project is backward compatible, and is being built with the 4.0 version of MSBuild.

Timeouts

MSBuildNodeConnectionTimeout

Specified in milliseconds, this value controls the default 15 minutes that child nodes stick around after a build. Using the /nodereuse:false command line option essentially sets this value to zero.

MSBuildEngineProxyInitialLeaseTime

Specified in minutes, with a default value of 1, this value is used by the remoting to control interprocess communications.

MSBuildEngineProxyLeaseExtensionTime

Separate from the initial least time, this value, which also defaults to 1, specifies the lease extension time.

MSBuildIdleRequestBuilderLimit,

Defaults to 10, setting a limit for the maximum number of builders available to service build requests.

MSBuildEndpointShutdownTimeout

Specified in milliseconds, with a default value of 0x7530, which is 30 seconds, a timeout for the shutdown of individual build engine nodes.

MSBuildEngineShutdownTimeout

Specified in milliseconds, with a default value of -1, which means infinite, the length of time to await build engine shutdown.

MSBuildLoggingThreadShutdownTimeout

Specified in milliseconds, with a default of 30 seconds, the timeout value for the thread on which logging operations are scheduled.

MSBuildRequestBuilderShutdownTimeout

Specified in milliseconds, with a default value of -1, the length of time to await the shutdown of a build request after it is cancelled.

MSBuildToolTaskCancelProcessWaitTimeout

Specified in milliseconds, with a default value of 5000, this is the timeout to wait before terminating a tool process when the tool is cancelled or when the timeout for the process expires.

Obsolete

MSBuildForceSTA

There is no longer any need for this, since you can use the [RunInSTA] attribute on your custom task if it must be run on an STA thread for some reason.

MSBuildUseNoSolutionCache

This is obsolete because the solution .cache files are not emitted any longer for 10.0 solution files, but are still used in Visual Studio 2005 and 2008 solutions. This used to force deletion of the solution.cache file created by MSBuild after the build completes.

Mechanics of Target and Execution

Targets embody the main units of execution when building MSBuild projects. There are many features that combine to determine how and when they are executed. The topic of batching, as it applies to targets and not tasks, is one of the most important features to understand with respect to target execution and overall execution flow within a build, so it is given some good introductory coverage in the mechanics tricks that follow.

35. Understand batched target execution

Target batching is a feature that allows a target to be executed, as if in a loop, with each loop iteration associated with a subset of an item array. Target batching is initiated when the target's Outputs parameter uses the metadata syntax to indicate which metadata value should be used to create the batches. A batch is a subset of an item array where all of the items in the subset share the same value for the chosen piece metadata. The batches can contain a single item if the metadata for all items in the item array were unique, or each batch may contain multiple items, if the selected metadata were replicated among multiple items.

For example, given the following item array,

```
<ItemGroup>
    <Item Include="One">
        <Meta>A</Meta>
    <Item>
    <Item Include="Two">
        <Meta>B</Meta>
    <Item>
    <Item Include="Three">
        <Meta>B</Meta>
    <Item>
</ItemGroup>
```

the following syntax describe two possible batches,

```
%(Item.Identity)
%(Item.Meta)
```

The first of these creates batches with the item specification, creating three batches, each with a single item in the batch, since the item specifications for all three items in the item array is unique. The second of these creates two batches, the first has a single item, "One" with the metadata value of "A," and a second batch with the remaining two items, which share the metadata value "B."

Within each "iteration" of the target, each with its own batch of the specified item array, that item array will only contain the subset of items in the batch. It won't contain the entire item array as it would in any other usage.

In other words, batching a target with items in an item array, using the identity value of those items for the batching argument to the Output attribute, as in `Outputs="%(Item.Identity)"` causes the value of `@(Item)` within each iteration to contain a single item and all the meta values associated with that instance. If the items did not have unique identity values, then `@(Item)` could contain multiple items as well. The same is true if the target batching is initiated on any other item metadata, not just the item specification.

You can create a compound batching declaration with multiple meta values to get to a single item in each iteration of a target, provided your items have enough information to be uniquely identified, as shown below.

Basic Batching.trkproj

```
<ItemGroup>                                              <!-- 1 -->
  <Batch Include="A">
    <Meta>1</Meta>
  </Batch>
  <Batch Include="A">
    <Meta>2</Meta>
  </Batch>
  <Batch Include="B">
    <Meta>1</Meta>
  </Batch>
</ItemGroup>

<Target Name="Batching">
  <Message Text="@(Batch) %(Batch.Meta)" />        <!-- 2 -->
</Target>

<Target Name="BatchIdentity"
  Outputs="%(Batch.Identity)">                     <!-- 3 -->
  <Message Text="@(Batch) %(Batch.Meta)" />
</Target>

<Target Name="BatchUnique"
  Outputs="%(Batch.Identity)+%(Batch.Meta)">       <!-- 4 -->
  <Message Text="@(Batch) %(Batch.Meta)" />
</Target>
```

Output

```
Batching:
  A;B 1
  A 2

BatchIdentity:
  A 1
  A 2
BatchIdentity:
  B 1

BatchUnique:
  A 1
BatchUnique:
  A 2
BatchUnique:
  B 1
```

An item array named @(Batch) is declared (1) with three items. The first two share the same item specification "A," the third is unique with "B." For custom metadata, the first and third share the same value, "1" while the second has the value "2."

The first target does not use target batching, which is indicated because it does not declare an Outputs value at all. However, the Message task (2) does use task batching. In the output for this target, note that the target header, the line that says "Batching:," is printed only once, indicating that the target ran one time. The Message task has output two separate lines, indicating that it was executed twice. Because the Message task used task batching with the %(Batch.Meta) metadata, the value of @(Batch) contained only the items in each batch. The first line shows that the batch contained the first and third items, the second batch contains the second.

The next target, BatchIdentity, is identical to the first, except that it uses target batching by specifying the Outputs parameter (3) using the batching expression %(Batch.Identity). The output is quite different. The target name header, "BatchIdentity:" is now displayed twice, once for each of the two batches created from unique identity values. Now, because @(Batch) contains only the batch subset, when the Message task is subsequently batched using task batching, it splits out the items individually, since when batched first by the item specification, there are no longer any items in the batch that share the same metadata value.

Finally, a third target "BatchUnique" is specified using a compound batching expression (4), referencing two separate metadata values. This could have been specified using either of these equivalent expressions,

```
%(Batch.Identity)+%(Batch.Meta)
%(Batch.Identity)+%(Meta)
%(Identity)+%(Batch.Meta)
```

These are equivalent because MSBuild recognizes the partially qualified item metadata name when it is found in an together with the same item fully qualified in the same expression. There is nothing special about the plus sign in the expression, other than that it merely serves as a visual clue that the batching is compound. The plus sign could be omitted with no change in behavior but would make casual observation a bit more confusing, so it is a useful convention to adopt. In this third target, note that the batching has broken the item array into three separate batches, each with a single item. This is because when both the item specification referenced by the %(Identity) metadata and the metadata value %(Meta) are combined, they form a "unique compound key" of sorts, since no two items in the array share the same combination of both values.

36. Use target inputs and outputs

By default, and according to the behavior in previous versions of MSBuild, build analysis is based on the target's Inputs and Outputs. If files specified as Outputs are older than the files specified as Inputs, then the target will be executed. MSBuild is pretty smart about this Inputs-Outputs analysis. If the Inputs and Outputs are defined where the Outputs are a one-to-one transformation of the Inputs, MSBuild is able to detect this one-to-one pairing. In this case, if some of the outputs are up-to-date, they are stripped from the set of Inputs. This optimization is known as "Incremental Build" analysis, where only the out-of-date items are processed. If all of the Outputs are up-to-date with respect to their inputs, MSBuild will skip the target.

Inputs and Outputs.trkproj

```
<ItemGroup>
    <InOut Include="PathTo\*.txt" />                    <!-- 1 -->
</ItemGroup>

<Target Name="InOut"
    Inputs="@(InOut)"
    Outputs="@(InOut->
        '%(RelativeDir)%(FileName)%(Extension).out')">  <!-- 2 -->
    <Message Text="InOut: '@(InOut)'" />
    <Copy
        SourceFiles="@(InOut)"
        DestinationFiles="@(InOut->
            '%(RelativeDir)%(FileName)%(Extension).out')"
    />
</Target>
```

Output from first execution

```
InOut:
  InOut: 'PathTo\One.txt;PathTo\Two.txt'
  Copying file from "PathTo\One.txt" to "PathTo\One.txt.out".
  Copying file from "PathTo\Two.txt" to "PathTo\Two.txt.out".
```

In the listing above, an item array is declared (1) that will pick up the same two text files in the PathTo folder as in previous examples. The InOut target declares this item array as its Inputs, and uses an item transformation of it (2) as its Outputs. The Output transformation is the same file as the Input, with an additional ".out" extension. The target simply displays the contents of @(InOut) and executes a file Copy task, using the same item transformation. Because a file copy is performed, the Input file and the newly copied Output file will share the same file date.

From the output the two files in the item array are seen to be copied to the transformed file names. If at this point the project were to be built again, the following output would be seen, indicating the up-to-date status:

```
InOut:
Skipping target "InOut" because all output files are up-to-date
with respect to the input files.
```

Following the initial execution in the listing above, an incremental build is performed, in the listing below.

Delete an output

```
> del PathTo\One.txt.out
```

Output from next execution

```
InOut:
Building target "InOut" partially, because some output files are out
of date with respect to their input files.
  InOut: 'PathTo\One.txt'
  Copying file from "PathTo\One.txt" to "PathTo\One.txt.out".
```

When one of the output files is deleted, the target is put in a partially built state. When the project is built again, MSBuild reports this state. Note that when @(InOut) is displayed, this time it only shows the out of date file, the up-to-date file has been removed. The output shows that only the removed file is copied.

Furthermore, MSBuild can handle other Input-Output pairings beyond a simple one-to-one transformation. Consider the following example,

Inputs and Outputs.trkproj, InOutPairing target

```
<ItemGroup>
                                                    <!-- 1 -->
    <InOutPair Include="PathTo\One.txt">
        <Out>OutPath\A.out</Out>
    </InOutPair>
    <InOutPair Include="PathTo\Two.txt">
        <Out>OutPath\A.out</Out>
    </InOutPair>
                                                    <!-- 2 -->
    <InOutPair Include="PathTo\Recurse\Three.txt">
        <Out>OutPath\B.out</Out>
    </InOutPair>
</ItemGroup>
<Target Name="InOutPairing"
    Inputs="@(InOutPair)"
    Outputs="%(InOutPair.Out)">                     <!-- 3 -->
    <Message Text="InOutPair: '@(InOutPair)'" />
```

```
    <Copy
        SourceFiles="@(InOutPair)"
        DestinationFiles="@(InOutPair->'%(Out)')"
        />
    </Target>
```

In this example, instead of an item transformation based on well-known item metadata, the output is declared as a custom item metadata value. The item will be the output, and the file declared in the %(Out) metadata for each item will be the paired output. Significantly, the first two items (1) share the same value for %(Out), which will become paired with both items as their output. The third item (2) has a distinct value for the %(Out) item metadata. Examining the target declaration (3) notice that the @(InOutPair) Input item array is transformed using nothing but the value of %(Out). MSBuild recognizes this as a form of Output target batching. When executed the following output results:

Output

```
InOutPairing:
  InOutPair: 'PathTo\One.txt;PathTo\Two.txt'
  Creating directory "OutPath".
  Copying file from "PathTo\One.txt" to "OutPath\A.out".
  Copying file from "PathTo\Two.txt" to "OutPath\A.out".
InOutPairing:
  InOutPair: 'PathTo\Recurse\Three.txt'
  Copying file from "PathTo\Recurse\Three.txt" to "OutPath\B.out".
```

Notice that from the output, the target header "InOutPairing:" appears twice, indicating that the target has been batched. This batching was performed using the items containing the same value for %(Out), so the first two items are in the first batch and the third item is in its own batch.

Finally, as shown in the next example, if the Inputs and Outputs are not related to one another through a transformation or through metadata references on the same item, MSBuild will not perform the incremental optimizations.

Inputs and Outputs.trkproj, InOutUnpaired target

```
    <ItemGroup>
      <UnpairedIn Include="PathTo\One.txt" />
      <UnpairedIn Include="PathTo\Two.txt" />
      <UnpairedOut Include="PathTo\A.out" />
      <UnpairedOut Include="PathTo\B.out" />
    </ItemGroup>
    <Target Name="InOutUnpaired"
      Inputs="@(UnpairedIn)"
      Outputs="@(UnpairedOut)">
```

```
    <Message Text="UnpairedIn: '@(UnpairedIn)'" />
    <Touch
        Files="PathTo\A.out"
        AlwaysCreate="true"
        />
    <Touch
        Files="PathTo\B.out"
        AlwaysCreate="true"
        />
 </Target>
```

In the listing above, there are two inputs declared in @(UnpairedIn) and two unrelated outputs declared in @(UnpairedOut). The target just executes the Touch task, to either create or update the output files. Assuming that the output files A.out and B.out do not exist prior to the first execution of this target, the initial execution would give,

```
InOutUnpaired:
  UnpairedIn: 'PathTo\One.txt;PathTo\Two.txt'
  Creating "PathTo\A.out" because "AlwaysCreate" was specified.
  Creating "PathTo\B.out" because "AlwaysCreate" was specified.
```

A subsequent execution indicates that normal Input-Ouptut analysis causes the target to be skipped,

```
  InOutUnpaired:
  Skipping target "InOutUnpaired" because all output files are
  up-to-date with respect to the input files.
```

Unlike the previous examples, if one of the output files is deleted and the other is left alone,

```
> del PathTo\A.out
```

A subsequent execution will still indicate that the entire Inputs item array is passed to the task.

```
InOutUnpaired:
  UnpairedIn: 'PathTo\One.txt;PathTo\Two.txt'
  Creating "PathTo\A.out" because "AlwaysCreate" was specified.
  Touching "PathTo\B.out".
```

In this case, the deleted output file is recreated and the existing one is updated, as the incremental build optimization can't be applied to uncorrelated Inputs and Outputs.

37. Understand target Returns

While powerful, the incremental build approach described above doesn't always scale well to huge collections of projects with file counts numbering in the thousands or tens of thousands being processed.

Sometimes, it is important for an individual target to maintain its numerous Inputs and Outputs, but knowledge of those potentially huge lists of files, many of which may be intermediate, is not needed outside the scope of the target. In other words, MSBuild needs to know if the target is up-to-date, but there may be a reduced set of resulting output files that are needed for dependency analysis with other targets. With multiple dependent targets all processing a huge collection of files, the bloat in the internally maintained sets of target input and output meta-data can consume large amounts of memory and slow down build execution.

To improve scalability, there are new attributes that can be used on the target element. The first is a Boolean attribute named KeepDuplicate-Outputs. The default value is false; setting this to true will cause MSBuild to discard any files that appear more than once in the Outputs.

A second new attribute, "Returns" can also be used to optimize your build. The use of the "Returns" attribute is examined globally in a build. If there are no "Returns" attributes present in an entire project, MSBuild will accumulate all Outputs declared by the target and retain them in memory treating the "Outputs" as the target return items. As discussed earlier, even if a target is up-to-date and skipped, these Outputs, in the form of items, are always remembered. This is also true for any items captured as Output parameters on any tasks in the target, as well as any dynamic items declared in the target. If, on the other hand, even a single target anywhere in the project or any of its imported project files declares a Returns attribute, this is a global signal to MSBuild that a different form of Output collection should be used.

Now for all of this talk about target Outputs being remembered by MSBuild, you may be wondering how can you get access to these items? It turns out that both the MSBuild task and the CallTarget task have an output parameter named TargetOutputs, which makes these items available.

While the CallTarget task is generally something to be avoided with preference given to creating dependent targets, it turns out that this output parameter does provide this useful built-in mechanism for gathering the outputs of a target, as shown below.

Target outputs.trkproj

```
<ItemGroup>
    <CalledTargetIn Include="PathTo\*.in" />          <!-- 1 -->
</ItemGroup>
<Target Name="CalledTarget"
```

```
      Inputs="@(CalledTargetIn)"
      Outputs="@(CalledTargetIn->'%(Fullpath).out')">      <!-- 2 -->
      <ItemGroup>
        <CalledTargetOut
          Include="@(CalledTargetIn->'%(Fullpath).out')"
        />                                                  <!-- 3 -->
      </ItemGroup>
      <Message Text="@(CalledTargetOut)" />
  </Target>

  <Target Name="TargetOutputs">
      <CallTarget Targets="CalledTarget">
        <Output
          TaskParameter="TargetOutputs"
          ItemName="TargetOut"
        />                                                  <!-- 4 -->
      </CallTarget>
      <Message Text="Out: '%(TargetOut.Identity)'" />
  </Target>
```

Output

```
CalledTarget:
  ...\PathTo\A.in.out;...\PathTo\B.in.out;...\PathTo\C.in.out
TargetReturns:
  Out: 'F:\...\PathTo\A.in.out'
  Out: 'F:\...\PathTo\B.in.out'
  Out: 'F:\...\PathTo\C.in.out'
```

An item array is declared (1) to serve as the Inputs for the target "CalledTargets" and is transformed (2) into the Outputs as well. In the target, these Outputs are not actually created in any way, but the same transformation (3) is applied to a new item array @(CalledTargetOut) solely for the purpose of displaying the transformed items. Because the files identified by the Outputs parameter to the target will never exist, this target will never be declared up-to-date, by the way. The main target uses the CallTarget task to call this child target, gathering the TargetOutputs output parameter (4) into a new item array named @(TargetOut), which is then displayed. From the output, the three transformed—and fictional—files are shown.

This next example is a clone of the one just shown with a single change. In addition to the Inputs and Outputs, a new attribute on the target named "Returns" is declared, with a path to a new file that will be considered the actual result of the target.

Target returns.trkproj, difference from Target outputs.trkproj

```
  <Target Name="CalledTarget"
    Inputs="@(CalledTargetIn)"
    Outputs="@(CalledTargetIn->'%(Fullpath).out')"
```

```
          Returns="PathTo\CalledTarget.returns">
```

Output

```
TargetReturns:
  Out: 'PathTo\CalledTarget.returns'
```

The Inputs and Outputs are still analyzed in the same manner, and since the Outputs are files that won't ever exist, it doesn't matter whether or not the CalledTarget.returns file specified in the Returns attribute is up-to-date, it is not used for the up-to-date analysis. From the output, it can be seen that MSBuild no longer considers the Outputs parameter of the target to be the TargetOutputs; it has instead used the Returns.

Notice that the use of the output parameter on the CallTarget task is one way to get around the item publishing limitation of that task, whereby items populated in a target executed by CallTarget are not made available until the calling target completes and returns to a higher scope, as discussed in *trick #31, Understand how dynamic values are published*.

The MSBuild task has the same output as the CallTarget task, so the CallTarget task above could have been replaced by the MSBuild task as shown below, with the same result,

```
<MSBuild
    Projects="$(MSBuildThisFile)"
    Targets="CalledTarget">
    <Output
        TaskParameter="TargetOutputs"
        ItemName="TargetOut"
        />
</MSBuild>
```

Consider also how these target outputs are aggregated when multiple targets are executed, whether using the CallTarget or the MSBuild task,

Target returns.trkproj, TargetReturnsFromMSBuild target

```
<Target Name="AnotherTarget"
    Returns="@(AnotherReturns)">
    <ItemGroup>
        <AnotherReturns Include="PathTo\*.txt" />          <!-- 2 -->
    </ItemGroup>
</Target>
<Target Name="TargetReturnsFromMSBuild">
    <MSBuild
        Projects="$(MSBuildThisFile)"
        Targets="CalledTarget;AnotherTarget">              <!-- 1 -->
        <Output
            TaskParameter="TargetOutputs"
            ItemName="TargetOut"
```

```
            />
        </MSBuild>
        <Message Text="Out: '%(TargetOut.Identity)'" />
    </Target>
```

Output

```
Out: 'PathTo\CalledTarget.returns'
Out: 'PathTo\One.txt'
Out: 'PathTo\Two.txt'
```

In the listing above, the MSBuild task specified (1) the CalledTarget from the previous examples, plus a new target named AnotherTarget, which can be seen to do nothing more than populate a new item array (2) that it also lists as its Returns attribute. The Returns from both of these targets are aggregated into the @(TargetOut) item array returned from the MSBuild task execution.

It is significant that the MSBuild task specifies both targets. If instead, the new target AnotherTarget had been made a dependent target of CalledTarget, and only CalledTarget had been specified in the MSBuild task, both targets would still have been executed. The TargetOutputs output parameter of the MSBuild task execution, however, would then only show the Outputs from the one target specified in the MSBuild task. Outputs from dependent targets, or initial targets, even when they are executed, are not aggregated into the result set being accumulated by MSBuild.

It is not possible to show these two variations—one declaring just Inputs and Outputs and having the TargetOutputs parameter populated with the Outputs, and the other using Inputs, Outputs and Returns where the Returns parameter is used to populate the TargetOutputs—together in the same project file. This is because if one target declares the Returns attribute, then MSBuild will assume that the entire project is using this optimization, and any targets that don't declare a Returns attribute will in effect have no outputs to report.

All of these examples have shown only items referenced in the Outputs and Returns attributes, and even then only a single item array. It is quite possible to specify multiple items and even properties, all of which will be aggregated into the collection of output values for a target.

Target outputs many.trkproj

```
<ItemGroup>
    <Item Include="PathTo\*.in" />                      <!-- 1 -->
</ItemGroup>
```

```
<Target Name="CalledTarget"
    Returns="@(Out1);@(Out2);$(Out)">                    <!-- 2 -->
    <ItemGroup>
        <Out1
            Include="@(Item->'%(Fullpath).out1')"
            />                                           <!-- 3 -->
        <Out2
            Include="@(Item->'%(Fullpath).out2')"
            />                                           <!-- 4 -->
    </ItemGroup>
    <PropertyGroup>
        <Out>ArbitraryOutput</Out>                       <!-- 5 -->
    </PropertyGroup>
</Target>

<Target Name="TargetReturnsMany">
    <!-- 7 -->
    <MSBuild
        Projects="$(MSBuildThisFile)"
        Targets="CalledTarget">
        <Output
            TaskParameter="TargetOutputs"
            ItemName="TargetOut"
            />
    </MSBuild>
    <Message Text="Out: '%(TargetOut.Identity)'" />
</Target>
```

Output, paths abbreviated

```
Out: 'F:\...\PathTo\A.in.out1'
Out: 'F:\...\PathTo\B.in.out1'
Out: 'F:\...\PathTo\C.in.out1'
Out: 'F:\...\PathTo\A.in.out2'
Out: 'F:\...\PathTo\B.in.out2'
Out: 'F:\...\PathTo\C.in.out2'
Out: 'ArbitraryOutput'
```

An item array—the same pattern used previously—is declared (1) which will capture the three ".in" files under PathTo. Unlike the previous examples, this target (2) is declared with three separate elements in the Returns attribute; two item arrays @(Out1) and @(Out2) and a single property $(Out). All three of these are defined within the target at (3, 4, 5). This target is executed with the MSBuild task (7) and the output parameter TargetOutputs is captured and then displayed. From the output, it can be seen that all three elements are represented, the two item transforms for the two item arrays, as well as the additional property referenced in the Returns attribute. Had the called target done the same thing with Inputs and Outputs, the same aggregate expression could have been used in the Outputs attribute as well.

As has just been shown throughout this section, the use of the Returns attribute is therefore available as an extreme optimization for the entire build. It allows you to precisely control target Input-Output analysis, and separately declare target "results" using Returns, to have targets operating on lots of files not be slowed down in cases where other targets do not need access to their outputs, and as a result dramatically reduce the memory footprint of massive scale builds.

38. Understand up-to-date targets and inferred properties

In the previous section, in *trick #36, Use target inputs and outputs*, it was shown how MSBuild may skip targets when it detects they are up-to-date.

When skipping a target, however, MSBuild will still examine the target looking for any dynamic ItemGroup or PropertyGroup declarations within the target, or their odd step-siblings, the CreateProperty and CreateItem tasks. Thus, even though MSBuild has optimized away the execution of the target, it is still in the same state as if the target had been inefficiently executed.

This is termed "Output inference," where MSBuild infers the values of Properties and Items properly even when a target is skipped. This target inference is only performed when the target would have run otherwise but was skipped due to up-to-date input-output analysis. If the target had a Condition that evaluated to false, it would not have run no matter what the input-output analysis indicated, and in this case output inference is not performed.

There is also an extra behavior in the CreateProperty task that side-steps the inference system, which will be shown below.

Up-to-date Inferred Properties.trkproj, Inferred target

```
<PropertyGroup>
    <A>A</A>
    <B>B</B>
    <C>C</C>
    <D>D</D>
    <E>E</E>
</PropertyGroup>
<Target Name="Inferred"
    DependsOnTargets="Create A;Create BCDE">        <!-- 1 -->
    <Message Text="A: $(A)" />
    <Message Text="B: $(B)" />
    <Message Text="C: $(C)" />
    <Message Text="D: $(D)" />
```

```
        <Message Text="E: $(E)" />
    </Target>
```

The basic target above is simple; five properties A through E are declared, with a value matching the static name. In the Inferred target these properties are printed out. The interesting part happens in the two dependent targets (1) "Create A" and "Create BCDE" which are shown below.

Up-to-date Inferred Properties.trkproj, Create A target

```
<Target Name="Create A"
    Inputs="$(FileThatDoesNotExist)"
    Outputs="$(MSBuildProjectFullPath)">          <!-- 2 -->
    <PropertyGroup>
        <A>Create Inferred A</A>                  <!-- 3 -->
    </PropertyGroup>
</Target>
```

In this first dependent target, notice that (2) the input is set to a non-existent file via an empty property, and the output is set to the current file. There is an attempt made (3) to override property A with a new value. When executed, MSBuild will issue the following notice:

```
Skipping target "Create A" because it has no inputs.
```

Since MSBuild is skipping the target for a reason other than the target being up-to-date, the value inference for property A will not occur.

Up-to-date Inferred Properties.trkproj, Create BCDE target

```
<Target Name="Create BCDE"
    Inputs="$(MSBuildProjectFullPath)"
    Outputs="$(MSBuildProjectFullPath)">                <!-- 4 -->
    <CallTarget Targets="Create B" />                   <!-- 5 -->
    <PropertyGroup>
        <C>Create Inferred C</C>                        <!-- 7 -->
    </PropertyGroup>
    <CreateProperty Value="Create Inferred D">          <!-- 8 -->
        <Output PropertyName="D" TaskParameter="Value" />
    </CreateProperty>
    <CreateProperty Value="Create Inferred E">          <!-- 9 -->
        <Output PropertyName="E" TaskParameter="ValueSetByTask" />
    </CreateProperty>
</Target>

<Target Name="Create B">
    <PropertyGroup>
        <B>Create Inferred B</B>                        <!-- 6 -->
    </PropertyGroup>
</Target>
```

```
Create A:
  Skipping target "Create A" because it has no inputs.
Create BCDE:
  Skipping target "Create BCDE" because all output files are up- ⤸
  to-date with respect to the input files.
Inferred:
  A: A
  B: B
  C: Create Inferred C
  D: Create Inferred D
  E: E
```

In this listing, for target "Create BCDE" notice that the current project file is listed (4) as both the Input and the Output. This forces MSBuild to consider the target up-to-date, so that we can see how the inference rules apply to property changes within up-to-date targets. First, the target "Create B" is called (5) with the CallTarget task. In the output, in addition to A maintaining its original value because target "Create A" was skipped, property B also retains its original value. Even though in target "Create B" there is a new value given (6) to property B, property inference does not cascade to additional targets executed in this manner. Since the "Create BCDE" target is not actually being executed, this CallTarget task is also not executed. Subsequently though, property C is given a new value (7) which does appear in the output. Property inference allows MSBuild to capture this new value. Property D is changed also (9) using a CreateProperty, which is just a different syntax for the same declaration as for property C, and the new value for property D likewise is captured. For the final property, note that instead of specifying the "Value" parameter for the CreateProperty task, as was done for property D, the alteration of Property E using the same task specifies the "ValueSetByTask" parameter. This parameter name essentially means "the value is only set by task execution, not by property inference," and it can be seen in the output that the original value for this property is unaltered. It is notable that this single extra parameter in the CreateProperty task is the only reason that it can't be completely discarded, since dynamically declaring a PropertyGroup doesn't yet permit this distinction with respect to property inference.

39. Understand CallTarget target execution

It's actually quite common when just starting out with your own customizations in MSBuild to think of targets as if they were functions, which generally leads to a misconception about how the CallTarget task operates. While targets do have some resemblance to functions—they have Inputs and Outputs, though they aren't parameters, they can specify a Returns attribute which is similar to a return value, and their bodies are made up of tasks which resemble program statements—their execution mechanics are quite different. The biggest difference is that they can't be executed like a subroutine more than once. They can be called more than once, but only one attempt will ever cause execution to complete. Several different usage patterns are presented below, to summarize the subtle behavior of the CallTarget task.

CallTarget Execution.trkproj

```
<Project ...>
  <Target Name="TargetOne">                          <!-- 1 -->
    <Message Text="TargetOne" />
  </Target>
```

CallTargetTwice target

```
  <Target Name="CallTargetTwice">
    <Message Text="first..." />
    <CallTarget Targets="TargetOne" />               <!-- 2 -->
    <Message Text="...then..." />
    <CallTarget Targets="TargetOne" />               <!-- 3 -->
  </Target>
```

Output of CallTargetTwice target

```
CallTargetTwice:
  first...
TargetOne:
  TargetOne
CallTargetTwice:
  ...then...
```

In this first example, a simple target named TargetOne (1) is executed twice with separate invocations (2, 3) of the CallTarget task. This same TargetOne target will be used throughout these examples. Examining the output, notice that the initial message is printed, then TargetOne executes as expected. After the second message is displayed, the second CallTarget execution leaves no trace in the output. This is because MSBuild will only execute targets a single time. The engine detects that the requested target has already been executed and skips it. If the output verbosity is cranked up to at least "detailed," the following additional messages would be displayed for the second execution.

```
Task "CallTarget"
Target "TargetOne" skipped. Previously built successfully.
Done executing task "CallTarget".
```

CallTargetTwiceWithDepends target

```
<Target Name="CallTargetTwiceWithDepends"
    DependsOnTargets="TargetOne">                          <!-- 4 -->
    <Message Text="...then..." />
    <CallTarget Targets="TargetOne" />
</Target>
```

Output of CallTargetTwiceWithDepends target

```
TargetOne:
  TargetOne
CallTargetTwiceWithDepends:
  ...then...
```

In this next listing, essentially the same behavior results, except that the first execution of TargetOne occurs because the target specified it as a dependent target (4) instead of calling it explicitly with CallTarget. It makes no difference how a target is executed; it will only be executed once.

This next set of targets shows an interesting twist on this single execution behavior.

CallTargetTwiceWithCondition (Fail) target

```
<Target Name="TargetTwo"
    Condition="'$(EnableTargetTwo)' == 'true'">            <!-- 5 -->
    <Message Text="TargetTwo" />
</Target>

<Target Name="CallTargetTwiceWithConditionFail">
    <CallTarget Targets="TargetTwo" />                     <!-- 6 -->
    <Message Text="...then..." />
    <PropertyGroup>
        <EnableTargetTwo>true</EnableTargetTwo>            <!-- 7 -->
    </PropertyGroup>
    <CallTarget Targets="TargetTwo" />                     <!-- 8 -->
</Target>
```

Output of CallTargetTwiceWithConditionFail target

```
CallTargetTwiceWithConditionFail:
  ...then...
```

A new target named TargetTwo is defined (5) with a condition. Initially this condition will evaluate false, since there is no default value for the $(EnableTargetTwo) property. The subsequent target attempts an initial execution with CallTarget (6). This attempt will not trigger an execution because the condition on TargetTwo evaluates to false. Subsequently, the

$(EnableTargetTwo) property is given a new value (7) which should cause the TargetTwo condition to now evaluate to true. However, from the output, it can be seen that the second attempt to execute TargetTwo with another CallTarget task (8) doesn't appear to work.

The reason for this was covered previously in *trick #31, Understand how dynamic values are published*. Because the CallTargetTwiceWtih-ConditionFail target has not yet completed execution, the new property value has not been published for visibility from within other targets, so when the TargetTwo condition is evaluated for the second time, after the property has been changed, the evaluation of the condition won't change, because the new value for the property is not yet visible. The next example shows how to get around this limitation.

CallTargetTwiceWithCondition (Success) target

```
   <Target Name="PublishEnableTargetTwo">
      <PropertyGroup>
         <EnableTargetTwo>true</EnableTargetTwo>          <!-- 10 -->
      </PropertyGroup>
   </Target>
   <Target Name="CallTargetTwiceWithCondition"
      DependsOnTargets="
         TargetTwo;
         PublishEnableTargetTwo">                         <!-- 9 -->
      <Message Text="...then..." />
      <CallTarget Targets="TargetTwo" />                  <!-- 11 -->
   </Target>
</Project>
```

Output of CallTargetTwiceWithCondition target

```
CallTargetTwiceWithCondition:
  ...then...
TargetTwo:
  TargetTwo
```

In this final example, the initial execution of TargetTwo, and a new target responsible for altering the property used in the TargetTwo condition are both executed (9) by virtue of being a dependent target. This dependent first execution of TargetTwo is skipped due to the condition, but when the property is altered in the next dependent target (10), the new value is immediately published and available. Now, when the subsequent second execution of TargetTwo is attempted (11) via the CallTarget task, TargetTwo finally executes for its first and only time.

This distinction clearly shows that it is an actual execution that will happen only once, not just an attempt. MSBuild attempted the first execution but skipped it due to the false target condition. This did not "burn" the targets one-and-only chance to execute, which could occur after the conditional property was altered.

40. Know how the engine works

MSBuild operates according to a precise set of rules governing the order of operations and evaluations. Understanding these is crucial to getting the most out of the engine. The sequence of operations is straightforward, starting with the first evaluation pass,

1. MSBuild captures the current environment, which freezes the values of any environment variables with valid XML token names to be referenced through properties. Even if these environment variables are later changed, the properties representing them will maintain the values at the start of the processing.
2. MSBuild begins parsing the project file passed on the command line.
3. Starting at the top of the file, any global PropertyGroup and Import statements are processed.
4. Any Conditions on these PropertyGroup elements or Property declarations within the groups are based only on the value of the properties seen up until that point.
5. Imported files are processed in-line at the point of the Import statement. Imports within these imported files are recursively processed as well.

This completes phase one, which is an evaluation phase only. Up until this point, ItemGroup elements have been ignored. This explains the error you would get if you had attempted to structure an import like this,

```
<ItemGroup>
  <Item Include="SomeValue" />
</ItemGroup>
<Import
  Condition="'@(Item)' != ''"
  Project="SomeProject.imp"
  />
```

The result would be an error, which makes sense considering Imports are processed in the first phase, with Properties, prior to MSBuild evaluating any Items,

```
F:\...\Check.proj(15,5): error MSB4099: A reference to an item list
at position 2 is not allowed in this condition "'@(Item)' != ''".
```

The next evaluation passes capture globally declared static items,

6. Global ItemDefinitionGroup declarations are processed from top-to-bottom.

7. ItemGroup declarations are processed from top-to-bottom.
8. Recall that all imported files have already been aggregated into a single document object model at this point, which is still being evaluated.

The subtlety expressed between the lines in these rules is that you can't use the values of items or item metadata *from another item* in an ItemDefinitionGroup. You can, however, reference meta values from the same item. In other words, you can reference values that items based on this item definition group will eventually have. For example,

```
<ItemDefinitionGroup>
   <Item>
      <Meta>%(Identity)456</Meta>
   </Item>
</ItemDefinitionGroup>
<ItemGroup>
   <Item Include="123" />
</ItemGroup>

<Target Name="Target">
   <Message Text="Item.Meta '%(Item.Meta)'" />
</Target>
```

This will properly report that %(Item.Meta) contains the value "123456," declared in the ItemDefinitionGroup in the first item evaluation pass, then populated later with the evaluation of %(Identity) from the declaration of the single member of @(Item) in the second pass.

Recall that Properties can derive their value from items, being expressed by default as a comma delimited list. Properties whose value is based on an item array can be deceiving when you consider the evaluation sequence. Early on, their value may just be an item expression, for example the literal strings shown below,

```
@(Item)
@(Item->'%(Meta)')
```

Because these are non-empty strings, conditions based on these values, if compared to an empty string, will always be true. But the actual values won't be what you might think. If you know the value that the item would have if evaluated and compared to that value instead, the condition would fail, because the property at this point will only contain the literal string value shown above, essentially an unevaluated item expression.

This notion of unevaluated expressions only applies to the part of the expression derived from an item. If the property were declared as,

```
@(Item->'$(Prop)%(Meta)')
```

and $(Prop) currently held the value "123" then the unevaluated portion of the property after the first evaluation pass would actually be,

```
@(Item->'123%(Meta)')
```

because MSBuild is able to replace the properties, just not the portion derived from an item or item transformation.

If you later use the value of these properties, for example in a diagnostic Message task, MSBuild will evaluate the expression and report the value you would expect to see, adding confusion to a failure based on a conditional expression, based itself on the unevaluated content of the property. The diagnostic message will show evaluated values, while the condition may be based on unevaluated ones. Be careful that you don't expect them to match.

For example, consider this rogue attempt to import a file based on the contents of an item, expressed as a property,

```
<ItemGroup>
  <Item Include="SomeValue" />
</ItemGroup>
<PropertyGroup>
  <PropFromItem>@(Item)</PropFromItem>
</PropertyGroup>
<Import
  Condition="'$(PropFromItem)' != ''"
  Project="Import.proj"
  />
```

It turns out of course that the import will always evaluate to true, but not because MSBuild has determined that @(Item) contains anything. Rather it is because $(PropFromItem) contains the literal string "@(Item)" instead. You could have just as easily done the following import, which would also succeed, but is not what you would ever intend.

```
<Import
  Condition="$(PropFromItem.Equals('@(Item)'))"
  Project="CheckImport.proj"
  />
```

Likewise, the following will always fail, even though $(PropFromValue) will eventually have the value being tested in the condition; it hasn't yet had its value expression evaluated when Imports are being processed in the first pass of evaluation.

```
<Import
  Condition="'$(PropFromItem)' == 'SomeValue'"
  Project="CheckImport.proj"
  />
```

This brings us to the final stages of processing. At this point, the evaluation phases are complete. MSBuild has a single document object model and has evaluated to some extent a complete set of global static properties and items. Some of these properties may contain unevaluated expressions. Some of the items may also contain expressions based on their own item metadata. The next and final phases are considered the execution phase, which are covered in the next section.

41. Understand target execution sequencing

In the execution phase, MSBuild begins its analysis of the dependencies between targets, starting with the targets that it has already determined will be processed, according to the rules governing DefaultTargets and InitialTargets. Execution will start with all of the collected InitialTargets, in the order they were discovered. Execution will then proceed with the targets specified on the command line, or if there were none, with the DefaultTargets.

All of the targets have already been analyzed and placed into a graph with respect to their dependencies on one another. The following example will help illustrate how this analysis proceeds.

Target execution.trkproj

```
<Target Name="BeforeTarget"
  BeforeTargets="Target">
  <Message Text="BeforeTarget" />
</Target>

<Target Name="AfterTarget"
  AfterTargets="Target">
  <Message Text="AfterTarget" />
</Target>

<Target Name="DependsOnAlpha">
  <Message Text="DependsOnAlpha" />
</Target>

<Target Name="DependsOnBravo">
  <Message Text="DependsOnBravo" />
</Target>

<Target Name="Target"
  DependsOnTargets="DependsOnAlpha;DependsOnBravo">
```

```
    <Message Text="Target" />
  </Target>
```

Output sequence

```
DependsOnAlpha
DependsOnBravo
BeforeTarget
Target
AfterTarget
```

For a given target, any targets it declares with DependsOnTargets will be placed into the dependency graph, also taking into consideration any targets they in turn specify with their own DependsOnTargets. Then, having access to the declarations on all targets in the processed project, the build engine looks for any targets that have declared a dependency with BeforeTargets or AfterTargets attributte to any target already in the dependency tree. These targets are placed in the dependency tree to guarantee that their dependency injection requests are respected, as shown with BeforeTargets and AfterTargets in the output above.

An important distinction to know is that while DependsOnTargets sets up a target dependency that forces the listed targets to execute, the BeforeTargets and AfterTargets don't work the same way. For example, if the following command is executed with the project above,

```
> msbuild "Target execution.trkproj" /t:AfterTarget
```

the output would only be the single AfterTarget target,

```
AfterTarget:
  AfterTarget
```

Just because that target specifies it runs after the "Target" target doesn't mean that it will force it to execute. It is only declaring a target ordering that will be respected if the mentioned targets happen to be in the list of targets that will be executed, but it doesn't force the mentioned targets to be added to the execution list.

Taking the example above and associating a dependency between target "Alpha" and target "Bravo" as shown below will alter the sequence as expected.

Alteration of DependsOnAlpha

```
  <Target Name="DependsOnAlpha" DependsOnTargets="DependsOnBravo">
```

Output sequence

```
DependsOnBravo
```

```
DependsOnAlpha
BeforeTarget
Target
AfterTarget
```

If instead, the dependency between these two targets were expressed using BeforeTargets or AfterTargets, the sequence would not be altered in the same way,

Alteration of DependsOnAlpha

```
<Target Name="DependsOnAlpha" AfterTargets="DependsOnBravo">
```

Output sequence (unchanged from original)

```
DependsOnAlpha
DependsOnBravo
BeforeTarget
Target
AfterTarget
```

What is going on here? Well, because the dependency analysis is constructing a target execution sequence based on DependsOnTargets, and has discovered these two additional targets as a result of the DependsOnTargets declaration in the main target, it will ignore any of the BeforeTargets or AfterTargets that these targets have on other targets. This may seem counter-intuitive, but if both types of target dependency ordering were to be considered, you would more easily get into impossible circular references that MSBuild would not be able to work out, and that would be difficult to rewire. For this reason, the choice between explicit DependsOnTargets declarations or Before-AfterTargets dependency injection should be reserved for different types of target ordering, and are generally not mixed.

Going back to the original sequence, what will happen if a circular dependency is injected?

Alteration of AfterTarget

```
<Target Name="AfterTarget"
    AfterTargets="Target" BeforeTargets="BeforeTarget">
```

With this change, the "AfterTarget" which currently executes after the main "Target" and the "BeforeTarget" which currently executes before it, are given a dependency that makes the sequence impossible,

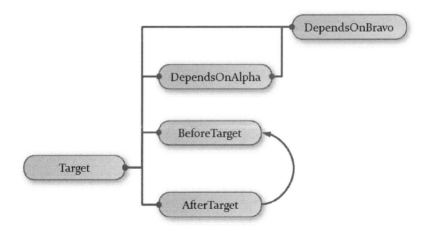

When MSBuild discovers this new dependency, it breaks the existing dependency between Target and AfterTarget, resulting in the following sequence,

Output sequence

```
DependsOnBravo
DependsOnAlpha
AfterTarget
BeforeTarget
Target
```

Again going back to the original sequence, a pair of additional targets are added, showing what happens when a target injects itself with the Before or AfterTargets attribute on one of the other targets already in the dependency tree as a result of it being listed in DependsOnTargets for the main target of execution. This is the opposite sequence of the request that was skipped previously, when a DependsOnTargets target tried to also use Before or AfterTargets.

Additional targets

```
<Target Name="BeforeDependsOnAlpha"
   BeforeTargets="DependsOnAlpha">
   <Message Text="BeforeDependsOnAlpha" />
</Target>
<Target Name="AfterDependsOnBravo"
   BeforeTargets="DependsOnBravo">
   <Message Text="AfterDependsOnBravo" />
</Target>
```

Output sequence

```
DependsOnBravo
```

```
AfterDependsOnBravo
BeforeDependsOnAlpha
DependsOnAlpha
BeforeTarget
Target
AfterTarget
```

These two new targets declared that they should run before one or the other of the two DependsOnTargets, "Alpha" or "Bravo." In this instance, MSBuild is able to place these targets into the existing dependency tree respecting all dependency requests discovered thus far.

Now up to this point, InitialTargets were presumed to have run first, in the order in which they were discovered while the projects were being imported. It turns out that you can use DependsOnTargets among InitialTargets—as well as other targets in the dependency sequence—to rearrange the ordering of their execution. It isn't possible to use Before and AfterTargets to rearrange InitialTargets with respect to one another, but it is possible to inject additional targets before or in-between InitialTargets. This follows the same pattern as was just seen with DependsOnTargets.

So, in summary, the MSBuild execution engine will build the target dependency graph first by placing InitialTargets, respecting their DependsOnTargets requests, then placing into the graph the top level execution targets and any additional targets they depend on. Following that, all other targets are placed into the graph using Before and AfterTargets injection. This target injection allows targets to be placed anywhere in the sequence, however, if a circular dependency is specified, the older link in the circular chain is discarded so that the most recently discovered one can be satisfied.

42. Investigate the standard build files

When you look into a typical C# or C++ project file that hasn't been the subject of extensive customizations, and follow all the standard imports declared therein, you begin a file spelunking adventure that can expose most of the inner workings of the standard builds for these project types. We've already covered how to wire your own extensions into this import hierarchy, in *trick #20, Consider the supported import patterns*. Now let's examine the import hierarchy for these two common project types.

Because there are a few targets that the IDE has special knowledge of, notably Build, Clean and Rebuild, as well as Package and Publish, these are a good place to start this investigation.

C# Project

We'll start with an examination of the standard C# project file imports, to find where the standard "Build" target is defined. From a new C# project file from a generic template, there is the first clue where to look in the single import it contains,

```
<Import Project="$(MSBuildToolsPath)\Microsoft.CSharp.targets" />
```

This corresponds to the following folder, which is easy enough to discover with a call to the Message task, supplying $(MSBuildToolsPath) as the Text parameter:

```
C:\Windows\Microsoft.NET\Framework\v4.0.30319\
```

The Microsoft.CSharp.targets file located there starts off by importing via wildcards any properly placed customization files in the "ImportsBefore" folder, as was shown in *trick #20, Consider the supported import patterns*, here again,

```
<Import
   Project="$(MSBuildExtensionsPath)\$(MSBuildToolsVersion)\
      $(MSBuildThisFile)\ImportBefore\*"
   Condition="..."
   />
```

Next is an interesting property definition, $(MSBuildAllProjects), into which the file places itself. This property is listed as an Input to the CoreCompile target, which is a dependent of the Build target, and provides an opportunity to make your project state "dirty" by inclusion of project files that will be modified. To extend this property to include your own files, redefine the property like this,

```
<PropertyGroup>
   <MSBuildAllProjects>
      $(MSBuildAllProjects);
      $(MSBuildProjectFullPath);
      $(ImportsPath)\My.props;
   </MSBuildAllProjects>
</PropertyGroup>
```

After the CoreCompile target we'll find the first standard import,

```
<Import Project="Microsoft.Common.targets" />
```

And toward the bottom, the bookend for ImportBefore, the ImportAfter wildcard extension point.

It is inside this Microsoft.Common.targets where, appropriately, the well-known targets "Build," "Rebuild," "Clean," and "Publish" are defined.

C++ Project

A C++ project file is similar, but starts with two property file imports,

```
<Import Project="$(VCTargetsPath)\Microsoft.Cpp.Default.props" />
<Import Project="$(VCTargetsPath)\Microsoft.Cpp.props" />
```

and a conditional import on a third user-specific property file, which won't exist until you create it,

```
<Import
   Project="$(UserRootDir)\Microsoft.Cpp.$(Platform).user.props"
   Condition="exists(
      '$(UserRootDir)\Microsoft.Cpp.$(Platform).user.props')"
   Label="LocalAppDataPlatform" />
```

Near the very bottom of the project file is a third import, for targets,

```
<Import Project="$(VCTargetsPath)\Microsoft.Cpp.targets" />
```

The $(VCTargetsPath) property however, is quite different from the reserved property $(MSBuildToolsPath) used by C# projects. It is maintained in the registry, at,

```
HKEY_LOCAL_MACHINE\SOFTWARE\Microsoft\MSBuild\ToolsVersions\4.0
```

which contains the following value,

```
$(MSBuildExtensionsPath32)\Microsoft.Cpp\v4.0\
```

which itself evaluates to

```
$(PROGRAMFILES)\MSBuild\Microsoft.Cpp\v4.0\
```

This and the few other properties defined in the registry will be read by MSBuild when the build engine is created. They can be overridden from the command line, since command line supplied properties always take precedence, but modifying them in your project file won't work, if you want to change it, you need to alter the registry, which is ill-advised— better off using your own property and leaving these alone.

The two standard property file imports, Microsoft.Cpp.Default.props and Microsoft.Cpp.props are separated by a pair of PropertyGroups, one for each Configuration in the project. The pattern provides first for the importing of default values for properties, then a section to alter the default values with project-plus-configuration-specific properties. These altered values, which indicate what kind of project it is and various other high level control properties, are used in the final property file Microsoft.Cpp.props to conditionally set the values of remaining properties. For example, the import of Microsoft.Cpp.Default.props sets the value of $(ConfigurationType) to the default value "Application."

Inside your C# project file, this value can be altered, for example to "StaticLibrary." Once this is done, when Microsoft.Cpp.props is imported this value is then used to pick up additional altered properties,

```
<PropertyGroup Condition="'$(ConfigurationType)' == 'StaticLibrary'">
   <LibCompiled>true</LibCompiled>
   <TargetExt>.lib</TargetExt>
   <OutputType>staticlibrary</OutputType>
</PropertyGroup>
```

Also in this property file, some additional property files are picked up, including these two, whose purpose is obvious,

```
<Import Project="$(VCTargetsPath)\Microsoft.Cl.Common.props" />
<Import Project="$(VCTargetsPath)\Microsoft.Link.Common.props" />
```

Returning to your C++ project, all the properties and items are defined and toward the bottom of the project the Microsoft.Cpp.targets file is imported.

The most important file imported from Microsoft.Cpp.targets is one whose name is computed from project properties,

```
$(VCTargetsPath)\Platforms\$(Platform)\ ⮑
    Microsoft.Cpp.$(Platform).Targets
```

Because the C++ compiler has more complexity to deal with in relation to compilation for different platforms, each platform has a separate targets file, which in turn will lead to a file for the toolset, in this case either 9.0 or 10.0, the version of the compiler specified with $(PlatformToolset). This file implements the ClCompile and Link targets, then begins an import chain that pulls in the following files,

```
$(VCTargetsPath)\Microsoft.CppCommon.targets
```

which contains the Lib, ImpLib, Midl and ResourceCompile targets, among others, then imports,

```
$(VCTargetsPath)\Microsoft.CppBuild.targets
```

This file is a treasure trove of property declarations that control the minutia of the build behavior. Many of the "Before" and "After" properties that set up the ordering of target dependencies for various build features are declared here, with comments indicating which can be extended, for example,

```
<!-- Easy to override before/after targets -->
<PropertyGroup>
  <BeforeClCompileTargets>
    $(BeforeClCompileTargets);
    BeforeClCompile;
  </BeforeClCompileTargets>
```

```
    <AfterClCompileTargets>
      $(AfterClCompileTargets);
      AfterClCompile;
    </AfterClCompileTargets>
  </PropertyGroup>
```

Also in this file is the import of,

```
$(VCTargetsPath)\Microsoft.BuildSteps.Targets
```

in which is found the import of,

```
$(MSBuildToolsPath)\Microsoft.Common.Targets
```

which is the very same file file described above for C# projects. Although the Microsoft.Common.targets file has already defined the "Build" and "Rebuild" targets, in C++ files, the Microsoft.BuildSteps.targets file replaces them with trivially overridden versions.

The import hierarchy can involve what are often very small files that declare only a few properties or import only a single additional file based on another property, then import a more generic file, working its way up the folder hierarchy under $(VCTargetsPath)\Platforms.

It's a fair bet that the next iteration of the C# project system will itself move away from reliance on project imports in the .NET Framework folder and also move these files under the MSBuild extension point folder in a manner similar to how C++ projects—which are using a newer project system core—are doing, so even if you're not using C++ this may still be a good pattern to understand.

Microsoft.Common.targets

At this point, the behavior of the C# and C++ projects become unified, as they both share this common target file. Not surprisingly, Microsoft.-Common.targets and most of the imports that follow start off and finish the same way that Microsoft.CSharp.targets did, with wildcard imports of the ImportBefore and ImportAfter files.

The first standard import is,

```
<Import Project="Microsoft.NETFramework.props" ...
```

which is used to deduce the version numbers and paths related to targeting various versions of the .NET Framework. Toward the bottom of Microsoft.Common.targets is the target half of this property-file target-file import pair,

```
<Import Project="$(MSBuildToolsPath)\Microsoft.NETFramework.targets"
```

which dynamically creates an item array containing the various paths required based on the value of $(TargetFrameworkVersion). After that final standard target import are a whole mess of feature-specific targets files, for example XAML, Silverlight, Team Test and the like.

The body of Microsoft.Common.targets is dedicated primarily to implementing the well-known targets. In general, these are junction point targets that execute dependent targets, eventually reaching a dependent target that is project system specific. For example, the "Build" target as shown in detail in *trick #23, Use BeforeBuild and AfterBuild only for local customizations*, depends on "CoreBuild" which depends on "Compile." The commonality completed, this final "Compile" target relies on an implementation of "CoreCompile" that would have been declared in either Microsoft.CSharp.targets or in the equivalent file for other .NET languages.

If you are trying to find an obscure junction point for your own customizations, digging through these files may not seem so mystical once you understand the basic patterns on which they are defined. Often, starting with knowledge of only a single related property name and a quick find-in-files, you can deduce the inner workings of the build operations related to the feature, opening up more opportunities for automation and extensibility.

43. How to wire into the standard build

In the previous *trick #42, Investigate the standard build files,* there was an introduction into the inner workings of the C# and C++ project system build targets. It was mentioned that with some thoughtful searching, you can find junction points into which you can wire your own customizations. This next section shows some of the specific options available.

The main chains of target execution dependencies described in the previous mechanics trick are:

```
C#: Build → CoreBuild  → Compile → CoreCompile
C++: Build → ( PrepareForBuild → BuildCompile → BuildLink )
Both: Clean → CoreClean
```

Each of these targets declare and depend on a property to run dependent targets, for example $(BuildDependsOn) or $(CoreCleanDependsOn). It is in these properties that the build systems can diverge. For example,

Cloud projects will add a Cloud specific target into the Clean target dependency tree by modifying the $(CoreCleanDependsOn) property,

```
<PropertyGroup>
  <CoreCleanDependsOn>
    DeleteCurrentDeployment;
    $(CoreCleanDependsOn)
  </CoreCleanDependsOn>
</PropertyGroup>
```

By examining log files created with diagnostic level logging in your build, you can often discover the specific target you need to extend. A simple text search in the MSBuild folder set,

```
C:\Windows\Microsoft.NET\Framework\v4.0.30319
C:\Windows\Microsoft.NET\Framework64\v4.0.30319
C:\Program Files (x86)\MSBuild
C:\Program Files\MSBuild
```

using the wildcard pattern,

```
*.targets;*.props;*.*proj
```

looking for the string "*TargetName*DependsOn" will usually get you right to the spot in the standard build files you need to examine to find the build logic of interest for your customization. Then, in your own project file, simply redeclare the property, keeping the current values and adding your own,

```
<PropertyGroup>
  <TargetNameDependsOn>
    MyEarlyCustomizationTarget;
    $(TargetNameDependsOn);
    MyLateCustomizationTarget;
  </TargetNameDependsOn>
</PropertyGroup>
```

In the standard build sequences, there are two obvious customization points already in place. One is the BeforeBuild and AfterBuild pair of targets, and the other is the PreBuildEvent and PostBuildEvent properties. Supposing you had a simple file copy operation you wanted to incorporate at some point after the build, what would be the difference between these two options? Besides the obvious that one is using an MSBuild task and the other a command shell command,

```
<Target Name="AfterBuild">
  <Copy
    SourceFiles="$(ProjectDir)\Extra.dll"
    DestinationFolder="$(OutDir)"
    />
</Target>
```

and,

```
<PropertyGroup>
  <PostBuildEvent
      >copy "$(ProjectDir)\Extra.dll" $(OutDir)</PostBuildEvent>
</PropertyGroup>
```

The $(PostBuildEvent) property is able to hold any command that can be passed as the Command attribute to an Exec task. Essentially, this will evaluate to a target that looks like this,

```
<Target Name="PostBuildEvent">
  <Exec Command="$(PostBuildEvent)" />
</Target>
```

It is declared in the property page for the project configuration. You can configure the conditions when this will be run with a setting in the IDE, by default it only runs on a successful build.

The AfterBuild target on the other hand is able to contain arbitrary MSBuild tasks, including one or more Exec tasks or any other task available to MSBuild, which allows for greater complexity. Unlike the Pre and PostBuildEvent properties, it doesn't have custom UI in the IDE, which means you'll have to unload the project file and edit it as XML to author the MSBuild customization.

The most interesting difference though is in terms of when they are executed. The PostBuildEvent target runs just prior to "CoreBuild" while the "AfterBuild" target will run after "CoreBuild."

If the placement is critical, you can make your own target and wire it into wherever in the build you need it to run, using the various $(...DependsOn) declarations, or by specifying BeforeTargets and AfterTargets on your new target.

from Microsoft.Common.targets

```
<PropertyGroup>
  <CoreBuildDependsOn>
      BuildOnlySettings;
      PrepareForBuild;                            <!-- 1 -->
      PreBuildEvent;                              <!-- 2 -->
      ResolveReferences;
      PrepareResources;
      ResolveKeySource;
      Compile;                                    <!-- 3 -->
      UnmanagedUnregistration;
      GenerateSerializationAssemblies;
      CreateSatelliteAssemblies;
      GenerateManifests;
      GetTargetPath;
      PrepareForRun;                              <!-- 4 -->
      UnmanagedRegistration;
```

```
                IncrementalClean;
                PostBuildEvent                                    <!-- 5 -->
            </CoreBuildDependsOn>
        </PropertyGroup>
        <Target
            Name="CoreBuild"
            DependsOnTargets="$(CoreBuildDependsOn)">
            <OnError ... />
            <OnError ... />
        </Target>

    ...

        <PropertyGroup>
            <BuildDependsOn>
                BeforeBuild;                                      <!-- 6 -->
                CoreBuild;                                        <!-- 7 -->
                AfterBuild                                        <!-- 8 -->
            </BuildDependsOn>
        </PropertyGroup>
        <Target
            Name="Build"
            Condition=" '$(_InvalidConfigurationWarning)' != 'true' "
            DependsOnTargets="$(BuildDependsOn)"
            Returns="$(TargetPath)" />
```

The really interesting targets that are often the junction points in the
dependency tree for customizations are indicated above.

- PrepareForBuild (1) – good place to wire in staging or code generation

- PreBuildEvent (2) – uses the $(PreBuildEvent) property

- Compile (3)

- PrepareForRun (4) – last chance to move files around

- PostBuild event (5) – uses the $(PostBuildEvent) property

Notice that the "Build" target is just a placeholder, it doesn't do anything
except execute dependent targets (6, 7, 8), the first and last which are
empty by default and available to be overridden in project files, with the
real meat of the build taking place in the "CoreBuild" target, which itself
is a do-nothing target that executes dependencies.

Chapter 5
Tips

We've reached about the halfway point in the book. By now you should have a complete understanding of the basic structure of an MSBuild file. Some basic guidance has been provided for how to structure your project files, with special attention paid to factoring common code with shared files and well-placed imports. You should also be well aware of the basic mechanics that will underpin everything that will follow from this point until the end. This chapter includes what I'd call "best practices" for MSBuild, things that you should be able to put to use in your own project files right away.

44. Use a response file named @

MSBuild accepts a response file in lieu of or in addition to command line parameters. Command line options can get pretty lengthy, especially if you are using custom loggers or commonly use other than the default log verbosity or attach multiple loggers. This is also handy if you have more than one .*proj or .sln file in your main build folder. The use of a response file can get the command line back to a manageable size.

There is built-in knowledge of an auto response file named MSBuild.rsp that seems appealing, but since it must reside in the same folder as MSBuild.exe, it loses its appeal, since the MSBuild executable is part of the Microsoft .NET Framework, which is installed under the C:\Windows\Microsoft.NET\Frameworks folder, and it is atypical to place build customizations in such a location. See the note on **MSBuild_Exe_Path** in *trick #34 Know some other secret environment variables* for an alternative approach.

The syntax for a response file is @<file>, where <file> is the name of a file containing command line options in the same format they would be supplied on the command line. You aren't limited to just a single line though, and can place each option on a separate line to increase the readability and maintenance of your response file.

Rather than choose a lengthy file name—or even use the .rsp file extension—I name response files '@' which is a valid single character file system name. This makes the command easy to invoke.

```
> msbuild @@
```

The first '@' indicates a response file name will follow, the second '@' is itself the file name. You can supplement the response file with additional options as well.

```
> msbuild @@ /t:TargetName
```

A typical response file is shown below. Notice that blank lines and comments are allowed.

Response File @

```
# specify a default project
SomeProject.trkproj

# console parameters
/verbosity:normal

# file logger zero, detailed
/filelogger
/fileloggerparameters:logfile=SomeProject.trkproj.Detailed.log
/fileloggerparameters:verbosity=detailed

# file logger one, diagnostic
/filelogger1
/fileloggerparameters1:logfile=SomeProject.trkproj.Diagnostic.log
/fileloggerparameters1:verbosity=diagnostic

# ignore pattern
/ignoreprojectextensions:.sln
```

The first non-comment line in the file shown above is the project name, SomeProject.trkproj. If there is only one file in the folder that MSBuild will pick up by default this line can be omitted.

If you supply additional arguments *after* the response file, they will replace the same values if they appear in the response file. Using the listing above, the default verbosity is set to normal. This can be altered, as shown below; it will override the response file setting and set the verbosity to quiet.

```
> msbuild @@ /v:q
```

Reversing this won't work, in the command below, since the response file appears on the command line after the verbosity, it overrides the explicit value that appears on the command line before it.

```
> msbuild /v:q @@
```

I tend to fully qualify the arguments in a response file rather than use the command line shortcuts (e.g. /v for /verbosity), and to split out to multiple lines values that the command line accepts as a semicolon delimited list (e.g. the multiple /fileloggerparameters) but that is just a matter of preference. Note that I've forced the attachment of two diagnostic file loggers, one detailed and one diagnostic, with the log file names based on both the name of the project file and the diagnostic level.

A response file can include additional response files by specifying their name, prefixed with @, just like on the command line.

When different combinations are needed, I tend to still use @ as the first character of the response file, to keep them together in an alphabetical file list for the folder. For example, @64 would be a response file adding in properties needed for a 64-bit build, if it were not included in whatever the default build were.

45. Make public property declarations conditional

For this discussion, the term "public property" means "a property you would expect to possibly be modified via the command line."

```
<PropertyGroup>
  <PublicProperty
    Condition="'$(PublicProperty)' == ''"
    >default</PublicProperty>
</PropertyGroup>
```

Generally, public properties assignments should be protected with a condition. By doing so they can be overridden from other import files but still pick up default values later on. Any properties provided on the command line will always override properties declared in this manner, but as we've already seen, there are numerous extension points where property values can be set. Any properties that a developer may override using any of these mechanisms should respect that ability by declaring their default value with a condition that preserves any values already present.

46. Know how to construct complex property usage patterns

On occasion, you may discover a need for a target that should only be run in certain situations, such as a lengthy operation. If it is possible to detect the condition absolutely, you can use simple condition on the target. Sometimes though, due to flaky behavior of a third party component, a foolproof system is elusive. This pattern will allow for the normal operation of lengthy targets, while still allowing a user supplied override of the default behavior, for cases when the execution detection is faulty.

To demonstrate this, consider the contrived inline task below that returns 'true' or 'false' with equal probability. The real meat of the pattern follows, where a property named SkipLengthyOperation will be set to one of four values:

```
true - explicitly set by the user on the command line
false - explicitly set by the user on the command line
null - not explicitly specified and the condition was not met
auto - not explicitly specified but the condition was met
```

AutoProperty.props, Contrived setup for phony flaky detection

```xml
                                                        <!-- 1 -->
<UsingTask
    TaskName="RandomChance"
    TaskFactory="CodeTaskFactory"
    AssemblyFile=
    "$(MSBuildToolsPath)\Microsoft.Build.Tasks.v4.0.dll">
    <ParameterGroup>
      <Result
          ParameterType="System.Boolean"
          Output="true"
          />
    </ParameterGroup>
    <Task>
      <Using Namespace="System" />
      <Code Type="Fragment" Language="cs">
        <![CDATA[
        Result = ((new Random().NextDouble() * 100) > 50);
        Log.LogMessage("Result = '{0}'", Result);
        ]]>
      </Code>
    </Task>
</UsingTask>

<Target Name="PhonyCheckForCondition">          <!-- 2 -->
    <RandomChance>
      <Output
```

```
            TaskParameter="Result"
            PropertyName="CheckForCondition"
            />
    </RandomChance>
</Target>
```

Auto property pattern

```
<PropertyGroup>
    <SkipLengthyOperation>null</SkipLengthyOperation>          <!-- 3 -->
</PropertyGroup>

<Target Name="SetupLengthyOperation"
    DependsOnTargets="PhonyCheckForCondition">
    <PropertyGroup>                                           <!-- 4 -->
        <SkipLengthyOperation
            Condition="
                (
                    '$(CheckForCondition)' == 'true' AND
                    '$(SkipLengthyOperation)' != 'true' AND
                    '$(SkipLengthyOperation)' != 'false'
                )"
            >auto</SkipLengthyOperation>
    </PropertyGroup>
    <PropertyGroup>                                           <!-- 5 -->
        <SkipMessage
            Condition="'$(SkipLengthyOperation)' == 'null'"
            >Skipping operation due to detection</SkipMessage>
        <SkipMessage
            Condition="'$(SkipLengthyOperation)' == 'auto'"
            >Performing operation due to detection</SkipMessage>
        <SkipMessage
            Condition="'$(SkipLengthyOperation)' == 'false'"
            >Skipping operation at user's request</SkipMessage>
        <SkipMessage
            Condition="'$(SkipLengthyOperation)' == 'true'"
            >Forcing operation at user's request</SkipMessage>
    </PropertyGroup>
</Target>
                                                             <!-- 6 -->
<Target Name="LengthyOperation"
    DependsOnTargets="SetupLengthyOperation">
    <Message
        Text="CheckForCondition is '$(CheckForCondition)'"
        />
    <Message
        Text="SkipLengthyOperation is '$(SkipLengthyOperation)'"
        />
    <Message
        Text="$(SkipMessage)"
        />
                                                             <!-- 7 -->
    <CallTarget
        Condition="
            (
                '$(SkipLengthyOperation)' == 'true' OR
```

```
                    '$(SkipLengthyOperation)' == 'auto'
            )"
        Targets="PerformLengthyOperation"
            />
</Target>

<Target Name="PerformLengthyOperation">
    <!-- ... -->
</Target>
                                                        <!-- 8 -->
<Target Name="Build"
    DependsOnTargets="LengthyOperation"
    />
```

Output for successive runs, without setting property

```
PhonyCheckForCondition:
  Result = 'False'
LengthyOperation:
  CheckForCondition is 'False'
  SkipLengthyOperation is 'null'
  Skipping operation due to detection

PhonyCheckForCondition:
  Result = 'True'
LengthyOperation:
  CheckForCondition is 'True'
  SkipLengthyOperation is 'auto'
  Performing operation due to detection
```

Output for runs, passing explicit true or false

```
> msbuild AutoProperty.props /p:SkipLengthyOperation=true

PhonyCheckForCondition:
  Result = 'False'
LengthyOperation:
  CheckForCondition is 'True'
  SkipLengthyOperation is 'true'
  Forcing operation at user's request

> msbuild AutoProperty.props /p:SkipLengthyOperation=false

PhonyCheckForCondition:
  Result = 'True'
LengthyOperation:
  CheckForCondition is 'False'
  SkipLengthyOperation is 'false'
  Skipping operation at user's request
```

The contrived inline task (1) named "RandomChance" produces a single Boolean output named "Result" that is "true" or "false" with equal probability. Consider this task, as it is called (2) in the dependent target "PhonyCheckForCondition" to be a detection of the "built" state of something in the build that requires a lengthy operation to complete. Furthermore, consider that due to issues beyond your control this lengthy operation may fail on occasion, but due to its duration you don't want to cover up the intermittent behavior of the operation by running it every time.

Basically you need a mechanism whereby the operation will attempt to run when the detection succeeds, won't attempt to run when the detection indicates (perhaps wrongly) that the operation isn't needed, but also has the ability to be overridden explicitly with a normal "true" and "false" property. Furthermore, the build—being aware of the flaky behavior of the long running task—needs to be very explicit about why the operation ran or was not run, to assist users when everything breaks down due to the failure of the detection.

The auto-property $(SkipLengthyOperation) is given a default state (3) of "null" which will indicate that the operation should not be run. Recall that if the user explicitly specifies this property on the command line, the build engine will use the value they supply, and will not overwrite the command-line-supplied value with the "null" value. If you want this to be configurable in a per-user My.props file—which will be fully covered in *trick #75, How to customize developer builds with My.props*—then you will need to add a guarding condition on this property declaration, since a value from another property file will be happily overwritten by the build engine.

Before (4) the dependent check will have run the inline task and the $(CheckForCondition) property will be either "true" or "false." At (4) the value of $(SkipLengthyOperation) will be promoted from "null" to "auto," but only if the condition check indicates the operation should be run, and only if the user did not explicitly specify a "true" or "false" from the command line, overriding the "null" value default.

At this point (5) the $(SkipLengthyOperation) property can have any of the four possible values. The property group sets a $(SkipMessage) property to a unique message string for each of the four possible states.

All of this setup (4, 5) is performed as the dependency of (6) the "LengthyOperation," itself a dependency (8) of the "Build" target. Within the "LengthyOperation" the condition check property and the skip message explaining exactly what state was detected are emitted, and then a CallTarget is used to conditionally call (7) the target that will actually perform the operation. By using a CallTarget, you can guarantee that the operation executes only a single time in the project build, regardless of how many paths of the call graph lead to the "LengthyOperation" target.

The next two sections of the listing show the output for each of the four possible states; the first two showing the default behavior, the last two showing the behavior when specifying the skip property explicitly. As a final thought, you should consider using a consistent naming pattern for the "auto" and "null" messages, so that they can be easily seen in the build.

47. Know the common escaped character values

The following table lists values you may commonly escape in your MSBuild files.

```
%    %25
$    %24
@    %40
(    %28
)    %29
'    %27
"    %22
;    %3b
?    %3f
*    %2a
```

Nothing special, these are just hex codes for the character values. Do a Bing search on "MSBuild special" to find this list quickly. If you plan on using these throughout your build files, place them in a table of defined properties so you don't have to keep looking them up, unless you are already fluent in hex.

SpecialCharacters.props

```
<PropertyGroup>
    <_pc_>%25</_pc_> <!-- % percent -->
    <_dl_>%24</_dl_> <!-- $ dollar -->
    <_at_>%40</_at_> <!-- @ at -->
    <_op_>%28</_op_> <!-- ( open paren -->
    <_cp_>%29</_cp_> <!-- ) close paren -->
    <_qt_>%27</_qt_> <!-- ' quote -->
    <_dq_>%22</_dq_> <!-- " double quote -->
    <_sc_>%3b</_sc_> <!-- ; semicolon -->
    <_qm_>%3f</_qm_> <!-- ? question mark -->
    <_as_>%2a</_as_> <!-- * asterisk -->
</PropertyGroup>
```

These can be used when writing out messages or writing text to files using the WriteLinesToFile task. While longer names could be helpful, they tend to add clutter when heavily used, which is often the case when writing out XML values to files.

Using Special Characters in Messages

```
<Message
  Text="The value of $(_dl_)(PropertyName) is '$(PropertyName)'"
  />
<Message
  Text="The value of $(_at_)(ItemName) is '@(ItemName)'"
  />
```

Output

```
The value of $(PropertyName) is 'value'
The value of @(ItemName) is 'value;value'
```

The next listing shows an important consideration of escaped special characters when using the WriteLinesToFile task. It uses an XML `<![CDATA[ ]]>` section to reduce the necessity of special characters in most instances, but pay special attention to the treatment of the semicolon.

It is important to note is that the WriteLinesToFile task, treating input lines as MSBuild items, will replace explicit semicolons with newlines if they are not escaped. It appears as though the WriteLinesToFiles first parses the input and creates individual items using explicit semicolons as an item delimiter, and then once the items are created, performs the replacement for escaped special characters.

The listing below writes out an MSBuild project file, so pay careful attention as you read through this as there is a property defined that contains the contents of the second file, itself an MSBuild file, so if you are not careful it may appear as though the XML elements are not properly nested.

Writing Lines To File.trkproj, source listing

```
<Target Name="WriteLines">
  <PropertyGroup>
    <_sc_>%3b</_sc_> <!-- ; semicolon -->
    <Item01>alpha</Item01>                              <!-- 1 -->
    <Item02>bravo</Item02>
    <Item03>charlie</Item03>
    <Item04>delta</Item04>
    <WriteFileContents>
                                                        <!-- 2a -->
<![CDATA[<?xml version="1.0" encoding="utf-8"?>
<Project xmlns="http://schemas.microsoft.com/developer/msbuild/2003"
  ToolsVersion="4.0"
```

```
   DefaultTargets="Build">
   <ItemGroup>
      <Item01 Include="$(Item01);$(Item02)" /> <!-- 3 -->
      <Item02 Include="$(Item03)$(_sc_)$(Item04)" /> <!-- 4 -->
   </ItemGroup>
</Project>
]]>
                                                      <!-- 2b -->
      </WriteFileContents>
   </PropertyGroup>

   <ItemGroup>                                        <!-- 5 -->
      <WriteFileLine Include="$(WriteFileContents)" />
   </ItemGroup>
   <WriteLinesToFile
      File="./WrittenLines.trkproj"
      Lines="@(WriteFileLine)"
      Overwrite="true"
      />
</Target>
```

Listing of file just written, WrittenLines.proj

```
<?xml version="1.0" encoding="utf-8"?>
<Project xmlns="http://schemas.microsoft.com/developer/msbuild/2003"
   ToolsVersion="4.0"
   DefaultTargets="Build">
   <ItemGroup>
      <Item01 Include="alpha
bravo" /> <!-- 3 -->
      <Item02 Include="charlie;delta" /> <!-- 4 -->
   </ItemGroup>
</Project>
```

Starting at (1) four properties are defined which will be written out to the file. This is done to demonstrate that even though the file content is within a CDATA section, the MSBuild property evaluation and substitution still takes place. The file contents are defined in a CDATA section between (2a) and (2b) in the property named WriteFileContents. This is a single property containing multi-line text.

At (5) this multi-line property is used as the identity for an item named WriteFileLine. This is important because the WriteLinesToFile task expects the file contents to be supplied in an item array. This item array is then passed to the WriteLinesToFile task. The contents of the file this task writes out are shown in the listing.

Two of the lines in the multi-line property WriteFileContents are significant, shown as (3) and (4) in the original source listing. Because the line number comments are within the property, these also show up in the written file contents. Line (3) in the source listing contains a semicolon, which in the written file is translated to a carriage return at (3). Line (4) in the source listing contains the $(_sc_) property declared previously as %3b, and shows up properly as a semicolon in line (4) of the written file contents. Although it may appear as though line (3) would be written out in the same manner what actually occurs is quite different.

The WriteLinesToFiles task, taking the entire CDATA defined property as an input parameter of type Item, performs processing on the supplied Include value, discovering the semicolon at line (3). It then splits the contents into two separate items, essentially everything before the semicolon and everything after the semicolon all the way to the final line in the CDATA section. After splitting the items, it then performs the property value replacement, which is when the values for $(Item01) through $(Item04) are replaced as well as the value of $(_sc_), which happens to be a semicolon, but which doesn't impact the item creation because that phase of processing has already completed. The net result in the generated file is thus three items, the first with the value "alpha<newline>bravo" and the second and third with "charlie" and "delta" respectively, likely not the intent.

It is possible to end up in a situation where a property unavoidably contains special characters, but you need to pass that property to another construct that will misinterpret it, for instance passing a property containing a semicolon to the Include attribute of an item array when your intent is not to create multiple items. To avoid this, you can use an MSBuild property function to escape (or unescape) the special characters using MSBuild escaping syntax.

```
<PropertyGroup>
    <ContainsSpecialChars>CONNECT:one;two;</ContainsSpecialChars>
    <Escaped>$([MSBuild]::Escape($(ContainsSpecialChars)))</Escaped>
    <Unescaped>$([MSBuild]::Unescape($(Escaped)))</Unescaped>
<PropertyGroup>
```

While demonstrated previously by showing the creation of an XML file that happens to also be valid MSBuild, this technique is also valuable for generating all sorts of file formats beyond the simple lists of files declared in file system item arrays for which WriteLinesToFile and ReadLines-FromFile appear to have been initially created.

An interesting side note about CDATA usage is needed. MSBuild will only accept a CDATA declaration when it appears as the first non-whitespace value in a property. Examine the following test,

```
<Target Name="CDATA Test">
    <PropertyGroup>
        <All><![CDATA[inside cdata]]></All>
```

```
            <Whitespace>
                <![CDATA[inside cdata]]></Whitespace>
            <Initial><![CDATA[inside cdata]]> after</Initial>
            <Interior>before <![CDATA[inside cdata]]> after</Interior>
        </PropertyGroup>
        <Message Text="All:          $(All)" />
        <Message Text="Whitespace: $(Whitespace)" />
        <Message Text="Initial:      $(Initial)" />
        <Message Text="Interior:     $(Interior)" />
    </Target>

CDATA Test:
  All:        inside cdata
  Whitespace: inside cdata
  Initial:    inside cdata after
  Interior:   before <![CDATA[inside cdata]]> after
```

Notice that the first three declarations work because the CDATA is preceded by only whitespace, but in the final one, where there are characters before the CDATA, MSBuild interprets the text literally.

Similarly, MSBuild can recognize property content that is valid XML in a similar manner,

```
    <Target Name="XML Test">
        <PropertyGroup>
            <Xml><element attribute="value">text</element></Xml>
        </PropertyGroup>
        <Message Text="Interior:     $(Xml)" />
    </Target>

XML Test:
  Interior:   <element attribute="value" xmlns="http://schemas.  ↘
microsoft.com/developer/msbuild/2003">text</element>
```

In this case, MSBuild recognized that the value of the property was valid XML and read it as such.

In these last two examples, you may have noticed that the target names had spaces in them. That caught me by surprise one time, and I've shown it here mostly as a novelty, to execute them, the target names were surrounded in quotes on the command line,

```
> msbuild Scratch.proj /t"CDATA Test";"XML Test"
```

48. Prefer inline syntax to CreateProperty/CreateItem

Dynamic Properties and Items are those declared inside a target body.

```
<Target Name="SomeTarget">
    <!-- inline property group form -->
    <PropertyGroup>
        <SomeProperty>Dynamic!</SomeProperty>
```

```
    </PropertyGroup>
    ...
```

The old syntax for this used to be to use the CreateProperty task, which is still available, but far less convenient than the newer syntax in MSBuild 3.5, which allows you simply to declare a PropertyGroup within the body of a target. The following is identical, though a bit wordier than the above:

```
<Target Name="SomeTarget">
    <!-- explicit task form -->
    <CreateProperty
        Value="Dynamic!">
        <Output
            TaskParameter="Value"
            PropertyName="SomeProperty" />
    </CreateProperty>
    ...
```

To decipher the use of the CreateProperty task, the Value attribute holds the value of the property being created, and the Output element is used to extract that value and give a name to the newly created property. The TaskParameter in the Output element will always be "Value" since that is the name of the output property on the CreateProperty task. As the inline property group syntax is always preferred, you generally only need to understand this form to the extent that you may run across it in some of the Microsoft supplied targets files, or in legacy builds. When I see these in my own files, and MSBuild 2.0 compatibility is irrelevant, I always convert them to the new form, for readability's sake".

49. Ensure Messages always print something

Consider this Message task invocation,

```
<Message Text="@(MyItems)" />
```

If this is the only output in a target, and if @(MyItems) happens to be empty, then the message will print nothing. MSBuild notices this, and instead of printing your message, it skips it altogether. With the default logging level, MSBuild also notices that the target had no console output at all. The potential problem here is that when a target produces no output, MSBuild omits the output that indicates that the target was run. This makes sense, because for C# or C++ project builds you would be inundated with a bunch of null output. If however, you are writing a custom target that is significant to your build, or in the case where you

---

" I'm being polite here, it's not just for readability. The designers of MSBuild will use words like "abomination" when they speak of these tasks. They were a quick workaround in the 2.0 version for the harder-to-implement inline syntax that arrived in version 3.5

are debugging it, you need to make sure you supply some additional text that will force the message output, and therefore force the target output. Adding some quotes around the possibly empty item,

```
<Message Text="'@(MyItems)'" />
```

or even adding some explanatory text,

```
<Message Text="MyItems = '@(MyItems)'" />
```

will change the output to this, even if MyItems is empty:

```
YourTargetName:
  MyItems = ''
```

50. Use System.IO.Path for path comparisons

If you need to compare two paths, it is easy to form a condition such as,

```
Condition="'$(PathOne)' == '$(PathTwo)'"
```

This will cause difficult to diagnose issues though, if you consider the following possible values for these properties,

```
C:\Code\CurrentDir\PathTo\SomeFolder
.\PathTo\SomeFolder
.\PathTo\SomeFolder\
.\PathTo\SOMEFOLDER
PathTo\SomeFolder
.\OtherPath\..\PathTo\SomeFolder
```

It is possible that all of the paths above actually refer to the same location. They may have been composed of other path parts from other properties or well-known metadata on file based items. Since MSBuild conditions will be evaluated using a string comparison it won't have any idea what the intent is. Instead, use a property function,

```
<PropertyGroup>
  <PathsAreEqual Condition="
    '$([System.IO.Path]::GetFullPath($(PathOne)))' ==
    '$([System.IO.Path]::GetFullPath($(PathTwo)))'"
    >true</PathsAreEqual>
</PropertyGroup>
<Message
  Condition="'$(PathsAreEqual)' == 'true'"
  Text="'$(PathOne)' is equal to '$(PathTwo)'"
  />
```

The code above uses property functions for comparison, which will normalize the paths. A property containing the comparison result is then used in the conditional expression, but the initial conditional expression could have just as easily been used directly in the Message task, if it doesn't need to be duplicated elsewhere.

While we're on the topic of comparing paths, there is yet another special property function available that can help. The property function MakeRelative will take two paths and compose a representation of one that is a relative path to the other. For example, given the two paths in properties,

```
<PropertyGroup>
    <Root>C:\Code\Root</Root>
    <Child>C:\Code\Root\Child</Child>
</PropertyGroup>
```

you can produce the relative path from one to the other, as,

```
$([MSBuild]::MakeRelative(`$(Root)`, `$(Child)`))
```

which will produce the relative path "Child" which is the path of the second argument relative to the path of the first.

Tips for Naming

As your build becomes more complex, you'll want to avoid naming conflicts between the contents of the many files in your build. I've used some standard naming patterns to help avoid this.

MSBuild does not permit custom XML namespaces for your property and item element names, giving a parse error on your project file if you attempt it. If you want to incorporate some sort of name collision avoidance of the sort provided by namespaces, you'll need to mangle the names yourself. Other techniques for this can be borrowed from the .NET Framework Design Guidelines[12], and are illustrated below in *trick #51* through *trick #56*.

51. Name public and private properties differently

Complex build files can contain many properties used for creating bits of content to be aggregated later, or for controlling the flow of the build code at a lower level of granularity than you wish to expose at higher

---

[12] http://bit.ly/netfdg

levels. I've generally used the convention of using an underscore prefix for private, internal properties and items.

```
<PropertyGroup>
    <PublicProperty Condition="'$(PublicProperty)' == ''">...
    <_PrivateProperty>...
</PropertyGroup>
```

Compared to public property declarations, there is generally no need for the same conditional override protection for private properties, unless they are being used as internal variables that can get their initial value from multiple disjoint locations in the build project files.

In addition to being a useful convention, similar to the Framework Design Guide convention for private members in a C# class, the leading underscore also has another feature. The Visual Studio IDE has a bit of knowledge about the contents of project files. By convention, the C++ project will filter out from its user interface any properties or targets that are named with a leading underscore.

52. Use 'Skip' properties

In a complex build there will inevitably be portions of the build that are time consuming and generally not interesting for developers during the course of their daily work. This would include things such as compiling the installer, or deploying all of the end user documentation, which are used as examples in this trick. Typically the targets that handle these operations will be written with a conditional based on the value of a property.

```
<PropertyGroup>
    <SkipProperty>... <!-- 1 -->
    <ForceProperty>... <!-- 2 -->
</PropertyGroup>

<!-- 3 -->
<Target Name="CompileInstaller"
    Condition="'$(SkipCompileInstaller)' == 'false'"
    ...

<!-- 4 -->
<Target Name="DeployDocumentation"
    Condition="'$(SkipDeployDocumentation)' != 'true'"
    ...
```

It is most often convenient to keep these properties consistently named with the same prefix (1), in this case "Skip." It doesn't matter whether the default value of a Skip property is "true" or "false" as long as the check for the property is consistent. I tend to always check against the non-default value either with a positive check against "false" (3) or negative check (4) against "true." This allows "Skip" properties to have a natural default value of either true or false.

Since it is inconvenient to change the default value for these properties after the logic for testing them is spread throughout various build files, and since double-negative logic is confusing, consider using "Force" (2) as a prefix for logic opposite that of "Skip," for actions that would be typically skipped by default but which the user may wish to explicitly trigger with a parameter property.

53. Cascade 'Skip' properties

For multi-part sequences of operations in the build, it may be convenient to have a single property that allows users to opt-out of the entire sequence, while still maintaining granular properties for each individual step.

Imagine the build steps for generating documentation.

1. Documentation is compiled using a 3rd party documentation tool.
2. Documentation is deployed for inclusion in the installer.
3. Documentation is copied to a local server for review.

These steps may dramatically increase the turnaround for individual developer builds. Documentation compilers tend to be notoriously slow, documentation is usually very large, which slows the creation of installers with every build—you do build installers with every build, don't you?—and copying large files to a remote server will add extra time as well. All that and your work for the next several days may not even touch the end user documentation. Set up your build so that you can turn it all off with a single switch, but can later add in individual elements to ensure you are getting proper local build coverage when needed.

```
<!-- $(SkipDocumentation) -->
<PropertyGroup
    Condition="'$(SkipDocumentation)' == 'true'">
    <SkipDocumentationCompile>true</SkipDocumentationCompile>
    <SkipDocumentationDeploy>true</SkipDocumentationDeploy>
    <SkipDocumentationStaging>true</SkipDocumentationStaging>
</PropertyGroup>
```

Because the entire property group is conditional, setting the primary Skip property automatically assigns the individual Skip properties that are used conditionally to execute the targets in the sequence.

54. Make conditions true opposites

Because properties can acquire values from so many different points, it is difficult to ensure the fidelity of how they are used. It may very well be that a Boolean property likely has two values, but not "true" and "false" as you would expect. It is more likely that the two values are "true" and an empty string. In many cases, you need to expect three values, "true," "false," and the empty string, with one of "true" or "false" being the desired default, and either of the other two being the exceptional case. If that is the case, then build scripts with both of the conditions below will have issues:

```
Condition="'$(Property)' == 'true'"
Condition="'$(Property)' == 'false'"
```

Don't think that you will be able to find every property and supply a default value for it, for example:

```
<Property Condition="'$(Property)' != 'true'>false</Property>
```

It will become a never-ending hunt, cause untold noise, and not buy you all that much. You'd also likely be in the situation of having to bundle up hundreds of properties to pass into calls to the MSBuild task, rather than just rely on a consistent interpretation of a default empty value.

Instead, ensure that when writing conditions on the value of a property, always use true opposite values by inverting the comparison operator. Doing so will work for both possible opposites, whether or not the opposite of the value tested against is "true," "false," or a string that is likely empty.

Comparison pairs for 'true' vs. empty string

```
Condition="'$(Property)' == 'true'"
Condition="'$(Property)' != 'true'"
```

Comparison against 'false' vs. empty string

```
Condition="'$(Property)' == 'false'"
Condition="'$(Property)' != 'false'"
```

In summary, take care to set default values meaningfully, using conditions where warranted—or not if you need to enforce a particular value and don't care about values that may be inherited from environment variables—and be sure that in your use of conditional expressions for the property, you are not comparing with a two values where one value would suffice.

55. Keep item names singular

When constructing lists of items in an item array, be consistent with the naming pattern used for items in the standard build files. Notice that in C++ projects the main item array driving the project compilation is named ClCompile, not ClCompiles, and in C# projects the main items are named Compile and None. For your own item arrays, whether for items to be Built, Deployed or Staged, keep the singular name.

```
<ItemGroup>
    <BuildItem Include="..." />
    <BuildItem Include="..." />
    <BuildItem Include="..." />

    <DeployItem Include="..." />
    <DeployItem Include="..." />
    <DeployItem Include="..." />

    <StageItem Include="..." />
    <StageItem Include="..." />
    <StageItem Include="..." />
</ItemGroup>
```

A good way to keep this consistent is to think of the item array symbol '@' as reading "array of" or "set of." With this reading convention, @(Build) is read "array of Build item." By the same token, @(BuildItem) can also be read "array of Build item," either convention will work just fine. This naming follows to targets, which often operate on individual items in an array, and tasks, which are often performed on a per-file basis, which are also commonly named singular. As an example, consider the naming of "GenerateResource" task and several targets named "GenerateResource..." as opposed to the plural "GenerateResources."

In the interest of readability, I tend to name the more significant items in one of two ways, either named after the target and task that will be used to perform the operation, as is the case with ClCompile for C++ targets, or as shown above, named after the target with an "Item" suffix.

I find that using the "Item" suffix prevents naming conflicts with just about any other standard extension and helps me to differentiate items that are part of my custom build from items that are part of the standard build. Regardless, if the "Item" suffix seems too redundant for your tastes, consider some common form that lends itself to a wildcard search, which can help out in a pinch when you need to dig through all of your projects and imports.

56. Recycle names for targets, properties and items

Names for targets, properties and items do not collide with each other. It can be convenient to reuse the exact same name for all three when together they form a single expression of functionality.

```
<PropertyGroup>
    <SomeTarget>...                               <!-- 1 -->
    <SomeTargetAdditional>...                     <!-- 2 -->
</PropertyGroup>

<ItemGroup>
    <SomeTarget Include="...                      <!-- 3 -->
</ItemGroup>

<Target Name="SomeTarget"
    Condition="'$(SkipSomeTarget)' != 'true'>     <!-- 4,5 -->
    <SomeTargetTask
        Items="@(SomeTarget)"
        Property="$(SomeTarget)"
        AdditionalProperty="$(SomeTargetAdditional)"
    />                                            <!-- 6 -->
```

In the code snippet above, the central theme of "SomeTarget" is apparent in the property names (1, 2), the item array (3), the name of the target (4) and the Skip property controlling the target (5), as well as the primary custom task (6) in the target. In the case of the properties and items, since they are each accessed with a unique syntax, $(SomeTarget) or @(SomeTarget), there is little chance for confusion, and keeping the names identical provides useful continuity and reduces the clutter that would appear if you forced unique—and probably redundantly formed— names, such as $(SomeTargetProperty) and @(SomeTargetItem).

Chapter 6
Tricks

Any programming language will have some nifty tricks available to a black belt programmer. Sometimes they involve doing in one line what normally takes a dozen. Sometimes their useful patterns, not always obvious from knowledge of the syntax. The best ones make your code more readable and maintainable, or faster. Since MSBuild is a bit of an oddball "language," most of these tricks that follow—the ones that have lent their usefulness to the title of this book—involve a manipulation of two or more basic mechanical features of the language in order to perform tasks that might seem simple in a more robust language, but that don't seem obvious at all to someone who's just poked around in a C# project file a few times.

Now of course it is always best to use the plainest, most conventional syntax and semantics you can—if only to help the developers that will have to read and maintain the build later, or dig through the log file. Nevertheless, sometimes to get something done, you just have to get Tricky, and this chapter will show you how to do just that. The tricks that follow are loosely grouped into sections, and occasionally build upon those that have preceded it.

Property Tricks

The basic property mechanics has already been fully discussed. But up until this point, only the default set of property functions—the set deemed "safe" and always available by default—have been covered. More are available, and this first set of tricks will explain how to set up your builds to take advantage of the full richness of the .NET Framework.

57. Know how to enable more property functions

The documentation for property functions lists the types and methods in the .NET Framework that are made available by default. This set of operations has been deemed safe for use in a build file; there isn't really a security risk inherent in allowing a build script to format a date. The general pattern established defines a syntax for the execution of static methods in these particular classes.

It turns out that there is an unsupported mechanism for opening up the whole world of the .NET Framework to MSBuild property functions, through the use of an environment variable. The primary reason this is considered unsupported is more likely than not the huge security hole this can open up. While formatting a date is benign, formatting a hard drive is pretty sinister, and this tweak opens that door a bit.

I'll start with a rather direct if not well-factored mechanism for triggering this functionality, and eventually show you a more concise way to wire this into your build in subsequent tricks.

The following target attempts to access a static property on System.Environment. As was shown earlier in *trick #9, Use property functions,* although the syntax below is valid, the particular property being referenced, ProcessorCount, is not on the list of allowed property functions, so a failure results.

TryToUseAnyStaticMethod (fails)

```
<Target Name="TryToUseAnyStaticMethod">
  <Message
    Text="ProcessorCount = '$([System.Environment]::
      ProcessorCount)'"
    /> <!-- Text="..." above is on line 44 -->
</Target>
```

Output

```
Project "...\Use Any Static in Property Function.trkproj" on node ↝
 1 (TryToUseAnyStaticMethod target(s)).
...\Use Any Static in Property Function.trkproj(44,13): error    ↝
MSB4185: The function "ProcessorCount" on type               ↝
"System.Environment" is not available for execution as an MSBuild ↝
property function.
```

MSBuild provides a backdoor for us though, which we'll sneak up on in a couple small steps.

Below is a generic mechanism for changing any environment variable, using an inline task.

Use Any Static in Property Function.trkproj

```
<UsingTask
  TaskName="SetEnvironmentVariable"
  TaskFactory="CodeTaskFactory"
  AssemblyFile="$(MSBuildToolsPath)\Microsoft.Build.Tasks./wrap ↪
v4.0.dll" >
  <ParameterGroup>                                        <!-- 1 -->
    <Variable ParameterType="System.String" Required="true" />
    <Value ParameterType="System.String" />
  </ParameterGroup>
  <Task>
    <Using Namespace="System" />
    <Code Type="Fragment" Language="cs">
    <![CDATA[
    // why this kind of try/catch isn't needed
    try
    {
        Log.LogMessage(                                    // 2
          "Current {0} is '{1}'",
          Variable,
          System.Environment.GetEnvironmentVariable(Variable));
        Log.LogMessage("Setting {0} to '{1}'",             // 3
          Variable,
          Value);
        System.Environment.SetEnvironmentVariable(         // 4
          Variable,
          Value,
          System.EnvironmentVariableTarget.Process);
    }
    catch (Exception e)
    {
        Log.LogMessage(e.Message);
    }
    ]]>
    </Code>
  </Task>
</UsingTask>
```

This inline task accepts (1) two strings, the first an environment variable name, the second a value for that variable. It then logs the current value of the specified environment variable (2), then another line showing what value will be set (3) before using System.Environment to change the value for the duration of the current process (4).

There is a comment in the code above that says, "why this kind of try/catch isn't needed." In the simple example above, there are no specific exceptions being captured, only a generic exception handler that logs the exception message. It happens that the task execution engine in

MSBuild is already wrapping the call to ITask.Execute in every task with a try/catch block. Any exceptions thrown out of a task will be caught and logged, either as an error or as a warning if ContinueOnError had been set for the task being executed.

It turns out that the backdoor MSBuild provides for us is triggered by another environment variable, in this case the rather descriptively named MSBuildEnableAllPropertyFunctions. The inline task above will be used to temporarily set this environment variable for the duration of the MSBuild process, so that all static methods and properties are available using the normal property function syntax.

EnableUseAnyStaticMethod

```
<Target Name="EnableUseAnyStaticMethod">
  <Message
    Text="NOTE: All property functions enabled "
    />
  <SetEnvironmentVariable
    Variable="MSBuildEnableAllPropertyFunctions"
    Value="1"
    />
  <Message Text="ProcessorCount = '$([System.Environment]::
    ProcessorCount)'"
    />
</Target>
```

Output

```
EnableUseAnyStaticMethod:
  NOTE: All property functions enabled
  Current MSBuildEnableAllPropertyFunctions is ''
  Setting MSBuildEnableAllPropertyFunctions to '1'
  ProcessorCount = '4'
```

Many of the tricks that follow rely on other non-standard property functions, and will need to ensure this environment variable is properly set up. Rather than have this become a tedious task, the next trick shows how to wrap up this behavior in a single import declaration.

58. Know how to alter environment variables

In your own build, instead of having to ensure the inline UsingTask is first defined locally or imported and then is properly called prior to any use of a property function requiring it, you can automate the behavior in a rather simple way. Also, to avoid possible typos in the rather lengthy names, and to formalize the use of the MSBuildEnableAllProperty-Functions environment variable, create an inline task specifically for this behavior, and set it up in such a manner that it executes automatically, as shown below:

EnableAllPropertyFunctions.tasks

```
<Project ...
    InitialTargets="ExecuteEnableAllPropertyFunctions">    <!-- 1 -->

    <UsingTask
       TaskName="EnableAllPropertyFunctions"
       TaskFactory="CodeTaskFactory"
       AssemblyFile="$(MSBuildToolsPath)\Microsoft.Build.Tasks    ⮑
.v4.0.dll">
       <ParameterGroup />
       <Task>
          <Using Namespace="System" />
          <Code Type="Fragment" Language="cs">
          <![CDATA[
          {
             string variable = "MSBuildEnableAllPropertyFunctions";
             string value = "1";
             string current = System.Environment
                .GetEnvironmentVariable(variable);

             if (current != null && current.Equals(value))
                return true;

             Log.LogMessage(
                "Current {0} is '{1}'",
                variable,
                current);
             Log.LogMessage("Setting {0} to '{1}'",
                variable,
                value);
             System.Environment.SetEnvironmentVariable(
                variable,
                value,
                System.EnvironmentVariableTarget.Process);
          }
          ]]>
          </Code>
       </Task>
    </UsingTask>

    <Target Name="ExecuteEnableAllPropertyFunctions">
       <EnableAllPropertyFunctions />                     <!-- 2 -->
       <PropertyGroup>
          <MSBuildEnableAllPropertyFunctions
             >1</MSBuildEnableAllPropertyFunctions>        <!-- 3 -->
       </PropertyGroup>
    </Target>
</Project>
```

This is essentially a duplicate of the SetEnvironmentVariable inline task defined above, but hardcodes the Variable and Value parameters, and it adds in some simple validation to ensure that the environment variable alteration and the display of the log messages only occur if the value isn't already set, so as not to clutter up your output logs. What makes this work, though, is the definition of the InitialTargets attribute (1) and the trivial implementation (2) of the initial target in which the custom inline task is called. Because of this, any project that imports this .tasks file, either directly or indirectly through a series of imports, can be assured that the environment variable will be set when any target executes, with one exception.

The exception is that any *other* InitialTargets that are imported prior to the import of this one will be executed too early to rest on the guarantee that the environment variable has been set by the execution of this initial target. Dependencies between one initial target and another are best avoided, but can be dealt with if your build files are structured in a manner that gives you control over the import sequence. It is also possible to use DependsOnTargets from one InitialTarget to another, so if a target needs to be specified as an InitialTarget and also requires that this property function enabling target is also executed, just list ExecuteEnableAllPropertyFunctions in the new target's DependsOn-Targets attribute.

What follows the call to the inline task in the listing above may seem a bit odd. An MSBuild property of the same name as the environment variable just set (3) is defined and set to the value "1," the same value the environment variable already holds. Since MSBuild already makes the values of environment variables available as properties, wouldn't a property of that name already have that value?

```
<EnableAllPropertyFunctions />
<Message
  Text="Value is '$(MSBuildEnableAllPropertyFunctions)'"
  />
```

It turns out that the above code would change the environment variable to "1," and then print out:

```
Value is ''
```

What is happening? Well, although MSBuild does allow the use of environment variables as properties, that particular usage is limited to the values those environment variables had when the environment was handed off to the MSBuild process. In this case, MSBuild has a copy of the original environment variable listing, and the change made to the current value isn't reflected in the environment variable based properties it knows about. To properly reflect the value of the environment-variable-turned-property, just setting a property to the expected value, as done in (3), will publish the property to MSBuild, or will overwrite MSBuild's now outdated value it picked up from whatever the value of the environment variable was when the build process started up and it cached them all. This technique should always be done when altering environment variables from within the build, as the C++ project system build also does when it uses its own custom "SetEnv" task in the Microsoft.Cpp.targets file.

Each project's environment block is segregated from that of other projects, so that build ordering doesn't affect the outcome. A single project can be used in several build requests in a single build, for example when building all projects in phases, and you'd expect that when a single project modifies its own environment in one pass that the modification would be present for a subsequent pass. Well, for 4.0 that behavior isn't complete, so you'll need to be sure you alter environment variables for each pass separately.

What follows are some additional property functions that couldn't be covered previously when the safe set of property functions was introduced, since they all require the use of the MSBuildEnable-AllPropertyFunctions environment variable in order to function. There are also some property functions that are always available, but which don't serve any useful purpose without relying on additional property functions that are only available with this particular tweak in place.

59. Know even more property functions

Each of the following target listings also requires the use of MSBuildEnableAllPropertyFunctions in order to function. They have done so using the .tasks file trick described in the previous trick, with the following import:

```
<Import Project="EnableAllPropertyFunctions.tasks" />
```

These two lines that follow have been removed from the output shown for these targets in the cases where they occurred, so if you run locally, you may see them as well as the output from the listing:

```
Current MSBuildEnableAllPropertyFunctions is ''
Setting MSBuildEnableAllPropertyFunctions to '1'
```

As was mentioned previously, the System.Enum property functions aren't of much use generally. With the extended property function set it is now possible to make use of them after all. Since some of these extended set of property functions are non-destructive, they may appear in the default set in future versions of MSBuild.

Enum Property Functions (reprise)

The System.Enum class is advertised as being available for use with property functions. However, many of the static functions, including System.Enum.GetNames take arguments that reject normal attempts to use them with MSBuild, which is limited to strings and such. Extending property functions to other types makes it possible to call such functions.

Even More Property Functions.trkproj, EnumPropertyFunctions target

```
<Import Project="EnableAllPropertyFunctions.tasks" />

<Target Name="EnumPropertyFunctions">
  <PropertyGroup>                                    <!-- 1 -->
    <SpecialFolderTypeName>System.Environment+SpecialFolder,
mscorlib, Version=4.0.0.0, Culture=neutral,
PublicKeyToken=b77a5c561934e089</SpecialFolderTypeName>
                                                     <!-- 2 -->
    <EnumGetNames>$([System.Enum]::
      GetNames($([System.Type]::
        GetType($(SpecialFolderTypeName)))))</EnumGetNames>
  </PropertyGroup>
  <ItemGroup>
    <SpecialFolder Include="$(EnumGetNames)" />      <!-- 3 -->
  </ItemGroup>
  <Message Text="%(SpecialFolder.Identity)" />       <!-- 4 -->
</Target>
```

Output

```
EnumPropertyFunctions:
  Desktop
  Programs
  Personal
  MyDocuments
  Favorites
  Startup
  Recent
  SendTo
  StartMenu
  MyMusic
  (etc...)
```

In this case, the EnumPropertyFunctions target above mimics a call to,

```
System.Enum.GetNames(typeof(System.Environment.SpecialFolder))
```

by nesting property functions.

A property named SpecialFolderTypeName (1) containing the strong name of the type is first declared. This can be simplified to just "System.Environment+SpecialFolder" if desired. The next property named EnumGetNames (2) is then declared. Notice that this uses a nested call to System.Type.GetType, in place of the *typeof* that was shown in the line of C# code above, since typeof is not available from within an MSBuild property function. Since SystemEnum.GetNames returns a value that is enumerable, MSBuild can convert it to a semicolon-delimited list which is then packed into the property EnumGetNames. This list is then split apart (3) into an item, and each element of the item set is displayed using a task-batched Message task.

Using the ::new Syntax

In addition to class static functions, class constructors can be called using ::new, followed by the constructor argument list.

UsingNewSyntax target

```
<Target Name="UsingNewSyntax">
    <Message Text="$([System.UriBuilder]::
        new('k7ranch.net').ToString())" />              <!-- 1 -->
    <Message Text="$([System.UriBuilder]::
        new('https', 'k7ranch.net', 8080).ToString())" /> <!-- 2 -->
</Target>
```

Output

```
UsingNewSyntax:
  http://k7ranch.net:80/
  https://k7ranch.net:8080/
```

In this case, a new instance (1) of System.UriBuilder is created, a partial Uri is passed to the constructor, and then ToString() is called on the UriBuilder instance that is created, in order to have a string to pass to the Message task. Noticing that the default "http" scheme and default port 80 was supplied; it is possible to construct other forms (2) using other constructors.

Using the ::set_ Syntax

Now it is also possible to alter properties on the returned instance using other syntax, but it leaves some interesting questions. To call the setter on a property, use the form ::set_, as shown below.

UsingSetSyntax target

```
<Target Name="UsingSetSyntax">
  <Message Text="$([System.UriBuilder]::
    new('http://k7ranch.net').set_Port(8080))" />
</Target>
```

Output

```
UsingSetSyntax:
```

In this case, after the instance is created, set_Port is called. Since the return type of set_Port is essentially void however, the Message task has nothing to log. Changing the call to create a syntax error, for example calling "SetPort" instead, creates an error:

```
...\Even More Property Function.trkproj(31,16): error MSB4184: The
expression ""http://k7ranch.net:80/".SetPort(8080)" cannot be
evaluated. Method 'System.UriBuilder.SetPort' not found.
```

This error indicates that the set_Port(8080) in the original is probably being called, however, there really doesn't seem to be much use for this in most cases, since you can't capture the intervening instance in an MSBuild variable and make use of it later on, for example as a parameter to another property function call. The set_ syntax is therefore probably only useful in cases where you are calling the setter on a static property, right?

Well it turns out that isn't all that useful either, without some interesting trickery, as will be shown next.

Using the ::set_ Syntax in Process

One static property with a public setter that could be considered of dubious use in a build is the process's current directory. I say dubious because relying on it is something you'd probably only do if you were also relying on a not-so-well-written external tool, one that you hadn't yet converted to a custom MSBuild task (note to Sheldon[13], this is one of those forms of speech you find troublesome).

UsingSetSyntaxInProcess target

```
<Target Name="UsingSetSyntaxInProcess">
  <PropertyGroup>
    <Current>$([System.Environment]::
      CurrentDirectory)\PathTo</Current>        <!-- 1 -->
  </PropertyGroup>
                                                <!-- 2 -->
  <Message
    Text="Change CurrentDirectory to '$(Current)'"
    />
                                                <!-- 3 -->
  <Message
    Text="$([System.Environment]::
      set_CurrentDirectory('$(Current)'))"
    />
                                                <!-- 4 -->
  <Message
    Text="CurrentDirectory is '$([System.Environment]::
      CurrentDirectory)'"
    />

  <Message Text="%0d" />                        <!-- 5 -->
  <Exec
    Command="cd $([System.Environment]::
      set_CurrentDirectory('$(Current)'))"
    />

  <Message Text="%0d" />                        <!-- 6 -->
  <Message
    Text="CurrentDirectory is '$([System.Environment]::
      CurrentDirectory)'"
    />
</Target>
```

Output

```
UsingSetSyntaxInProcess:
  Change CurrentDirectory to 'F:\Trickery\Source Code\PathTo'
  CurrentDirectory is 'F:\Trickery\Source Code'

  cd
  F:\Trickery\Source Code\PathTo

  CurrentDirectory is 'F:\Trickery\Source Code'
```

In this target, a dynamic property is declared (1) that captures the value of a folder beneath the current directory. In the code distribution, the

---

[13] Note to anyone who does not watch "The Big Bang Theory," Sheldon is, oh, never mind, you won't understand anyway, why do I even try. This footnote is recursive.

"PathTo" folder exists and is used in various examples, and this behavior requires that MSBuild is run from the folder containing the project file. Next a message is printed out (2) indicating what change is about to be attempted. This is followed by an odd usage of the Message task (3) which has a Text parameter consisting of a property function call that returns void. The Message task will not print anything if the Text parameter is empty, making it an oddly useful container for arbitrary property function calls in this example. Immediately thereafter (4) another Message task prints the current directory. As can be seen from the Output in the first message starting with "CurrentDirectory is," the directory appears not to have been changed.

It turns out that the directory was changed, but only for the duration of the Message task. This seems absurd until you consider what mechanism MSBuild must be employing in order to execute arbitrary code. Theorizing that it must have created a separate process or AppDomain in which the current directory was inherited, then changed, then discarded when the task execution completed, you can design an experiment to test this. The next steps of the example do exactly this. Instead of a Message task, the property function is embedded in the Command attribute (5) of an Exec task. Note that the command passed to the Exec task is a "cd" command followed by the set_CurrentDirectory property function. Since the property function returns a void, the net result passed to the Exec task is just the "cd " string. Looking at the output though, it can be seen that the cd command, which when called without argument displays the current directory, indicates that the current directory was indeed changed during the lifetime of the Exec task. A subsequent Message task (6) again reveals that the current directory has reverted to the value it had when the MSBuild execution from the command line started.

The way the Exec task operates internally is that the contents of the Command parameter are packed into a dynamically generated batch file and executed. It is possible then, to group together multiple commands for sequential execution,

```
<Exec
  Command="pushd . &amp; cd &amp; cd.. &amp; cd &amp; popd &amp; cd"
  />
```

which is an XML encoded sequence of commands more clearly seen as,

```
pushd . & cd
cd.. & cd
popd & cd
```

which will output the following,

```
ExecTest:
  pushd . & cd & cd.. & cd & popd & cd
  F:\Code\Trickery
  F:\Code
  F:\Code\Trickery
```

Using this knowledge, plus an understanding of how inline property functions behave when mixed in, you should be able to easily arrive at whatever behavior you're looking for.

Case Insensitive String Comparisons

While MSBuild performs Condition comparisons in a case insensitive manner, and is generally very forgiving when it comes to case sensitivity, there are times in your build where explicit control of string comparisons may be needed. The next target demonstrates a way to use property functions with the System.String class to perform them.

CaseInsensitiveComparison target

```xml
<Target Name="CaseInsensitiveComparison">
  <ItemGroup>
    <Cased Include="Mixed Case Item Number One" />      <!-- 1 -->
    <Cased Include="Mixed Case Item Number Two" />
    <Cased>                                             <!-- 2 -->
      <ToLower>$([System.String]::
          new('%(Identity)').
          ToLower())</ToLower>
    </Cased>
  </ItemGroup>

  <PropertyGroup>
    <StartsWith>mixed case</StartsWith>                 <!-- 3 -->
  </PropertyGroup>

  <ItemGroup>
    <Cased>                                             <!-- 4 -->
      <StartsWith>$([System.String]::
          new('%(ToLower)').
            StartsWith(
              '$(StartsWith)',
              System.StringComparison.OrdinalIgnoreCase)
            )</StartsWith>
    </Cased>
  </ItemGroup>

  <Message Text="StartsWith='$(StartsWith)'" />         <!-- 5 -->

  <Message Text="%0d" />
  <Message Text="Identity='%(Cased.Identity)'" />       <!-- 6 -->
```

```
    <Message Text="%0d" />
    <Message Text="ToLower='%(Cased.ToLower)'" />                    <!-- 7 -->

    <Message Text="%0d" />                                          <!-- 8 -->
    <Message
        Text="'%(Cased.Identity)' starts with '$(StartsWith)' = '%(
        Cased.StartsWith)'"
        />
  </Target>
```

Output

```
CaseInsensitiveComparison:
  StartsWith='mixed case'

  Identity='Mixed Case Item Number One'
  Identity='Mixed Case Item Number Two'

  ToLower='mixed case item number one'
  ToLower='mixed case item number two'

  'Mixed Case Item Number One' starts with 'mixed case' = 'True'
  'Mixed Case Item Number Two' starts with 'mixed case' = 'True'
```

In this example, an item array (1) containing mixed case strings is created. An item meta value named ToLower is then added to all items in the set (2) which contains the original identity transformed to lower case. As an aside, note the particular placement of the "." Before the call to ToLower, and later before the call to StartsWith. In other forms, the dot can be moved to the next line, but in this particular usage MSBuild requires the dot on the previous line, if you desire to form these using a mutli-line style.

Since each of the items starts with the mixed case string "Mixed Case," and since this is setting up a case insensitive comparison, a property named $(StartsWith) (3) is defined containing the lower case version of the string, to be used in the comparison later on. Next, a new item meta value is created, this one named "StartsWith" which contains the evaluation of the System.String.StartsWith method as called in a property function, which will return a Boolean result which will be converted to a string and held in this meta value.

Here is another aside; the PropertyGroup interlude between the first item meta created, the one named "ToLower" and the next one named "StartsWith" was intentional. If both of the item meta values were attempted in the same ItemGroup, as shown below,

```
    <ItemGroup>
      <Cased Include="Mixed Case Item Number One" />
      <Cased Include="Mixed Case Item Number Two" />
```

```
<Cased>
    <ToLower>...</ToLower>
    <StartsWith>...StartsWith>
</Cased>
</ItemGroup>
```

MSBuild would have issued the following error:

```
...\Even More Property Function.trkproj(112,7): error MSB4096: The
item "Mixed Case Item Number One" in item list "Cased" does not
define a value for metadata "ToLower".  In order to use this
metadata, either qualify it by specifying %(Cased.ToLower), or
ensure that all items in this list define a value for this metadata.
```

I've segregated them into separate PropertyGroup declarations, but even doing something as simple as this below would work:

```
<ItemGroup>
    <Cased Include="Mixed Case Item Number One" />
    <Cased Include="Mixed Case Item Number Two" />
    <Cased>
        <ToLower>...</ToLower>
    </Cased>
    <Cased>
        <StartsWith>...StartsWith>
    </Cased>
</ItemGroup>
```

MSBuild requires that the item being modified, in this case the one named @(Cased), be "closed off" with an intervening </Cased> before it publishes the new meta to the item. Since the second meta "StartsWith" makes reference to the one just created, it needs to be fully created and published before it can be referenced in the next one.

Careening wildly back to the point[14], we've now got ourselves an item array with one meta value containing the lowercased version of the identity string, another meta value containing the results of the case insensitive property function comparison. The comparison property (5) the item (6) and the first meta value (7) are logged for each item, followed by the second meta value (8) in sentence form, indicating the results of the case insensitive comparison.

File and Folder discrimination

It was mentioned briefly in the introductory section on Conditions that there is no way when using the Exists condition to determine whether or

---

[14] As David T. would say.

not the path being tested is a file or a folder; the result is "true" either way. Using File IO property functions these two can be distinguished.

IsFileOrFolder target

```
<Target Name="IsFileOrFolder">
  <Exec Command="dir /d PathTo\*.*" />                    <!-- 1 -->
  <Message
    Condition="$([System.IO.Directory]::
      Exists('./PathTo'))"
    Text="'PathTo' is a folder."
    />
  <Message
    Condition="$([System.IO.File]::
      Exists('./PathTo'))"
    Text="'PathTo' is a file."
    />
  <Message
    Condition="$([System.IO.Directory]::
      Exists('./PathTo/one.txt'))"
    Text="'PathTo\one.txt' is a folder."
    />
  <Message
    Condition="$([System.IO.File]::
      Exists('./PathTo/one.txt'))"
    Text="'PathTo\one.txt' is a file."
    />
</Target>
```

Output

```
IsFileOrFolder:
  dir /d PathTo\*.*

  Directory of F:\Code\Trickery\Source Code\PathTo

  [.]        [..]       One.txt    [Recurse] Two.txt
                  2 File(s)               0 bytes
             3 Dir(s)   430,871,515,136 bytes free

  'PathTo' is a folder.
  'PathTo\one.txt' is a file.
```

The listing above shows the use of System.IO.Directory.Exists and System.IO.Path.Exists. The current path is shown with an execution of the dir command (1), followed by tests of "PathTo" which is a folder, and "one.txt" which is a file within the folder; both of these are used in other sample scripts. Important to note is that although the Exists condition is always available, it can't discriminate between the two, but the use of these static methods requires activation of the MSBuildEnableAll-PropertyFunctions environment variable.

32 and 64 Bitness

If you've not yet suffered the joy of mixed 32 and 64–bit development consider yourself lucky. The mess of environment variable checking hinted at in *trick #19, Consider using the standard extensions path,* can be put behind us though, with what may be the most useful property functions with respect to mixed platform building, two new properties made available on System.Environment in the .NET 4.0 Framework.

Bitness target

```
<Target Name="Bitness">
  <Message Text="Is64BitOperatingSystem = '$([System.Environment]::
    Is64BitOperatingSystem)'"
    />
  <Message Text="Is64BitProcess = '$([System.Environment]::
    Is64BitProcess)'"
    />
</Target>
```

Output, when run from the standard VS command prompt on 64-bit OS

```
Bitness:
  Is64BitOperatingSystem = 'True'
  Is64BitProcess = 'False'
```

Output, when run from the 64-bit VS command prompt on 64-bit OS

```
Bitness:
  Is64BitOperatingSystem = 'True'
  Is64BitProcess = 'Trus'
```

These are really quite self-explanatory. What isn't so obvious is how you would use them in a multi-platform build. Although for a production build it isn't such a concern, since the build machines will likely be properly provisioned, for developer builds it can be a different story.

Item Array Membership Tricks

Items are the most complex data type available in MSBuild, and are central to the more interesting tricks available to developers. We're about to start a series of sections covering all of the possible manipulations, starting with tricks that demonstrate control over the membership of data items in item arrays.

60. How to exclude items from an existing item array

In the listing that follows, a static item array is set up that contains several files (1). Later, in the execution of the Filter target, two different techniques are shown for excluding items based on a file pattern. First, some of these items are effectively removed by filtering (2) during the creation of a new item array. Next, the items are removed (3) from the original item array. Message tasks are used to display the contents of the item arrays at various points in the execution.

Directory listing

```
one.txt
one.extra.txt
two.txt
```

Items/Exclude Items.trkproj

```
<Project ... InitialTargets="Initial">
  <ItemGroup>                                        <!-- 1 -->
    <Item Include="one.txt" />
    <Item Include="two.txt" />
    <Item Include="one.extra.txt" />
    <Item Include="one.file.doesn't.exist" />
  </ItemGroup>

  <Target Name="Initial">
    <Message Text="@(Item)" />
  </Target>

  <Target Name="ExcludeItems">
    <ItemGroup>
      <ItemCopy
        Include="@(Item)"
        Exclude="one.*" />                           <!-- 2 -->
      <Item
        Remove="one.*" />                            <!-- 3 -->
    </ItemGroup>
    <Message Text="Copy: @(ItemCopy)" />
    <Message Text="Orig: @(Item)" />
    <ItemGroup>
      <Item Remove="one.file.doesn't.exist" />       <!-- 4 -->
    </ItemGroup>
    <Message Text="Then: @(Item)" />
  </Target>
</Project>
```

Output of target ExcludeItems

```
Initial:
  one.txt;two.txt;one.extra.txt;one.file.doesn't.exist
ExcludeItems:
  Copy: two.txt;one.file.doesn't.exist
```

```
Orig: two.txt;one.file.doesn't.exist
Then: two.txt
```

Take note that in the original directory listing, the file referenced in the item array named "one.file.doesn't.exist" does not actually exist on disk, while the other three files in the item array do. The files that exist are treated as items differently than those that do not, when it comes to the use of wildcards, which are a notion specific only to items representing files and directories. The Exclude and Remove attributes in (2) and (3) both use wildcards to cause the removal. Since the item with the identity "one.file.doesn't.exist" isn't related to a file system object, the exclusion based on a file system pattern does not apply to it. In other words, don't assume that those patterns will be used to find matches on the identity values for non-file system items, even if the pattern would match it if it were a file.

Finally, at (4) this non-file item is removed using the full identity value, as shown in the final message.

Note that the Remove attribute can only be used on an existing item array. The following, as a replacement for line (2) above, would not work since prior to that line the item array named @(ItemCopy) does not exist. Said more precisely, even if the item array exists you can't specify both an Include and a Remove attribute on the same item declaration at the same time. As a result, you can't swap out the content of a list in a single line. Similarly, because the Remove attribute doesn't exist for an Output element, you'll likewise need to use a temporary item array to swap out the contents of any item array output by a task.

You can also remove items from one item array based on their membership in a second item array, when the identity values are the same.

Items/Exclude Items from Other.trkproj

```
<ItemGroup>
  <These Include="*.txt" />                           <!-- 1 -->
  <Other Include="one.txt" />                          <!-- 2 -->
</ItemGroup>

<Target Name="ExcludeItemsFromOther">
  <Message Text="These: @(These)" />                   <!-- 3 -->
  <Message Text="Other: @(Other)" />                   <!-- 4 -->
  <ItemGroup>
    <These Remove="@(Other)" />
  </ItemGroup>
  <Message Text="These: @(These)" />
</Target>
```

Output

```
ExcludeItemsFromOther:
  These: one.extra.txt;one.txt;two.txt
  Other: one.txt
  These: one.extra.txt;two.txt
```

The target above declares two item arrays, @(These) and @(Other), (1) and (2). The *Other* array contains a single file, which is one of the several files in the *These* array. The contents of the initial arrays is shown at the start of the target (3) and (4). Next, the Remove attribute of an item definition is used, to operate on the @(These) array, removing any members of this array that are in the specified @(Other) array. This removal is performed in-place on the array; when printed it shows the item has been removed.

61. How to exclude items based on meta values

It is possible to use the Exclude attribute in an item declaration to filter items based on particular built-in or custom meta values, as well as using an item specification as was just shown.

Items/Exclude Items with Meta.trkproj

```
<Project ...
  InitialTargets="InitialExcludeItems">

  <Target Name="InitialExcludeItems">
    <Message Text="@(ItemWithMeta)" />
  </Target>

  <ItemGroup>
    <ItemWithMeta Include="one.txt">
      <Ignore>true</Ignore>
    </ItemWithMeta>
    <ItemWithMeta Include="two.txt">
      <Ignore>false</Ignore>
    </ItemWithMeta>
    <ItemWithMeta Include="one.extra.txt" />
    <ItemWithMeta Include="file.doesn't.exist">
      <Ignore>true</Ignore>
    </ItemWithMeta>
  </ItemGroup>

  <Target Name="ExcludeItems">
    <Message
      Condition="'@(ItemWithMeta->'%(Ignore)')' ==
        'true;false;;true'"
      Text="Ignored: @(ItemWithMeta->'%(Ignore)')"
      />
    <ItemGroup>
```

```
    <ItemWithMeta
        Condition="'%(ItemWithMeta.Ignore)' == 'true'"
        Remove="%(Identity)"
        />                                              <!-- 3 -->
    </ItemGroup>
    <Message Text="Ignored: @(ItemWithMeta)" />
    <Message
        Condition="'@(ItemWithMeta->'%(Ignore)')' != 'Foo'"
        Text="Ignored: @(ItemWithMeta->'%(Ignore)')"
        />
</Target
```

Output of target ExcludeItems

```
InitialExcludeItems:
  one.txt;two.txt;one.extra.txt;file.doesn't.exist
ExcludeItems:
  Ignored: two.txt;one.extra.txt
```

In this listing, only items with a meta value of Ignore=true are excluded (3). In this case, notice that because meta values instead of identity wildcards are being used, the treatment of file versus non-file items is identical.

Note that the meta value in the Condition at (3) could have been specified using the alternate syntax @(ItemWithMeta->'%(Ignore)') instead. Given the semantics of the use of that syntax in other situations, it appears as though this form is given slightly different treatment in Conditions on Item declarations than used elsewhere. For the confusion this seems to add, I stick with the batching syntax, since it is more obvious. Effectively, as a result of batching, the item array at (3) can be thought of as being expanded to multiple individual declarations:

Original

```
<ItemGroup>
  <ItemWithMeta
      Condition="'%(ItemWithMeta.Ignore)' == 'true'"
      Remove="%(Identity)" />
</ItemGroup>
```

Effectively expanded to (pseudo-code, not valid MSBuild)

```
<ItemGroup>
  <ItemWithMeta
      Condition="'one.txt.%(Ignore)' == 'true'"
      Remove="one.txt" />
  <ItemWithMeta
      Condition="'two.txt.%(Ignore)' == 'true'"
      Remove="two.txt" />
  <ItemWithMeta
      Condition="'one.extra.txt.%(Ignore)' == 'true'"
```

```
                Remove="one.extra.txt" />
        <ItemWithMeta
            Condition="'file.doesn't.exist.%(Ignore)' == 'true'"
            Remove="file.doesn't.exist" />
    </ItemGroup>
```

In this pseudo-code, the first and last conditions evaluate to 'true' ==
'true' and those named items are removed.

When you consider this technique in terms of file-based item arrays, and
consider the use of well-known meta values in addition to custom values,
you get some powerful item manipulation techniques. The following
takes an item array with many file types and splits them out to several
groups specific to a file extension.

Items/Exclude Items with BuiltIn Meta.trkproj

```
<Project ...>
   <ItemGroup>
      <AllFiles Include="*.cs" />
      <AllFiles Include="*.fs" />
      <AllFiles Include="*.cpp" />
   </ItemGroup>
   <Target Name="ExcludeItemsUsingBuiltInMeta">
      <ItemGroup>
         <CsFiles Include="@(AllFiles)" />
         <FsFiles Include="@(AllFiles)" />
         <CppFiles Include="@(AllFiles)" />

         ...some processing skipped...

         <CsFiles
            Condition="'%(CsFiles.Extension)' != '.cs'"
            Remove="%(Identity)"
            />
         <FsFiles
            Condition="'%(FsFiles.Extension)' != '.fs'"
            Remove="%(Identity)"
            />
         <CppFiles
            Condition="'%(CppFiles.Extension)' != '.cpp'"
            Remove="%(Identity)"
            />
      </ItemGroup>
      <Message Text="All: @(AllFiles)" />
      <Message Text="C#: @(CsFiles)" />
      <Message Text="F#: @(FsFiles)" />
      <Message Text="C++: @(CppFiles)" />
   </Target>
</Project>
```

Output

```
All: 1.cs;2.cs;1.fs;2.fs;1.cpp;2.cpp
C#: 1.cs;2.cs
F#: 1.fs;2.fs
C++: 1.cpp;2.cpp
```

In this case, the meta value %(Extension) is a well-known value that exists because each of the items is an actual file on the file system. Notice that the Extension value always begins with the dot and the dot is required in the comparison expression.

62. How to include items that don't exist when the build starts

Way back in Chapter 2, in *trick #5, Consider complex items for task parameters*, a brief discussion about declaring complex items with the paths encoded in metadata instead of the item specification was introduced, for the purpose of describing an alternative mechanism for passing item information into custom tasks. Taking this one step further, we'll now consider a similar processing of the same sort of items, this time without custom coding of any sort, in order to fully explore some more advanced item array manipulations.

From Items/Complex Items.trkproj

```
<Project ...
  DefaultTargets="Build">

  <ItemGroup>                                    <!-- 1 -->
    <Complex Include="Item01">
      <Path>./complex</Path>
      <File>Item01.txt</File>
      <Tag>alpha</Tag>
    </Complex>
    <Complex Include="Item02">
      <Path>./complex</Path>
      <File>Item02.txt</File>
      <Tag>bravo</Tag>
    </Complex>
    <Complex Include="Item03">
      <Path>./complex</Path>
      <File>Item03.txt</File>
    </Complex>
  </ItemGroup>
  <ItemDefinitionGroup>
    <Complex>
      <Tag>default-tag</Tag>                      <!-- 2 -->
    </Complex>
  </ItemDefinitionGroup>
```

```xml
<!-- ensure the files don't exist -->
<Target Name="DeleteItems"
    Outputs="%(Complex.Identity)">                      <!-- 3 -->
    <Delete Files="%(Complex.Path)/%(File)"
        />
</Target>

<!-- report that the files don't exist -->
<Target Name="ReportItems"
    Outputs="%(Complex.Identity)">                      <!-- 4 -->
    <Message
        Condition="Exists('%(Complex.Path)/%(File)')"
        Text="file '%(Path)/%(File)' exists"
        />
    <Message
        Condition="!Exists('%(Complex.Path)/%(File)')"
        Text="no file '%(Path)/%(File)' exists"
        />
</Target>

<!-- create folders and files -->
<Target Name="CreateItems"
    Outputs="%(Complex.Identity)">                      <!-- 5 -->
    <MakeDir
        Condition="!Exists('%(Complex.Path)')"
        Directories="%(Path)"
        />
    <Touch
        Condition="!Exists('%(Complex.Path)/%(File)')"
        Files="%(Path)/%(File)"
        AlwaysCreate="true"
        />
    <Message
        Condition="Exists('%(Complex.Path)/%(File)')"
        Text="file '%(Path)/%(File)' created"
        />
</Target>

<!-- synthesize item spec for a renamed copy of the items -->
<Target Name="SynthesizeItems"
    Outputs="%(Complex.Identity)">                      <!-- 6 -->
    <ItemGroup>                                         <!-- 7 -->
        <_ComplexCopy Include="%(Complex.Path)/%(File)"><!-- 8 -->
            <Tag>%(Tag)</Tag>                           <!-- 9 -->
        </_ComplexCopy>
    </ItemGroup>
</Target>

<!-- report files with matching tag that exist -->
<Target Name="Build"
    DependsOnTargets="
        DeleteItems;
        ReportItems;
        CreateItems;
        SynthesizeItems">                               <!-- 10 -->
```

```
      <Message
        Condition="'%(_ComplexCopy.Tag)' != 'alpha'"
        Text="skipping '%(Identity)' tag is '%(Tag)'"
        />                                              <!-- 11 -->
      <Message
        Condition="Exists('%(_ComplexCopy.Identity)') AND
           '%(Tag)' == 'alpha'"
        Text="file '%(Identity)' exists with tag '%(Tag)'"
        />                                              <!-- 12 -->
      <Message
        Condition="!Exists('%(_ComplexCopy.Identity)') AND
           '%(Tag)' == 'alpha'"
        Text="no file '%(Identity)' exists"
        />                                              <!-- 13 -->
  </Target>
</Project>
```

Output

```
DeleteItems:
  Deleting file "./complex/Item01.txt".
DeleteItems:
  Deleting file "./complex/Item02.txt".
ReportItems:
  no file './complex/Item01.txt' exists
ReportItems:
  no file './complex/Item02.txt' exists
ReportItems:
  no file './complex/Item03.txt' exists
CreateItems:
  Creating "./complex/Item01.txt" because "AlwaysCreate" was spec...
  file './complex/Item01.txt' created
CreateItems:
  Creating "./complex/Item02.txt" because "AlwaysCreate" was spec...
  file './complex/Item02.txt' created
CreateItems:
  Creating "./complex/Item03.txt" because "AlwaysCreate" was spec...
  file './complex/Item03.txt' created
Build:
  skipping './complex/Item02.txt' tag is 'bravo'
  skipping './complex/Item03.txt' tag is 'default-tag'
  file './complex/Item01.txt' exists with tag 'alpha'
```

Notice that for each individual task, since only one item array is being referred to, the meta only needs to be fully qualified as %(Complex.Meta) the first time it is encountered, and can specify just the meta value as %(Meta) for each subsequent usage, but only within a single task. Thus, the full path can be specified with %(Complex.Path)/%(File).

Walking through the long listing, the complex item array is declared (1) each with a unique item specification and each with separate Path, File, and Tag meta, except for Item03 which does not declare a Tag, thus inheriting the default value (2) from the ItemDefinitionGroup that follows. Execution begins in the Build target (10) running the dependent targets in order, starting with DeleteItems (3). Each of these dependent targets executes in order using a similar mechanism. Because the target specifies Outputs using the %( ) syntax, and no inputs, the target is set up to use target batching, and will execute once for each item in the @(Complex) item array. Within the targets (3), (4), (5) the path to the transient files is synthesized from the item meta values for the Path and File. The DeleteItems target (3) deletes the files one-by-one if they already exist. The ReportItems target (4) reports whether or not each of the files exists, essentially to prove that DeleteItems worked, and also to demonstrate that @(Complex) can't possibly be composed of file based items, as if that were not obvious from the declaration. The CreateItems target (5) ensures that the folders specified in the Path meta values exist, then recreates the files using the Touch task with AlwaysCreate set to true, to create empty files.

In Synthesize items (6), a new dynamic item array named @(_ComplexCopy) is created (7). Each batched iteration of the target will add a single new item to this item array, one for each item in the @(Complex) item array that is used to drive the target batching. Significantly, this new item array is comprised of actual file based items, since the path and file name are specified as the item specification (8) in the Include attribute. The Tag meta value from the %(Complex) item is copied (9) to a meta value of the same name for the items in this new item array.

Finally, the Build target (10) executes, running one of three separate messages conditioned on whether or not the file exists, and also on whether or not the copied Tag meta value matches the string "alpha." The output listing demonstrates that all three files were deleted (as this was not the first time the target was run on my machine), but then all three were recreated, and the files then triggered two of the possible conditions, with only a single file matching the desired Tag value.

63. How to count items in an item array

Item functions can be used to do some interesting processing of lists of items, but there is no obvious way to get a simple count of how many items are in an item array. Using some trickery, it is possible.

This technique involves first making a new item array out of a transformation of the array to be counted, transforming the contents of this transformed item array into a property, and then using property functions to perform a count. This first example shows how to do this in with some heavy manipulation, followed up with a shortcut that does the same thing. The benefit of this longer version is, I surmise, that it shows some deft translation of an item array that might not otherwise be intuitive or possible. The benefit of the next version is, well, it's much easier.

Count of Items.trkproj

```xml
<!-- 1 -->
<ItemGroup>
   <Item Include="Item01" />
   <Item Include="Item02" />
   <Item Include="Item03" />
   <Item Include="Item04" />
</ItemGroup>

<Target Name="CountItems">
   <!-- 2 -->
   <Message Text="Item: '@(Item)'" />

   <!-- 3 -->
   <ItemGroup>
      <_Item Include=".">                          <!-- 4 -->
         <Fake>%(Item.Identity)</Fake>             <!-- 5 -->
      </_Item>
   </ItemGroup>
   <PropertyGroup>
      <_Item>@(_Item, '+')</_Item>                 <!-- 6 -->
   </PropertyGroup>

   <!-- 7 -->
   <Message Text="_Item: '$(_Item)'" />

   <!-- 8 -->
   <Message Text="_Item.Length: $(_Item.Length)" />

   <!-- 9 -->
   <Message Text="Count of Item is: $(
      [MSBuild]::Divide(
         $([MSBuild]::Add(
            1,
            $(_Item.Length))),
         2))"
      />
</Target>
```

Output

```
Item: 'Item01;Item02;Item03;Item04'
_Item: '.+.+.+.'
_Item.Length: 7
Count of Item is: 4
```

An item array @(Items) with four items (1) is declared. Note that each item has a unique item specification. These items are displayed using a message (2) that shows the list flattened to a semicolon delimited list, which is the default format used for item array. Next a new item array is created (3) from the original, named @(_Items), using task batching to iteratively create a new item from the original list. Because this is batched using %(Item.Identity), and because there are unique values for each of the original four items, the new item array ends up with four items also. The distinction is that each of these four items contains the same item specification (4), a single dot. The original item specification is placed into the new items in @(_Item) as an item meta value (5) named Fake.

This new item array, composed of four items each with the item specification "." is then flattened into a property (6), this time delimited by a plus sign. This property, named $(_Item) is then displayed (7), showing ".+.+." as the value. The length of this property is displayed (8) using the string property function Length, there are seven characters, four characters from the single character identities, and three delimiters.

Finally, it is simple integer math (9) to calculate the number of distinct items in the original item array, adding 1 and dividing by 2, using the built-in MSBuild property functions Add and Divide.

A shorter version of the same functionality is shown next.

Count of Items, CountItemsSplit target

```
<Target Name="CountItemsSplit">
    <PropertyGroup>
        <_Item>@(Item)</_Item>                       <!-- 10 -->
    </PropertyGroup>

    <Message
        Text="Count of Item is: $(_Item.Split(';').Length)"
        />                                           <!-- 11 -->
</Target>
```

This next version takes advantage of the evaluation of property functions. First, the item array is flattened into a property (10) which will become a semicolon-delimited list. The call to String.Split (11) passing this string, returns an array, and before MSBuild has a chance to convert the array back into the delimited string, the Length property is retrieved, which contains the dimension of the array, which is also the number of items in the original array.

For the even easier usage,

```
@(Item->Count())
```

well, we'll all just have to perform item array crunching while we wait for a future version of MSBuild!

64. How to merge two different item arrays

Two separate item arrays can easily be combined into a third; simply reference both in the Include attribute of a one-line declaration for a new item array.

Items/More Items.trkproj, MergeItems target

```
<ItemGroup>
    <Item Include="one" />                              <!-- 1 -->
    <Item Include="two" />
    <Item Include="three" />
    <Item Include="four" />
    <Add Include="three" />                             <!-- 2 -->
    <Add Include="four" />
    <Add Include="five" />
</ItemGroup>

<Target Name="MergeItems">
    <Message Text="Item: @(Item)" />                    <!-- 3 -->
    <Message Text="Add: @(Add)" />                      <!-- 4 -->
    <ItemGroup>
        <Merged Include="@(Item);@(Add)" />             <!-- 5 -->
    </ItemGroup>
    <Message Text="Merged: @(Merged)" />                <!-- 6 -->
    <ItemGroup>
        <Distinct Include="@(Merged->Distinct())" />    <!-- 7 -->
    </ItemGroup>
    <Message Text="Distinct: @(Distinct)" />
</Target>
```

Output

```
MergeItems:
  Item: one;two;three;four
  Add: three;four;five
  Merged: one;two;three;four;three;four;five
  Distinct: one;two;three;four;five
```

Two item arrays, @(Item) and @(Add), (1) and (2), are declared and then displayed in the target (3) and (4). A new item array, @(Merged) is then declared to include both (5). Although in this example this new item array is dynamically created, this works the same with statically declared arrays as well. When the new array is displayed (6) you can see that the repeated items have been duplicated, note that "three" and "four" appear in both of the original arrays, and each appears twice in the merged array.

The next lines (7) show the use of the Distinct item function to get the array back to a list of unique items.

This has just shown items with no metadata, the next example shows what happens to metadata when item arrays are merged:

Items/More Items.trkproj, MergeMeta target

```
<ItemGroup>
  <Alpha Include="A1">                                    <!-- 1 -->
    <MetaId>1</MetaId>
  </Alpha>
  <Alpha Include="A2">
    <MetaId>2</MetaId>
  </Alpha>

  <Bravo Include="B3">                                    <!-- 2 -->
    <MetaId>3</MetaId>
    <Extra>Extra1</Extra>
  </Bravo>
  <Bravo Include="B4">
    <MetaId>4</MetaId>
    <Extra>Extra2</Extra>
  </Bravo>
  <Bravo Include="A1">                                    <!-- 3 -->
    <MetaId>5</MetaId>
    <Extra>Extra3</Extra>
  </Bravo>
</ItemGroup>

<Target Name="MergeMeta">
  <ItemGroup>
    <AlphaBravo Include="@(Alpha);@(Bravo)" />            <!-- 4 -->
  </ItemGroup>
  <Message Text="AlphaBravo.MetaId: '%(
    Identity).%(AlphaBravo.MetaId)'" />
  <Message Text="AlphaBravo.Extra: '%(
    Identity).%(AlphaBravo.Extra)'" />
</Target>
```

Output

```
MergeMeta:
  AlphaBravo.MetaId: 'A1.1'
  AlphaBravo.MetaId: 'A2.2'
  AlphaBravo.MetaId: 'B3.3'
  AlphaBravo.MetaId: 'B4.4'
  AlphaBravo.MetaId: 'A1.5'
  AlphaBravo.Extra: 'A1.'
  AlphaBravo.Extra: 'A2.'
  AlphaBravo.Extra: 'B3.Extra1'
  AlphaBravo.Extra: 'B4.Extra2'
  AlphaBravo.Extra: 'A1.Extra3'
```

Two item arrays @(Alpha) and @(Bravo) are declared at (1, 2). All items in both arrays contain custom metadata named %(MetaId), each of which is unique across all items. The @(Bravo) array also declares an additional metadata item named %(Extra). Of note, in the *Bravo* item array (3) one of the items has the same item specification "A1" as an item previously declared in the *Alpha* item array. Pay attention to how these items are kept separate from one another, and not aggregated when the item arrays are merged, which will be evidenced by the item metadata that is preserved when items are copied into the merged item array.

In the target, both item arrays are merged (4), and the contents of the merged array are displayed. First notice that all of the metadata from all items was retained when the two item arrays were merged into a new one. New items were created in the new item array and all of the metadata was copied to these new items.

From the listing you can see that all items contain the %(MetaId) metadata, but the items originally from the Alpha array do not have an %(Extra) metadata value.

Also from the fifth and last lines of the listing, notice that the *Bravo* item created at (3) with the duplicated item specification, rather than being merged with the item from *Alpha* with the same identity, instead created a new item, with its own metadata.

65. How to set metadata on some items but not others

It is possible to modify existing metadata or add new metadata to existing items in an item array, using the metadata extension syntax in a dynamic item array. It is also possible to be selective, with the use of Condition attributes, so that new or altered metadata is only applied to some items and not to others.

Items/More Items.trkproj, ChangeMetaSometimes target

```
<ItemGroup>
  <Partial Include="P1">
    <MetaId>1</MetaId>
  </Partial>
  <Partial Include="P2">
    <MetaId>2</MetaId>
  </Partial>
</ItemGroup>
<Target Name="ChangeMetaSometimes">
  <ItemGroup>                                          <!-- 1 -->
```

```
        <Partial Condition="'%(MetaId)' > '1'">        <!-- 4 -->
            <MetaId>Changed</MetaId>                    <!-- 2 -->
            <New>%(MetaId)</New>                        <!-- 3 -->
        </Partial>
    </ItemGroup>
    <Message Text="Partial.MetaId.New: '%(Identity
        ).%(MetaId).%(Partial.New)'" />
  </Target>
```

Output

```
ChangeMetaSometimes:
  Alpha.MetaId.New: 'P1.1.'
  Alpha.MetaId.New: 'P2.Changed.2'
```

In the listing above a new item array is declared named @(Partial), where each item contains a unique %(MetaId) metadata value. Within the target, the metadata extension syntax form of a dynamic item array (1) alters the value of the %(MetaId) metadata (2) and adds a new metadata value (3). These changes though are conditionally applied (4) only to items where the value of %(MetaId) is greater than one, which in this example would only apply to the second item.

When the resulting values are displayed there are a number of interesting things to note. First it can be seen that only item P2 had the value of %(MetaId) changed, and only that item received the new metadata value, as would be expected from the conditional expression.

What is interesting is when you notice how the value of %(New) is applied,

```
            <MetaId>Changed</MetaId>
            <New>%(MetaId)</New>
```

Notice that %(New) captures its value from %(MetaId), which was just changed on the line above. However, you can see from the output that %(New) retained the value of %(MetaId) prior to the metadata alteration. If it had not, the output would read,

```
  Alpha.MetaId.New: 'P2.Changed.Changed'
```

All of the metadata values are captured prior to any changes, and those captured values are used throughout. The new metadata values are not "published" until the item declaration is closed. Understanding how this operates, an alternative becomes apparent, you could instead declare this as,

```
    <Partial>
      <MetaId Condition="'%(MetaId)' > '1'">Changed</MetaId>
    </Partial>
```

and still end up with the proper result, as the value used in the condition is the value prior to the alteration.

Also notable is the specific syntax used to display the items and their metadata,

```
%(Identity).%(MetaId).%(Partial.New)
```

It has been discussed previously that when using the metadata batching syntax, you only need to fully qualify one of the metadata expressions, and that MSBuild can figure out the rest as long as a single item is involved or there are no metadata name conflicts if multiple items are invoved. However, when you force MSBuild to deduce the values, MSBuild requires that the metadata actually exists. In other words, since the %(New) metadata does not exist on item P1, any of the following alternate syntax, where %(New) is not qualified but other parts of the expression are,

```
%(Partial.Identity).%(MetaId).%(New)
%(Identity).%(Partial.MetaId).%(New)
%(Partial.Identity).%(Partial.MetaId).%(New)
```

would have caused MSBuild to emit an error of the form,

```
F:\Code\...\More Items.trkproj(76,7): error MSB4096: The item "P1" in
item list "Partial" does not define a value for metadata "New".  In
order to use this metadata, either qualify it by specifying
%(Partial.New), or ensure that all items in this list define a value
for this metadata.
```

It is perfectly acceptable to fully qualify more than one item, but in this example at least one of them would need to be the value %(Partial.New), since it doesn't exist on all items.

Item Array Target Output Batching Tricks

For precise control of target execution, target output batching with item arrays, declared with item metadata references in the target Outputs parameter, is central to most advanced MSBuild usage. We've finally reached the point where all the fundamentals have been covered, and this next section of tricks reveals some interesting tricks based on target batching operations.

66. Use dependent targets creatively

This next trick can be a building block for all sorts of data driven build behavior. It will start out slow and obvious, with some hardcoded MSBuild, then peel it apart into a data driven—though still simplistic— target that alludes to some arbitrary build actions.

To start with, a target will create two folders directly,

Items/Creative use of items.trkproj, EnsureFolderExists target

```
<Target Name="EnsureFolderExists">
   <MakeDir
      Directories="hardcoded1"
      />
   <MakeDir
      Directories="hardcoded2"
      />
</Target>
```

Output

```
EnsureFolderExists:
  Creating directory "hardcoded1".
  Creating directory "hardcoded2".
```

The target above simply creates the folders if they don't already exist by using the built-in MakeDir task. The obvious first step in the generalization of this would be to use items for the folders, and create them indirectly by batching the MakeDir task on the items,

EnsureFolderExistsIndirect target

```
<ItemGroup>
   <Folder Include="indirect1" />
   <Folder Include="indirect2" />
</ItemGroup>
<Target Name="EnsureFolderExistsIndirect">
   <MakeDir
      Directories="%(Folder.Identity)"
      />
</Target>
```

Output

```
EnsureFolderExistsIndirect:
  Creating directory "indirect1".
  Creating directory "indirect2".
```

The functionality is intact, including the conditional check. This approach may be enough, but often the creation of folders if they don't exist is just one piece of a larger activity. Perhaps there are multiple items being used in a more sophisticated way—we'll get to some of these approaches in some tricks that follow—or perhaps, you are composing a complex operation, where the path is just one piece of the data, as shown below, where the folders are described as just one piece of item metadata.

Prepare target

```
<ItemGroup>
  <PrepareItem Include="Unique1">
    <Folder>folder1</Folder>                          <!-- 1 -->
    <Other>one.txt</Other>                            <!-- 2 -->
  </PrepareItem>
  <PrepareItem Include="Unique2">
    <Folder>folder2</Folder>
    <Other>two.txt</Other>
  </PrepareItem>
  <PrepareItem Include="Unique3">
    <Folder>folder1</Folder>                          <!-- 3 -->
    <Other>three.txt</Other>
  </PrepareItem>
</ItemGroup>

<Target Name="PrepareFolders"
    Outputs="%(PrepareItem.Folder)">                  <!-- 4 -->
  <Message Text="PrepareFolders: '%(PrepareItem.Folder)'" />
  <MakeDir
    Directories="%(PrepareItem.Folder)"
    />                                                <!-- 5 -->
</Target>

<Target Name="Prepare"
    DependsOnTargets="PrepareFolders">                <!-- 6 -->
  <Message Text="Preparing %(PrepareItem.Identity)..." />
  <Message Text="  Action 1, %(PrepareItem.Folder)/%(Other)" />
  <Message Text="  Action 2, %(PrepareItem.Folder)/%(Other)" />
</Target>
```

Output

```
PrepareFolders:
  PrepareFolders: 'folder1'
  Creating directory "folder1".
PrepareFolders:
  PrepareFolders: 'folder2'
  Creating directory "folder2".
Prepare:
  Preparing Unique1...
  Preparing Unique2...
    Action 1, folder1/one.txt
    Action 1, folder2/two.txt
    Action 2, folder1/one.txt
    Action 2, folder2/two.txt
```

The items named @(PrepareItem) are declared with item metadata named %(Folder) for the path (1) that needs to exist prior to other presumed operations that would use the %(Other) metadata (2). A third item (3) duplicates the use of "folder1" in its item metadata. This item is used for target output batching in the PrepareFolders target (4). It is batched using the Folder metadata and no other part of the item. This is because this particular target only needs unique folder metadata regardless of how many items there are. A Message task displays for each iteration in the batching loop, just to show the execution. From the output it can be seen that the target runs twice, once for each unique metadata item used for setting up the target batching. The MakeDir task operates only on the Folder metadata, ignoring the rest of the item.

This target is executed as a dependent target of some other operation (6), in this case representing what could be one of the primary targets in the build. Message tasks are used to simulate these other operations which presumably require that the folders exist.

In a complex build, the functionality wrapped up in this type of target is often going to be something along the lines of these:

- Unzip – Either unzipping large prebuilt third-party assemblies or entire SDK distributions, to save from lengthy version control operations. These distributions can be declared in an item array so that custom build actions aren't needed for each one. I've worked on projects that had many dozens of these, which cut version control source code synchronization by up to 15 minutes per clean build.

- Zip – Packaging up build artifacts for archiving, or as part of a deployment. The item describing these can be formed from items that describe locations in the build drop that may be aggregated and overlaid on top of each other from the build of multiple projects.

- Copy – Often at a certain point in the build, files may need to be staged from one location to another, for example to represent the final layout the product will have on an end user's machine after being installed.

- Validate – You can even declare a series of actions that need to be run to validate the build. Item metadata can be a command that is fed to an Exec task, perhaps even running a custom tool that was produced during the build. This mimics the way the built-in PostBuild steps work in project files, but rather than operating at one point and for one project, they operate on the entire build or deployment. Other parts of the item metadata can be used to filter when the operation occurs, which will be shown in *trick #70, How to enhance item-based action tricks*, trick that follows.

- Mimic – If a product needs to be installed, it may be useful for the build to mimic the actions of the installer, which can be described in MSBuild items, for example, consider registry changes, with an item declared as follows,

```
<ItemGroup>
  <RegistryItem>
    <Hive>HKLM</Hive>
    <Path>Software\</Path>
    <ValueName></ValueName>
    <Value></Value>
    <Type>String</Type>
  </RegistryItem>
</ItemGroup>
```

This is then fed to a target using the technique outlined above, where the target contains a task that can alter the registry in a developer build, and a task that can transform the data into the WiX or an include file for some other installer script for the installer build, giving a single point of maintenance for this information.

In subsequent tricks we'll expand upon this basic building block technique.

67. An alternative to $($(NestedProperty))

Okay, first a word of caution. I'm not suggesting that littering your build with deeply nested syntax like the title of this trick—which isn't even valid MSBuild—is a best practice. As I've said in the chapter introduction, using the simplest and most concise constructs has benefits. What this trick does is introduce an important concept when data needs to be translated from items to properties. When you need it, this can be the difference between composing behavior in raw MSBuild and having to create overly-complex custom tasks which themselves add an opaque barrier to understanding what the build is doing. When I've used this sort of thing in production builds, I've always been careful to provide lots of XML comments surrounding these tricky bits—there have been times when the line count of comments outnumbered the line count of the MSBuild it was describing by ten-to-one. The goal is that a casual observer—or someone who doesn't have this book—won't be left in the dark.

The names of properties can't easily be derived from other properties, as shown in the section on Static and Dynamic Properties; at least not without going through some hoops. For example, the nested property definition in the title of this section won't be evaluated properly. One technique for simulating this is demonstrated below.

Properties/Create Property From Item.trkproj

```
<PropertyGroup>                                                  <!-- 1 -->
  <Name01>Not it!</Name01>
  <Name02>No, Really!</Name02>                                   <!-- 2 -->
  <Name03>Not it again!!</Name03>
</PropertyGroup>
<ItemGroup>                                                      <!-- 3 -->
  <NestedPropertyItem Include="Name01" />
  <NestedPropertyItem Include="Name02" />
  <NestedPropertyItem Include="Name03" />
</ItemGroup>

<Target Name="FindNamedPropertyFromItem"
  Outputs="%(NestedPropertyItem.Identity)">                      <!-- 4 -->
  <Message
    Text="NestedPropertyItem = @(NestedPropertyItem)"
    />
                                                                 <!-- 5 -->
  <Message
    Text="NestedPropertyItemValue = $(%(
      NestedPropertyItem.Identity))"
    />
  <PropertyGroup
    Condition="'@(NestedPropertyItem->'%(Identity)')' ==
      '$(NestedPropertyName)'">                                  <!-- 6 -->
    <NestedProperty
      >$(%(
        NestedPropertyItem.Identity))</NestedProperty>  <!-- 7 -->
  </PropertyGroup>
</Target>

<PropertyGroup>
  <NestedPropertyName>Name02</NestedPropertyName>                <!-- 8 -->
</PropertyGroup>

<Target Name="MockNestedProperty"
  DependsOnTargets="FindNamedPropertyFromItem">                  <!-- 9 -->
  <Message
    Text="NestedPropertyName = $(NestedPropertyName)"
    />                                                           <!-- 10 -->
  <Message
    Text="NestedProperty = $(NestedProperty)"
    />
</Target>
```

Output

```
FindNamedPropertyFromItem:
  NestedPropertyItem = Name01
  NestedPropertyItemValue = Not it!
```

258

```
FindNamedPropertyFromItem:
  NestedPropertyItem = Name02
  NestedPropertyItemValue = No, Really!
FindNamedPropertyFromItem:
  NestedPropertyItem = Name03
  NestedPropertyItemValue = Not it again!!
MockNestedProperty:
  NestedPropertyName = Name02
  NestedProperty = No, Really!
```

Several properties are declared (1), and an item array is declared (3) that refers to these three separate properties by name. The second of these properties (2) is the one that is going to be the target of the property selection.

The main execution starts in the MockNestedProperty target (9) with a dependency on the FindNamedPropertyFromItem target. This dependent target has output batching (4) on the nested item array declared earlier. This batching performs an iteration over the three uniquely identified items in the array. From the output, it can be seen that the messages in the target display once for each of the three items, indicating that all members of the item array were involved in the iteration. Note in particular the syntax used in the second message (5), which is,

```
<Message
  Text="NestedPropertyItemValue = $(%(NestedPropertyItem.Identity))"
  />
```

While a property can't take the form $($(Prop)), it can take this form, where a property name is held in item metadata, in this case the item specification maintained in the %(Identity) metadata.

A dynamic property group then conditionally (6) declares a new property named $(NestedProperty). This condition is based on a value comparison between the current item iteration in the iteration batch, and a static property named $(NestedPropertyName). Essentially, this target serves as a loop. In pseudo-code form, it would have the following behavior,

```
foreach (item in @(NestedPropertyItem))
   if (item.ItemSpec == $(NestedPropertyName))
      $(NestedProperty) = <value of property named item.ItemSpec>;
```

The conditional property is declared statically (8) in this example, but it could be determined dynamically based on other conditions. This property holds the name of the "property" whose value is sought. Of course, since it isn't possible to do this, it is really the "name" in the form of an item specification of the item in a known item array that is referenced. When control returns to the initiating target (10) the correctly selected value is shown, properly contained in $(NestedProperty), effectively mimicking $($(NestedPropertyName)), but taking an assist from an iteration through an item array to perform the property lookup.

68. @($(CanYouDoThis))

We've just seen how much trouble you need to go through to use the value of a property named by another property, but with items, there is more flexibility. This is of course due to the order of operations in the processing, since properties are evaluated in a first pass, then items in a second.

Can You Do This.trkproj

```
<PropertyGroup>
   <CanYouDoThis>SomeItemName</CanYouDoThis>              <!-- 1 -->
</PropertyGroup>
<ItemGroup>
   <SomeItemName Include="Yep!" />                        <!-- 2 -->
</ItemGroup>

<Target Name="CanYouDoThis">
  <Message
     Text="CanYouDoThis = '@($(CanYouDoThis))'"
     />
</Target>
```

Output

```
CanYouDoThis:
  CanYouDoThis = 'Yep!'
```

This is almost too easy: the project declares a property (1) that "names" the item of interest, in this case @(SomeItemName) (2). When executed, the expression,

```
@($(CanYouDoThis))
```

is evaluated in the first pass to be,

```
@(SomeItemName),
```

which in the second pass properly refers to the item array of the same name. While simple, this trick plays a key role in several other tricks that follow.

69. How to flatten item array metadata

Having a totally data-driven build may seem like a pretty tall ambition.
The benefits can be considerable, not the least of which is that when you
can make it come down to essentially adding another "row of data" to
some definition file in order to add a new extension to your build, you've
just widened the population of the team who can do it, beyond just those
few who know how to customize the build scripts.

Quite a few of the remaining tricks in this book will rely on the technique
discussed here, which I've come to call the "flattening" of items and their
metadata. We've already seen how targets can be batched with Target
Output batching expressions in *trick #35, Understand batched target
execution*. What follows is a convenient way of getting past excessive
metadata access syntax and simplifying the operations within a batched
target operating on an item array. These item arrays can be used for just
about anything. The example below mimics the kind of thing that might
be done late in a build, to get the built binaries and other items copied to
staging servers.

Item/Creative use of items.trkproj, FlattenMetadata setup

```
<PropertyGroup>
    <OutDir Condition="'$(OutDir)' == ''">.</OutDir>
</PropertyGroup>
<ItemDefinitionGroup>
    <Server>
        <Password>$(Password)</Password>
    </Server>
</ItemDefinitionGroup>
<ItemGroup>
    <Server Include="Server">
        <Name>Arrakis</Name>
        <User>Paul</User>
        <Password>P@ssw0rd</Password>
        <OutFolder>$(OutDir)\Services</OutFolder>
        <DestFolder>DropFolder\Svc</DestFolder>
        <ChildItem>ArrakisConfig</ChildItem>
    </Server>
    <Server Include="Server">
        <Name>Caladan</Name>
        <User>Maud'Dib</User>
        <Password>Fr3men</Password>
        <OutFolder>$(OutDir)\Data</OutFolder>
        <DestFolder>DropFolder\Data</DestFolder>
        <ChildItem>CaladanData</ChildItem>
    </Server>
</ItemGroup>
```

In this example, all items of the main @(Server) item array have the same item specification. Their uniqueness can be determined by whatever combination of metadata that makes sense for the data, as long as the Output batching expression on the target contains enough parts to guarantee uniqueness. This example ignores the identity attribute and relies on a compound key of other metadata solely for illustrative purposes, to show an example where the item specification is completely irrelevant, to reinforce the notion that in some usage scenarios the item specification is nothing more than another piece of metadata. More often than not though, I will generally give each item a unique identifier. If you ever need to deal with individual items in a special way, having a single unique key to deal with can be useful. The item metadata for each of the two items in the @(Server) item array can be considered to be fields of a structure type represented by the item.

Flattened metadata child item lists

Additional referenced items

```
<ItemGroup>
    <ArrakisConfig Include="subfolder\server.config" />
    <ArrakisConfig Include="subfolder\web.config" />
    <CaladanData Include="subfolder\seed.dat" />
    <CaladanData Include="subfolder\test.dat" />
</ItemGroup>
```

One of the item metadata "fields" is named ChildItem. This field holds a value of "ArrakisConfig" for the first item and "CaladanData" for the second. These metadata values refer to related item arrays by name, which are declared in this second listing, showing the two separate item arrays named in the metadata. In C# pseudo-code, this sets up something along the lines of a child array, in this case,

```
struct Server
{
    string Name;
    string User;
    string Password;
    string OutFolder;
    string DestFolder;
    IList<string> ChildItem;
}
```

The "flattening" routine below will show how to access each member of this structure individually.

FlattenMetadata target

```
<Target Name="FlattenMetadata"
  Outputs="%(Server.Identity)+ %(Name)+%(OutFolder)
+%(DestFolder)+%(ChildItem)">                           <!-- 1 -->
    <PropertyGroup>
      <!-- 2 -->
      <_ThisName>%(Server.Name)</_ThisName>
      <_ThisUser>%(Server.User)</_ThisUser>
      <_ThisPassword>%(Server.Password)</_ThisPassword>
      <_ThisOutFolder>%(Server.OutFolder)</_ThisOutFolder>
      <_ThisDestFolder>%(Server.DestFolder)</_ThisDestFolder>
      <_ThisChildItem>%(Server.ChildItem)</_ThisChildItem>
    </PropertyGroup>
    <ItemGroup>
      <_ThisChildItem Include="@($(_ThisChildItem))" />  <!-- 3 -->
    </ItemGroup>
    <!-- 4 -->
    <Message Text="Connect: \\$(_ThisName)\$(_ThisDestFolder)
-user:$(_ThisUser);$(_ThisPassword)" />
    <Message Text="Copy from: '$(_ThisOutFolder)'" />
    <!-- 5 -->
    <Message Text="More Files %(_ThisChildItem.Identity)" />
</Target>
```

Output

```
FlattenMetadata:
  Connect: \\Arrakis\DropFolder\Svc -user:Paul;P@ssw0rd
  Copy from: '.\Services'
  Additional Files subfolder\server.config
  Additional Files subfolder\web.config
FlattenMetadata:
  Connect: \\Caladan\DropFolder\Data -user:Maud'Dib;Fr3men
  Copy from: '.\Data'
  Additional Files subfolder\seed.dat
  Additional Files subfolder\test.dat
```

Notice the rather verbose target output batching declaration (1) that refers to every available piece of metadata on the item. Because of how the data is defined, this will cause the target to be batched using each individual item in the item array. Immediately, properties are declared (2) for each of these metadata items. By convention, these property names have a leading underscore which indicates that they are to be considered private local variables for the target. Also by convention, because they are the local data storage elements for the "flattening" technique, they are given the prefix name "This" which indicates it is the value for "this iteration" of the batching. The property $(_ThisChildItem) now contains the name of the child item array referenced by the %(ChildItem) metadata value. An item array named @(_ThisChildItem) is declared next (3), using the "item from property" syntax of the previous trick as the item specification,

```
Include="@($(_ThisChildItem))"
```

Now if you're thinking that this dynamic item array will have one new set of members added to it for each iteration of the target, well, you'd be having a rational thought, but an incorrect one. Remember the rules governing how items and properties are published with respect to target execution, from *trick #31, Understand how dynamic values are published*? These rules also apply to batched target execution. With each iteration, a new set of items from the referenced item array is essentially staged for publication to the aggregating item array, but the entire aggregate item array containing these items, one set for each iteration, won't be published until the target completes execution. The target doesn't reach completion until after the final batch executes. So, during the batching, the @(_ThisChildItem) item array which is being created will only contain the items added at (3), within the same iteration. Once target execution completes, the @(_ThisChildItem) item array will contain a useless aggregation of all the items added by each batch, but it won't ever be referenced outside of the scope of the batched target; its utility is isolated to a single batch iteration in this case. If needed, you could control this by removing all the items in the item array at the end of the target, or by otherwise explicitly controlling the contents that will be exposed when the target item publication occurs.

The next two tasks in the target first print out messages using all the normal local iteration properties (4) which mimics some server oriented activity, perhaps connecting to the server using the username and password and gathering the source items to be deployed to the server. The final task uses task batching to display all the current items in the @(_ThisChildItem) item array, which in the output clearly shows how the child item array referenced by the original @(Server) metadata is fully realized, mimicking the copying of additional items needed for the server deployment.

This item flattening can become arbitrarily complex. Referenced item arrays can themselves contain metadata that can be flattened in a secondary iteration driven by a dependent target. Items can be combined to drive complex behavior. Metadata values can be used in conditions to determine the context of other values, or to trigger different task actions. Some of these tricks are covered in the next section.

70. How to enhance item-based action tricks

This next section expands on the "flattening" trick, showing a few novel enhancements that is useful when some additional sophistication or flexibility is needed.

Poor-man's switch

First up is a poor-man's switch statement, where the items in an array represent the data for multiple separate tasks, with one item metadata value serving as the discriminator. While it seems like it might be nicer to perform this sort of thing with dependent targets, with each dependent target having a condition filtering out all but one value in the discriminator, the item metadata value extraction syntax can't be used in target conditions in this manner. For example, trying to make a dependent target for the Exec task, where there is an item array declared with an action discriminator,

```
<ItemGroup>
  <Item Include="SomeExecAction">
    <Action>Exec</Action>
    ...
  </Item>
</ItemGroup>
```

and a target with a condition based on that metadata value,

```
<Target Name="ActionExec"
  Condition="'%(Item.Action)' == 'Exec'"
  Outputs="%(Item.Identity)">
```

This however would only reveal an error message,

```
C:\Code\... : error MSB4116: The condition "'%(Item.Action)'
 == 'Exec'" on the "Actions" target has a reference to item metadata.
References to item metadata are not allowed in target conditions
unless they are part of an item transform.
```

Reforming this condition using an item transform won't work though, as the result,

```
<Target Name="Actions"
  Condition="'@(Item->'%(Action)')' == 'Exec'"
  Outputs="%(Item.Identity)">
```

is premised on a misunderstanding. It might seem that @(Item) used in the transform of the conditional expression might refer to the single item in the batch created by the outputs batching expression, however, with detailed verbosity, you could see that with more than one item in the item array, it actually refers to all three, and breaks down with the diagnostic message,

```
Target "Actions" skipped, due to false condition; ('@(Item->
'%(Action)')' == 'Exec') was evaluated as ('Exec;Copy;Transform' ==
'Exec').
```

What we're left with is a choice between some overuse of conditions on tasks, or a bit of extra work and duplication in some targets, but for some rare occasions this trick really fits the bill with one or the other of these options.

Other item-based actions.trkproj, Actions data

```
<ItemGroup>
  <Item Include="IniFiles">
    <Action>None</Action>                          <!-- 1a -->
    <Sources>drop\*.ini</Sources>
    <LayoutFolder>Config\Ini</LayoutFolder>
  </Item>
  <Item Include="Documentation">
    <Action>Exec</Action>                           <!-- 1b -->
    <Sources>drop\*.doc</Sources>                   <!-- 2 -->
    <LayoutFolder>Docs</LayoutFolder>
    <Command>dir ${_ThisSources}</Command>          <!-- 3 -->
    <Message>Running %(Command)</Message>           <!-- 5 -->
  </Item>
  <Item Include="XmlFiles">
    <Action>Transform</Action>                      <!-- 1c -->
    <Sources>drop\*.xml</Sources>
    <LayoutFolder>Config\Xml</LayoutFolder>
    <Transform>transform.xsl</Transform>            <!-- 4 -->
    <Message>Transforming files with %(Transform)</Message>
  </Item>
</ItemGroup>
```

The scenario for the item array above is a series of configurable post build actions. The items each have a unique item specification, and define an %(Action) metadata value (1a), (1b), (1c), representing three possible activities, "Common," "Exec" and "Transform." Generally speaking these activities could each have their own independent item arrays, and their own targets driving them.

There are times however, when there is a parent activity that is identical across a broad array of items, with a minor sub-activity that reuses most of the data from the parent, adding only a small amount of customization. If each of the sub-activities required its own item array and target, there may be too much duplication among these independent item arrays. So the scenario for this trick centers on the varied activities being secondary to the primary one, both in the scope of data and the complexity of the task. This sort of thing appears most often in the pre-build setup of sources from source control or perhaps pulling from other locations, or in the post-build layout and deployment.

The shared data for each item starts at (2) and declares a source location—presumably where the drop folder of the build is located—and a layout folder, presumably where the built artifacts are being copied to for some post build processing, such as building an installer or setting up a configured drop for a test deployment.

Each of the items also contains some custom metadata specific to the specific sub-activity. For the Exec action these are the command (3) to be executed, and for the Transform task, it is an XSL transformation file (4). There is also optional metadata for a message. Although these are part of the common metadata listed at (2), they are declared last in the structure, after the action-specific metadata. This is because they reference the action-specific metadata in the message. Notice the last two metadata values in the Documentation item,

```
<Command>dir ${_ThisSources}</Command>
<Message>Running %(Command)</Message>
```

Because the %(Message) metadata makes reference to the %(Command) metadata of the same item, it needs to be declared afterword to pick up the value. Had it been declared at (2) with the other shared data, it would not have found a value to replace the reference. In this case, the message expands initially to,

```
Running dir ${_ThisSources}
```

Embedded in this string is a non-MSBuild "macro" of sorts, ${_ThisSources} which is the bases for a little trick shown below:

Other item-based actions.trkproj, Actions target

```
<Target Name="Actions"
    Outputs="%(Item.Identity)">                         <!-- 1 -->
    <PropertyGroup>
        <_ThisAction>%(Item.Action)</_ThisAction>
        <_ThisSources>%(Item.Sources)</_ThisSources>
        <_ThisLayoutFolder>%(Item.LayoutFolder)</_ThisLayoutFolder>
        <_ThisTransform>%(Item.Transform)</_ThisTransform>
        <_ThisCommand>%(Item.Command)</_ThisCommand>
        <_ThisMessage>%(Item.Message)</_ThisMessage>
    </PropertyGroup>                                     <!-- 2 -->

    <ItemGroup>
        <_ThisSources Include="$(_ThisSources)" />       <!-- 3 -->
    </ItemGroup>
```

```
                                                       <!-- 4 -->
    <Message
      Condition="'$(_ThisMessage)' != ''"
      Text="Message: $(_ThisMessage)"
      />
                                                       <!-- 5 -->
    <Message
      Condition="'@(_ThisSources)' != ''"
      Text="Common action: @(_ThisSources)"
      />
    <Copy
      SourceFiles="@(_ThisSources)"
      DestinationFolder="drop\Layout\$(_ThisLayoutFolder)"
      />

    <!-- Exec -->                                      <!-- 6 -->
    <PropertyGroup>
      <_ThisCommand>$(_ThisCommand.Replace(
        '${_ThisSources}',
        '$(_ThisSources)'))</_ThisCommand>
    </PropertyGroup>
    <Exec
      Condition="'$(_ThisAction)' == 'Exec'"
      Command="$(_ThisCommand)"
      />

    <!-- Transform -->                                 <!-- 7 -->
    <Message
      Condition="'$(_ThisAction)' == 'Transform'"
      Text="Simulate xsl $(_ThisSources) --> $(_ThisTransform)"
      />

  </Target>
```

The target operates on the action data items discussed previously, using the same batching and item flattening discussed in the previous trick, shown from (1) to (2) in the target listing above.

Because the %(Sources) metadata contains wildcards, it needs to be expanded to a per-iteration item array (3) named @(_ThisSources), just like the @(_ThisChildItem) array of the previous trick. The common activity is hinted at with an explicit message task (4), and also handled by the Copy task (5), which also has a separate message as well. These messages are conditioned on the existence of the optional %(Message) metadata value, or the existence of any items in the %(_ThisSources) item array, populated from the %(Sources) metadata. Each of the action types then gets its own series of tasks (6) and (7), with each task requiring a condition on the value of $(_ThisAction)—not ideal, but the only straightforward option not requiring a custom task. Even if these action task series were to be separated into dependent tasks, they would still need these conditions, because the batching would be on the entire item array using the technique. It is possible though, as will be shown in the next iteration in just a moment, but first let's examine the output of the script above.

```
Output
Actions:
  Common action: drop\user.ini
  Copying file from "drop\user.ini" to "drop\Layout\Config\Ini\   ↪
user.ini".
Actions:
  Message: Running dir ${_ThisSources}
  Common action: drop\feature.doc;drop\main.doc
  Copying file from "drop\feature.doc" to "drop\Layout\Docs\      ↪
feature.doc".
  Copying file from "drop\main.doc" to "drop\Layout\Docs\main.doc".
  dir drop\*.doc
  Volume in drive C has no label.
  Volume Serial Number is BEEF-7AC0

  Directory of C:\Code\...\Items\drop

06/09/2011  05:50 PM                    0 feature.doc
06/09/2011  05:50 PM                    0 main.doc
               2 File(s)              0 bytes
               0 Dir(s)   218,880,667,648 bytes free
Actions:
  Message: Transforming files with transform.xsl
  Common action: drop\machine.xml;drop\user.xml
  Copying file from "drop\machine.xml" to
"drop\Layout\Config\Xml\machine.xml".
  Copying file from "drop\user.xml" to
"drop\Layout\Config\Xml\user.xml".
  Simulate xsl drop\*.xml --> transform.xsl
```

The Actions target will run in three batches, each with a single item from the original item array. The three target header messages "Actions:" in the output above show these three iterations. The second and third of them display the explicit message; the optional %(Message) metadata was empty for the Common action, and they all display the "Common action:" message displaying the value of the iteration's @(_ThisSources) item array, as well as the output of the Copy task that operates on this item array. In the second action, the explicit message contains the literal text,

```
Message: Running dir ${_ThisSources}
```

This was composed in the original %(Message) metadata. The Exec action however, utilizes a string replacement (6) in the Exec task section, just prior to calling Exec, that looks like this,

```
<PropertyGroup>
  <_ThisCommand>$(_ThisCommand.Replace(
    '${_ThisSources}',
    '$(_ThisSources)'))</_ThisCommand>
</PropertyGroup>
```

This is an example of a simple macro substitution that you can employ in any script. Because MSBuild does not recognize the brace delimiters ${...}, they can be employed for your own value replacement. In this case, the macro name matches the desired property name, for delayed replacement. The command passed to exec is transformed from,

```
dir ${_ThisSources}
```

into,

```
dir drop\*.doc
```

...the result of which is shown in the output. Finally, the mimicked file transformation (7) is executed.

Sub-Activity Actions with dependent targets

Now it was mentioned earlier that there were two ways to go about this. This next set of targets shows how to perform essentially the same activity in dependent targets. This alternative way does have a bit of duplication, but it may be that the duplicated bits add less complexity than the poor-man's-condition-on-every-task alternative above.

ActionsWithDepends target

```
                                                        <!-- 1 -->
<Target Name="ActionsWithDepends"
  DependsOnTargets="
    SplitActions;
    ActionCommon;
    ActionExec;
    ActionTransform;
    ActionContrived"
  />

<Target Name="SplitActions"
  Outputs="%(Item.Identity)">                           <!-- 2 -->
  <PropertyGroup>
    <_ThisAction>%(Item.Action)</_ThisAction>
  </PropertyGroup>

  <ItemGroup>
    <_ActionTransform Include="@(Item)"
      Condition="'$(_ThisAction)' == 'Transform'"
```

```
            />                                    <!-- 3 -->
      <_ActionExec Include="@(Item)"
        Condition="'$(_ThisAction)' == 'Exec'"
            />                                    <!-- 4 -->
    </ItemGroup>
  </Target>
```

The primary target (1) is just a junction point for the dependent targets, the first of which, SplitActions, is shown above. It is batched with the entire set of @(Item) items (2) which is then split into separate dynamic item arrays for the two actions that require them separately from the common activity. These two item arrays (3) and (4) each have a condition which limits the membership to those items with the proper %(Action) metadata value. They each include all items that match the condition, and duplicate all of the metadata present in each item. For the common activities, which in this case are limited to the messages and the Copy task, the original @(Item) item array can be used, so a separate duplicate item array is not needed. The remaining dependent targets are shown below, which can operate on separate item array batching now that the original item array has been split into arrays with their membership filtered from the original array.

Common and action targets

```
<Target Name="ActionCommon"
  Outputs="%(Item.Identity)">
  <PropertyGroup>
    <_ThisMessage>%(_ActionCommon.Message)</_ThisMessage>
    <_ThisSources>%(Item.Sources)</_ThisSources>        <!-- 1a -->
  </PropertyGroup>
  <ItemGroup>
    <_ThisSources Include="$(_ThisSources)" />           <!-- 2a -->
  </ItemGroup>

  <Message
    Condition="'$(_ThisMessage)' != ''"
    Text="Message: $(_ThisMessage)"
    />
  <Message
    Condition="'@(_ThisSources)' != ''"
    Text="Common action: @(_ThisSources)"
    />
  <PropertyGroup>
    <_ThisSources>%(Item.Sources)</_ThisSources>        <!-- 1b -->
    <_ThisLayoutFolder>%(Item.LayoutFolder)</_ThisLayoutFolder>
  </PropertyGroup>
  <Copy
    SourceFiles="@(_ThisCopySources)"
    DestinationFolder="drop\Layout\$(_ThisLayoutFolder)"
    />
</Target>
```

```
<Target Name="ActionExec"
  Outputs="%(_ActionExec.Identity)">
  <PropertyGroup>
    <_ThisSources>%(_ActionExec.Sources)</_ThisSources><!-- 1c-->
    <_ThisCommand>%(_ActionExec.Command)</_ThisCommand>
    <_ThisCommand>$(_ThisCommand.Replace(
      '${_ThisSources}',
      '$(_ThisSources)'))</_ThisCommand>
  </PropertyGroup>
  <Exec
    Command="$(_ThisCommand)"
    />
</Target>

<Target Name="ActionTransform"
  Outputs="%(_ActionTransform.Identity)">
  <PropertyGroup>
    <_ThisSources>%(_ActionTransform.Sources)</_ThisSources>
    <_ThisTransform>%(_ActionTransform.Transform
      )</_ThisTransform>
  </PropertyGroup>
  <Message
    Text="Simulate xsl $(_ThisSources) --> $(_ThisTransform)"
    />
</Target>

<Target Name="ActionContrived">
  <PropertyGroup>
    <_ThisSources>%(_ActionTransform.Sources)</_ThisSources>
  </PropertyGroup>
  <ItemGroup>
    <_ThisContrivedSources Include="$(_ThisSources)" /><!-- 2b-->
  </ItemGroup>
  ...
</Target>
```

Without going over every line of the above, there are a few things that are important to note. First of all, most of the content of the first approach was used pretty much unchanged in this refactored example. One change is how the $(_ThisSources) property (1a) (1b) (1c) needs to be duplicated in each of the three targets. Since this property represents the primary metadata value in this example, this can't be avoided. It may however indicate a possible issue with this approach, if there were many other metadata values that would need to be duplicated in each dependent target.

To understand the possible glitch, the $(_ThisSources) property is used in two targets (2a) (2b)—the second of which is a contrived action not involved in the sample—to form the same item array in both targets. However, because of the item publication rules, and since the operations using this item array have been split into multiple targets, we can't rely on the delayed publication any longer. If we were to try to rely on this, the separate iterations of item creation (2a) would be aggregated into the item array, and by the time the second target was being executed in batches, the item array (2b) would already contain all the members from the previously batched target. Looking closely, you can see that the item array names for the two targets are unique, the first named @(_ThisSources), and the second named @(_ThisContrivedSources), so that the latter is not influenced by the publication of the values in the former.

The other notable difference is that since the item arrays were created using the conditional expression to filter only those items with the proper value for the %(Action) metadata, the tasks within the targets no longer require these conditions. In fact, the action metadata is not even stored into a local $(_ThisAction) property because it isn't referenced after the item array is split.

Output from ActionsWithDepends

```
ActionCommon:
  Common action: drop\user.ini
  Copying file from "drop\user.ini" to
"drop\Layout\Config\Ini\user.ini".
ActionCommon:
  Common action: drop\feature.doc;drop\main.doc
  Copying file from "drop\feature.doc" to
"drop\Layout\Docs\feature.doc".
  Copying file from "drop\main.doc" to "drop\Layout\Docs\main.doc".
ActionCommon:
  Common action: drop\machine.xml;drop\user.xml
  Copying file from "drop\machine.xml" to
"drop\Layout\Config\Xml\machine.xml".
  Copying file from "drop\user.xml" to
"drop\Layout\Config\Xml\user.xml".
ActionExec:
  dir drop\*.doc
   Volume in drive C has no label.
   Volume Serial Number is BEEF-7AC0

   Directory of C:\Code\Trickery\Source Code\Items\drop

  06/09/2011  05:50 PM                      0 feature.doc
  06/09/2011  05:50 PM                      0 main.doc
                 2 File(s)                  0 bytes
                 0 Dir(s)   218,874,474,496 bytes free
ActionTransform:
  Simulate xsl drop\*.xml --> transform.xsl
```

The output is similar, but represents the dependent target batching that occurs. First with the three iterations of the ActionCommon target, then a separate single batch for each of the two specific sub-action targets; but the results remain the same.

Phases

Generally, in a complex build, the "Build" is only one of several phases, typically somewhere in the middle. Before building, there may be a bunch of configuration, source manipulation, code generation and validation. After building there may be moving and copying of files into a deployment, interrogation of built assemblies, more code or documentation generation, packaging or installer creation, and unit and integration testing, as well as more validation. Each of these activities can often be thought of as a separate build phase.

The following trick shows a mechanism for sequencing these build phases with a unified set of items. While it may not be the most convenient trick to use for every phase of the end-to-end build, you may find it useful for certain sequences of actions. I've even used this trick extensively to separate early and late built projects just during the Build phase when inter-project dependencies grew beyond the scope of the built-in dependencies in C# projects.

Other item-based actions.trkproj, Phases data

```
<ItemGroup>
  <Phase Include="Initial" />                          <!-- 1 -->
  <Phase Include="During" />
  <Phase Include="Final" />
</ItemGroup>
<ItemGroup>
  <!-- sources -->                                     <!-- 2 -->
  <PhaseItem Include="PhaseItem">
    <Id>SourceSync</Id>
    <Phase>Initial</Phase>
    <Action>Fetch sources</Action>
  </PhaseItem>
  <PhaseItem Include="PhaseItem">
    <Id>ExpandSdk</Id>
    <Phase>Initial</Phase>
    <Action>Prepare third party SDKs</Action>
  </PhaseItem>
  <!-- analyze -->                                      <!-- 3 -->
  <PhaseItem Include="PhaseItem">
    <Id>AnalyzeProjects</Id>
    <Phase>Initial</Phase>
    <Action>Analyze project file conformance</Action>
  </PhaseItem>
  <PhaseItem Include="PhaseItem">
```

```
        <Id>AnalyzeDrop</Id>
        <Phase>Final</Phase>
        <Action>Analyze build drop</Action>
      </PhaseItem>
      <!-- build -->                                    <!-- 4 -->
      <PhaseItem Include="PhaseItem">
        <Id>Bootstrap</Id>
        <Phase>Initial</Phase>
        <Action>Build bootstrap</Action>
      </PhaseItem>
      <PhaseItem Include="PhaseItem">
        <Id>Tooling</Id>
        <Phase>During</Phase>
        <Action>Build tools</Action>
      </PhaseItem>
      <PhaseItem Include="PhaseItem">
        <Id>Build</Id>
        <Phase>During</Phase>
        <Action>Build normal projects</Action>
      </PhaseItem>
      <PhaseItem Include="PhaseItem">
        <Id>Installer</Id>
        <Phase>Final</Phase>
        <Action>Build installer</Action>
      </PhaseItem>
      <!-- deployment -->                               <!-- 5 -->
      <PhaseItem Include="PhaseItem">
        <Id>Staging</Id>
        <Phase>Final</Phase>
        <Action>Stage artifacts</Action>
      </PhaseItem>
      <PhaseItem Include="PhaseItem">
        <Id>Documentation</Id>
        <Phase>Final</Phase>
        <Action>Generate documentation</Action>
      </PhaseItem>
      <!-- testing -->                                  <!-- 6 -->
      <PhaseItem Include="PhaseItem">
        <Id>Testing</Id>
        <Phase>Final</Phase>
        <Action>Run tests</Action>
      </PhaseItem>
    </ItemGroup>
```

The listing above contains the data used to drive the phase-based execution. The data consists of two separate item arrays, the first named @(Phase) which lists (1) three simple phases named "Initial," "During" and "Final." These three phases can be thought of as placeholders for an arbitrarily complex set of phased steps specific to your own build requirements. The second item array is named @(PhaseItem), which describes various operations, each labeled with a comment; "sources" (2), "analyze" (3), "build" (4), "deployment" (5) and "testing (6). Each of these operations may have some representation in any of the phases declared in the previous item array. The phases are sequential, while the phase items are grouped by the particular operation they are responsible for completing.

Within each phase item there are defined three separate pieces of metadata, "Id," "Phase," and "Action." The Id is a unique identifier for the item, required to be unique because of the batching operation. This is one of those examples where the item specification could also be used for the same purpose by using the metadata access syntax for "Identity." The Phase metadata must match one of the available phases declared in the @(Phase) item array. The Action metadata in this example represents the data used by the build operation.

Other item-based actions.trkproj, Phases target

```
<Target Name="FlattenPhaseItems"
    Outputs="%(Phase.Identity)">                          <!-- 7 -->
    <Message Text="Flattning phase: '@(Phase)'" />
    <ItemGroup>
        <!-- 8 -->
        <_OrganizedPhaseItem Include="%(PhaseItem.Id)"
            Condition="'@(Phase)' == '@(PhaseItem->'%(Phase)')'">
            <Id>%(PhaseItem.Id)</Id>
            <Phase>%(PhaseItem.Phase)</Phase>            <!-- 9 -->
            <Action>%(PhaseItem.Action)</Action>
        </_OrganizedPhaseItem>
    </ItemGroup>
</Target>

<Target Name="Phases"
    DependsOnTargets="FlattenPhaseItems"
    Outputs="%(_OrganizedPhaseItem.Id)">                  <!-- 10 -->
    <PropertyGroup>                                       <!-- 11 -->
        <_Phase>%(_OrganizedPhaseItem.Phase)</_Phase>
        <_Id>%(_OrganizedPhaseItem.Id)</_Id>
        <_Action>%(_OrganizedPhaseItem.Action)</_Action>
    </PropertyGroup>
    <Message
        Text="Action: $(_Phase), $(_Id), $(_Action)"
        />
</Target>
```

Output

```
FlattenPhaseItems:
  Flattening phase: 'Initial'
FlattenPhaseItems:
  Flattening phase: 'During'
FlattenPhaseItems:
  Flattening phase: 'Final'
RunPhases:
  Action: Initial, SourceSync, Fetch sources
RunPhases:
```

```
  Action: Initial, ExpandSdk, Prepare third party SDKs
RunPhases:
  Action: Initial, AnalyzeProjects, Analyze project file conformance
RunPhases:
  Action: Initial, Bootstrap, Build bootstrap
RunPhases:
  Action: During, Tooling, build tools
RunPhases:
  Action: During, Build, Build normal projects
RunPhases:
  Action: Final, AnalizeDrop, Analyze build drop
RunPhases:
  Action: Final, Installer, Build installer
RunPhases:
  Action: Final, Staging, Stage artifacts
RunPhases:
  Action: Final, Documentation, Generate documentation
RunPhases:
  Action: Final, Testing, Run tests
```

The dependent target "FlattenPhaseItems" is the key to this trick. It expands on *trick #69, How to flatten item array metadata*, in which a target is batched with an item array, and individual properties are declared for the item metadata for each batched item. In this expanded use of that technique, a new item array is created.

First, examine the output batching on the target (7), which segregates the target execution into three separate passes, one for each of the individual phases declared in the @(Phase) item array. Next, notice that the new item array being created, @(_OrganizedPhaseItem), is itself "task batched" by the declaration of its item specification,

```
<_OrganizedPhaseItem Include="%(PhaseItem.Id)" ...
```

Carefully consider that this batching is on the second of the two item arrays, the @(PhaseItem) array, and that the batching is using the unique-by-convention "Id" metadata value. This creates an iteration of each and every member of @(PhaseItem), each of which could add a new item to the @(_OrganizedPhaseItem) item array. Since the enclosing target is being executed three times, one for each member of @(Phase), this could potentially result in each and every member of @(PhaseItem) being added three times to the newly created @(_OrganizedPhaseItem). This duplication is avoided, and more importantly the PhaseItem members are sequenced *into the proper phases*, however, because of the Condition attribute also declared on the item declaration (8),

```
Condition="'@(Phase)' == '@(PhaseItem->'%(Phase)')'"
```

This condition limits the inclusion of each PhaseItem into the _OrganizedPhaseItem array for the target iteration where the PhaseItem's

Phase metadata matches the @(Phase) item specification batch being used to drive the current target iteration. In other words, three separate passes of item creation are set up, and with each pass, a second inner iteration of the PhaseItem's is executed, but only the PhaseItems matching the outer loops Phase are included each time, the others are filtered out. The three metadata values for the original PhaseItem is simply copied into the newly created item (9).

Because target batching will always execute in the sequence in which the items are declared, the original declaration of @(Phase) at (1) determines the ordering of the individual phase items in the newly created item array. In pseudo-code, this dependent target has done essentially this operation,

```
void FlattenPhaseItems()
{
    foreach (var phase in @(Phase))
        foreach (var item in @(PhaseItem))
            if (phase == item.Phase)
                _OrganizedPhaseItem.Add(item.Clone());
}
```

Once the items are flattened and sorted by phase, the Phases target performs item flattening by batching with the newly created and published @(_OrganizedPhaseItem) array (10), creating temporary properties (11) which are then passed to a Message task. In the output listing, notice the three separate invocations of the dependent FlattenPhaseItems target, batched with the @(Phase) item array, followed by the properly phase-sorted execution of the Action message in the RunPhases target, with just a single separate batched iteration for each of the original @(PhaseItem) members.

Since this is a shortened example intended only to show the batching operation to get this sort of approach working, the Message task is used for the build action. You can substitute any other action though, for instance,

```
<PhaseItem>
    <Id>Documentation</Id>
    <Phase>Final</Phase>
    <Action>PathTo/Docs.proj</Action>
</PhaseItem>
```

In this case, the action is a reference to a project file, and in the Phase target, instead of printing a message, you could build the project,

```
<PropertyGroup>
    <_Phase>%(_OrganizedPhaseItem.Phase)</_Phase>
    <_Id>%(_OrganizedPhaseItem.Id)</_Id>
```

```
        <_Action>%(_OrganizedPhaseItem.Action)</_Action>
    </PropertyGroup>
    <MSBuild
        Project="$(_Action)"
        />
```

Then, using the enhancements discussed above, in *Poor-man's switch* or
Sub-Activity Actions with dependent targets, you can build more complex
stage items with varied execution policies.

71. Forming delimited lists for repeated arguments

When using the Exec task to call out to custom grown or third-party
tools, you will inevitably find yourself composing sometimes long lists of
parameters. Often these parameters are composed of one or more
properties, and often you may find you're calling the same program in
multiple Exec tasks with conditions; it can get a bit unwieldy.

You'll also likely find yourself composing similar lists of property
arguments to the MSBuild task, with the repeating /p:name=value form.
You might even find yourself, like I have, composing the same lists of
parameters in both forms, to call out to MSBuild using the MSBuild task,
or to call MSBuild using the Exec task so that you can alter command line
options.

This trick shows how to manipulate an item array defining your
parameters to form any type of command line list you need, with a
pattern that can help keep some sanity in your build files where long lists
of parameters are needed.

The listing below contains just two parameters for brevity, to highlight
the argument forming technique,

```
Forming Arguments.trkproj
<ItemGroup>
    <Param Include="param01">                        <!-- 1 -->
        <Value>value01</Value>
    </Param>
    <Param Include="param02">
        <Value>value02</Value>
    </Param>
</ItemGroup>
<PropertyGroup>
    <ParamsAsProperties>@(Param->
        '%(Identity)=%(Value)',
        ';')</ParamsAsProperties>                    <!-- 2 -->
    <ParamsAsSwitches>@(Param->
        '/p:%(Identity)=%(Value)',
```

```
        ' ')</ParamsAsSwitches>                                <!-- 3 -->
</PropertyGroup>
<Target Name="Params">
    <Message Text="As Properties = '$(ParamsAsProperties)'" />
    <Message Text="As Switches   = '$(ParamsAsSwitches)'" />
</Target>
```

Output

```
Params:
  As Properties = 'param01=value01;param02=value02'
  As Switches   = '/p:param01=value01 /p:param02=value02'
```

Any property that will be needed in the child process—whether it is via a call through Exec or through the MSBuild task—is listed (1) as an item. In this example the identity for the item is the parameter or property name, and the value is shown as metadata. Refer to *trick #143*, *Understand the limitations of the MSBuild task, Passing properties to an MSBuild task target*, for a similar technique that doesn't need metadata values when all the values are already present in MSBuild properties, and the property name is used as the item specification, from which the property can later be discovered.

Two separate properties are created showing both ways of forming the argument lists. Both of these (2, 3) use the item transformation syntax that allows you to specify a delimiter to replace the default semicolon. Each of these properties is then printed out, to show how they are formed; the first showing the syntax for passing to the Properties attribute of the MSBuild task, the second showing the form that would be used to pass the same properties to MSBuild.exe using the Exec task. For other command line tools you can adjust the property definition to get the parameter passing syntax just right.

Since some parameter values may have spaces in them, you may need to surround the values with quotes. This variation is shown below.

ParamsQuoted target

```
<Target Name="ParamsQuoted">
    <ItemGroup>
        <Param>
            <QuotedValue>"%(Value)"</QuotedValue>              <!-- 4 -->
        </Param>
    </ItemGroup>
    <PropertyGroup>
        <ParamsAsQuotedProperties>@(Param->
            '%(Identity)=%(QuotedValue)',
            ';')</ParamsAsQuotedProperties>
        <ParamsAsQuotedSwitches>@(Param->
```

```
        '/p:%(Identity)=%(QuotedValue)',
        ' ')</ParamsAsQuotedSwitches>
  </PropertyGroup>
  <Message Text="As Properties = '$(ParamsAsQuotedProperties)'" />
  <Message Text="As Switches   = '$(ParamsAsQuotedSwitches)'" />
</Target>
```

Output

```
ParamsQuoted:
  As Properties = 'param01="value01";param02="value02"'
  As Switches   = '/p:param01="value01" /p:param02="value02"'
```

The item metadata creation form of a dynamic item is used to add an additional metadata value (4) containing the %(Value) metadata with enclosing quotes, which is then substituted for the use of %(Value) when the property argument lists are formed. This same technique can be used conditionally as well, to form arguments where the syntax varies depending on the argument type.

The script below shows the formation of several different command line argument types using a fairly generic and extensible method. The different argument forms in this example include:

```
-arg:value    Use argument name, a standard delimiter, and value
-arg          Use argument name if true, ignore otherwise, no value
-arg value    Use argument name, a non-standard delimiter, and value
 value        Use only the argument value, no name or delimiter
```

ParamsVaried data

```
<PropertyGroup>                                          <!-- 1 -->
  <argNormal>normal</argNormal>
  <argShowIfTrue>true</argShowIfTrue>
  <argDoNotShow>false</argDoNotShow>
  <argSeparatedValue>value</argSeparatedValue>
  <argUnnamed>unnamed</argUnnamed>
</PropertyGroup>

<ItemDefinitionGroup>                                    <!-- 2 -->
  <ParamVaried>
    <Type>Normal</Type>
    <Delimit>:</Delimit>
    <Switch>-</Switch>
  </ParamVaried>
</ItemDefinitionGroup>

<ItemGroup>                                              <!-- 3 -->
  <ParamVaried Include="argNormal" />                    <!-- 4 -->
  <ParamVaried Include="argSeparatedValue">              <!-- 5 -->
    <Delimit>%20</Delimit>                               <!-- 6 -->
  </ParamVaried>
  <ParamVaried Include="argShowIfTrue">                  <!-- 7 -->
```

```
      <Type>Boolean</Type>
    </ParamVaried>
    <ParamVaried Include="argDoNotShow">
      <Type>Boolean</Type>
    </ParamVaried>
    <ParamVaried Include="argUnnamed">                    <!-- 8 -->
      <Type>Unnamed</Type>
    </ParamVaried>
  </ItemGroup>
```

The parameters for this example are described using items and properties. First, the argument names are used as property names (1) and the parameter values are contained a the property value, duplicating the techniques shown above. Since each parameter will need additional item metadata to be able to form them differently on a command line, each property has a corresponding entry in an item array named @(ParamVaried), which has an item definition (2) to supply default values for some of the metadata, and separate entries for each of the arguments being used.

For a normal argument (3) the Type does not need to be specified as it takes the default from the item definition. For an argument with a unique delimiter (5), the delimiter text is declared in a metadata value named %(Delimit), which in this case (6) contains a space character, escaped using the MSBuild escaped character syntax. A third argument (7) of type "Boolean" will be shown only if the value is true, and a final one (8) of type "Unnamed" which will show the value only.

ParamsVaried target

```
  <Target Name="FormArgs">                               <!-- 9 -->
    <ItemGroup>
      <ParamVaried>                                       <!-- 10 -->
        <!-- 11 -->
        <Formed Condition="'%(Type)' == 'Normal'"
          >%(Switch)%(Identity)%(Delimit)$(%(Identity))</Formed>
        <!-- 12 -->
        <Formed Condition="'%(Type)' == 'Boolean'
          AND '$(%(Identity))' == 'true'"
          >%(Switch)%(Identity)</Formed>
        <!-- 13 -->
        <Formed Condition="'%(Type)' == 'Unnamed'"
          >$(%(Identity))</Formed>
      </ParamVaried>
    </ItemGroup>
  </Target>

  <Target Name="ParamsVaried"
    DependsOnTargets="FormArgs">
    <PropertyGroup>
      <ParamsFormed>@(ParamVaried->
```

```
          '%(Formed)',
          ' ')</ParamsFormed>                              <!-- 14 -->
    </PropertyGroup>
    <Message
      Text="ParamsFormed:
$(ParamsFormed)"
      />
  </Target>
</Project>
```

Output

```
ParamsVaried:
  ParamsFormed:
  -argNormal:normal -argSeparatedValue value -argShowIfTrue unnamed
```

The target execution begins with a dependent target (9) named "FormArgs." This target adds a new metadata value to each entry in the @(ParamVaried) item array (10), named %(Formed). This metadata contains the properly formed text for this argument as it will appear on the command line which will be constructed later. The %(Formed) metadata is declared three times, each with a different conditional expression keyed on the %(Type) metadata.

The "Normal" type composes (11) the metadata with the values of the %(Switch) and %(Delimit), along with the argument name and value, which uses the metadata variant of *trick #68, @($(CanYouDoThis))*. If the argument were tagged with the type "Boolean," the condition (12) also requires that the value is 'true' before it will declare this metadata. In this example, of the two Boolean arguments, only one, $(ShowIfTrue) has the value true, the other $(DoNotShow) is false. The %(Formed) metadata for an "Unnamed" type argument (13) contains only the property value.

Inside the main "ParamsVaried" target, the arguments are formed into an argument string (14) using the same technique as previously discussed, then printed via the Message task. The extra carriage return in the Text attribute of the Message task only serves to separate the parameter property value from the message header in the output. From the output, it can be seen that all of the arguments are properly formed, with the exception of the $(DoNotShow) argument that was skipped because it was a Boolean type with the value "false."

In the above script, it is also possible to override the switch value used, though this is not shown. For example,

```
<ItemGroup>
  <ParamVaried Include="argSwitch">
    <Switch>/</Switch>
  </ParamVaried>
```

```
</ItemGroup>
```

The snippet above would form an argument with an alternate argument switch, as,

```
/argSwitch:value
```

You could also use *trick #69, How to flatten item array metadata* technique to form repeated arguments, for example,

```
-argRepeated:value1;value2;value3
```

In this case, a new argument type of "Repeated" could be declared, and the value, which would be composed of a separate item array declared as,

```
<ItemGroup>
  <ParamVaried Include="argRepeated">
    <Type>Repeated</Type>
    <ChildItem>RepeatedChild</ChildItem>
  </ParamVaried>
  <RepeatedChild Include="value1" />
  <RepeatedChild Include="value2" />
  <RepeatedChild Include="value3" />
</ItemGroup>
```

Remembering to add a default value to the item definition group, this could then be computed by adding an additional condition,

```
<Formed Condition="'%(Type)' == 'Repeated'"
  >%(Switch)%(Identity)%(Delimit)@(%(ChildItem))</Formed>
```

The number and form of the variations possible is quite broad, making it possible to declaratively drive nearly any command line tool by composing the values out of properties that already exist in your build.

More Item Array Tricks

To round out the coverage of item arrays here are a trio of additional tricks, one using the Returns attribute, and a couple more showing data selection techniques for filtering item data.

72. How to capture items not returned from a target

In *trick #37, Understand target Returns,* it was shown how you can use the TargetOutputs from the MSBuild task to capture the items declared in a the Returns attribute of the target being called. Remembering that the usage of the Returns attribute triggers a global change in how it is handled, if there are no Returns attributes in use, MSBuild would instead capture the items declared in the Outputs attribute. But what if you were interested in some other item that wasn't declared, and what if it were in one of the stock target import files and you couldn't modify it?

One example of these potentially useful item arrays can be seen in the ResolveAssemblyReferences target in Microsoft.Common.targets. In this target a call is made to the ResolveAssemblyReference task. Nine separate item arrays are captured from output parameters to this task, only one of which, @(ReferencePath), is listed as the target output.

Consider if for instance you wanted to be able to capture one of the other output parameters, the @(ReferenceCopyLocalPaths) item array. One undesirable option would be to cut-and-paste the entire target. Instead, realizing that the target of interest is actually part of a dependency listing for the ResolveReferences target, which performs other processing, you could simply wire a new target to your project,

```
<Target Name="ResolveCopyLocalPaths"
   DependsOnTargets="ResolveReferences"
   Returns="@(ReferenceCopyLocalPaths)">
</Target>
```

This new target has the built-in ResolveReferences target as a dependency. When this new target is executed, it will only run after ResolveReferences has been executed, which in turn forces the execution of ResolveAssemblyReferences, which will populate the item arrays of interest. The new target doesn't actually do anything—other than declaring the item array created by its dependency as its own Returns value, thus making it available for examination.

Then, in your build where you needed access to this item array, you could simply add a call to this target, capturing the target output,

```
<Target Name="GetReferenceCopyLocalPaths">
  <MSBuild
    Projects="@(Project)"
    Targets="ResolveCopyLocalPaths">
    <Output
      TaskParameter="TargetOutputs"
      ItemName="CopyLocalPaths"
      />
  </MSBuild>
  <Message Text="Paths = '@(CopyLocalPaths)'" />
</Target>
```

The target above, when executed with any set of projects in the @(Project) item array, will capture all of the assembly references marked with the "CopyLocal" attribute set to "true."

73. Picking from multiple data sets to drive build functionality

It has often come up that a particular operation that can be driven by the build in a data driven way needs to be parameterized out the wazoo to make it suitable for an ever-changing build and test environment. Consider a product that, after being built, needs to be deployed to multiple machines for testing. Each of these machines may have certain specific data, for instance:

- The operating system in use

- Different versions of other related tools, to create a testing or compatibility matrix

- Different security configurations and account credentials for access

- Different physical locations, either local machines on the internal network, or remote hosted machines

What's more, the machine names, OS etc. will likely change over time, and all of this information needs a place to be configured. There are likely to be three main usage scenarios for these operations:

- Continuous integration builds

- Typical daily (or rather hourly, or every couple minutes) developer builds

- Atypical developer builds, where a developer is working on something specific, and needs to push a local build (or a CI build of a particular change set) to a particular environment of their choosing

As has been shown, items and item metadata are great for storing all of the various data needed to drive targets like these. What follows is a simple example, showing deployment to remote machines, which allows for proper default behavior as well as user selectable parameterization from the command line.

The terminology used in the example below includes "Zone," which represents a particular place on a specific target machine, "Site" which refers to one of several possible configurations on that Zone, and

"Artifact," which refers to a subset of all available build artifacts of a particular type that are going to be pushed to a specific Zone.

This first listing presents only the data, in item arrays.

Pick.trkproj, data

```
<PropertyGroup>
  <RemoteDrive
    Condition="'$(RemoteDrive)' == ''">Z:</RemoteDrive>
</PropertyGroup>

<ItemDefinitionGroup>                                    <!-- 1 -->
  <Zone>
    <RemoteDrive>$(RemoteDrive)</RemoteDrive>
    <DropFolderRoot>d:\Data\Drop</DropFolderRoot>
    <DbInstance>.</DbInstance>
  </Zone>
</ItemDefinitionGroup>
<ItemGroup>
  <Zone Include="Test">                                  <!-- 2 -->
    <RemoteComputer>PICARD</RemoteComputer>
    <RemoteShare>\\%(RemoteComputer)\Drop</RemoteShare>
    <RemoteDomain>PICARD.dmz.k7ranch.net</RemoteDomain>
    <RemoteUser>PICARD\ServiceAccount</RemoteUser>
  </Zone>
  <Zone Include="Staging">                               <!-- 3 -->
    <RemoteComputer>KIRK</RemoteComputer>
    <RemoteShare>\\%(RemoteComputer)\Drop</RemoteShare> <!-- 6 -->
    <RemoteDomain>KIRK.azure.local</RemoteDomain>
    <RemoteUser>azure\BuildServiceAccount</RemoteUser>
    <DbInstance>SQLPROD01</DbInstance>
  </Zone>
</ItemGroup>

<ItemGroup>
  <Site Include="Admin">                                 <!-- 4 -->
    <Site>Web.Admin</Site>
    <DropFolder>Web\%(Site)</DropFolder>                 <!-- 7 -->
    <Port>81</Port>
  </Site>
  <Site Include="Public">                                <!-- 5 -->
    <Site>Web.Public</Site>
    <DropFolder>Web\%(Site)</DropFolder>
    <Port>82</Port>
  </Site>
</ItemGroup>

<ItemGroup>
  <PublicSiteArtifact Include="WebProject.Forum" />
  <PublicSiteArtifact Include="WebProject.Storefront" />
  <PublicSiteArtifact Include="Service.EmailQueue" />

  <AdminSiteArtifact Include="WebProject.Admin" />
  <AdminSiteArtifact Include="WebProject.Data" />
```

```
    <AdminSiteArtifact Include="Service.MembershipQueue" />
    <AdminSiteArtifact Include="Service.FlaggedItemQueue" />
  </ItemGroup>
```

An item definition is used (1) to supply default values for @(Zone) metadata, which can be overridden in individual items. Two Zone items are declared, one for a Test server (1) and another for a Staging server (2). Following this pattern, additional zones could be defined for Development, additional layers of QA validatation, and even production. Two separate Site items are declared, one for an Admin site (4) and one for a Public site (5). Note that some of the item metadata (6, 7) uses other metadata to compose new values. The final sets of items are declared using a naming convention. The @(PublicSiteArtifact) and @(AdminSiteArtifact) items are a composition of the Site identity, plus the literal string "SiteArtifact." In the data picking targets that follow this pattern will take shape.

Pick.trkproj, main target

```
<Target Name="PushToZone"
  DependsOnTargets="
    ValidateArguments;
    PickZone;
    PickSite;
    PickArtifacts;
    ConnectToRemoteShare;
    DeployArtifacts;
    ResetWebServer;
    DisconnectFromRemoteShare;
    ">
</Target>
<Target Name="ResetWebServer" />
<Target Name="DisconnectFromRemoteShare" />
```

The main target sets up a dependent target junction point. There are two empty targets in this example, ResetWebServer would be filled in with custom tasks or calls to Exec using a tool such as PsExec. For a detailed example of what you would do in the DisconnectFromRemoteShare target, see *trick #103, How to safely connect to remote machines*.

Pick.trkproj, data picking targets

```
<Target Name="ValidateArguments">
  <Error
    Condition="'$(Zone)' == '' OR '$(Site)' == ''"
    Text="Must supply /p:Zone=value and /p:Site=value"
    />                                              <!-- 1 -->
</Target>
```

```xml
<Target Name="PickZone"
  Outputs="%(Zone.Identity)">                              <!-- 2 -->
  <PropertyGroup Condition="'@(Zone)' == '$(Zone)'">
    <_RemoteComputer>%(Zone.RemoteComputer)</_RemoteComputer>
    <_RemoteDomain>%(Zone.RemoteDomain)</_RemoteDomain>
    <_RemoteUser>%(Zone.RemoteUser)</_RemoteUser>
    <_RemoteDrive>%(Zone.RemoteDrive)</_RemoteDrive>
    <_RemoteShare>%(Zone.RemoteShare)</_RemoteShare>
    <_DropFolderRoot>%(Zone.DropFolderRoot)</_DropFolderRoot>
    <_DbInstance>%(Zone.DbInstance)</_DbInstance>
  </PropertyGroup>
</Target>

<Target Name="PickSite"
  Outputs="%(Site.Identity)">                              <!-- 3 -->
  <PropertyGroup Condition="'@(Site)' == '$(Site)'">
    <_Artifacts>%(Site.Identity)SiteArtifact</_Artifacts>
    <_Site>%(Site.Site)</_Site>
    <_DropFolder>%(Site.DropFolder)</_DropFolder>
    <_Port>%(Site.Port)</_Port>
  </PropertyGroup>
</Target>

<Target Name="PickArtifacts">
  <ItemGroup>
    <_Artifacts Include="@($(_Artifacts))" />              <!-- 4 -->
  </ItemGroup>
</Target>
```

To start off, the required arguments are validated, in this case (1) simply with an Error task. This is a trivial implementation of error checking, which is expanded upon in the next *trick #74, Gathering errors from multiple failures*. Next, the @(Zone) item array is flattened (2) and filtered with a condition based on the value of $(Zone), resulting in a single set of properties for the specified Zone. The same thing is done for the @(Site) item array, filtering on the specified $(Site). Finally, an @(_Artifacts) item array (4) is constructed from the $(_Artifacts) property that was composed in (3). In this example it will cause @(_Artifacts) to be a copy of either @(PublicSiteArtifact) or @(AdminSiteArtifact).

Pick.trkproj, execution targets

```xml
<Target Name="ConnectToRemoteShare">
  <Message Text="Connect to '$(_RemoteShare)'" />
  ...
</Target>

<Target Name="DeployArtifacts">
  <Message
    Text="Deploy to '$(_DropFolder) for port $(_Port)'"
    />
  <Message
```

```
        Text="@(_Artifacts->'  %(Identity)', '%0a')"
        />                                              <!-- 5 -->
     ...
  </Target>
```

Output

```
ConnectToRemoteShare:
  Connect to '\\PICARD\Drop' as 'Z:'
DeployArtifacts:
  Deploy to 'Web\Web.Admin for port 81'
    WebProject.Admin
    WebProject.Data
    Service.MembershipQueue
    Service.FlaggedItemQueue
```

The execution targets display the data that would be used in Exec tasks calling MSDeploy, a third party deployment tool, or simple file copying. Notice that the message displaying all of the items in the calculated @(_Artifacts) item array (5) is formatting the value with a couple leading spaces so that they are indented, and separating the items with the value '%0a' which is an MSBuild escaped carriage return, so that in the output they appear on separate lines.

74. Gathering errors from multiple failures

In the previous trick, all of the missing parameters were tested in a single target, in a single condition. A more sophisticated approach to this type of validation is to aggregate all possible errors among several different validation targets. Validation targets may be spread throughout the build and it can be difficult to combine them into a single spot, so you can instead collect them in two different ways, depending on how your build is structured. The easiest would be to make use of the InitialTargets execution path, essentially letting MSBuild gather and execute them for you. If that is too early in the dependency chain, you can gather the validation targets yourself with a "DependsOn" property list,

```
<PropertyGroup>
   <ValidateArgumentsDependsOn>
      $(ValidateArgumentsDependsOn);
      ValidatePickZoneArguments
   </ValidateArgumentsDependsOn>
</PropertyGroup>
```

Within each validation target, you can further aggregate error messages, one at a time, by adding them to an item array,

```
<Target Name="ValidatePickZoneArguments">
    <ItemGroup>
        <ValidationError
            Condition="'$(Zone)' == ''"
            Include="Must supply /p:Zone=value"
            />
        <ValidationError
            Condition="'$(Site)' == ''"
            Include="Must supply /p:Site=value"
            />
    </ItemGroup>
</Target>
```

Within the junction point Validation target that runs the dependent target list, you can make a final check and display all of the errors, which is better than just displaying the first error and having the build quit, when there may be additional errors that need to be resolved as well,

```
<Target Name="ValidateArguments"
    DependsOnTargets="$(ValidateArgumentsDependsOn)">
    <Warning
        Condition="'@(ValidationError)' != ''"
        Text="%(ValidationError.Identity)"
        />
    <Error
        Condition="'@(ValidationError)' != ''"
        Text="See warnings above"
        />
</Target>
```

In the snippet above, the Warning uses task batching and will be called once for each item in the @(ValidationError) array, if there are any items in it at all. A warning task is used instead of an error task because when executed with task batching, the first item in the array will force an error, and the build will stop before any of the other items in the array are processed. A final error task follows the batched warning with a note to check the warnings that would have just been issued.

75. How to customize developer builds with My.props

I don't like maintaining multiple builds for the same product. Having a build used only by the build machine seems like it is not only going to end up being a one-off pain to maintain, but it is also a source for hard-to-find errors, since the developers won't be using it. Instead, I prefer to maintain a single end-to-end build that is used by developers during their daily edit-compile-release cycles, as well as by the build machines for churning out continuous builds. Eventually, the exact same build script is used for final production builds as well, so that there is no chance for a new error creeping into an already stable and continually run build system.

As your build becomes more comprehensive though, there will likely be some steps that are optional for some developers, or that are too time consuming to interrupt every build performed throughout the day. There may also be build steps that require software that is not licensed for use by every member of the development staff. Using a per-user file that can globally alter the build is a good way to control these options.

It is always possible to control various build stages by passing properties on the command line, or with a response file. When building from the IDE however, there isn't a good way to pass command line options to MSBuild. There are also cases where you may need to alter items or item metadata, which is very cumbersome to pull off using properties on the command line. You may also want to be able to add in your own customizations in targets. Not to mention that remembering and setting up multiple properties on the command line isn't really all that useable for quick iterations.

For this technique I use the name "My.props" for the per-user property file. The "My" prefix indicates by naming convention that the file should never be checked into version control. Since this file is not checked into version control, its use needs to be optional, so that a build is functional when it is absent. The file should be imported into every project as well as into any custom MSBuild projects used to drive the full build. The exact mechanism for this import was covered in *trick #18, Import properties first, targets last*.

Conditional import of My.props

```
<Import
  Condition="Exists('./My.props')"
  Project="'./My.props'"
  />
```

Configurable conditional import, with recursion guard

```
<PropertyGroup>
  <MyPropsPath Condition="'$(MyPropsPath)' == ''">.</MyPropsPath>
</PropertyGroup>
<Import
  Condition="Exists('$(MyPropsPath)/My.props') AND
    '$(MyPropsImported)' != 'imported'"
  Project="'$(MyPropsPath)/My.props'"
  />
```

My.props

```
<Project ...>
  <PropertyGroup>
    <MyPropsImported>imported</MyPropsImported>
  </PropertyGroup>
  <!-- place local customizations here -->
  <PropertyGroup>
    <SkipDocumentation>true</SkipDocumentation>
    <SkipInstaller>true</SkipInstaller>
  </PropertyGroup>
</Project>
```

The listing above shows a simple conditional import, which covers the basic case where the file has not been created, or when sources are newly pulled from version control. The second listing shows the use of the recursion guard described in *trick #81, How to avoid the circular import warning.*

Better still, developers can combine sets of property values, all controlled with a "build profile" property, as shown below,

Build profiles, from My.props

```
<PropertyGroup>
  <Profile Condition="'$(Profile)' == ''">Standard</Profile>
</PropertyGroup>
<PropertyGroup Condition="'$(Profile)' == 'Quick'">
  <SkipDocumentation>true</SkipDocumentation>
  <SkipInstaller>true</SkipInstaller>
  <SkipTests>true</SkipTests>
</PropertyGroup>
<PropertyGroup Condition="'$(Profile)' == 'Full'">
  <SkipDocumentation>false</SkipDocumentation>
  <SkipInstaller>false</SkipInstaller>
  <SkipReleaseBuild>false</SkipReleaseBuild>
</PropertyGroup>
...
```

These build profiles can now be maintained individually, and controlled with a single option,

```
> msbuild Project.proj /p:Profile=Quick
```

Depending on the default value for the various "Skip" properties, some of these can be omitted from various profiles, but the idea remains the same; it is available for developers to tweak as the features they are working on demand.

To extend this trick even further, consider that instead of using a fixed name as is shown here with "My.props," you could instead use an import wildcard on a convention-based file name,

```
<Import Project="$(MyPropsPath)/My.*.props" />
```

First of all, since the import contains a wildcard, there is no need for the Exists condition; if no files exist that match the wildcard there is no error. Secondly, this allows you to establish multiple types of files, for example, My.User.props, My.Team.props, My.Branch.props, each of which could be a more obvious place for particular customizations.

Execution Tricks

Typically MSBuild extensions are developed with heavy use of the command line. For teams making heavy use of Visual Studio though, you need to know a couple things. First, how to make full use of the command line, and second how to make the full power of your scripts available inside the IDE. Here's a pair of tricks that show how to begin.

76. Know the detailed & performance summary logs

When you cross the boundary of twenty or so projects, the amount of time spent building each one can become significant. A three second delay in each project will cost you a minute in the whole build. When you reach 200 projects, it will consume ten extra minutes, which is a long time for a developer to wait around.

To see where all the time has gone, run with diagnostic level logging (/verbosity:diagnostic, or /v:diag). You will be given a performance summary at the end of the build log that can help you to understand where the performance bottlenecks are. You can also force this summary with any verbosity by using one of the console logger parameters. The project file below imports five of the largest project files from other tricks in the book and executes all of their primary targets by declaring them as the DefaultTargets for the importing file.

Detailed Summary.trkproj

```
<Project ...
```

```
    DefaultTargets="
       UsePropertyFunctions;
       UseItemFunctions;
       EnableUseAnyStaticMethod;
       JoinManyToManyWithLinq;
       JoinWithLinq">
   <Import Project="Use Property Functions.trkproj" />
   <Import Project="Use Item Functions.trkproj" />
   <Import Project="Use Any Static in Property Function.trkproj" />
   <Import Project="Many-to-Many With LINQ.trkproj" />
   <Import Project="Join With LINQ.trkproj" />
   ...
</Project>
```

Execute with /v:diag or /clp:PerformanceSummary

```
> msbuild "Detailed Summary.trkproj" /v:diag
> msbuild "Detailed Summary.trkproj" /clp:PerformanceSummary
```

Summary Output (at the very end)

```
Project Performance Summary:
    1859 ms  F:\Code\Trickery\Source Code\Detailed Summary.trkproj
1 calls

Target Performance Summary:
        0 ms  UsePropertyFunctions                          1 calls
        0 ms  EnumPropertyFunctions                         1 calls
       20 ms  RegexPropertyFunctions                        1 calls
       20 ms  DateTimePropertyFunctions                     1 calls
       20 ms  GuidPropertyFunctions                         1 calls
       20 ms  MathPropertyFunctions                         1 calls
       20 ms  ConvertPropertyFunctions                      1 calls
       25 ms  ReadEscapedFromFile                           1 calls
       30 ms  UseItemFunctions                              1 calls
       40 ms  DoublePropertyFunctions                       1 calls
       40 ms  IoPropertyFunctions                           1 calls
       43 ms  EscapePropertyFunctions                       1 calls
       50 ms  CharacterPropertyFunctions                    1 calls
       80 ms  NumericConstantPropertyFunctions              1 calls
      142 ms  EnableUseAnyStaticMethod                      1 calls
      170 ms  JoinWithLinq                                  1 calls
      220 ms  JoinManyToManyWithLinq                        1 calls
      250 ms  BitwisePropertyFunctions                      1 calls
      384 ms  EnvironmentPropertyFunctions                  1 calls

Task Performance Summary:
        0 ms  SetEnvironmentVariable                        1 calls
        0 ms  ReadLinesFromFile                             1 calls
       10 ms  AsBinary                                      7 calls
       20 ms  JoinWithLinqFromItems                         1 calls
       30 ms  JoinManyToManyWithLinqFromItems               1 calls
      511 ms  Message                                     181 calls
```

When run with diagnostic level logging, or with the /clp:PerformanceSummary option, a report showing how much time was spent in each target is displayed, organized from the fastest targets to the slowest. Not surprisingly, the property functions that manipulate environment variables took the most time, followed by the inline tasks that perform complex data joins. Next, a summary is shown by task, showing the total time spent as well as the number of calls made to the task. From this you can see that although the JoinWithLinq targets took a fair amount of time to execute, the inline task was actually very quick, indicating that the processing of the data may have been the bottleneck. Although the Message task consumed a fair amount of time, the time per call was quite small. Still, message display consumed over 25% of the time in the build, indicating that for quick developer builds, running with minimal logging can speed up the build.

These same project files, when collected into an item array, can also be built in parallel, so that we can see another summary report in action:

Detailed Summary.trkproj, BuildInParallel target

```
<ItemGroup>
  <Project Include="Use Property Functions.trkproj" />
  <Project Include="Use Item Functions.trkproj" />
  <Project Include="Use Any Static in Property Function.trkproj"
/>
  <Project Include="Many-to-Many With LINQ.trkproj" />
  <Project Include="Join With LINQ.trkproj" />
</ItemGroup>
<Target Name="BuildInParallel">
  <MSBuild
    Projects="@(Project)"
    BuildInParallel="true"
    />
</Target>
```

Execute with /ds

```
> msbuild "Detailed Summary.trkproj" /t:BuildInParallel /ds
```

Summary Output, reformatted

```
Deferred Messages

 Detailed Build Summary
 =======================


================ Build Hierarchy (IDs represent configurations)===
 Id  : Exclusive Total Path (Targets)
       Time     Time
 ----------------------------------------------------------------
 0   : 0.346s  5.524s  F:\...\Detailed Summary...(BuildInParallel)
```

```
| 1 : 3.658s  3.658s  F:\...\Use Property Functions.trkproj ()
| 2 : 0.036s  0.036s  F:\...\Use Item Functions.trkproj ()
| 3 : 0.182s  0.182s  F:\...\Use Any Static in Property Functi...
| 4 : 0.939s  0.939s  F:\...\Many-to-Many With LINQ.trkproj ()
. 5 : 0.283s  0.283s  F:\...\Join With LINQ.trkproj ()


============= Node Utilization (IDs represent configurations) =====
Timestamp:              1      Duration   Cumulative
-------------------------------------------------------------------
634455675819803552:     0      0.330s     0.330s ######
634455675823104559:     1      3.648s     3.978s ###################
####################################################################
634455675859587640:     2      0.126s     4.104s ##
634455675860843642:     3      0.182s     4.286s ###
634455675862664650:     4      0.939s     5.225s ##################
634455675872049667:     5      0.283s     5.508s #####
634455675874882672:     0      0.016s     5.524s
-------------------------------------------------------------------
Utilization:          100.0   Average Utilization: 100.0
```

In this summary, the column named "Id" shows a text-mode representation of the tree of build nodes created, in this case with node zero as the
parent, with one node for each of the individual files being compiled in
parallel. The next two columns show the execution time for that project
alone, and cumulatively with all of its child nodes. The final column
shows which project was executed, and in parenthesis which target called'
empty parenthesis mean that no target was specified and thus the default
targets were executed. The second part of the chart shows the node
utilization, with a text-mode bar chart using hash marks to indicate
relative duration. From this listing we can see that the most time is
consumed by the "Use Property Functions.trkproj" project, which
matches the performance summary findings.

If build timings are really a concern for you though, you are almost
certainly performing a muti-processor build to get the benefit of
parallelization. The same project above, when run with an extra
command line option, will run across three processors,

```
> msbuild "Detailed Summary.trkproj" /t:BuildInParallel /m:3 /ds
```

In the detailed summary this will be presented in the "Node Utilization"
section of the summary report, with one column for each processor,

Output with /m:3

```
============= Node Utilization (IDs represent configurations) ======
Timestamp:             1    2    3      Duration   Cumulative
-------------------------------------------------------------------
634468100541449444:    0    x    x      0.046s     0.046s
634468100541909470:    1    x    x      0.040s     0.086s
```

```
634468100542309493:  |       3       2      0.055s     0.141s #
634468100542859525:  |       |       4      0.366s     0.507s #######
634468100546519734:  |       |       5      0.099s     0.606s #
634468100547509791:  x       |       |      0.022s     0.628s
634468100547729803:  x       x       |      0.146s     0.774s ##
634468100549189887:  0       x       x      0.002s     0.776s
                    ----------------------------------------------------------
Utilization:        78.4  78.6  99.7        Average Utilization: 85.5
```

The listing above shows a fair distribution across three processors. In this case, the first two processors are starved which is why their utilization is low, adding more projects would start to balance out the build a bit more.

For a more detailed analysis, what follows is a rather verbose listing of the detailed summary report for a large and rather complex build. This listing has been formatted a bit to better fit the page, and has been somewhat obfuscated to hide its origin, but the timings are all real. It is from a product that has been upgraded through several versions of Visual Studio, and it turns out that the age is showing a bit as it doesn't parallelize very well. The first part of the listing shows how the tree of build nodes is created. To understand how the tree structure is displayed, in the left hand column, nodes 1, 14 and 15 etc. are children of node 0, while nodes 22 through 27 are children of node 1, as indicated by the continuation vertical bar starting with the first child, and the dot for the final child node of each parent.

Detailed Summary, large build

```
====================== Build Hierarchy (IDs represent configurations) ======
Id              : Exclusive  Total      Path (Targets)
                  Time       Time
                ----------------------------------------------------------------
0               : 0.749s     270.208s   f:..\dirs.proj (BuildAll...)
| 1             : 0.203s     3.339s     f:..\dirs.proj (Build)
| | 22          : 1.232s     1.232s     f:..\Runtime\Publish.nproj (Build)
| | 24          : 0.265s     0.265s     f:..\Runtime\Dyn.nproj (Build)
| | 23          : 0.078s     0.078s     f:..\Runtime\Custom.nproj (Build)
| | 25          : 0.343s     0.343s     f:..\Runtime\DynUni.nproj (Build)
| | 26          : 0.577s     0.577s     f:..\Runtime\Common.nproj (Build)
| . 27          : 0.343s     0.343s     f:..\Runtime\CommonUni.nproj (Build)
| 14            : 0.811s     0.811s     f:..\Hooks2\Hooks2.nproj (Build)
| 15            : 0.406s     0.406s     f:..\Hooks3\Hooks3.nproj (Build)
| 7             : 128.636s   269.256s   f:..\Interop\Interop.nproj (Build)
| . 30          : 138.826s   140.620s   f:..\Iface\Ids\Ids.nproj (Build)
| | . 61        : 1.794s     1.794s     f:..\Imports\Imports.nproj (Build)
| 10            : 0.749s     0.749s     f:..\CheckFx\CheckFx.nproj (Build)
| 12            : 0.437s     0.437s     f:..\Themes\Themes.nproj (Build)
| 4             : 0.546s     0.749s     f:..\Check\Check.nproj (Build)
| | 2           : 0.000s     0.000s     f:..\Debug\Debug.nproj (Build)
| . 3           : 0.000s     0.000s     f:..\Hooks\Hooks.nproj (Build)
| 2             : 0.608s     0.608s     f:..\Debug\Debug.nproj (Build)
```

```
| 3             : 0.530s    0.530s      f:..\Hooks\Hooks.nproj (Build)
| 5             : 0.031s    3.167s      f:..\Tools\dirs.proj (Build)
| . 28          : 0.094s    3.136s      f:..\Tools\Log\dirs.proj (Build)
|| . 29         : 0.359s    1.310s      f:..\Tools\Log\Query.nproj (Build)
||| | 22        : 0.000s    0.000s      f:..\Runtime\Publish.nproj (Build)
||| . 70        : 0.000s    0.000s      f:..\Check\Check.nproj (Build)
| 6             : 0.016s    267.557s    f:..\Iface\dirs.proj (Build)
|| 30           : 0.000s    0.000s      f:..\Iface\Ids.nproj (Build)
| . 31          : 126.624s  265.918s    f:..\Iface\IdsCustom.nproj (Build)
||| | 61        : 0.000s    0.000s      f:..\Imports\Imports.nproj (Build)
|| . 30         : 0.000s    0.000s      f:..\Iface\Ids.nproj (Build)
| 8             : 0.062s    2.824s      f:..\Tree\dirs.proj (Build)
| . 32          : 0.000s    0.000s      f:..\Tree\Publish.nproj (Build)
| 9             : 0.047s    4.477s      f:..\Util\dirs.proj (Build)
|| 33          : 0.156s    3.339s      f:..\Util\UtilDyn.proj (Build)
||| 62         : 0.250s    1.279s      f:..\Util\UtilDyn.nproj (Build)
||| . 32       : 0.000s    0.000s      f:..\Tree\Publish.nproj (Build)
||| . 63       : 0.187s    1.217s      f:..\Util\UtilDyn2.nproj (Build)
||| . 32       : 0.000s    0.000s      f:..\Tree\Publish.nproj (Build)
|| 34          : 0.156s    2.387s      f:..\Util\Utils.proj (Build)
||| 66         : 0.952s    2.231s      f:..\Util\Utils\Utils.nproj (Build)
||| . 32       : 0.000s    0.000s      f:..\Tree\Publish.nproj (Build)
|| . 67        : 0.172s    1.388s      f:..\Util\Utils2.nproj (Build)
||| . 32       : 0.000s    0.000s      f:..\Tree\Publish.nproj (Build)
|| 35          : 0.125s    1.810s      f:..\Util\UtilDynUni.proj (Build)
||| 68         : 0.218s    1.685s      f:..\Util\UtilDynUni.nproj (Build)
||| . 32       : 0.000s    0.000s      f:..\Tree\Publish.nproj (Build)
|| . 69        : 0.203s    1.388s      f:..\Util\Util2dynUni.nproj (Build)
||| . 32       : 0.000s    0.000s      f:..\Tree\Publish.nproj (Build)
| . 36         : 0.062s    1.732s      f:..\Util\UtilsUni.proj (Build)
||| 64         : 0.094s    1.466s      f:..\Util\UtilsUni.nproj (Build)
||| . 32       : 1.373s    1.373s      f:..\Tree\Publish.nproj (Build)
|| . 65        : 0.234s    1.466s      f:..\Util\UtilsUni2.nproj (Build)
||| . 32       : 0.000s    0.000s      f:..\Tree\Publish.nproj (Build)
| 11           : 0.047s    2.715s      f:..\Ui\dirs.proj (Build)
|| 37          : 0.312s    0.312s      f:..\Ui\Publish.nproj (Build)
|| 38          : 0.125s    0.125s      f:..\Ui\RuntimeDyn.nproj (Build)
| . 39         : 0.265s    0.265s      f:..\Ui\RuntimeCommon.nproj (Build)
| 13           : 0.047s    14.634s     f:..\Edit\dirs.proj (Build)
|| 40          : 1.045s    1.045s      f:..\Edit\Publish.nproj (Build)
|| 41          : 0.218s    0.218s      f:..\Edit\PerfHost.nproj (Build)
|| 43          : 0.234s    0.234s      f:..\Edit\DesignTime2.csproj (Build)
|| 42          : 0.125s    0.125s      f:..\Edit\DesignTime.csproj (Build)
|| 44          : 0.125s    0.125s      f:..\Edit\DesignTime4.csproj (Build)
|| 45          : 13.916s   13.916s     f:..\Edit\EditEtwRc.nproj (Build)
|| 46          : 0.218s    0.218s      f:..\Edit\PerfQA.nproj (Build)
|| 47          : 0.312s    0.312s      f:..\Edit\PerfQA2.nproj (Build)
|| 48          : 0.265s    0.265s      f:..\Edit\Listener.nproj (Build)
|| 49          : 3.417s    3.557s      f:..\Edit\Editink.nproj (Build)
|| . 48        : 0.000s    0.000s      f:..\Edit\Listener.nproj (Build)
| . 50         : 0.125s    0.125s      f:..\Edit\ListenerInterop.csproj (Build)
| 18           : 0.031s    0.983s      f:..\Addin\dirs.proj (Build)
|| 51          : 0.203s    0.203s      f:..\Addin\ConfigReader.csproj (Build)
| . 52         : 0.374s    0.374s      f:..\Addin\Addins\Addins.nproj (Build)
| 19           : 0.094s    0.967s      f:..\Design\dirs.proj (Build)
|| 53          : 0.515s    0.515s      f:..\Design\Design.nproj (Build)
```

```
| | 54      : 0.203s     0.203s     f:..\Design\MockDesign.nproj (Build)
| | 55      : 0.296s     0.671s     f:..\Design\PrivateDesign.nproj (Build)
| | . 53    : 0.000s     0.000s     f:..\Design\Design.nproj (Build)
| | 56      : 0.250s     0.250s     f:..\Design\DesignCert.nproj (Build)
| | 57      : 0.234s     0.234s     f:..\Design\DumpCurrent.nproj (Build)
| | 59      : 0.296s     0.296s     f:..\Design\UnitTest.nproj (Build)
| . 58      : 0.094s     0.094s     f:..\Design\ValidationGen.csproj (Build)
| 20        : 0.062s     0.874s     f:..\Startup\dirs.proj (Build)
| . 60      : 0.796s     0.796s     f:..\Startup\Publish.nproj (Build)
| 16        : 0.374s     0.374s     f:..\Private.nproj (Build)
| 17        : 0.343s     0.343s     f:..\Log\Log.nproj (Build)
. 21        : 0.234s     0.234s     f:..\Licensing\Licensing.nproj (Build)
```

Continued below...

Note that there are "dirs.proj" files highlighted in the listing above. These MSBuild project files—which will be discussed in a section coming up shortly—are like little custom solution files, responsible for building collections of projects. This is easy to see because each of these files is associated with a parent node for the several project files beneath it. The Id numbers assigned to each project are important when you get to the second part of the listing, continued below:

Continued from above, Node Utilization Swimlanes

```
==================== Node Utilization (IDs represent configurations) =====
Timestamp:      1   2   3   4   5   6   7   8   9   Duration  Cumulative
-------------------------------------------------------------------------
63..3317098072: 0   x   x   x   x   x   x   x   x   0.749s    0.749s ###
                                                              ##############
63..3324586456: 1   x   x   x   x   x   x   x   x   0.187s    0.936s ###
63..3326458552: |   12  15  14  10  3   2   7   4   0.016s    0.952s
63..3326614560: 5   |   |   |   |   |   |   |   |   0.031s    0.983s
63..3326926576: 28  |   |   |   |   |   |   |   |   0.094s    1.076s #
63..3327862624: 6   |   |   |   |   |   |   |   |   0.016s    1.092s
63..3328018632: 8   |   |   |   |   |   |   |   |   0.047s    1.139s
63..3328486656: 9   |   |   |   |   |   |   |   |   0.047s    1.186s
63..3328954680: 11  |   |   |   |   |   |   |   |   0.047s    1.232s
63..3329422704: 13  |   |   |   |   |   |   |   |   0.031s    1.264s
63..3329734720: 18  |   |   |   |   |   |   |   |   0.016s    1.279s
63..3329890728: 19  |   |   |   |   |   |   |   |   0.078s    1.357s #
63..3330670768: |   |   51  |   |   |   |   |   |   0.016s    1.373s
63..3330826776: 20  |   |   |   |   |   |   |   |   0.016s    1.388s
63..3330982784: |   53  |   |   |   |   |   |   |   0.031s    1.420s
63..3331294800: |   |   |   |   |   |   |   |   54  0.016s    1.435s
63..3331450808: 60  |   |   |   |   |   |   |   |   0.047s    1.482s
63..3331918832: |   |   |   |   55  |   |   |   |   0.078s    1.560s #
63..3332698872: |   |   |   |   |   |   56  |   |   0.016s    1.576s
63..3332854880: |   |   57  |   |   |   |   30  |   0.047s    1.622s
63..3333322904: |   |   |   |   |   |   |   |   4   0.078s    1.700s #
63..3334102944: |   |   |   |   58  |   |   |   59  0.047s    1.747s
63..3334570968: |   |   |   |   |   52  |   |   |   0.016s    1.763s
63..3334726976: |   |   |   40  |   |   |   |   |   0.016s    1.778s
63..3334882984: |   |   |   |   |   |   |   61  |   0.016s    1.794s
```

```
63..3335038992:  |   |   |   | 41 |   |   |   |   0.016s   1.810s
63..3335195000:  |   | 42 |   |   |   | 43 |   |   0.094s   1.903s #
63..3336131048:  | 44 |   |   |   |   |   |   |   0.031s   1.934s
63..3336443064:  |   | 45 |   |   |   |   |   |   0.062s   1.997s #
63..3337067096:  |   |   |   |   |   |   | 46 0.016s   2.013s
63..3337223104:  |   |   |   | 47 |   |   |   |   0.016s   2.028s
63..3337379112:  | 48 |   |   |   |   |   |   |   0.016s   2.044s
63..3337535120:  |   |   |   |   |   | 49 |   |   0.078s   2.122s #
63..3338315160:  |   |   |   |   | 55 |   |   |   0.031s   2.153s
63..3338627176:  |   |   |   |   | 50 |   |   |   0.062s   2.215s #
63..3339251208:  |   |   |   |   |   |   | 37 0.016s   2.231s
63..3339407216:  18 |   |   |   |   |   |   |   |   0.016s   2.247s
63..3339563224:  38 |   |   |   |   |   |   |   |   0.031s   2.278s
63..3339875240:  |   |   |   |   | 39 33 |   |   0.016s   2.293s
63..3340031248:  | 34 |   |   |   |   |   |   |   0.031s   2.325s
63..3340343264:  |   |   |   | 35 |   |   |   |   0.047s   2.371s
63..3340811288:  36 |   |   |   |   |   |   |   |   0.047s   2.418s
63..3341279312:  |   |   |   |   |   | 49 |   |   0.016s   2.434s
63..3341435320:  64 66 |   | 68 |   |   |   |   0.094s   2.527s #
63..3342371368:  32 |   |   |   |   |   | 69 0.016s   2.543s
63..3342527376:  |   |   |   |   | 67 |   |   |   0.094s   2.637s #
63..3343463424:  |   |   |   | 65 |   |   |   |   0.016s   2.652s
63..3343619432:  | 62 |   |   |   |   |   |   |   0.047s   2.699s
63..3344087456:  |   |   |   |   | 63 |   |   |   0.016s   2.715s
63..3344243464:  |   |   |   |   |   |   | 31 0.094s   2.808s #
63..3345179512:  |   |   | 29 |   |   |   |   |   0.047s   2.855s
63..3345647536:  |   |   |   | 22 |   |   |   |   0.016s   2.871s
63..3345803544:  | 23 |   |   | 24 |   |   |   0.031s   2.902s
63..3346115560:  |   |   |   |   |   |   | 25 0.047s   2.949s
63..3346583584:  | 26 |   |   |   |   |   |   |   0.187s   3.136s ###
63..3348455680:  |   |   | 27 | 16 |   |   |   0.109s   3.245s ##
63..3349547736:  |   |   |   |   |   |   | 17 0.234s   3.479s ####
63..3351887856:  |   |   | 21 |   |   |   |   |   0.031s   3.510s
63..3352199872:  |   |   |   | x |   |   |   0.016s   3.526s
63..3352355880:  | x |   |   | x |   |   |   0.047s   3.573s
```

Continued below...

As painful as it is to read this text-based chart, you can determine quite a bit about the behavior of the build. It is easy to spot which projects are the bottlenecks by looking at the "swimlane" graph in the second part of the listing, which shows the node utilization. The nodes above for the most part have relatively quick timings, but notice how long the lanes become for some nodes. It isn't possible to deduce from this data why some builds are taking so long compared to other builds. For native project types, this is typically the time waiting for link.exe to complete, and sometimes there are disk I/O delays. Notice that on the last line of the listing above, two processors are starved as indicated by the "x" marks. In the continuation of the listing below, those processors eventually are occupied with new work. This indicates that all the remaining projects had to await a bottleneck until they could be scheduled, which is a good thing to try to identify and fix.

The remainder of the swimlane listing continues below, showing the final nodes with an abbreviated notation, since some of them take a remarkable amount of time. For example, the graphic "#+2525" means one timing tick mark "#" followed by 2,252 more that were omitted so that they didn't fill the entire printed page.

```
Continued from above...

63…3352823904:  |  x  |  |  |  x  |  30  |   0.016s    3.588s
63…3352979912:  |  x  |  |  |  x  |  |   x  0.125s    3.713s ##
63…3354227976:  |  x  |  x  |  x  |  |   x  0.187s    3.900s ###
63…3356100072:  8  62 |  x  |  63 |  |  69  0.016s    3.916s
63…3356256080:  x  |  |  x  |  67 |  |   x  0.016s    3.931s
63…3356412088:  x  66 |  x  |  x  |  |   x  0.156s    4.087s ###
63…3357972168:  1  |  |  29 65 x  |  |   x  0.016s    4.103s
63…3358128176:  36 |  |  |  68 x  |  |   x  0.016s    4.119s
63…3358284184:  5  |  |  x  35 x  |  |   x  0.016s    4.134s
63…3358440192:  |  |  |  x  x  x  |  |   x  0.530s    4.665s #######
63…3363744464:  |  34 |  x  x  x  |  |   x  0.016s    4.680s
63…3363900472:  |  x  |  x  x  x  |  |   x  0.920s    5.601s ####+14
63…3373104944:  |  x  |  x  x  x  33 |   x  0.016s    5.616s
63…3373260952:  9  x  |  x  x  x  x  |   x  10.234s   15.850s ##+205
63…3475602200:  13 x  x  x  x  x  x  |   x  0.016s    15.866s
63…3475758208:  x  x  x  x  x  x  x  |   x  126.330s  142.196s #+2525
63…4739058662:  x  x  x  x  x  x  x  7  31  126.437s  268.633s #+2528
63…6003428290:  6  x  x  x  x  x  x  |   x  1.575s    270.208s ###+28
63…6019178331:  0  x  x  x  x  x  x  x   x  0.016s    270.224s
-------------------------------------------------------------------
Utilization:  1.5 1.3 5.5 1.0 1.2 1.0 1.7 100 47.9
                     Average Utilization: 17.9
```

This final part of the build ends up with some incredibly long duration build nodes. Only two of the processors, the eighth and ninth columns, achieve more than 5% occupancy during the build. The main culprits appear to be nodes 30, 31, 7 and possibly 9. From the first listing, the one with the build node tree hierarchy, we can see that these nodes are identified as:

```
Node 30,  f:..\Iface\Ids.nproj
Node 31,  f:..\Iface\IdsCustom.nproj
Node 7,   f:..\Interop\Interop.nproj
Node 9,   f:..\Util\dirs.proj
```

Right away it is easy to hone in on which projects are messing with the build performance. Notice how many of the other processors are starved when these final steps in the build are being processed. The first line of attack would be to try to break up these long-building projects into smaller chunks, or to adjust the number of processors used so that all of them are fully utilized. There are a number of things you can do to deal with the outliers:

1. You can also look for ways to break up inter-project dependencies, which prevent building a project while waiting for the build of a dependent project to complete.
2. Find a way to move them earlier in the build, probably by reducing the dependencies they have on other projects. This may involve building against header files in a C++ project, or using assemblies from a previous build pass, or by removing unused assemblies (JetBrains ReSharper can help).
3. On rare occasions, you may have caught MSBuild making some poor scheduling choices. Since it currently doesn't keep any data about previous builds, it can't tell ahead of time which projects are the expensive ones. It may arbitrarily be building them last. In this case you may be able to coerce the build order by juggling the order the projects are listed in your outer build or dirs.proj project.
4. In the worst case, you can literally invoke the build of the long-running projects separately before building the rest of the projects. You can leave them in the main build as well, which should discover them already up to date.

So, there are many of options, and once you've gotten the interdependencies worked out, you can then work on analyzing individual projects using the task summary performance log to find out how to speed them up as well.

For build machines with more than eight processors, you may find that until such optimizations are done, there is little difference between an 8–way and a 16–way build. It isn't that MSBuild doesn't scale—it can handle this scaling quite well—it is that your project architecture may not lend itself to aggressive scaling without some custom tuning of your projects.

After cleaning up the parallelization of your build, even when there are outlier nodes that require quite a bit more time than all the rest, and even with some intermittent starvation, especially at the end of the build, you should strive to see a utilization summary that looks more like this:

```
Utilization:  95.8  96.0  95.3  99.6  94.5  95.4  95.8  96.9  94.8
                                       Average Utilization: 96.0
```

Looking at the utilization, when numbers are near 100% as they were in the real-life build utilization of a large set of projects shown above, your build may have been scheduled close to optimally. But these timings include all the time spent waiting for file IO, which can be considerable. You may want to experiment by reducing the CPU count by one to get additional timings, since this may actually decrease the file IO contention in the build and increase the overall performance.

77. How to make an item array available in the IDE

When you add item array types directly to your project file in an item group, rather than in an imported file, any file items in the item arrays in those item groups will appear in the solution explorer. If you open the Properties window when one of these files is selected, the "Build Action" for the file will be the name of the item type in which it is a member. But what if you want to make it possible to add files to the item array from within the IDE?

There is a special item type that contains the collection of named items that is to appear in the "Build Action" drop down. Simply add an entry to this item type with the name of your custom item array for which you've already wired build behavior into the project, typically through imported .props and .targets files you've authored.

```
<ItemGroup>
    <AvailableItemName Include="MyItem" />
</ItemGroup>
```

That's it. Add any file to your project, then right click and select Properties. At this point, if the file extension is not yet associated with a particular item type, the file will be in the "None" item type and the Build Action will be "None."

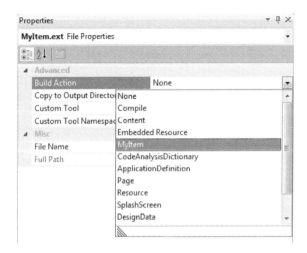

In the Properties window, click on the Build Action drop down and your registered item name should be available. Selecting this or any item in the drop-down causes the project system to move the file from the "None" item array to the selected one, creating the new item array if it doesn't already exist in the project.

The @(AvailableItemName) item array above will make your custom item arrays available for the purpose of associating them with a build action. There is also a related bit of functionality in the IDE with respect to your custom item arrays, which is the specially treated "Visible" metadata value. When items are declared in an item array, the state of this metadata determines whether or not items in the array will appear in the solution explorer hierarchy. For items that are in the project file itself, the default value of this metadata is assumed to be the value "true," which indicates that the item should be shown. To omit any particular item, just set this value to false,

```
<ItemGroup>
   <MyItemGroup Include="My.file">
      <Visible>false</Visible>
   </MyItemGroup>
</ItemGroup>
```

To omit all items, you can set this non-default value in an item definition group,

```
<ItemDefinitionGroup>
   <MyItemGroup>
      <Visible>false</Visible>
   </MyItemGroup>
</ItemDefinitionGroup>
```

Now above you may have missed that I said that this is the behavior for items "in the project file itself." It turns out that for items that arrive in the project file by way of an import, the behavior was reversed, in order to get the correct default behavior with regard to the IDE features. For imported items, the value of %(Visible) is presumed to be false. If you want those to show up, be sure to explicitly set this metadata value to "true," either on individual items or on the item definition.

78. How to run custom targets from the IDE

There is a simple (though not all that satisfying) way to run targets from the IDE using a custom external tool. Assuming your project file has the following modification:

```
<Target Name="CalledFromIde">
  <Message
      Importance="High"
      Text="Called from the IDE!"
      />
</Target>
```

Remember that if the project had been loaded in the IDE previously, you will need to reload the project, and if you put the customization into an imported file, you will need to reload the solution.

Next, after the modification above has been made to a project file, in the IDE navigate to the Tools | External Tools command and add an external tool with these values,

```
Title: Called from IDE
Command: C:\Windows\Microsoft.NET\Framework64\v4.0.30319\MSBuild.exe
Arguments: $(ProjectDir)$(ProjectFileName) /t:CalledFromIde
Initial directory: $(ProjectDir)
Use Output window: checked
```

To run the command, select the new Tools | Called from IDE command that will have been just created. You will either need to select the project in the Solution Explorer or have one of the files in the project open in the editor, either of which will set the properties referenced in the external tool command to the proper project.

Running this command, with a loaded project containing the CalledFromIde target customization above, will produce the following output,

```
Build started 6/4/2011 10:59:30 PM.
Project "F:\Code\...\CsProject.csproj" on node 1 (CalledFromIde ⇥
target(s)).
CalledFromIde:
  Called from the IDE!
Done Building Project "F:\Code\...\CsProject.csproj"          ⇥
(CalledFromIde target(s)).
```

This will appear in the Output tool window, in a new output channel named "Called from IDE" which can be selected in the combo box in the Output tool window toolbar. What you are doing is calling out to MSBuild as an external tool and having it run the target directly. You have to supply the full path to MSBuild because the IDE doesn't maintain the same properties that are available from within the build environment it creates for normal IDE builds.

Note that the Message task sets the message importance to "high" which makes it appear in the Output Window with the default IDE settings. See *trick #33, Know how to control MSBuild from the IDE,* for more details on settings to control output visibility.

You can also hook up this external tool to a shortcut key. First select the Tools | Customize command, then click the Keyboard... button at the bottom of the dialog. When the dialog appears, enter the following text in the search box labeled "Show commands containing"

```
Tools.ExternalCommand
```

You will see a list of external commands numbered 1 through 24. All you need to do now is figure out which of the 24 commands is your new one. This is not as easy as it would seem, but a nice trick is to create a new temporary toolbar (Tools | Customize | New...) then make sure the toolbar is visible on a line of its own, then one-by-one add the External Command commands to it, with,

- Tools | Customize | Commands tab | Toolbar

- select your new temporary toolbar

- Add Command...

- select Tools

- scroll down to Tools.ExternalCommand1

- repeat

As they are added to the temporary toolbar, the name of the external command will appear. In my case it ended up being #3, go figure?

Now, knowing the correct command number, it is easy to hook up the keyboard shortcut.

Now building with an arbitrary target is one thing, but this trick can really come in handy to speed up builds from within the IDE. When built inside Visual Studio, C# and Visual Basic projects will be built on a single processor. There is no particular reason for this, and hopefully Microsoft will correct this omission in the next version of Visual Studio. For now, try configuring an external tool as shown above, but with the following command line,

```
Title: Called from IDE
Command: C:\Windows\Microsoft.NET\Framework64\v4.0.30319\MSBuild.exe
Arguments: $(ProjectDir)$(ProjectFileName) /t:Build /m
Initial directory: $(ProjectDir)
Use Output window: checked
```

Notice that the target has been set to the standard "Build" target, and also that the /m multiprocessor command line option has been used. By default this will use all available processors. You may want to set this to the number of processors plus or minus one to get better performance. See *trick #9, Use property functions*, for an example of this calculation being performed on the fly. It is not unheard of to double the speed of the build using this technique.

This is just a quick IDE extension that can be useful for certain repetitive tasks, but may not provide enough customization. To see something more advanced, you need to get ahold of the companion book, *More MSBuild Trickery*, which describes these more advanced topics and how to perform tighter integrations with Visual Studio.

79. Know what should make you feel queasy

The solution file in Visual Studio serves as a workspace with a collection of projects. It isn't an MSBuild file, though it is known to the engine, which needs to convert it into an MSBuild compatible file when building. As such, there are a few features available in the solution that are essentially an end-run around the MSBuild in the project. These features are available with just a few clicks in the IDE, making them pretty enticing to use. They are best avoided though, as each has a better expression in the MSBuild in the projects themselves.

Avoid the Solution Configuration Manager

The solution file provides a mechanism for associating a specific platform in one project with a platform in another, and controlling these with the Platform combo box in an IDE toolbar. This feature, known as the Configuration Manager, is something that you really want to avoid for a couple reasons. First of all, it specifies build parameters outside of your projects and relies on a file format that is incompatible with MSBuild. Second of all, it allows for some really horrible combinations that are difficult to diagnose. It is possible to configure the solution so that when building with "Win32" and "Debug" selected, you are really getting "x64" and "Release" built for some or even all projects.

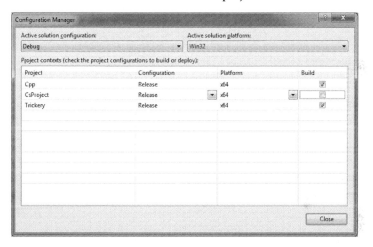

Worse, as shown above, if the checkmark in the Build column happens to get unchecked, nothing in that project will get built, and you'll have tough to diagnose issues related to having an out-of-date assembly from a prior build, or will be left scratching your head as to why the program doesn't work. Your best chance of long term success, especially as the build grows in size and project count, is to leave the Configuration Manager alone, except for a periodic check to ensure that there aren't rogue configurations. Rely instead on an MSBuild based command line build that can be integrated into the IDE using the previous *trick #78, How to run custom targets from the IDE*, replacing the solution build altogether.

Just to be clear here, whatever you set up in the Configuration Manager will be fully respected by MSBuild when it generates the "metaproj" MSBuild file based on the solution settings. If you are planning on defining your own "solution mechanics" in a custom MSBuild file though, this feature—and its evil twin known as the solution Batch Build feature—are best avoided.

Avoid Solution Dependencies

Worse still than the Configuration Manager is the solution level Project Dependencies feature. This allows you to declare inter-project dependencies from the solution file. The project files become unaware of dependencies among one another. When you use this feature, your build is hopelessly tied to the solution file. To properly specify inter-project dependencies, make sure that they are always specified using either the @(Reference) or @(ProjectReference) item arrays in the project file itself or in a shared file imported by the project files.

On the Visual Studio Blog there is an entry titled "Incorrect solution build ordering when using MSBuild.exe[15]." It describes in detail some of the issues that can arise as a result of using solution-based dependencies.

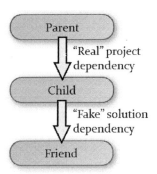

If a project "Parent" has an actual project dependency on another project "Child," while in the solution there is a solution dependency from "Child" to "Friend," the build will likely fail. The solution will launch the build of "Parent" and "Child" concurrently. This launch of the build for "Child" will await the build of "Friend," but when the simultaneously launched build of the "Parent" project discovers the real project dependency on "Child," it will immediately schedule a second build of that project, unaware of the behind the scenes "meta" build already set up by the solution. I say it will likely fail because in a concurrent build among several projects, there is no way to know whether or not the "fake" dependency from "Child" to "Friend" will trigger "Friend" to be built in

---

[15] Available at http://bit.ly/depfail

time for the real dependency from "Parent" to "Child" to succeed, since "Child" can't successfully build until "Friend" is built.

A common reason people rely on the solution dependency mechanism instead of using project references is the case where you need a build-time dependency, but not the runtime dependency that is typically inherited when setting up a project reference. If this is the case, it is very easy to set up the dependency properly, using a special metadata value on the reference. For C# or C++/CLI projects, specify the dependency like this,

```
<ProjectReference Include=".../Dependency.csproj">
   <ReferenceOutputAssembly>false</ReferenceOutputAssembly>
</ProjectReference>
```

and for C++ projects like this,

```
<ProjectReference Include=".../Dependency.vcxproj">
   <LinkLibraryDependencies>false</LinkLibraryDependencies>
</ProjectReference>
```

Both of these will cause the proper build ordering while avoiding any sort of dependency on the resulting build target of the reference project.

Watch for Rogue Platforms

If you keep a close eye on check-ins on the solution files, you may at times notice an incredible bloat in the size of the solution caused by the addition of a single project file. Whereas the solution file's configuration section may have looked like this for a single project, shown with the project Guids truncated,

```
{9D17E40C...1019D68D}.Debug|Win32.ActiveCfg = Debug|x86
{9D17E40C...1019D68D}.Debug|x64.ActiveCfg = Debug|x86
{9D17E40C...1019D68D}.Release|Win32.ActiveCfg = Release|x86
{9D17E40C...1019D68D}.Release|x64.ActiveCfg = Release|x86
```

become this,

```
{9D17E40C...1019D68D}.Debug|Mixed Platforms.ActiveCfg = Debug|x86
{9D17E40C...1019D68D}.Debug|Mixed Platforms.Build.0 = Debug|x86
{9D17E40C...1019D68D}.Debug|Win32.ActiveCfg = Debug|x86
{9D17E40C...1019D68D}.Debug|x86.ActiveCfg = Debug|x86
{9D17E40C...1019D68D}.Debug|x86.Build.0 = Debug|x86
{9D17E40C...1019D68D}.Release|Mixed Platforms.ActiveCfg = Release|x86
{9D17E40C...1019D68D}.Release|Mixed Platforms.Build.0 = Release|x86
{9D17E40C...1019D68D}.Release|Win32.ActiveCfg = Release|x86
{9D17E40C...1019D68D}.Release|x86.ActiveCfg = Release|x86
{9D17E40C...1019D68D}.Release|x86.Build.0 = Release|x86
```

not just for one project, but for every project in the solution. For solutions with hundreds of projects, the bloat can be enormous. What has happened? Likely, a project was created using a project template that was incompatible with your existing projects. In order for the solution file to have contained only the "Win32" and "x64" Platforms, every project in the solution could have only contained those two. The newly added project however, instead of having a matching "Win32" platform, contained an "x86" platform. This introduces an incompatibility that causes several things to happen. First, the "x86" platform needed to be matched to an existing platform in all of the other projects. Second, because there is a mismatch, the solution creates the "Mixed Platforms" entries.

When you see this sort of change in the check-in log, you need to get aggressive about cleaning it up. First, identify the new offending project. Next, fix the platforms in that project to match those that are already in use. Finally, revert the solution file and add the cleaned up project to the solution in a second time.

The best practice that needs to evolve on the team is this, "always perform a line-by-line visual diff for every change to project files or solution files, looking for rogue patterns." Every change seen in the diff during check-in operation should be intentional and expected.

80. Define your own solution mechanics

Solution files tend to become troublesome in large projects.

Second class citizens. Not even the Microsoft developers building Visual Studio use them for their builds.

I'm going to let you in on a little secret. I'm no fan of solution files, they've caused me more build trouble than any other part of the build chain. Okay, that's not the secret. What is though is that my dislike of this feature has been confirmed in a way, when I found out that internally in Microsoft, many products that use MSBuild—like those in the Developer Division team—don't use solution files for building. A solution file is best thought of as an artifact of the old build systems—the only artifact not yet ported to the new technology of MSBuild. Sure it is dealt with by MSBuild in a special case way, but there are limitations as we've already gone over.

At Microsoft, there are a few very simple techniques that are widely used to build the many projects that make up a product build, what you'd typically think of as a solution. The source trees of products at Microsoft can be quite large—including tests the build of Visual Studio .NET involves somewhere on the order of 15,000 projects and is built without solution files. Products aren't monolithic, they are collections of individually built assemblies, often worked on by different teams, each who owns a portion of the source tree. To pull everything together in a single build, each directory in the source tree is given a special file. In one technique, this file—called a "traversal project"—is used to walk the directory structure and build any projects it can find, using a wildcard search. In another technique, this special file is named by convention "dirs.proj" and contains lists of project files. The project files in the list can be individual C# or C++ project files, or conveniently, other "dirs.proj" projects in child folders. An example in its simplest form would look something like this,

```
dirs.proj

<Project ...>
   <ItemGroup>
      <Project Include="Source\Main.csproj" />
      <Project Include="Source\Secondary.csproj" />
      <Project Include="Source\FeatureOne\dirs.proj" />
      <Project Include="Source\FeatureTwo\dirs.proj" />
   </ItemGroup>
   <Target Name="Build">
      <MSBuild
         Projects="@(Project)"
         Targets="Build"
         BuildInParallel="true"
         />
   </Target>
</Project>
```

From the command line in any folder in the source tree, provided that there is only a single *.*proj file in the folder, all you need to do is type "msbuild" and you will build everything from that part of the source tree on down. The "dirs.proj" files can incorporate all of the tricks in this book to create your own solution-free build system. Both of these techniques reinforce how important it is to use only project references to declare all inter-project dependencies.

Of special mention would be the use of the AdditionalProperties metadata on items passed to the MSBuild task, for example,

```
<ItemGroup>
   <SolutionItem Include="..."
      Condition="...">
      <AdditionalProperties>Prop=value;...</AdditionalProperties>
   </solutionItem>
```

```
</ItemGroup>
```

These AdditionalProperties are covered in the *trick #19, Consider using the standard extensions path*, and *trick #32, Understand the limitations of the MSBuild task*.

Also remember that if you choose to use imports to construct your solution mechanics, relative paths found in imported project files are composed from the main project file, not the project file in which they happen to be defined. In cases where an imported project file—and in this case I'm referring to any MSBuild project file, not necessarily a C# or C++ project file—is in a folder separate from the main project file, and there are several main project files in use that all import the same secondary file, you may need to discriminate which location you wish to use as the root for files placed relative to one file or another.

```
$(MSBuildThisFileDirectory)
$(MSBuildStartupDirectory)
$(MSBuildProjectDirectory)
```

Of course, you'll need a solution file for your daily work, and you won't want to have to maintain one separately. Any solution file that is checked into source control will inevitably get corrupted with rogue platform, solution-file-only "fake" project dependencies, and unexpected config-uration options, leaving you, the guy trying to get the build working perfectly, in a bit of a bind. The best solution I've ever come across is also one used at Microsoft, which is to generate the solution files dynamically. You can use the data in the dirs.proj file, along with data extracted from the project files it references, to synthesize one at any level of the source tree. This will be given coverage in depth in the companion book, *More MSBuild Trickery*.

Important to note with this notion of rolling your own solution file mechanics is that there is no easy—or even recommended—way to encode all of the inter-project dependencies in a dirs.proj file, which further clarifies that all dependencies should really be properly declared in the project files themselves using project-to-project references.

Project Import Tricks

Next is a pair of tricks related to the Import element. The first one shows how to avoid a commonly seen warning, followed by a trick that tries to help the developers making modifications to imported projects.

81. How to avoid the circular import warning

It is fair to say that you should structure your build files in a normalized way that prevents circular or repeated imports from occurring. It is also fair to say that even if goals are worthwhile, they are sometimes at odds with other concerns such as legacy support or time constraints. Having an error and warning free build is always important though, so this tip is presented in that light.

As was noted in the introductory section on Imports, importing the same file twice will produce a warning. You can use a Condition on an import to avoid this provided you are able to stick with a simple pattern.

The pattern involves setting a unique sentry property for each imported file, which will be familiar if you've ever seen an inclusion guard around a C++ header file.

Imported file, ImportMe.trkprops

```
<Project ...>
   <PropertyGroup>
      <ImportMePropsImported>imported<ImportMePropsImported>
   </PropertyGroup>
   ...
</Project>
```

Importing file, Master.trkproj

```
<Project ...>
   <Import
      Condition="'$(ImportMePropsImported)' != 'imported'"
      Project="ImportMe.trkprops"
      />
   ...
</Project>
```

The first time the import statement for the file is reached, the $(...Imported) property will not be set, the condition on the Import will succeed, and the file will be imported. When processing the import file, the $(...Imported) property is set to the value "imported." Upon the subsequent Import statement for the same file, the condition will now fail, avoiding the second attempt to import the same file and preventing the warning from appearing. Needless to say, this will really only work if every Import statement for the offending files is properly structured with the conditional import based on the same property name.

82. How to force Visual Studio to build properly when using imports

In a team environment all your projects and customizations—except for your "My file" customizations—will be checked into version control. It is also pretty likely that folks will want to build from the solution file inside Visual Studio. Unfortunately, the importation of property files can cause issues when building in the IDE, requiring some additional trickery to make it work.

The problem is that Visual Studio, when loading projects containing imports, caches the imported property files. If a solution is kept open while the imported property or target files are updated from version control, Visual Studio doesn't notice the update to the file. Subsequent project builds will occur using the older cached version of the updated import file's contents. When the changes to the imported file are ignored, the build will either fail, or even worse, it will complete with unexpected results. This is true even when Team Foundation is the version control system, even though it has special understanding of project file updates.

This can cause disruption every time the import files are updated, requiring developers to close and reopen solution files, typically after wasting time trying to discover the source of the build error they encounter.

To demonstrate this, consider a simple C# project file with an imported targets file.

Forced Build With Imports/ForcedBuildWithImports.csproj

```xml
<Project ...>
  ...
  <Import Project="Common.targets" />
</Project>
```

Forced Build With Imports/Common.targets

```xml
<Project ...
  InitialTargets="Verify">                                  <!-- 1 -->
  <Target Name="Verify">
    <Message Importance="High" Text="***" />                <!-- 2 -->
    <Message Importance="High" Text="*** VERIFIED" />
    <!--Error Text="*** ERROR" /-->                         <!-- 3 -->
    <Message Importance="High" Text="***" />
  </Target>
</Project>
```

Output built from Command Line (partial)

```
...
Verify:
  ***
  *** VERIFIED
  ***
```

Output Window inside Visual Studio

```
------ Build started: Project: ForcedBuildWithImports,            ➥
Configuration: Debug Any CPU ------
  ForcedBuildWithImports -> C:\Dev\...\ForcedBuildWithImports.exe
  ***
  *** VERIFIED
  ***
========== Build: 1 succeeded or up-to-date, 0 failed, 0 skipped  ➥
==========
```

Because the imported targets file declares an InitialTargets (1) named "Verify," the Verify target will run with every build. In order to get the message to show up in the Visual Studio Output Window by default, the Importance (2) is set to "High." The target at first only prints out a message. Initially the Error task is commented out (3) as shown.

When this project is loaded in the Visual Studio IDE and built, the Output Window should present the message from the imported targets file when the Verify target is run. Build a second time and notice that even when the project is up-to-date the Verify target will still be run. Now, without closing the solution, open the Common.targets file and edit it to remove the comments around the Error task. Save the file and rebuild. Although the Error task is now active in the Verify target, the build result is the same as it was prior to the modification. At this point, building from the command line will produce the expected result with the error.

Only after a close and reopen of the solution file will the result match that of the command line build, as shown below:

Output with Error built from Command Line (partial)

```
Verify:
  ***
  *** VERIFIED
C:\Dev\...\Common.targets(8,5): error : *** ERROR            ➥
[C:\Dev\...\ForcedBuildWithImports.csproj]
```

Output Window with Error, after Close/Reopen of Solution

```
------ Build started: Project: ForcedBuildWithImports,            ➥
Configuration: Debug Any CPU ------
```

```
ForcedBuildWithImports -> C:\Dev\...\ForcedBuildWithImports.exe
***
 *** VERIFIED
C:\Dev\...\Common.targets(8,5): error : *** ERROR
========== Build: 0 succeeded or up-to-date, 1 failed, 0 skipped ⟲
==========
```

That the Verify target always runs, even when the project is up-to-date,
provides a clue as to how we can make a further modification to force the
Visual Studio IDE build to behave. Part of the sequence of operations
when processing the "Build" target in standard project files is the
determination of whether or not the project is up-to-date. By wiring into
this process, we can add the imported file into the list of files whose dates
are being checked. When the target file is newer than the output file, the
project will be considered "dirty" and rebuilt as would be expected.

To locate the right place to wire this in, you may need to refer to
trick #42, Investigate the standard build files.

The standard targets file for C# projects, Microsoft.CSharp.targets,
declares a property named $(MSBuildAllProjects). Each of the standard
Microsoft supplied build files involved in the build add themselves to this
property, which becomes a semicolon delimited list of file names. This
property is then aggregated into the Inputs attribute on the CoreCompile
target. The project file and all of its imports are considered inputs to the
build in the same manner as the source files. You would think that this
property could be extended with your own project imports files. The
problem is that even though the build may be able to recognize that the
file date has changed and trigger a build, because the contents of the file
are cached, it doesn't really matter if the project is rebuilt, it won't have
access to any of the changes in the imported file, it will continue to use
the stale imported version.

The only useful trick I've discovered to get around this is really a
workaround for the aggressive caching behavior of the IDE.

In Common.targets

```
<Target Name="UpToDateImport"
  BeforeTargets="PrepareForBuild"
  Inputs="$(MSBuildThisFileFullPath)"
  Outputs="$(MSBuildThisFileFullPath).cache"
  Condition="
    '$(BuildingProject)' == 'true' AND
    '$(BuildingInsideVisualStudio)' == 'true' AND
    '$(SolutionPath)' != '*Undefined*' AND
    '$(SolutionPath)' != '' AND
    Exists('$(SolutionPath)')"
```

```
      >                                           <!-- 1 -->
    <Message
      Importance="High"
      Text="*** The imported file $(MSBuildThisFile) has changed.
*** The solution file $(SolutionFile) will be reloaded in order
*** to use the new version of the imported file, which has been
*** previously cached by the IDE."
      />                                          <!-- 2 -->
    <Touch
      AlwaysCreate="true"
      Files="$(MSBuildThisFileFullPath).cache"
      />                                          <!-- 3 -->
    <Touch
      Files="$(SolutionPath)"
      />                                          <!-- 4 -->
  </Target>
```

Essentially, a target is wired into the build in Common.targets that checks for the state where the custom import file has a file date newer than the most recent build. When this is detected, the solution file containing the offending project is touched, which forces the IDE to prompt you to reload it. When reloading a solution file, the IDE gets rid of the cached version of all imported files. The next build will include the newly loaded version of the custom import file containing the detected modifications.

In the code listing above, quite a bit is going on that is worth mentioning. The target is wired into the standard C# build by setting the BeforeTargets attribute (1) to PrepareForBuild, a target declared in the standard Microsoft.Common.targets file, making it one of the first targets to be executed.

The Condition on the Target (also at 1) first checks the value of $(BuildingProject). This property is set to true only when the project is being built, as opposed to other operations that occur at load time that may execute targets for other purposes. Because this issue occurs only when building from within the IDE and not when building from the command line, the $(BuildingInsideVisualStudio) property is checked. The project system sets this property explicitly when using the internal call to MSBuild, it is not declared in the standard project files. Since this target needs to touch the solution file, the $(SolutionPath) property is checked. When building from the command line, this and other properties available as macros when in the IDE are set to the value "*Undefined*." An additional check to ensure this property isn't empty is also included due to paranoia, and finally a condition is added to ensure that any value for $(SolutionPath) actually refers to a file that exists.

What drives this target, (also at 1) is the declaration of the Inputs and Outputs. For input, file date of the file referred to by the reserved property $(MSBuildThisFileFullPath), which refers to the file in which the declaration occurs, in this case the Common.targets file, is compared against the modification date of an empty "cache" file named $(MSBuildThisFileFullPath).cache that is expected to sit beside the imported project file. You may think that a file like this should be placed into the intermediate output folder of the project from which it is imported, but in a solution with multiple files, this could result in multiple solution file reloads being triggered during a single build.

A detailed high importance message is printed (2), explaining to the user why the project is being forcibly reloaded. Next an empty cache file named $(MSBuildThisFileFullPath).cache is touched (3) to prevent an endless loop of reloads, and finally the solution file itself (4) is touched. If your version control system requires you to get a lock on the solution file before touching it, you'll need to include an Exec task or two to run whatever command line is needed to either perform the lock or work around it. But then, checking in solution files is another topic unto itself, if you can generate them from build metadata you'll be in a better place overall.

There is a bit of a bootstrapping problem in this trick because the $(MSBuildThisFileFullPath).cache file will not exist the first time the solution is pulled from source control. Because projects are partially built during their initial load, though not fully compiled, there don't appear to be any checks available to set up the cache file in time, so upon the first load of the solution from a fresh checkout, it will always reload itself. Since the $(MSBuildThisFileFullPath).cache file is not written out to the @(FileWrites) item array, and not included in the ProjectName.FileList-Absolute.txt listing in the intermediate output file, it won't be removed when the project is cleaned, so this bootstrapping reload should only occur one time, as long as you haven't done extra work to delete the "obj" folders outside of what occurs in the Clean target, thus removing the $(MSBuildThisFileFullPath).cache sentry file as well.

To expand this to be able to deal with multiple import files, just alter the Inputs to work off of an item array into which each of your import files can place their own path.

```
<!-- place this ItemGroup declaration in every import file -->
<ItemGroup>
  <UpToDateCheck Include="$(MSBuildThisFileFullPath)" />
<ItemGroup>

<!-- this target needs to be defined only once -->
```

```
<Target Name="UpToDateImport"
    BeforeTargets="PrepareForBuild"
    Inputs="@(UpToDateCheck)"
    ...
```

For any file type other than MSBuild files imported by the project, there is a much less aggressive approach. In addition to the not-really-useful $(MSBuildAllProjects) property, there is another one reserved for your use, named $(CustomAdditionalCompileInputs). Just add any non-build-file files to this property, as follows:

```
<PropertyGroup>
    <CustomAdditionalCompileInputs>
        MyFileToTriggerBuilds.file;
        $(CustomAdditionalCompileInputs)
    </CustomAdditionalCompileInputs>
</PropertyGroup>
```

At this point, the previous experiment should prove successful. Close and reopen the solution file containing the project with the imported Common.targets file. Now open the Common.targets file and remove the comments around the Error task, then save the file. Next perform a build. Early in the build, the Inputs and Outputs dependency detection triggers the UpToDateImport target, causing the IDE to prompt for a reload of the solution file, as shown below in the screenshot of the solution and project file related to this trick from the online download companion content for this book.

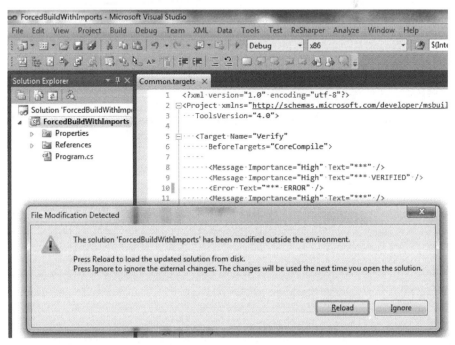

At this point, if you click the Reload button and build again the new contents of the reloaded targets file cause the forced error to occur.

Item Array Looping and Data Joining Tricks

If one thing is clear by now it should be this: item arrays are the data that both drive the build behavior and are consumed by it. The combination of item metadata, item transforms, item functions and batching provide enough power and flexibility to express rich data relationships that can be used to drive the entire build from end-to-end.

The tricks in this next section are a bit of a change from most of the other examples thus far. They treat item arrays as raw data, and show how to perform some basic data operations on them; operations that will be particularly familiar if you've used relational databases. The hope is that by learning these tricks just as they relate to the data structures themselves, you will gain insight into how they can be used when you come upon a particularly aggressive operation you want to encode into your build.

83. How to execute a target more than once

Generally a target only gets a single shot at execution. They are not like function calls in a procedural language in that regard. They can't be called more than once in the execution on a single build node in the engine. This question comes up so often though that it is deserving of its own section here, even though this is really just a reference to various techniques covered elsewhere.

There are however a couple things that can simulate repeated calls to a target. Many of these techniques are covered elsewhere; here are references to a few that fall into this category,

- Use target batching, see *trick #35, Understand batched target execution*

- Rely on target Conditional reevaluation; see *trick #39, Understand CallTarget target execution*. The target won't actually execute more than once, but you can get several attempts to get it to execute one time based on a changing conditional expression.

- Another technique, covered in *trick #85, How to drive targets as if in a loop*, discusses how to set up item data in a way that can simulate iterating over the data in a target, a technique that leads to discussions of how to nest these loops in various ways in subsequent sections.

In the end though, you may find that none of this works as you need. There are really two options left. The first—and in many cases the best option—is to create a custom task to handle the behavior, since there is no limit to how often a task can be invoked. The other option is to use the MSBuild task to call recursively into the project containing the target and run it on a separate node in the build engine. In order to do this of course, you will need to provide all the properties and items needed for the task to execute properly. All of this is discussed in *trick #32, Understand the limitations of the MSBuild task*.

84. How to force target execution with fake outputs

We've already examined target dependency execution using Inputs and Outputs. This trick is a useful extension to the normal target execution mechanics. The example that follows relies on the directory structure below,

```
./InputsOutputs/
  One.in
  Two.in
```

These files are referenced directly in an item array that declares @(Input), as shown in (1) below.

Target Inputs and Outputs.trkproj

```
<ItemGroup>                                         <!-- 1 -->
    <Input Include="InputsOutputs\One.in" />
    <Input Include="InputsOutputs\Two.in" />
</ItemGroup>


                                                    <!-- 2 -->
<Target Name="UsingRealInputsOutputs"
    Inputs="@(Input)"
    Outputs="@(Input->'%(RootDir)%(Directory)%(Filename).out')">
    <Copy
        SourceFiles="@(Input)"
        DestinationFiles="@(Input->
          '%(RootDir)%(Directory)%(Filename).out')"
        />                                          <!-- 3 -->
</Target>
```

Output after initial call

```
UsingRealInputsOutputs:
  Copying file from "InputsOutputs\One.in" to "F:\Trickery\Source ⮐
Code\InputsOutputs\One.out".
  Copying file from "InputsOutputs\Two.in" to "F:\Trickery\Source ⮐
Code\InputsOutputs\Two.out".
```

Output after subsequent call

```
UsingRealInputsOutputs:
Skipping target "UsingRealInputsOutputs" because all output files ⮐
are up-to-date with respect to the input files.
```

The "UsingRealInputsOutputs" target above (2) uses this item array for its Inputs attribute, and a transformation of the same item array for the Outputs attribute. The transformation, declared as,

```
@(Input->'%(RootDir)%(Directory)%(Filename).out')
```

specifies a file that will sit beside the original, with an altered file extension, in other words,

```
./InputsOutputs/
  One.in
  Two.in
```

becomes through transformation,

```
./InputsOutputs/
  One.out
  Two.out
```

The target has one task, the Copy task (3) is used to copy the input file to the output file. Note that the target Outputs attribute specifies the exact same item transformation as the DestinationFiles attribute of the Copy task.

When the target executes for the first time, both of the input files are copied to the output files, as shown in the first output listing. If the target is then executed again without any intervening changes, the target will be skipped because the output files are "up-to-date with respect to the input files" as stated in the second output listing.

In some situations though, you may want to force the execution of the target ignoring whether or not the output files are up-to-date. In the following variation, the only difference in the target, other than the target name, is the target Outputs attribute, which is declared as,

```
Outputs="@(Input->'%(Identity).nofile')"
```

The use of "nofile" is a convention I like to use to indicate that a transformation is being constructed that intentionally will not ever match an actual file. In this case, the outputs with respect to the inputs will be,

```
./InputsOutputs/One.in → ./InputsOutputs/One.in.nofile
./InputsOutputs/Two.in → ./InputsOutputs/Two.in.nofile
```

neither of which refers to a file. The full listing is shown below,

UsingRealInputsAndFakeOutputs target

```xml
<Target Name="UsingRealInputsAndFakeOutputs"
    Inputs="@(Input)"
    Outputs="@(Input->'%(Identity).nofile')">
    <Copy
        SourceFiles="@(Input)"
        DestinationFiles="@(Input->
            '%(RootDir)%(Directory)%(Filename).out')"
        />
</Target>
```

Output after initial call and subsequent call

```
UsingRealInputsAndFakeOutputs:
  Copying file from "InputsOutputs\One.in" to "F:\Trickery\Source ⤷
Code\InputsOutputs\One.out".
  Copying file from "InputsOutputs\Two.in" to "F:\Trickery\Source ⤷
Code\InputsOutputs\Two.out".
```

In the outputs for this variation, the Copy task will always execute, since the Input-Output analysis performed by MSBuild can't cause the target to be skipped, lacking outputs that refer to actual files.

This technique is also useful when using target output batching.

UsingOnlyFakeOutputs target

```xml
<Target Name="UsingOnlyFakeOutputs"
    Outputs="%(Input.Identity).nofile">
    <Copy
        SourceFiles="@(Input)"
        DestinationFiles="@(Input->
            '%(RootDir)%(Directory)%(Filename).out')"
        />
</Target>
```

Output

```
UsingOnlyFakeOutputs:
  Copying file from "InputsOutputs\One.in" to
"F:\Code\Trickery\Source Code\InputsOutputs\One.out".
UsingOnlyFakeOutputs:
```

```
Copying file from "InputsOutputs\Two.in" to
"F:\Code\Trickery\Source Code\InputsOutputs\Two.out".
```

The variation above is using target outputs only for the purpose of batching the target, and like the previous example it has formed a "nofile" expression for the output. In this particular example it is shown to complete the thought started with the previous two targets, however it may be noted that removing the ".nofile" from the Outputs attribute on the target would not alter the behavior in any way. In this usage, it is strictly for convention, to act as a visual clue that the output batching is not related to any specific file, but is correlated only to the unique batchable values in the referenced item array. This form adds additional clarity when the target output batching expression is being formed from multiple metadata values for the purpose of establishing uniqueness, as in the following,

```
Outputs="%(Item.Identity).%(PartialKeyOne).%(PartialKeyTwo).nofile"
```

In the above expression, @(Item) presumably does not have a unique item specification for each array member, but uniqueness can be guaranteed when composing a compound key from the identity and two metadata values PartialKeyOne and PartialKeyTwo. Because this composition is not related to a particular file, the addition of .nofile—which adds no additional uniqueness—serves as an indicator of this. You could go further by using other delimiters in the expression, for example,

```
Outputs="%(Item.Identity)+%(PartialKeyOne)+%(PartialKeyTwo)+nofile"
```

85. How to drive targets as if in a loop

The previous trick introduced in a simplified way the notion of target batching. This trick expands on that technique just a bit since it is such an important feature of MSBuild and since it can be used in so many different ways. Loops are generally driven by iterating over a range of numbers or enumerating items in a collection. Consider the following pseudo-code snippet for inspiration,

```
foreach (var phase in phases)
{
   foreach (var project in phase.Projects)
   {
      foreach (var stage in project.StagingItems)
         Stage(stage);
      project.Build();
      foreach (var deploy in project.DeployItems)
         Deploy(deploy);
   }
}
```

Or these, for post build activities,

```
foreach (var folder in outputFolders)
   foreach (var file in folder.Files)
      installer.Add(file);

foreach (var type in documentTypes)
   foreach (var document in documents)
      GenerateDocumentation(type, document);
```

These snippets make sense when you consider the types of activities generally performed in a rich build. They are easy to consider as loops or nested loops. But MSBuild doesn't have looping constructs, or does it?

Suppose you have a target that will execute two tasks, iterating over the items of an item array, as follows:

```
<ItemGroup>
   <Iteration Include="A" />
   <Iteration Include="B" />
   <Iteration Include="C" />
</ItemGroup>
<Target Name="Loop">
   <FirstTask Value="...Iteration Item..." />
   <SecondTask Value="...Iteration Item..." />
</Target>
```

Using the two forms of batching, you can "loop" over the items two different ways, effectively producing one of the two following sequences of operations.

Target Batching sequence

```
First Task with Iteration A
Second Task with Iteration A

First Task with Iteration B
Second Task with Iteration B

First Task with Iteration C
Second Task with Iteration C
```

Task Batching sequence

```
First Task with Iteration A
First Task with Iteration B
First Task with Iteration C

Second Task with Iteration A
```

```
Second Task with Iteration B
Second Task with Iteration C
```

Depending on the operation, one or the other may be preferred, or as is often the case, the result might be the same regardless.

To set this up for target batching, define the target as follows:

```
<Target Name="LoopTargetBatching"
   Outputs="%(Iteration.Identity)">
   <FirstTask Value="%(Iteration.Identity)" />
   <SecondTask Value="%(Iteration.Identity)" />
</Target>
```

By specifying an Outputs parameter with the %() syntax, keyed on the Identity, which is unique for all entries in the item array, and by not specifying any corresponding Inputs parameter, target batching is initiated. Once inside each iteration of the target, the value of @(Iteration) is restricted to the items in the batch matching the target batching declaration item, which in this example means that @(Iteration) will always contain a single item. There are three alternate versions of syntax that can be used in this situation, all with equivalent behavior:

```
<FirstTask Value="%(Iteration.Identity)" />
<FirstTask Value="@(Iteration->'%(Identity)')" />
<FirstTask Value="@(Iteration)" />
```

The first form is actually initiating task batching on FirstTask, but since the item array is known to contain a single item, the task batching will always be performed with a single item, resulting in a single execution per loop. The second form is the item transformation syntax, explicitly specifying the Identity metadata. The third form will take the identities of all items in the item array, again in this case a single item, and prepare the identity values as a semicolon delimited list. Since this example passes the identity metadata to the task, it is sufficient. Were a different metadata value needed for an argument, this form would not be appropriate. To see this distinction, consider this variation, where FirstTask and SecondTask just print out which task is executing and what Value is passed to it.

Drive Targets in Loop.trkproj, Loops with Meta

```
<ItemGroup>
  <IterationWithMeta Include="A">
    <Meta>Aye</Meta>
  </IterationWithMeta>
  <IterationWithMeta Include="B1">
    <Meta>Bee</Meta>                                <!-- 1 -->
  </IterationWithMeta>
  <IterationWithMeta Include="B2">
```

```
        <Meta>Bee</Meta>                                    <!-- 2 -->
      </IterationWithMeta>
    </ItemGroup>
    <Target Name="LoopTargetBatchingWithMeta"
       Outputs="%(IterationWithMeta.Identity)">             <!-- 3 -->
      <FirstTask Value="%(IterationWithMeta.Meta)" />
      <SecondTask Value="%(IterationWithMeta.Meta)" />
    </Target>
    <Target Name="LoopTaskBatchingWithMeta">                <!-- 4 -->
      <FirstTask Value="%(IterationWithMeta.Meta)" />
      <SecondTask Value="%(IterationWithMeta.Meta)" />
    </Target>
```

Output

```
LoopTargetBatchingWithMeta:
  1st Task Value is Aye
  2nd Task Value is Aye
LoopTargetBatchingWithMeta:
  1st Task Value is Bee
  2nd Task Value is Bee
LoopTargetBatchingWithMeta:
  1st Task Value is Bee
  2nd Task Value is Bee
LoopTaskBatchingWithMeta:
  1st Task Value is Aye
  1st Task Value is Bee
  2nd Task Value is Aye
  2nd Task Value is Bee
```

Notice that the values for Meta (1, 2) in items B1 and B2 are identical. The target batching is driven by the unique values of the items' identity, but since the Meta value is the same for the last two items the output repeats two sets of "Value is Bee" pairs for the second and third iteration of the LoopTaskBatchingWithMeta target, one for item B1 and the second for item B2.

Using task batching in this situation produces quite a different result however. Because the target does not have batching driven by the unique values for Identity, and because the Meta value is used to drive the task batching, the non-unique values for Meta, in this case items B1 and B2 that both share "Bee" as their Meta value, cause the task to only execute a single time. The batching is based on the collection of values for Meta, not on the collection of values for the items based on the uniqueness of the Identity values.

To correct this, consider the following variation, which adds a second meta value, which demonstrates how the task batching can be controlled by the combination of values, kind of like a compound key in database terms.

Drive Targets in Loop.trkproj, Loops with Two Meta Values

```
<ItemGroup>
  <IterationWithTwoMeta Include="A">
    <Meta>Aye</Meta>
    <MetaTwo></MetaTwo>                                   <!-- 3 -->
  </IterationWithTwoMeta>
  <IterationWithTwoMeta Include="B1">
    <Meta>Bee</Meta>
    <MetaTwo>One</MetaTwo>                                <!-- 1 -->
  </IterationWithTwoMeta>
  <IterationWithTwoMeta Include="B2">
    <Meta>Bee</Meta>
    <MetaTwo>Two</MetaTwo>                                <!-- 2 -->
  </IterationWithTwoMeta>
</ItemGroup>
<Target Name="LoopTaskBatchingWithTwoMeta">
  <FirstTask Value="%(IterationWithTwoMeta.Meta) %(MetaTwo)" />
  <SecondTask Value="%(IterationWithTwoMeta.Meta) %(MetaTwo)" />
</Target>
```

Output

```
LoopTaskBatchingWithTwoMeta:
  1st Task Value is Aye
  1st Task Value is Bee One
  1st Task Value is Bee Two
  2nd Task Value is Aye
  2nd Task Value is Bee One
  2nd Task Value is Bee Two
```

In this target, both %(Meta) and %(MetaTwo) are referenced when passed into the Value properties of the tasks. The build engine, when evaluating the items and specific values driving the batching, ensure that every combination that is unique is satisfied. Since the MetaTwo values (1, 2) provide uniqueness when combined with the Meta values, even though they are the same, the third item reappears in the output. Note that the first item (3) is given an empty value for MetaTwo. Failure to provide a value causes an error since MetaTwo is reference without an identity. Other than specifying empty meta values, which would quickly become cumbersome, there are two alternatives to avoiding this error. One is to provide an empty value in an ItemDefnitionGroup, which serves as a default for any item that doesn't explicitly define one. The other would be to fully qualify the use of %(IterationWithTwoMeta.MetaTwo) in the task, allowing the build engine to determine the specific intent—even though in this case there is no possible confusion since only one item is involved in the batching in this example—because it is explicitly qualified.

The next trick builds on this to discuss the implications of driving loops with data from two separate item arrays.

86. How to mimic multiple nested loops (Compound)

The previous two tricks dealt with target batching, but we still haven't gone deep enough yet to have a foundation for the advanced tricks, so this trick takes us one step closer. Target batching in essence runs a target as if in a single loop, iterating over the items in a group. If what you really need to do is iterate over two separate item arrays, in essence two "for" loops, one nested inside the other, there isn't an obvious way to get the behavior you want.

Compound Loop.trkproj, target + task batching, incorrect

```xml
<ItemGroup>
    <i Include="i1" />
    <i Include="i2" />
</ItemGroup>

<ItemGroup>
    <j Include="j1" />
    <j Include="j2" />
    <j Include="j3" />
</ItemGroup>

<Target Name="SimpleCartesianLoopIncorrect"
    Outputs="%(i.Identity)">
    <FirstTask Value="%(i.Identity)" />
                                                    <!-- 1 -->
    <SecondTask Value="[%(i.Identity)] [%(j.Identity)]" />
</Target>
```

Outputs

```
SimpleCartesianLoopIncorrect:                       // 2
    1st Task Value is i1
    2nd Task Value is [i1] []
    2nd Task Value is [] [j1]
    2nd Task Value is [] [j2]
    2nd Task Value is [] [j3]
SimpleCartesianLoopIncorrect:                       // 3
    1st Task Value is i2
    2nd Task Value is [i2] []
    2nd Task Value is [] [j1]
    2nd Task Value is [] [j2]
    2nd Task Value is [] [j3]
```

In this example, the first set of items *i* is used to drive the target batching. The second set *j* is merely referenced in the second task in the target, to demonstrate how this type of compound batching is evaluated.

In the first target, the execution of FirstTask is no different than in the previous *trick #85, How to drive targets as if in a loop*. But for the execution of SecondTask (1) the Value parameter is a combination of the *i* item being used to drive the target batching, which will be unique for each target iteration, and the *j* item. Notice the square brackets placed around the two identity values as they are passed as the task parameter. The first two target listings in the Output (2, 3) show the results of this combination. The FirstTask executes as expected, showing *i1* in the first iteration (2), and *i2* in the second (3). The second task containing the identity for both *i* and *j*, however shows something a bit different. The task batching for this task notices that there are two separate items involved, and it creates a separate iteration of the task for each unique item, without doing any sort of combination on them, keeping them distinct and separate from one another. In the first iteration of the target (2), the SecondTask will execute four times. The first time the unique value for *i* in this target iteration is used, and the *j* value is empty. In the next three iterations, *i* is ignored, and the three separate values for *j* are each given an iteration of the task. This does not give the desired result of mimicking a nested loop.

Compound Loop.trkproj, target + task batching, correct

```
<Target Name="SimpleCartesianLoopCorrect"
    Outputs="%(i.Identity)">
    <FirstTask Value="%(i.Identity)" />

                                              <!-- 4 -->

    <SecondTask Value="[@(i)][%(j.Identity)]" />
</Target>
```

Outputs

```
SimpleCartesianLoopCorrect:                                 // 5
    1st Task Value is i1
    2nd Task Value is [i1][j1]
    2nd Task Value is [i1][j2]
    2nd Task Value is [i1][j3]
SimpleCartesianLoopCorrect:                                 // 6
    1st Task Value is i2
    2nd Task Value is [i2][j1]
    2nd Task Value is [i2][j2]
    2nd Task Value is [i2][j3]
```

In the second target in this example, the second task (4) specifies the value for the *i* item using the set syntax @(*i*), which causes it to be excluded from the batch iteration determination for the task, and the result (6) is the concatenation of the value for the current iteration *i* item and each of the *j* items, which are used to drive the task batching.

This is a fairly trivial example, but reliance on the combination of target and task batching to provide for the outer and inner loop is a bit restrictive. It is likely to be insufficient when the target needs to execute multiple tasks in sequence and can't rely on performing separate task batching for multiple tasks resulting in the wrong order of operations. This next trick shows how to overcome this limitation.

87. How to mimic multiple nested loops (Cartesian)

The Cartesian product of two sets is a new set containing all possible pairs where the first element of each pair in the result set is from the first set and the second element of each pair in the result set is from the second set. For the following two item arrays, the Cartesian set is shown.

```
<ItemGroup>
    <i Include="i1" />
    <i Include="i2" />
</ItemGroup>
<ItemGroup>
    <j Include="j1" />
    <j Include="j2" />
    <j Include="j3" />
</ItemGroup>
```

The Cartesian product of these two, described in set notation as,

```
{ i1, i2 } x { j1, j2, j3 }
```

is,

```
{ (i1, j1), (i1, j2), (i1, j3), (i2, j1), (i2, j2), (i2, j3) }
```

Knowing this, it is reasonable to pattern the combination of two sets into a third in MSBuild by combining two separate item arrays into a third. This can be accomplished using dependent targets that dynamically create the direct product, using the flattening technique described earlier in *trick #69, How to flatten item array metadata*. Unlike many of the previous looping examples, the resulting set will be an item array where each item shares the same identity, but whose members can be fully discriminated from one another based on the aggregate values of their metadata. In pseudo-code, this formation of the Cartesian product would look like this,

```
foreach (var i in @(i))
    foreach (var j in @(j))
```

```
    @(product).Add(new { i, j });
```

As the two loops are uncorrelated, @(i) and @(j) in the pseudo-code above can be interchanged. The listing that follows shows the same thing in MSBuild.

Looping Cartesian.trkproj

```
<ItemGroup>                                        <!-- 1 -->
    <i Include="i1" />
    <i Include="i2" />
</ItemGroup>

<ItemGroup>                                        <!-- 2 -->
    <j Include="j1" />
    <j Include="j2" />
    <j Include="j3" />
</ItemGroup>

<Target Name="CreateCartesianProduct"
    Outputs="%(i.Identity)">                       <!-- 3 -->
    <ItemGroup>
      <_ij Include="ij">
        <i>@(i)</i>                                 <!-- 4 -->
        <j>%(j.Identity)</j>                        <!-- 5 -->
      </_ij>
    </ItemGroup>
</Target>

<Target Name="CartesianLoop"
    DependsOnTargets="CreateCartesianProduct">
    <Message Text="(%(_ij.i),%(j))" />             <!-- 6 -->
</Target>

<Target Name="CartesianLoopBatched"
    DependsOnTargets="CreateCartesianProduct"
    Outputs="%(_ij.i)+%(_ij.j)+nofile">           <!-- 7 -->
    <Message Text="@(_ij->'(%(i),%(j))')" />       <!-- 8 -->
</Target>
```

Output

```
CartesianLoop:
  (i1,j1)
  (i1,j2)
  (i1,j3)
  (i2,j1)
  (i2,j2)
  (i2,j3)
CartesianLoopBatched:
  (i1,j1)
CartesianLoopBatched:
  (i1,j2)
CartesianLoopBatched:
  (i1,j3)
```

```
CartesianLoopBatched:
  (i2,j1)
CartesianLoopBatched:
  (i2,j2)
CartesianLoopBatched:
  (i2,j3)
```

Two sets *i* (1) and *j* (2) are declared as item arrays, with two and three items in each respectively. A dependent target "CreateCartesianProduct" is first executed using target output batching (3) with the individual items in the first set. An item array named @(ij) is declared in this target, using task batching (5) in the individual items in the second set, referencing the unique items in the batched first set (4) to form the pair. The resulting product set created, it is now iterated using two different techniques.

When the main "CartesianLoop" target executes, it uses task batching (6) in the Message task to display both element values in each pair. When the main "CartesianLoopBatched" target executes, it instead (7) uses target output batching with a fake output to perform the result set iteration. Each batched execution of the target will contain a single item since the output batching expression,

```
%(_ij.i)+%(_ij.j)+nofile
```

uniquely identifies each item. The Message task in this case can use the item transform syntax to display the pair.

88. How to mimic multiple nested loops (Tree)

A different kind of looping relies on a tree construction. Given the following tree of data,

```
parent p1
    child c1
    child c2
    child c3
parent p2
    child c4
    child c5
```

the pseudo-code for iterating on this data to create a result set representing the data flattened to an array,

```
foreach (var p in @(parents))
    foreach (var c in p.@(children))
        @(result).Add(new {p, c});
```

This is similar to the Cartesian product above, except that in this case the inner loop is constrained by the parent data, while in the Cartesian product the two loops are uncorrelated. In MSBuild, first the tree data must be defined.

Looping Tree.trkproj, data

```xml
<ItemGroup>
    <Parent Include="p1" />
    <Parent Include="p2" />
</ItemGroup>
<ItemGroup>
    <Child Include="c1">
        <Parent>p1</Parent>                          <!-- 1 -->
    </Child>
    <Child Include="c2">
        <Parent>p1</Parent>
    </Child>
    <Child Include="c3">
        <Parent>p1</Parent>
    </Child>
    <Child Include="c4">
        <Parent>p2</Parent>
    </Child>
    <Child Include="c5">
        <Parent>p2</Parent>
    </Child>
</ItemGroup>
```

Note that each child item in the @(Child) item array associates itself with its parent (1) using item metadata. The item metadata value %(Child.Parent) is populated with the identity of the item in @(Parent) of the same name.

Looping Tree.trkproj, targets

```xml
<Target Name="CreateTreeResult"
    Outputs="%(Parent.Identity)">                    <!-- 2 -->
    <ItemGroup>
        <_ParentChild Include="ParentChild"
          Condition="'%(Child.Parent)' == '@(Parent)'">  <!-- 3 -->
            <Parent>@(Parent)</Parent>               <!-- 4 -->
            <Child>%(Child.Identity)</Child>         <!-- 5 -->
        </_ParentChild>
    </ItemGroup>
</Target>

<Target Name="TreeLoop"
    DependsOnTargets="CreateTreeResult">
    <Message
        Text="(%(_ParentChild.Parent),%(Child))" />  <!-- 6 -->
</Target>

<Target Name="TreeLoopBatched"
    DependsOnTargets="CreateTreeResult"
```

```
         Outputs="%(_ParentChild.Parent)">              <!-- 7 -->
         <Message Text="parent %(_ParentChild.Parent)" />    <!-- 8 -->
         <Message Text="  child %(_ParentChild.Child)" />    <!-- 9 -->
      </Target>
```

Output

```
TreeLoop:
  (p1,c1)
  (p1,c2)
  (p1,c3)
  (p2,c4)
  (p2,c5)
TreeLoopBatched:
  parent p1
    child c1
    child c2
    child c3
TreeLoopBatched:
  parent p2
    child c4
    child c5
```

Once again the result item array is created by a dependent target, "CreateTreeResult," that uses target output batching (2) on the Parent item array. The resulting @(_ParentChild) item array encodes the parent-child constraint with a conditional expression (3)—the key distinction in this example—on the item declaration, then duplicates the identity values of each item in two metadata values (4, 5).

There are two different main targets shown, each of which takes a slightly different approach. The first of these, "TreeLoop," follows the pattern shown in the previous looping trick, with simple task batching on a Message task (6) to dump all of the data pairs in the newly created item array. The second of these, "TreeLoopBatched," uses target output batching (7) on the outer loop variable—which is the Parent metadata value from the combined item array—with this expression,

```
Outputs="%(_ParentChild.Parent)"
```

This more closely matches the original pseudo-code line,

```
foreach (var p in @(parents))
```

which may be important if the target will perform additional tasks on the parent item. The first message uses task batching (8) on the target batch which will contain one item for each unique parent. Looking at the output, you can see that this first message is executed once for each batch. For the inner loop, task batching is again used, but this time on the secondary loop variable—the %(Child) metadata. Notice that the output format from these two batched Message tasks properly reflects the form of the original data tree.

You may find yourself in need of this technique where the parent item array is formed with item specifications that can't be easily encoded in a child metadata value, for example if the parent items are fully qualified paths to files. For a variation that can handle this type of data, instead of using the parent item specification in target CreateTreeResult to correlate the child items with their parents, you could also use item metadata on the parent. In this case, declare the parent item array as,

```
<ItemGroup>
  <Parent Include="parent.one">
    <Id>p1</Id>
  </Parent>
  <Parent Include="parent.two">
    <Id>p2</Id>
  </Parent>
</ItemGroup>
```

essentially moving the previously used item specification into a metadata key value named %(Id). Keeping the child item definitions unchanged— their %(Parent) metadata now referring to the parent's %(Id) metadata— the target would work identically if you were to change the result item array filtering condition from,

```
'%(Child.Parent)' == '@(Parent)'
```

in which @(Parent) refers by default to the item specification value, to,

```
'%(Child.Parent)' == '@(Parent->'%(Id)')'
```

in which the new parent metadata containing the referenced key value is explicitly declared using the item transformation syntax, knowing that in each batch of target execution there is a single unique item in the batching item array.

89. How to mimic multiple nested loops (Join)

Imagine two data tables, Group and Membership, where each data row in each table contains a unique key and an arbitrary value. The Membership table also has a foreign key relationship with the Group table. In the diagram of this data structure below, the table instance data is shown for the values, two items in the Group table with the values "Alpha" and "Beta," and 5 different "Location" values in the Membership table.

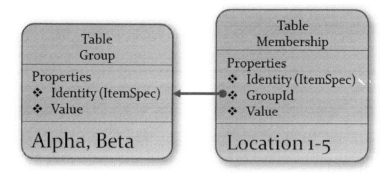

Expressing this data as two MSBuild item arrays, this would look like the following tables, in item form:

Looping Join.trkproj, data

```
<ItemGroup>
  <TableGroup Include="B">                          <!-- 1a -->
    <Value>Beta</Value>                             <!-- 2a -->
  </TableGroup>
  <TableGroup Include="A">                          <!-- 3b -->
    <Value>Alpha</Value>
  </TableGroup>
</ItemGroup>
<ItemGroup>
  <TableMembership Include="1">                     <!-- 1b -->
    <GroupId>A</GroupId>
    <Value>Location1</Value>                         <!-- 2b -->
  </TableMembership>
  <TableMembership Include="2">
    <GroupId>A</GroupId>
    <Value>Location2</Value>                         <!-- 3a -->
  </TableMembership>
  <TableMembership Include="3">
    <GroupId>A</GroupId>
    <Value>Location3</Value>
  </TableMembership>
  <TableMembership Include="4">
    <GroupId>B</GroupId>
    <Value>Location4</Value>
  </TableMembership>
  <TableMembership Include="5">
    <GroupId>B</GroupId>
    <Value>Location5</Value>
  </TableMembership>
</ItemGroup>
```

Some things to note that are important for the discussion that follows, is first the unique keys for each item (1a, 1b), in this case item "B" for the TableGroup item array and item "1" for the TableMembership item. Note that for @(TableGroup), the two items are listed in reverse alphabetical order, with "B" first and "A" second. This will be important in the subsequent trick, which builds on this one. Each item in both item arrays contains a %(Value) metadata value (2a, 2b). Finally, the two item arrays are correlated when the %(GroupId) metadata value of an item in the TableMembership array (3a) matches the item specification of an item in the TableGroup array (3b).

The target execution will create a new item array named @(Joined) which contains the result of performing a database-like "join" on these two item array "tables."

Looping Join.trkproj, targets

```
<Target Name="LoopJoinResult"
  Outputs="%(TableGroup.Identity).nofile">          <!-- 4 -->
  <PropertyGroup>
    <_ThisTable>@(TableGroup)</_ThisTable>          <!-- 6 -->
  </PropertyGroup>

  <ItemGroup>
                                                     <!-- 5 -->
    <Joined
      Include="$(_ThisTable)%(TableMembership.Identity)"
      Condition="'%(TableMembership.GroupId)'
        == '@(TableGroup)'">
      <GroupValue>@(TableGroup->'%(Value)')</GroupValue>
      <MemberValue>%(TableMembership.Value)</MemberValue>
    </Joined>
  </ItemGroup>
</Target>

<Target Name="LoopJoin"
  DependsOnTargets="LoopJoinResult">
  <Message
    Text="Join: '%(Joined.Identity) %(GroupValue) %(MemberValue)'"
    />
</Target>
```

Output

```
LoopJoin:
  Join: 'B4 Beta Location4'
  Join: 'B5 Beta Location5'
  Join: 'A1 Alpha Location1'
  Join: 'A2 Alpha Location2'
  Join: 'A3 Alpha Location3'
```

This is very similar to the previous *trick #88, How to mimic multiple nested loops (Tree),* with an interesting distinction. The dependent target output batching using a fake item transformation (4) is unchanged. The @(Joined) array is created using task batching on the Membership table, as evidenced by the batching notation %(TableMembership...) in both the Condition and MemberValue metadata declaration

Where previous examples of this created items in a new item array with a meaningless repeated item specification, in this example, a meaningful identity value for the items in the @(Joined) item array is declared. Each item in the table join will have a unique identity formed from the item specifications of the two rows being matched, for example "A1" or "B4." Note the item specification for this item (5), which composes this string,

```
Include="$(_ThisTable)%(TableMembership.Identity)"
```

This relies on the flattened batch property $(_ThisTable), created in the property group (6) above. The actual join is represented by the condition on this item creation, which matches the GroupId of the Membership table with the Group table identity. The item created contains the two values, one from each item array table involved in the join. The property flattening was required because MSBuild won't allow one item array to be combined with another string in an item specification, which is what would happen if you tried to use the flattened property directly,

```
Include="@(TableGroup)%(TableMembership.Identity)"
```

MSBuild interprets the above as an attempt to clone the TableGroup array but also adding in some additional text, which it doesn't allow. It presumes the presence of the @(TableGroup) in the item specification is intended to represent the entire array, not the semicolon-delimited-list-of-item-specifications for the single item in the batch that we're going for. By flattening this into a property, it can be used to form an arbitrary item specification without MSBuild misinterpreting the intent.

You also can't use the batching syntax for this,

```
Include="%(TableGroup.Identity)%(TableMembership.Identity)"
```

Since the above batches on two separate items, instead of getting a single value named "A1," following the batching sequence rules of MSBuild, you would get two separate values, one named "A" and the other named "1," clearly not what is intended. Once the dependent target executes, the resulting joined item array is displayed, showing the newly created identity and the two values, one pulled from each table in the join. As you move on to the next trick, notice that the output listing above has the "B" values first, followed by the "A" values, since the items are processed in the order in which they are declared.

90. How to do a real join with inline LINQ on items

The previous example showed how to perform a join using simple MSBuild constructs. However, there are limits to what you can easily do with this technique. In database queries and LINQ expressions, there are a wealth of other features available that become cumbersome to try to mimic in raw MSBuild. For example, the join performed in the previous trick can't sort the result set. You can get more power and flexibility, not to mention a possibly easier to maintain build script, by using the integrated query mechanisms in C#. For example, a trivial join that filters items from a candidate item array that match items in a filtering item array is only a couple lines of code,

```
<UsingTask
    TaskName="FilterCandidatesBasedOnItemSpec"
    TaskFactory="CodeTaskFactory"
    AssemblyFile="...">
    <ParameterGroup>
        <CandidateItemList
            ParameterType="Microsoft.Build.Framework.ITaskItem[]" />
        <FilterItemSpecList
            ParameterType="Microsoft.Build.Framework.ITaskItem[]" />
        <Result
            ParameterType="Microsoft.Build.Framework.ITaskItem[]"
            Output="true" />
    </ParameterGroup>

    <Task>
        <Code Type="Fragment" Language="cs">
            <![CDATA[
                var matches = from candidate in CandidateItemList
                    join spec in FilterItemSpecList
                    on candidate.ItemSpec.ToUpperInvariant()
                        equals spec.ItemSpec.ToUpperInvariant()
                    select candidate;

                Result = matches.ToArray();]]>
        </Code>
    </Task>
</UsingTask>
```

Without trying to become a complete LINQ tutorial, the listing above is pretty straightforward if you've ever used LINQ or even SQL. Two lists are passed in, one is returned, the result being formed from the join on the two lists with a clause that matches their item specifications. Only items in both the filter item array and the candidate list will match the clause and be returned.

Starting with the exact same data as the previous trick, but adding in a new "row" in the Group table, we'll perform a more robust implementation. Adding the Sort metadata to the items in the group array, the data becomes,

Join With Link.trkproj, data

```
<ItemGroup>
  <TableGroup Include="B">
    <Value>Beta</Value>
    <Sort>200</Sort>                                    <!-- 1a -->
  </TableGroup>
  <TableGroup Include="A">
    <Value>Alpha</Value>
    <Sort>100</Sort>                                    <!-- 1b -->
  </TableGroup>
</ItemGroup>
<ItemGroup>
  <TableMembership Include="1">
    <GroupId>A</GroupId>
    <Value>Location1</Value>
  </TableMembership>
  <TableMembership Include="2">
    <GroupId>A</GroupId>
    <Value>Location2</Value>
  </TableMembership>
  <TableMembership Include="3">
    <GroupId>A</GroupId>
    <Value>Location3</Value>
  </TableMembership>
  <TableMembership Include="4">
    <GroupId>B</GroupId>
    <Value>Location4</Value>
  </TableMembership>
  <TableMembership Include="5">
    <GroupId>B</GroupId>
    <Value>Location5</Value>
  </TableMembership>
</ItemGroup>
```

Note the new %(Sort) metadata value (1a, 1b), which if sorted numerically, would properly alphabetize the two entries. To start off, we'll create an inline task that performs the same kind of database join, but this time we'll use LINQ on the ITaskItem arrays, and we'll add in the ability to sort the output by specifying an "OrderBy" column. In pseudo-code, the inline task we want to create is,

```
TableData JoinWithLinqFromItems(
    TableData LeftItems,
    ColumnName LeftName,
    ColumnName LeftOrderBy,
    TableData RightItems,
    ColumnName RightName,
    ColumnName RightForeignKey)
```

343

which with the data described above, would be called as,

```
var @(InnerItems) = JoinWithLinqFromItems(
    @(TableGroup),
    "Group",
    "Sort",
    @(TableMembership),
    "Member",
    "GroupId");
```

The two item array tables are passed into the task in the LeftItems and RightItems parameters, to become the left and right tables in the join. Because the task is going to create a new item array in a generic way, and because it is going to populate the new items with all of the item metadata from joined rows in two tables, it needs some help naming the item metadata values in the newly created items. If it were to just use the original metadata names, there could be conflicts if both tables had metadata with the same name. To avoid this, the metadata names from each table will be prefixed with the table name. However, since item arrays are passed into MSBuild task as the type ITaskItem[], there is no way to deduce the original item name. The two custom task parameters LeftName and RightName are used to contain the table names of their respective item arrays, to be used for prefixing the aggregated metadata names.

To support the new sorting functionality, the LeftOrderBy parameter names the metadata name on the left table by which the results are to be sorted. Finally, the RightForeignKey parameter provides the name of the metadata value on the right-side item array table that should be joined with the item specification of the left table. Of course, if you wish to join to some other metadata value on the left table you could easily change the code that follows, but you'd need to add a parameter to indicate which metadata value to use, or else establish some other convention for the task operation.

This next partial listing shows the beginning of the custom inline task code as well as the encoding of the task parameters.

...Continued from above, inline task parameters

```
<Project ...
    ToolsVersion="4.0"
    DefaultTargets="JoinWithLinq">

    <UsingTask
        TaskName="JoinWithLinqFromItems"
        TaskFactory="CodeTaskFactory"
        AssemblyFile=
            "$(MSBuildToolsPath)\Microsoft.Build.Tasks.v4.0.dll">
```

```
    <ParameterGroup>
        <LeftItems
            ParameterType="Microsoft.Build.Framework.ITaskItem[]"
            Required="true"
            />
        <LeftName
            ParameterType="System.String"
            Required="true"
            />
        <LeftOrderBy
            ParameterType="System.String"
            Required="true"
            />

        <RightItems
            ParameterType="Microsoft.Build.Framework.ITaskItem[]"
            Required="true"
            />
        <RightName
            ParameterType="System.String"
            Required="true"
            />
        <RightForeignKey
            ParameterType="System.String"
            Required="true"
            />

        <InnerItems
            ParameterType="Microsoft.Build.Framework.ITaskItem[]"
            Output="true"
            />
    </ParameterGroup>
```

What follows is the inline task Code body,

...Continued from above, inline task parameters

```
<Task>
    <Code Type="Fragment" Language="cs">
        <![CDATA[
            Log.LogMessage("Left {0}", LeftItems.Count());   // 1
            Log.LogMessage("Right {0}", RightItems.Count());

            // Left-Right join performed using the value of
            // the foreign key found in metadata
            //
            var result =
                from left in LeftItems                       // 2
                join right in RightItems
                on left.ItemSpec
                    equals right.GetMetadata(RightForeignKey)
                orderby left.GetMetadata(LeftOrderBy)        // 3
                select new                                   // 4
                {
                    _itemSpec = string.Format(
```

```
                          "{0}{1}",
                          left.ItemSpec,
                          right.ItemSpec),
                    _leftMeta = left.CloneCustomMetadata(),
                    _rightMeta = right.CloneCustomMetadata(),
                    _leftKey = string.Format(
                          "{0}{1}",
                          LeftName,
                          left.ItemSpec),
                    _rightKey = string.Format(
                          "{0}{1}",
                          RightName,
                          right.ItemSpec),
                };

        // 6
        // Create an MSBuild Item collection, copying
        // all metadata from both item arrays, and
        // mangling the meta key names using the
        // provided Name attributes
        //
        IList<TaskItem> join = new List<TaskItem>();
        foreach (var i in result)
        {
            Log.LogMessage(
                "result {0} {{ {1}, {2} }}",
                i._itemSpec,
                i._leftKey,                                // 5a
                i._rightKey);                              // 5b

            var item = new TaskItem(i._itemSpec);          // 7

            foreach (DictionaryEntry l in i._leftMeta)     // 8
                item.SetMetadata(
                    string.Format(
                        "{0}{1}",
                        LeftName,
                        l.Key.ToString()),
                    l.Value.ToString());

            foreach (DictionaryEntry r in i._rightMeta)    // 9
                item.SetMetadata(
                    string.Format(
                        "{0}{1}",
                        RightName,
                        r.Key.ToString()),
                    r.Value.ToString());

            join.Add(item);                                // 10
        }
        InnerItems = join.ToArray();                       // 11

        Log.LogMessage("Inner {0}", InnerItems.Count());
    ]]>
  </Code>
</Task>
```

346

```
    </UsingTask>
```

Initially (1) some log messages are printed out to show how many items populate each of the item arrays passed in for the left and right data tables. The LINQ statement (2) from, join and on clauses establish the basic join operation; from and on identify the left and right tables, and the on clause establishes the foreign key relationship. The sorting functionality is added with a simple *orderby* clause (3) using the provided metadata value. Since in this usage a numeric value is used, which has a natural sort order, no further expression is required.

The line starting with "select new" at (4) actually creates the result as an anonymous type. This type will contain five different members, named _itemSpec, _leftMeta, _rightMeta, _leftKey and _rightKey, with values pulled from the left or right rows in the join, or from formatting strings from various properties. Similar to how the compound item specification was created using property flattening in the previous trick with raw MSBuild, in this case the item specification is the result of a string format on the two identity strings. The _leftMeta and _rightMeta are copies of the entire set of custom metadata for each of the two rows in the join. The _leftKey and _rightKey are composed from the passed in prefixes and the item specifications, to be used later (5a, 5b) in a message, but otherwise not used.

The result is now populated as an enumerable set of anonymous types. The next phase of the task (6) iterates each item in this result set, logging some of the transient values (5), and creating a new MSBuild item for each member (7). The cloned metadata sets in the anonymous type are then iterated (8, 9), and their names are mangled with the corresponding passed in table name prefix before being added to the new item, and then to the item array (10). Finally, the output parameter (11) is created from the list of ITaskItem, and the final count of the joined item array is displayed.

As all of the complexity formerly in the MSBuild target is now completely contained within the inline task, the target becomes quite simple, as shown below, a call to the task (12) and a capture of the output (13).

...Continued from above, target

```
<Target Name="JoinWithLinq">
                                                    <!-- 12 -->
  <JoinWithLinqFromItems
    LeftItems="@(TableGroup)"
    LeftName="Group"
```

347

```
        LeftOrderBy="Sort"
        RightItems="@(TableMembership)"
        RightName="Member"
        RightForeignKey="GroupId">
        <Output
          TaskParameter="InnerItems"
          ItemName="Joined"
          />                                          <!-- 13 -->
    </JoinWithLinqFromItems>

    <Message
      Text="Join: '%(Joined.Identity) %(GroupValue) %(MemberValue)'"
      />
  </Target>

</Project>
```

Output

```
JoinWithLinq:
  Left 2
  Right 5
  result A1 { GroupA, Member1 }
  result A2 { GroupA, Member2 }
  result A3 { GroupA, Member3 }
  result B4 { GroupB, Member4 }
  result B5 { GroupB, Member5 }
  Inner 5
  Join: 'A1 Alpha Location1'
  Join: 'A2 Alpha Location2'
  Join: 'A3 Alpha Location3'
  Join: 'B4 Beta Location4'
  Join: 'B5 Beta Location5'
```

The output resembles the output from the raw MSBuild interpretation of
this exercise, with the addition of the logging messages in the inline task.

You should consider whether or not your data is supposed to be case
insensitive, and modify the LINQ statement accordingly, for example,

```
from left in LeftItems
join right in RightItems
on left.ItemSpec.ToUpperInvariant()
    equals right.GetMetadata(RightForeignKey).ToUpperInvariant()
```

You could easily extend this basic example with additional LINQ
functionality, for example, providing a data filter,

Additional task parameters

```
    <RightFilterName
        ParameterType="System.String"
        Required="true"
        />
```

```
<RightFilterValue
    ParameterType="System.String"
    Required="true"
    />
```

Additional LINQ clause

```
where right.GetMetadata(RightFilterName)
    .Equals(RightFilterValue)
```

These expressions could even be made arbitrarily complex, passing in an expression in C# code, and specifying that the code body of the inline task should preprocess the properties. For example—and yes, I know that self-evaluating code opens up a whole Pandora's box, but this is pretty cool—make the following simple changes,

Task body change, add evaluation

```
<Task Evaluate="true">
```

Global property

```
<PropertyGroup>
    <RightWhereClause>
        // this is C# code!
        (RightForeignKey).Equals("B")
    </RightWhereClause>
</PropertyGroup>
```

Additional LINQ clause

```
where right.GetMetadata$(WhereClause)
```

New Output, showing only the "B" matches

```
JoinWithLinq:
  Left 2
  Right 5
  result B4 { GroupB, Member4 }
  result B5 { GroupB, Member5 }
  Inner 2
  Join: 'B4 Beta Location4'
  Join: 'B5 Beta Location5'
```

By turning on task evaluation, MSBuild will replace properties found within the body of the task code. A global property in the project named $(WhereClause) is declared that contains C# code, in this case some hard-coded data in an expression, then just adds the clause right into the C# code of the inline task, becoming,

```
// this is C# code!
where right.GetMetadata(RightForeignKey).Equals("B")
```

When evaluated, the *where* clause is placed into the body of the inline task and executed. Although this may seem a bit odd, it would be easier than constructing a complete set of parameters that would be needed to add increasingly complex filtering, can you imagine what kind of complexity would be required in order to pass "GreaterThan" and "RValueName" and "LValue," plus all the other combinations and permuations? With the establishment of some code conventions, this could be made usable in limited fashion.

91. How to do a LINQ many-to-many join

The last in this set of data relationships and join operations that may be useful in creating data-driven sequences of build operations, this one is conceptually only slightly more complex than the previous simple join, but does require a bit more code to complete. What follows below is a generic mechanism for establishing many-to-many data relationships as a mechanism for filtering item-based datasets and combining them into a result item array.

Whereas the previous join allowed the secondary "table" to contain a "foreign key" metadata value referring to the related item in the primary table, a many-to-many relationship requires a third "table" to allow for multiple, bi-directional relationships. Since neither table is primary in the relationship, the two data table input item arrays being joined have been given the generic names "East" and "West" in the task in this example. The specific data passed into the task has two tables related to source files; the first is a collection of paths, and the second is a collection of file wildcards. These make up the east "Path" table and the west "Pattern" table.

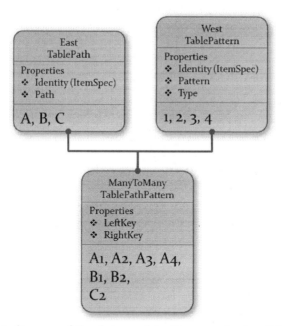

A diagram of the data used in the example that follows is shown above, showing these two data tables along with a third table that holds foreign keys to both data tables, to establish the many-to-many binding. For example, in the data instances shown at the bottom of the many-to-many table named TablePathPattern, item "B|2" indicates a relationship between item "B" in the East table and item "2" in the West table.

This data, represented in MSBuild item arrays, is shown below.

Many-to-Many With LINQ.trkproj, data

```
<ItemGroup>                                          <!-- 1 -->
  <TablePath Include="A">
    <Path>./Path/Alpha</Path>
  </TablePath>
  <TablePath Include="B">
    <Path>./Path/Bravo</Path>
  </TablePath>
  <TablePath Include="C">
    <Path>./Path/Charlie</Path>
  </TablePath>
</ItemGroup>
<ItemGroup>
  <TablePathPattern Include="A|1" />                 <!-- 3 -->
  <TablePathPattern Include="A|2" />
  <TablePathPattern Include="A|3" />
  <TablePathPattern Include="A|4" />
  <TablePathPattern Include="B|1" />
  <TablePathPattern Include="B|2" />
  <TablePathPattern Include="C|2" />
```

```
    </ItemGroup>
    <ItemGroup>
      <TablePattern Include="1">                           <!-- 2 -->
        <Pattern>*.txt</Pattern>
        <Type>Text</Type>
      </TablePattern>
      <TablePattern Include="2">
        <Pattern>*.cs</Pattern>
        <Type>C#</Type>
      </TablePattern>
      <TablePattern Include="3">
        <Pattern>*.cpp</Pattern>
        <Type>C++ Source</Type>
      </TablePattern>
      <TablePattern Include="4">
        <Pattern>*.h</Pattern>
        <Type>C++ Header</Type>
      </TablePattern>
    </ItemGroup>
```

Continued below...

The two main item arrays, one for the Path (1) and one for the Pattern (2) are declared, with obvious metadata values that will be included in the joined item array.

Note that for the many-to-many relationship table TablePathPattern, rather than using two metadata values for the keys, for example,

```
<TablePathPattern Include="A|1">
```

is declared, with both values composed (3) using a simple syntax, with each key separated by a vertical bar rather than,

```
<TablePathPattern Include="Unused">
   <Path>A</Path>
   <Pattern>1</Pattern>
</TablePathPattern>
```

Since the item array is passed into an inline task, pulling apart the values is trivial, and maintaining the table of data where each "row" uses only a single line rather than four lines of XML seems a bit friendlier. There is otherwise nothing special about this technique, it is just a simplification for visual appeal in the MSBuild file.

The pseudo-code for this join operation could be expressed as,

```
foreach (mapping in @(MapItems))
{
   if (@(EastKeyFilter).Contains(mapping.EastKey) AND
      @(WestKeyFilter).Contains(mapping.WestKey)
   {
      var east = @(East).Find(mapping.EastKey);
```

```
        var west = @(West).Find(mapping.WestKey);
        @(Joined).Add(east, west);
    }
}
```

The pseudo-code for a task to implement the above functionality could be something along these lines,

```
TableData JoinManyToManyWithLinq(
    TableData EastItems,
    ColumnName EastKeyFilter,
    TableData WestItems,
    ColumnName WestKeyFilter,
    TableData MapItems,
    string EastKey,
    string EastName,
    string WestKey,
    string WestName)
```

which with the data described above, would be called as,

```
var @(JoinedItems) = JoinManyToManyWithLinq(
    @(TablePath),
    "A;B",
    @(TablePattern),
    "2;3;4",
    "PathId",
    "",
    "PatternId",
    "");
```

Note that in the pseudo-code above, the two data filtering items are passed as hard-coded strings, and that in each case they do not contain all of the possible values for their respective keys, the first omitting "C" and the second omitting "1."

Converting the pseudo-code into an MSBuild task, the parameter declarations would be,

... Continued from above, task parameters

```
<Project...
    ToolsVersion="4.0"
    DefaultTargets="JoinManyToManyWithLinq">

    <UsingTask
        TaskName="JoinManyToManyWithLinqFromItems"
        TaskFactory="CodeTaskFactory"
        AssemblyFile=
            "$(MSBuildToolsPath)\Microsoft.Build.Tasks.v4.0.dll">
        <ParameterGroup>
            <EastItems
                ParameterType="Microsoft.Build.Framework.ITaskItem[]"
                Required="true" />
            <EastKeyFilter
```

```
          ParameterType="Microsoft.Build.Framework.ITaskItem[]"
          Required="true" />
      <WestItems
          ParameterType="Microsoft.Build.Framework.ITaskItem[]"
          Required="true" />
      <WestKeyFilter
          ParameterType="Microsoft.Build.Framework.ITaskItem[]"
          Required="true" />
      <MapItems
          ParameterType="Microsoft.Build.Framework.ITaskItem[]"
          Required="true" />
      <EastKey
          ParameterType="System.String"
          Required="true" />
      <EastName
          ParameterType="System.String"
          Required="false" />
      <WestKey
          ParameterType="System.String"
          Required="true" />
      <WestName
          ParameterType="System.String"
          Required="false" />

      <JoinedItems
          ParameterType="Microsoft.Build.Framework.ITaskItem[]"
          Output="true" />
    </ParameterGroup>
```

Continued below ...

These parameters are a straightforward mapping of the pseudo-code representation, using only ITaskItem arrays and strings as the required inputs, and an item array for the single task output. The code for the join operation, which is the first part of the task, continues below,

... Continued from above, task code join operation

```
<Task>
  <Code Type="Fragment" Language="cs">
    <![CDATA[

      // Split the map Identity into left and right keys
      //
      var mapItems =
          from map in MapItems                          // 4
          select new
          {
              _eastKey = map.ItemSpec.Split(
                  new [] { '|' })[0],
              _westKey = map.ItemSpec.Split(
                  new [] { '|' })[1],
          };
```

```
// 5
// Find all East keys in also in the map
//
Log.LogMessage("East # {0}", EastItems.Count());// 7
foreach (var east in EastKeyFilter)
   Log.LogMessage(" Select {0}", east);        // 8
var eastKeys = from eastKey in EastKeyFilter
   select eastKey.ItemSpec;                     // 9
var eastSet =                                    // 10
   from east in EastItems
   join map in mapItems
   on east.ItemSpec
      equals map._eastKey
   where eastKeys.AsEnumerable()
      .Contains(east.ItemSpec)
   select new
   {
      _eastKey = east.ItemSpec,
      _westKey = map._westKey,
      _customMeta = east.CloneCustomMetadata(),
   };

// 6
// Find all West keys in also in the map
//
Log.LogMessage("West # {0}", WestItems.Count());
foreach (var west in WestKeyFilter)
   Log.LogMessage(" Select {0}", west);
var westKeys = from westKey in WestKeyFilter
   select westKey.ItemSpec;
var westSet =
   from west in WestItems
   join map in mapItems
   on west.ItemSpec
      equals map._westKey
   where westKeys.AsEnumerable()
      .Contains(west.ItemSpec)
   select new
   {
      _westKey = west.ItemSpec,
      _eastKey = map._eastKey,
      _customMeta = west.CloneCustomMetadata(),
   };

// 11
Log.LogMessage("East-West # {0}", eastSet.Count());
Log.LogMessage("West-East # {0}", westSet.Count());

// 12
// Join the East and West sets, keeping only
// items properly mapped
//
var result =
   from east in eastSet
   join west in westSet
   on
```

```
                east._eastKey equals west._eastKey
            where
                east._westKey == west._westKey
            select new
            {
                _itemSpec = string.Format(
                    "{0}{1}",
                    east._eastKey,
                    west._westKey),
                _eastMeta = east._customMeta,
                _westMeta = west._customMeta,
            };
```

Continued below ...

The comments in the inline code above explain the basic operation, but some additional explanation may be needed, especially if you are unfamiliar with LINQ. The first LINQ expression (4) creates an enumerable array of an anonymous type that is essentially a structure containing the "east" and "west" parsed from the encoded map. The first map item, "A|1" will create an anonymous type of,

```
{ _eastKey = "A", _westKey = "1" }
```

The next two code blocks (5, 6), each perform the following operations, the first block working on the @(EastItems) parameter and the second block on @(WestItems), but otherwise the same:

- Log a diagnostic message showing the count of items in the provided source table item array (7).

- Log each item passed in the key filtering array, showing which values will be selected (8).

- Duplicate the filter, to create an enumerable type (9) that can later be used in a LINQ expression *where* clause.

- Perform the first join operation (10), joining the source table with the mapping table, to retrieve the subset of items in the original table that contain a key present in the filter.

Upon completion, each of these code blocks provides an array of anonymous types containing three pieces of data; the east and west keys for the mapped many-to-many item, and the cloned metadata from the primary table. The counts for these two transient arrays are then logged (11).

Next, the secondary join operation is performed, which combines these two sets rather easily (12) by ensuring that the east and west keys in the anonymous types are properly paired. This operation creates a new array of anonymous types that is identified with an item specification derived from the concatenation of the east and west keys, and which also contains the copied metadata that was carried along in the transient anonymous types created in the first join operation. This new array of anonymous types contains the result set desired. All that is left is to turn the result set into an item array for the output parameter.

... Continued from above, task code result item creation

```csharp
// Create an MSBuild Item collection, copying
// all metadata from the East and West sets,
// and mangling the meta key names if the Name
// attributes were provided
//
IList<TaskItem> join = new List<TaskItem>();

foreach (var i in result)
{
    var item = new TaskItem(i._itemSpec);

    foreach (DictionaryEntry l in i._eastMeta)
        item.SetMetadata(
            string.Format(
                "{0}{1}",
                EastName,
                l.Key.ToString()),
            l.Value.ToString());

    foreach (DictionaryEntry r in i._westMeta)
        item.SetMetadata(
            string.Format(
                "{0}{1}",
                WestName,
                r.Key.ToString()),
            r.Value.ToString());

    join.Add(item);
}

InnerItems = join.ToArray();
Log.LogMessage("Final # {0}", InnerItems.Count());
        ]]>
    </Code>
  </Task>
</UsingTask>
```

Continued below ...

The code above does just that, using the same metadata name-mangling trick discussed in the simple inner join from the previous trick. An MSBuild target to utilize this task is again quite trivial:

```
<Target Name=" JoinManyToManyWithLinq">
   <ItemGroup>
      <PathKeyFilter Include="A;B" />                     <!-- 13 -->
      <PatternKeyFilter Include="2;3;4" />
   </ItemGroup>
   <JoinManyToManyWithLinqFromItems
      EastItems="@(TablePath)"
      EastKeyFilter="@(PathKeyFilter)"
      WestItems="@(TablePattern)"
      WestKeyFilter="@(PatternKeyFilter)"
      MapItems="@(TablePathPattern)"
      EastKey="PathId"
      EastName=""
      WestKey="PatternId"
      WestName="">
      <Output
         TaskParameter="InnerItems"
         ItemName="JoinedItems"
         />
   </JoinManyToManyWithLinqFromItems>
   <Message
      Text="Join: '%(JoinedItems.Identity) - %(Type) - %(Path) ⏎
/%(Pattern)'"
      />

</Target>

</Project>
```

Output

```
JoinWithLinq:
  East # 3
   Select A
   Select B
  West # 4
   Select 2
   Select 3
   Select 4
  East-West # 6
  West-East # 5
  Final # 4
  Join: 'A2 - C# - ./Path/Alpha/*.cs'
  Join: 'A3 - C++ Source - ./Path/Alpha/*.cpp'
  Join: 'A4 - C++ Header - ./Path/Alpha/*.h'
  Join: 'B2 - C# - ./Path/Bravo/*.cs'
```

In this target, an item array for each of the filters is declared (13) in the target, as a placeholder for an actual item array that in a real build would likely be created from a dependent target or through some outer means, perhaps as the output of another task. It is interesting to note that when calling this inline task, you don't have to actually run these hard-coded values through an item array; you could just as easily call the task with,

```
<JoinManyToManyWithLinqFromItems
    EastItems="@(TablePath)"
    EastKeyFilter="A;B"
    WestItems="@(TablePattern)"
    WestKeyFilter="2;3;4"
```

MSBuild will take these strings and convert them to an item array for you.

Examining the output, you can see the diagnostic messages showing that there were three items in the @(TablePath) item array, but only two matching items in the east filter, and four items in the @(TablePattern) array, with three matching filter items. The two transient arrays from the initial join produced more items than the final result, since the East-West join contained items "A1" and "B1" and the West-East join contained item "C2," all of which were removed since they weren't present in both arrays, leaving the four final matching items, which are displayed with metadata pulled from both item arrays.

This ends the section on the various forms of data joins using both raw MSBuild and inline tasks with LINQ expressions. The use of these type of data-driven operations will be explored in various tricks throughout the remainder of the book, providing some insight into how to use data-driven techniques in a rich and full-featured build.

Task Tricks

This tricks in this next section all rely on or explain the use of specific built-in tasks, or on the creation of a custom inline task.

92. How to generate assembly attributes

Several of the common assembly attributes typically found in the file AssemblyInfo.cs lend themselves to being generated as part of the build. Keeping consistency between multiple assemblies is one reason, but a couple other reasons that come to mind are automatically generating version numbers or including the correct year in the Copyright.

The built-in task named WriteCodeFragment can assist in the generation of some of these attributes.

GenerateAssemblyAttributes.trkproj (first target)

```
<Target Name="GenerateAssemblyAttributes">
  <ItemGroup>                                        <!-- 1 -->
    <AssemblyAttributes Include="AssemblyVersion">
      <_Parameter1>1.2.3.4</_Parameter1>             <!-- 2 -->
    </AssemblyAttributes>
    <AssemblyAttributes Include="AssemblyTitle">
      <_Parameter1>My Title</_Parameter1>
    </AssemblyAttributes>
    <AssemblyAttributes Include="AssemblyCopyright">  <!-- 3 -->
      <_Parameter1>Copyright © 2010-$(
      [System.DateTime]::Now.Year)</_Parameter1>
    </AssemblyAttributes>
    <AssemblyAttributes Include="Guid">
      <_Parameter1
         >0ca6105a-7f2d-4314-91b7-6439b3e83724</_Parameter1>
    </AssemblyAttributes>
  </ItemGroup>

  <WriteCodeFragment
    Language="C#"
    OutputFile="_AssemblyInfo.cs"
    AssemblyAttributes="@(AssemblyAttributes)"
    />                                               <!-- 4 -->
  <Exec Command="type _AssemblyInfo.cs" />
</Target>
```

Listing of _AssemblyInfo.cs (partial)

```
[assembly: AssemblyVersion("1.2.3.4")]
[assembly: AssemblyTitle("My Title")]
[assembly: AssemblyCopyright("Copyright © 2010-2011")]
[assembly: Guid("0ca6105a-7f2d-4314-91b7-6439b3e83724")]
```

Create an item array (1) to hold the individual attributes you are interested in generating. For each generated attribute, you supply the attribute name as the item identity in the Include attribute. Attributes typically require parameters, and there are two mechanisms for supplying them. You supply unnamed attribute parameters by using the reserved meta name "_Parameter#" with "#" starting at "1" and increasing. You supply named arguments with any other meta name, which will become the argument name; this is shown below.

In this example, I've hard-coded the version number (2), but the next couple tricks will demonstrate a dynamic approach. Notice that the copyright date (3) has a fixed starting year but a calculated completion year using a property function. Notice that all of the attributes accept only arguments of string type.

When the WriteCodeFragment task is called (4) the attributes are passed in the AssemblyAttributes parameter of the task, along with the language to be used by the CodeDOM, and the file name of the file to be generated. I've used the mangled name _AssemblyInfo.cs, as the name AssemblyInfo.cs is typically going to be already used in the project, and should be retained for project-specific attributes. Also remember that assembly attributes can only be declared in a single location, so any attributes that will end up in the generated file may not also exist in the standard hand-authored file or a build error will occur. The listing above shows the resulting generated file.

It is then a simple matter to add some properties and items to your standard .props and .targets file imports to wire in the generation:

Standard .props file

```
<ItemGroup Condition="Exists('_AssemblyInfo.cs')">
  <Compile Include="_AssemblyInfo.cs"
</ItemGroup>
```

Standard .targets file

```
<Target Name="GenerateAssemblyAttributes"
  Condition="'$(SkipGenerateAssemblyAttributes)' != 'false'">
  ...
```

Now, in an individual project file the behavior will be enabled by default, but can be disabled by the definition of a single property, namely by setting SkipGenerateAssemblyAttributes to true. Once you are generating assembly attributes, you may discover that every project shares the same values. At that point you can rework the projects to use a shared file in which the shared attributes are defined.

There are some strange additional capabilities, seemingly appropriate for handling custom attributes, but probably not quite what you'd need. In addition to string arguments, some standard attributes require Boolean or enum values, and custom attributes can likewise accept arbitrary types. The listing below shows the result:

GenerateAssemblAttributes.trkproj (second target)

```
<Target Name="GenerateBadAssemblyAttributes">
  <ItemGroup>
    <BadAssemblyAttributes Include="ComVisible">
      <_Parameter1>true</_Parameter1>                    <!-- 1 -->
```

```
        </BadAssemblyAttributes>
        <BadAssemblyAttributes Include="SecurityPermission">
            <_Parameter1
                >SecurityAction.RequestMinimum</_Parameter1>   <!-- 2 -->
            <Flags>SecurityPermissionFlag.Execution</Flags> <!-- 3 -->
        </BadAssemblyAttributes>
    </ItemGroup>

    <WriteCodeFragment
        Language="C#"
        OutputFile="BadAssemblyInfo.cs"
        AssemblyAttributes="@(BadAssemblyAttributes)"
        />
    <Exec Command="type BadAssemblyInfo.cs" />
</Target>
```

Listing of BadAssemblyInfo.cs (partial)

```
[assembly: ComVisible("true")]
[assembly: SecurityPermission("SecurityAction.RequestMinimum",
Flags="SecurityPermissionFlag.Execution")]
```

In this example, an unnamed Boolean parameter (1) an unnamed enum value (2), and a named enum value (3) are declared. The result is less than spectacular, as the code generation will only emit string arguments. Thus, if you intend to use custom attributes, either use only those with string arguments, or roll your own custom attribute generator task.

93. The two types of copy (per file, or single destination)

The Copy task is quite simple, but there are two different ways that it can be used, and this often causes some confusion. This trick shows the difference between the two mutually exclusive task parameters that support these two different usages; DestinationFiles and Destination-Folders.

Copy.trkproj

```
<ItemGroup>
    <Source Include="PathTo\**\*.txt" />                   <!-- 1 -->
</ItemGroup>

<Target Name="CopyToFolder">                               <!-- 2 -->
    <Copy
        SourceFiles="@(Source)"
        DestinationFolder="OutPath\ByFolder"
        />
</Target>
```

```
<Target Name="CopyPerFile">                              <!-- 3 -->
  <Copy
    SourceFiles="@(Source)"
    DestinationFiles="@(Source->
      'OutPath\ByFile\%(RecursiveDir)%(FileName)%(Extension)')"
    />
</Target>
```

Output

```
CopyToFolder:
  Creating directory "OutPath\ByFolder".
  Copying file from "PathTo\One.txt" to "OutPath\ByFolder\One.txt".
  Copying file from "PathTo\Recurse\Three.txt" to                    ↴
    "OutPath\ByFolder\Three.txt".
  Copying file from "PathTo\Two.txt" to "OutPath\ByFolder\Two.txt".
CopyPerFile:
  Creating directory "OutPath\ByFile".
  Copying file from "PathTo\One.txt" to "OutPath\ByFile\One.txt".
  Creating directory "OutPath\ByFile\Recurse".
  Copying file from "PathTo\Recurse\Three.txt" to                    ↴
    "OutPath\ByFile\Recurse\Three.txt".
  Copying file from "PathTo\Two.txt" to "OutPath\ByFile\Two.txt".
```

Both copy options use the same input, the @(Source) item array used many times previously, that recursively picks up the three text files under the PathTo folder. Also note from the output, you can see that the Copy task created the folders needed for the destination in both cases. Because the source item array (1) is specified with the recursive wildcard, "**" the subfolder names for the files found are preserved. For review, these files, and the value of the recursive metadata are,

```
%(Identity)                   %(RecursiveDir)
./PathTo/One.txt              empty
./PathTo/Two.txt              empty
./PathTo/Recurse/Three.txt    Recurse
```

The first usage (2) of the Copy task specifies the DestinationFolder task parameter. From the output, it can be seen that all three folders are collected and placed directly in the output folder. The intervening recursive folder is ignored; all files regardless of their origin are dumped in the specified destination folder,

```
Source                        Destination
./PathTo/One.txt              ./OutPath/ByFolder/One.txt
./PathTo/Two.txt              ./OutPath/ByFolder/Two.txt
./PathTo/Recurse/Three.txt    ./OutPath/ByFolder/Three.txt
```

In the second usage (3), the DestinationFiles task parameter is used instead. Usage of this parameter typically involves performing an item transformation on the input Source item array, which in this case is the expression,

```
@(Source->'OutPath\ByFile\%(RecursiveDir)%(FileName)%(Extension)')
```

This transform is a combination of the literal portion of the output path, "OutPath\ByFile" with selected metadata from the source items. Because %(RecursiveDir) is specified in this transform, the result seen in the output is the following operation,

```
Source                        Destination
./PathTo/One.txt              ./OutPath/ByFile/One.txt
./PathTo/Two.txt              ./OutPath/ByFile/Two.txt
./PathTo/Recurse/Three.txt    ./OutPath/ByFile/Recurse/Three.txt
```

This is quite different from the first approach, since the recursive folder is maintained. If there is an even more complex folder hierarchy, it will be completely preserved using the item transformation with the DestinationFiles task parameter.

Finally, it is important to note that you don't need to perform an item transformation on the source item array, you can use a completely different one, provided it contains the same number of items as the source array, so that a one-to-one mapping can be determined,

Copy.trkproj, CopyPerItem target

```
<ItemGroup>                                        <!-- 4 -->
  <Destination Include="OutPath\ByItem\Odd\First.txt" />
  <Destination Include="OutPath\ByItem\Even\Second.txt" />
  <Destination Include="OutPath\ByItem\Odd\Third.txt" />
</ItemGroup>
<Target Name="CopyPerItem">
  <Copy
    SourceFiles="@(Source)"
    DestinationFiles="@(Destination)"
    />                                             <!-- 5 -->
</Target>
```

Output, CopyPerItem target

```
CopyPerItem:
  Creating directory "ByItem\Odd".
  Copying file from "PathTo\One.txt" to                    ⮑
    "OutPath\ByItem\Odd\First.txt".
  Creating directory "ByItem\Even".
  Copying file from "PathTo\Recurse\Three.txt" to          ⮑
    "OutPath\ByItem\Even\Second.txt".
  Copying file from "PathTo\Two.txt" to                    ⮑
    "OutPath\ByItem\Odd\Third.txt".
```

In this example, a new item array @(Destination) is declared (4). It contains three items, but customizes both the path and file name for each. When the Copy task executes (5), the result is a direct remapping of the files,

```
Source                       Destination
./PathTo/One.txt             ./OutPath/ByItem/Even/First.txt
./PathTo/Two.txt             ./OutPath/ByItem/Odd/Second.txt
./PathTo/Recurse/Three.txt   ./OutPath/ByItem/Even/Third.txt
```

Adding a fourth item to this new output array will cause an error,

```
F:\Code\...\Copy.trkproj(32,5): error MSB3094: "DestinationFiles"
refers to 4 item(s), and "SourceFiles" refers to 3 item(s). They must
have the same number of items.
```

Because the Copy task can't create a uniform one-to-one mapping, which is a requirement for using the DestinationFiles task parameter.

I'd be remiss if I didn't also point out that you aren't limited to the stock Copy task and have several other options. First, you can either create your own uniquely named task, e.g. FastCopy, or override the stock task by declaring your own Copy task by declaring a task of the same name in an imported .tasks file. In both cases you should keep the parameters identical to the built-in Copy task, but can add as many additional parameters as you'd like as long as their values are optional. If you are performing lots of copies, you may find the built-in task a bit on the slow side, as it seems to copy one file at a time in a leisurely way. To speed up bulk copies, you can use Xcopy.exe or RoboCopy.exe, either executed in a process inside your custom task, or called directly with Exec, and gain some significant performance improvements.

94. How to dynamically generate files

Generating files, either source files for your primary projects, sources for secondary tasks like installers or documentation, or metadata files to drive parts of the build, can be done in several ways using standard MSBuild tasks. Three of these are shown side-by-side here.

Each of the three approaches generates the same file, in this case a small C# source file with a bit of dynamic content. The MSBuild code shared by all three is shown first:

Dynamically Generate Files.trkproj, shared properties

```
<PropertyGroup>                                          <!-- 1 -->
  <GeneratedValue
    Condition="'$(GeneratedValue)' == ''">3.0</GeneratedValue>
                                                         <!-- 2 -->
  <FileContents><![CDATA[//
// Generated on $([System.DateTime]::Now)
```

```
// by '$(MSBuildThisFile)'
//
namespace Trickery
{
    public class Generated
    {
        public static float Value
        { get { return $(GeneratedValue); } }
    }
}
]]></FileContents>
                                                    <!-- 3 -->
    <FileContentsEscaped
        >$([MSBuild]::Escape($(FileContents)))</FileContentsEscaped>
    </PropertyGroup>
```

The file contents is declared within the $(FileContents) property. An additional property $(GeneratedValue) is also declared (1) above, but should be considered to be the dynamic portion of the file. It is only given a value if none is specified, either on the command line or as a result of some other processing. Note that the file contents (2) is contained within an XML CDATA declaration, and that it contains three additional MSBuild properties, all of which will be substituted,

```
$([System.DateTime]::Now)
$(MSBuildThisFile)
$(GeneratedValue)
```

The file contents, since it is C#, will contain semicolons and likely other reserved MSBuild characters. To encode the contents so that it can be properly processed by standard MSBuild tasks, it is passed through a property function (3) and stored in escaped form in a new property, $(FileContentsEscaped). It is this escaped version of the file contents that will be passed to the various tasks below.

using WriteLinesToFile task

```
<Target Name="WithWriteLinesTask">
    <WriteLinesToFile
        Lines="$(FileContentsEscaped)"
        File="Generated.WithWriteLinesTask.cs"
        Overwrite="true"
        />
</Target>
```

The first approach above passes the escaped contents to the WriteLines-ToFile task. Previously there have been examples where the property was first converted to items, then the items were passed to the Lines task parameter of this task,

```
<ItemGroup>
   <FileContentsEscaped ="$(FileContentsEscaped)" />
</ItemGroup>
<WriteLinesToFile
   Lines="@(FileContentsEscaped)"
   ...
```

but this isn't strictly needed, as the task will perform the conversion internally when a string datatype is passed to the ITaskItem[] parameter. If the Overwrite parameter were not set to true, the task would instead append any new lines to the file if it already existed.

This next version below uses an extended property function in System.IO.File, passing the escaped contents as a string.

using System.IO.File property function

```
<Import Project="EnableAllPropertyFunctions.tasks" /> <!-- 4 -->
<Target Name="WithSystemIo">
   <Message
      Text="$([System.IO.File]::WriteAllText(
         'Generated.WithSystemIo.cs',
         $(FileContentsEscaped)))"
         />
</Target>
```

If you have already enabled all property functions, as shown with the import of the tasks file (4) described in *trick #57, Know how to enable more property functions*, then this may be a more direct approach, one that makes additional functionality of System.IO available if needed.

Finally, if you need even more flexibility or wish to perform more processing than is easy to do with raw MSBuild, an inline task may be the best approach.

using a custom inline task

```
<UsingTask
   TaskName="GenerateFile"
   TaskFactory="CodeTaskFactory"
   AssemblyFile="$(MSBuildToolsPath)\Microsoft.Build.Tasks     ⤵
.v4.0.dll">
   <ParameterGroup>
      <FileName
         ParameterType="System.String"
         Required="true"
         />
      <Contents
         ParameterType="System.String"
         Required="true"
         />
   </ParameterGroup>
```

```xml
  <Task>
    <Using Namespace="System" />
    <Code Type="Fragment" Language="cs">
    <![CDATA[
    {
        Log.LogMessage(
            "Writing {0} characters to {1}",
            Contents.Length,
            FileName);
        System.IO.File.WriteAllText(FileName, Contents);
    }
    ]]>
    </Code>
  </Task>
</UsingTask>
<Target Name="WithCustomTask">
  <GenerateFile
      FileName="Generated.WithCustomTask.cs"
      Contents="$(FileContentsEscaped)"
      />
</Target>
```

Output

```
WithCustomTask:
  Writing 218 characters to OutPath\Generated.WithCustomTask.cs
```

The example above is a skeleton that only reproduces the functionality of the previous approach using extended property functions. It adds a log message indicating how many characters are being written, but otherwise uses the same method of System.IO.File to write out the text. All three approaches create the same output file, shown below.

Output file for all three methods

```csharp
//
// Generated on 7/1/2011 8:59:50 PM
// by 'Dynamically Generate Files.trkproj'
//
namespace Trickery
{
  public class Generated
  {
    public static float Value
    { get { return 3.0; } }
  }
}
```

Using CDATA properties to hold file contents, and a few trivial property functions, files that describe how and when they were created are easy to generate.

95. How to enhance logging with tell targets & trace

The Message task is invaluable for logging. As shown in this book, it also takes a primary role as a placeholder for more complex operations while they are being developed. But with only three levels of verbosity supported by the Importance task parameter it might not be as robust a diagnostic tool as you are used to. This trick shows you some enhancements and patterns to give you a better diagnostic experience.

Trace task

The first part of trick shows you a four line inline task—well, four functional lines of C# code that is—that can serve as a worthy substitute.

Trace.tasks

```
<UsingTask
    TaskName="Trace"
    TaskFactory="CodeTaskFactory"
    AssemblyFile="$(MSBuildToolsPath)\Microsoft.Build.Tasks
.v4.0.dll">
    <ParameterGroup>
        <Level
            ParameterType="System.Int32"
            Required="true"
            />                                          <!-- 1 -->
        <Text
            ParameterType="System.String"
            Required="true"
            />                                          <!-- 2 -->
        <Category
            ParameterType="System.String"
            Required="false"
            />                                          <!-- 3 -->
    </ParameterGroup>
    <Task Evaluate="true">                              <!-- 4 -->
        <Using Namespace="System" />
        <Code Type="Fragment" Language="cs">
        <![CDATA[
        {
            if ($(TraceLevel) >= Level)                 // 5
                if (string.IsNullOrWhiteSpace(Category) ||  // 6
                    "@(TraceCategory)".Contains(Category))  // 7
                    Log.LogMessage(Text);               // 8
        }
        ]]>
        </Code>
    </Task>
</UsingTask>
```

```
<PropertyGroup>
    <TraceLevel>0</TraceLevel>                            <!-- 9 -->
</PropertyGroup>
<ItemGroup>
    <TraceCategory Include="General" />                   <!-- 10 -->
</ItemGroup>
```

The task takes three parameters, Level (1), Text (2) and Category (3), that declare a task that in pseudo-code is,

```
void Trace(int Level, string Text, string Category)
```

Because the task element enables evaluation (4), the body of the first if statement (5) will have the current value of the $(TraceLevel) property injected into the code prior to compilation. The contents of the @(TraceCategory) item array is likewise converted to a literal string (7) right in the task code. Prior to tracing the message (8), the trace message level is compared to the current level (5), and if both a category is supplied (6), and if the @(TraceCategory) item array contained the supplied category (7), only then will the message be sent to the attached MSBuild loggers (8). The trace level is set to zero by default (9), which disables tracing, and the category array is prepopulated with the tag "General." An example project file that imports this task and shows an example of its use is shown below.

Trace.trkproj

```
<Import Project="Trace.tasks" />

<ItemGroup>
    <TraceCategory Include="TraceThis" />                <!-- 11 -->
    <TraceCategory Include="$(TraceCategory)" />         <!-- 12 -->
</ItemGroup>
<Target Name="Trace">
    <Trace Level="1" Text="Trace level 1" />
    <Trace Level="2" Text="Trace level 2" Category="TraceThis" />
    <Trace Level="3" Text="Trace level 3" Category="SkipThis"  />
    <Trace Level="4" Text="Trace level 4" />
</Target>
```

This example hardcodes in the MSBuild (11) the additional category "TraceThis" but not the "SkipThis" category referenced in the third trace message. The Trace target outputs four separate messages, each with an escalating value for the diagnostic level. The second and third trace messages also include the optional Category parameter. Note that the level "2" message specifies a category that has been included in the @(TraceCategory) item array, and the level "3" message specifies an unknown category that isn't included.

Since the default trace level is zero and all of the trace messages specify a level of one or higher, there would be no output at all, when run from the command line without specifying a value for TraceLevel,

```
> msbuild Trace.trkproj
```

Supplying a trace level on the command line, you will get varying levels of trace output,

Output with different command lines

```
> msbuild Trace.trkproj /p:TraceLevel=1

Trace:
  Trace level 1

> msbuild Trace.trkproj /p:TraceLevel=2

Trace:
  Trace level 1
  Trace level 2

> msbuild Trace.trkproj /p:TraceLevel=3

Trace:
  Trace level 1
  Trace level 2

> msbuild Trace.trkproj /p:TraceLevel=4

Trace:
  Trace level 1
  Trace level 2
  Trace level 4
```

One item that was skipped in the previous discussion is line (12), which aggregates into the @(TraceCategory) item array any additional categories contained in the $(TraceCategory) property. Since up until this point that property contained no value, it has no effect on the execution. Supplying this property from the command line however will alter the behavior as shown,

Output with additional categories

```
> msbuild Trace.trkproj /p:TraceLevel=4 /p:TraceCategory=SkipThis

Trace:
  Trace level 1
  Trace level 2
  Trace level 3
  Trace level 4
```

Notice that the level 3 trace message, previously skipped because the Category associated with it was "SkipThis" which was not declared originally, will now be displayed, since the @(TraceCategory) item array will now contain both the default item "General," the hardcoded item "TraceThis" and now will also include the item "SkipThis" as a result of the additional item introduced from the property.

Multiple additional categories could be specified from the command line by escaping the semicolon character needed to combine them into a single property, which would then be converted into additional items in the TraceCategory item array,

```
/p:TraceCategory=CategoryOne%3bCategoryTwo
```

Tell targets

By convention, I've used the target name "Tell" for targets whose sole purpose is to emit diagnostic information. When diagnostic level log files reach hundreds of thousands of lines in length, searching for my custom diagnostics becomes much easier with such a convention. In most cases, "Tell" is used as a prefix for several targets, most of which are declared in project files in an InitialTargets list on the Project element.

In addition to helping the developers maintaining the build to easily find their diagnostics, this trick is also useful for a team that isn't all that build savvy. If you can coerce a Tell target to execute as the very first target in the build, and load it up with diagnostics for any situation you've ever seen trip anyone up, it can be very helpful for novice build users.

Things that I typically put into a Tell target include,

- Interesting properties like $(Platform), $(OutDir) and $(OutPath), so that diagnostic level logging doesn't need to be enabled to see them.

- The values of all $(Skip...) properties supplied on the command line.

- The actual command line used to build, pulled out of from an Environment property function.

- Special properties that are computed when the projects are parsed, especially if they do not have one of the normally expected values.

- Complete listings of, or perhaps only the count of items in important item arrays.

Furthermore, having Tell targets available, and properly encoded in the self-documenting help metadata (to be shown soon in *trick #102, How to define self-documenting build files*), gives you a quick way to perform "dry runs" on complex or destructive build operations.

96. How to add file change detection beyond inputs/output

The mechanism for target dependency analysis in MSBuild is to check the file dates on the Inputs and Outputs of a target, and run the target when out-of-date outputs are detected. Sometimes build operations don't leave any trace in the file system. Often these are encoded in the build to operate always, without concern for whether or not the state of the operation is out of date. This trick discusses a technique for creating proxy files for operations so that they can be included in the dependency analysis.

To serve as an example, a target that manipulates the registry is used, since registry operations tend to be lengthy, and avoiding their execution is a desirable optimization. I've used the name "touch files" for these proxy files, since they are created and updated with the built-in Touch task in MSBuild.

The most convenient way to alter the local registry during a build may be to manipulate the registry directly with a property function operating on an item array, as shown in the generic case in *trick #87, How to mimic multiple nested loops (Cartesian)*.

You can even use this same item array to generate a registry script (.reg) if you need to distribute it with your application or reference it from an installer.

There are times however, when the registry script will be created by some other part of the build, or needs to be maintained separately. In those cases, the following example becomes relevant.

Because running the RegEdit.exe program in import mode—where you pass it a .reg file on the command line to be merged into the registry— can be such a time consuming operation, the use of a "touch file" can dramatically speed up the build.

Below are shown two different approaches for setting registry values in the build. A unique touch file is created for each approach, both of which manipulate their own unique registry entry.

Touch.trkproj, directly from items

```
<Import Project="EnableAllPropertyFunctions.tasks" />
<Target Name="TouchDirect"
  Inputs="$(MSBuildThisFile)"
  Outputs="OutPath/TouchDirect.reg.cache"
  Condition="'$(SkipRegistry)' != 'true'">         <!-- 2 -->
  <ItemGroup>
    <RegistryItem Include="RegistryItem">          <!-- 1 -->
      <KeyName>HKEY_CURRENT_USER\Trickery</KeyName>
      <ValueName>TestNumberFromItem</ValueName>
      <Value>1</Value>
      <Kind>DWord</Kind>
    </RegistryItem>
  </ItemGroup>
                                                    <!-- 3 -->
  <Message
    Text="$([Microsoft.Win32.Registry]::SetValue(
      '%(RegistryItem.KeyName)',
      '%(RegistryItem.ValueName)',
      %(RegistryItem.Value),
      Microsoft.Win32.RegistryValueKind.%(RegistryItem.Kind)))"
    />
                                                    <!-- 4 -->
  <Touch
    AlwaysCreate="true"
    Files="OutPath/TouchDirect.reg.cache">
    <Output TaskParameter="TouchedFiles" ItemName="FileWrites" />
  </Touch>
</Target>
```

This first target uses an item array (1) of @(RegistryItem) values encoded with all the metadata needed to call the Microsoft.Win32.Registry.Set-Value method. The target is attributed (2) with the containing MSBuild file as the sole member of the Inputs attribute, and a "touch file" with the name TouchDirect.reg.cache. Because the data being written to the registry is defined in this very same file, in the @(RegistryItem) array, it is proper to specify $(MSBuildThisFile) as the Inputs attribute. Any change to the contents of the file may require a new execution of the target. By convention, I've followed the pattern Visual Studio uses for temporary files it creates to deal with incremental building and use the file extension ".cache" for touch files.

The message file (3) doesn't ever display a message, it is only used to contain the property function that executes the call to Registry.SetValue, which is driven by task batching to iterate over all items in the @(RegistryItem) array. Finally, the touch file is created (4), being sure to specify the AlwaysCreate option, and capturing the write of the file in the @(FileWrites) item array, since it is a new file being created by the build.

Touch.trkproj, running RegEdit with a .reg file

```
<Target Name="Touch"
  Inputs="PathTo/Touch.reg"
  Outputs="OutPath/Touch.reg.cache"
  Condition="'$(SkipRegistry)' != 'true'">

  <Message
    Importance="high"
    Text="Populating registry with Touch.reg"
    />
  <Exec
    Command="RegEdit.exe /s /c PathTo\Touch.reg"
    />                                              <!-- 5 -->
  <Touch
    AlwaysCreate="true"
    Files="OutPath/Touch.reg.cache">
    <Output TaskParameter="TouchedFiles" ItemName="FileWrites" />
  </Touch>
</Target>
```

Touch.reg

```
Windows Registry Editor Version 5.00

[HKEY_CURRENT_USER\Trickery]
"TestNumberFromScript"=dword:00000001
```

This second listing shows an alternate technique, where a registry file presumably created by some other part of the build is used, passed as a parameter (5) to the RegEdit program. The contents of the registry file are listed as well. The Inputs and Outputs attributes mimic those of the previous example, except that the Touch.reg file which contains the data being written to the registry is used as the Inputs in place of the self-referencing use of the $(MSBuildThisFile) reserved property.

The two registry entries written are shown in the screenshot below.

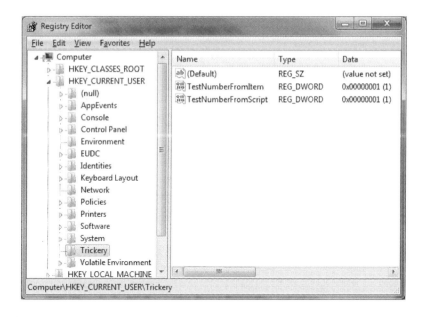

The output in both cases is essentially the same, shown below.

Output after first execution

```
TouchDirect:
  Creating "OutPath/TouchDirect.reg.cache" because "AlwaysCreate"
  was specified.
Touch:
  Populating registry with Touch.reg
  RegEdit.exe /s /c PathTo\Touch.reg
  Creating "OutPath/Touch.reg.cache" because "AlwaysCreate" was
specified.
```

Output after subsequent execution

```
TouchDirect:
Skipping target "TouchDirect" because all output files are up-to-
date with respect to the input files.
Touch:
Skipping target "Touch" because all output files are up-to-date with
respect to the input files.
```

On the first execution the touch files are created. If a second execution is initiated immediately with no changes, the targets are skipped, the touch file having been determined to be newer than the input files, and the lengthy registry operation is skipped.

To complete the discussion on this trick, take a look at the performance summary for the initial execution below:

```
Performance summary, running with /v:diag

Project Performance Summary:
     1110 ms   F:\Code\Trickery\Source Code\Touch.trkproj   1 calls

Target Performance Summary:
       90 ms   TouchDirect                                  1 calls
      180 ms   ExecuteEnableAllPropertyFunctions            1 calls
      700 ms   Touch                                        1 calls

Task Performance Summary:
        0 ms   EnableAllPropertyFunctions                   1 calls
       10 ms   Message                                      2 calls
      120 ms   Touch                                        2 calls
      650 ms   Exec                                         1 calls
```

The Touch target that runs the RegEdit program is about eight times slower than the direct registry manipulation done by the TouchDirect target with the property function. This is most likely due to the overhead of running a heavyweight executable in a separate process when compared to an in-process execution of a single method on a class in the .NET Framework.

97. The most useful inline task, TokenReplace

This quick trick pays homage to the most frequently used inline task I've ever come across. I had authored this task several times, then one day when looking up the syntax of inline tasks, came across this version, which was almost identical character for character to the ones I've been using, on the MSDN website.

```xml
<UsingTask
  TaskName="TokenReplace"
  TaskFactory="CodeTaskFactory"
  AssemblyFile="$(MSBuildToolsPath)\Microsoft.Build.Tasks.v4.0 ↱
.dll">
  <ParameterGroup>
    <Path ParameterType="System.String" Required="true" />
    <Token ParameterType="System.String" Required="true" />
    <Replacement ParameterType="System.String" Required="true" />
  </ParameterGroup>
  <Task>
    <Code Type="Fragment" Language="cs">
    <![CDATA[
      string content = File.ReadAllText(Path);
      content = content.Replace(Token, Replacement);
      File.WriteAllText(Path, content);
    ]]>
    </Code>
  </Task>
</UsingTask>
```

Quite simply, it takes as parameters a path to a file, a token to replace, and the string to replace it with. I typically encode tokens in a form that won't trip up MSBuild and are easy to see in template files or properties,

```
${Token}
```

and replace them with MSBuild properties of the same name,

```
$(Token)
```

This has come in handy for all sorts of things, notably transforming configuration files for web projects, and application settings files for services or executables, as well as composing strings within MSBuild files, as was shown in *trick #70, How to enhance item-based action tricks*.

98. How to build more than one configuration at a time

If you've heeded the advice in this book and on the MSBuild team blogs, and taken a step away from using solution files for your build, you may find this trick handy. In your solution-replacing main build driver project, you need a mechanism for building multiple configurations at the same time, similar to the way the solution's batch build feature works. This can also apply if you are using the "dirs.proj" technique discussed in *trick #80, Define your own solution mechanics*.

To start off, an item array named @(ConfigurationsToBuild) is declared, including conditionally all the various configurations that are available in the projects being built.

```
<ItemGroup>
    <ConfigurationToBuild Include="Debug"
        />
    <ConfigurationToBuild Include="Release"
        "'$(SkipRelease)' != 'true'"
        />
    <ConfigurationToBuild Include="Production"
        "'$(SkipRelease)' != 'true' AND
         '$(SkipProduction)' != 'true'"
        />
</ItemGroup>
```

The use of $(Skip...) properties makes it possible to turn on and off various configurations from the command line. These configurations can then be used to batch-execute an MSBuild task that will build the projects,

```
<MSBuild
    Projects="@(Project)"
```

```
Properties="Configuration=%(ConfigurationToBuild.Identity)"
...
/>
```

This will execute the MSBuild task for all projects one time for each unique configuration name that makes it into the @(ConfigurationTo-Build) item array.

Everyday Task Execution Tricks

In the tricks that follow, some common build challenges are demonstrated. The hope is that they are fully realized—enough so that you can take these examples and incorporate them directly into your own build with only minimal changes.

99. How to extract the branch name from a path

When checking out sources from version control, it is common that the branch name of the sources becomes a literal folder name in the path to which they are checked out. It is possible to extract this single folder in the path during the build and perform custom actions depending on the specific branch the sources are found in. This may also be useful to prevent certain combinations of actions, for example, publishing to a staging server from the development branch.

If your source tree looks like this,

```
Code/
   Dev/
      Source/
      ...
   Staging/
      Source/
      ...
```

you can extract "Dev" or "Staging" into a property from a file in either "Source" folder with the following property functions,

```
<PropertyGroup>
  <_ThisBranch>$([System.IO.Path]::
    GetFileName($([System.IO.Path]::
      GetDirectoryName(
        $(MSBuildThisFileDirectory)))))</_ThisBranch>
</PropertyGroup>
```

The property $(_ThisBranch) is then available for use within the target, for example,

```
<Error
  Condition="
    '$(_ThisBranch)' != 'Staging' AND
    '$(DeployZone)' == 'Staging'"
  Text="Can't deploy from '$(_ThisBranch)' to '$(DeployZone)'"
/>
```

Given the source code repository shown above, the $(_ThisBranch) property will have either the value "Dev" or "Stage," which can be used to customize the build behavior based on the location, without having to have different files checked into both branches.

100. How to manipulate version numbers[16]

There are all sorts of considerations regarding version numbering at build time. The approach I like to take is for the build to "brand" each build with a unique version number; so that there is no special handling of release builds in this regard that is any different from any other build

Version number formats have four numeric slots available, the first two reserved for the major and minor version numbers, which are treated specially in some cases, for example with installer upgrade and patch features. The last two fields are generally up for grabs. In the scheme detailed below, there are three different MSBuild features working together to demonstrate a simple framework for handling version numbers; an inline task to form the date, use of the MSBuild FormatVersion task to create two separate version properties to be used in the build, and use of the MSBuild WriteCodeFragment task to generate the assembly attribute for the version number, which can then be incorporated into your project.

GenerateVersionNumber.trkproj

```
<Project ...>
                                                           <!-- 1 -->
  <UsingTask
    TaskName="MakeDate"
    TaskFactory="CodeTaskFactory"
    AssemblyFile=
      "$(MSBuildToolsPath)\Microsoft.Build.Tasks.v4.0.dll">
    <ParameterGroup>
      <Year
        ParameterType="System.Int32"
        Output="true"
```

---

[16] See the Preface if you're wondering how a book subtitled "99 ways..." gets to 100.

```
            />
         <DayOfYear
            ParameterType="System.Int32"
            Required="true"
            />
         <YyDdd
            ParameterType="System.String"
            Output="true"
            />
      </ParameterGroup>
      <Task>
         <Using Namespace="System" />
         <Code Type="Fragment" Language="cs">
            <![CDATA[
               int currentYear = Year % 100;
               YyDdd = String.Format(
                  "{0:00}{1:000}",
                  currentYear,
                  DayOfYear);
            ]]>
         </Code>
      </Task>
   </UsingTask>

   <Target Name="GenerateVersionNumber">
      <!--
      use FormatVersion to form a version number
      -->
      <PropertyGroup>                                      <!-- 2 -->
         <VerMajor>1</VerMajor>
         <VerMinor>2</VerMinor>
         <_MajorDotMinor>$(VerMajor).$(VerMinor)</_MajorDotMinor>
         <!--
           YYDDD where
             YY is CurrentYear - 2000
             and DDD is between 1 and 365
         -->                                               <!-- 3 -->
         <_CurrentYear>$(
            [System.DateTime]::Now.Year)</_CurrentYear>
         <_DayOfYear>$(
            [System.DateTime]::Now.DayOfYear)</_DayOfYear>
         <BuildRevision>100</BuildRevision>                <!-- 4 -->
      </PropertyGroup>
                                                           <!-- 5 -->
      <MakeDate
         Year="$(_CurrentYear)"
         DayOfYear="$(_DayOfYear)">
         <Output
            TaskParameter="YyDdd"
            PropertyName="MyBuildDate"
            />
      </MakeDate>
                                                           <!-- 6 -->
      <FormatVersion
         Version="$(_MajorDotMinor).$(MyBuildDate).*"
         Revision="$(BuildRevision)"
```

```
            FormatType="Path">
            <Output
                TaskParameter="OutputVersion"
                PropertyName="MyAssemblyVersionPath"
                />
        </FormatVersion>
        <FormatVersion
            Version="$(VersionMajorDotMinor).$(MyBuildDate).*"
            Revision="$(BuildRevision)"
            FormatType="Version">
            <Output
                TaskParameter="OutputVersion"
                PropertyName="MyAssemblyVersionDotted"
                />
        </FormatVersion>

        <Message Text="CurrentYear:  '$(_CurrentYear)'" />
        <Message Text="DayOfYear:    '$(_DayOfYear)'" />
        <Message Text="Date:         '$(MyBuildDate)'" />
        <Message Text="as Path:      '$(MyAssemblyVersionPath)'" />
        <Message Text="as Version:   '$(MyAssemblyVersionDotted)'" />

        <!--
            generate assembly version attribute with WriteCodeFragment
        -->
        <ItemGroup>                                    <!-- 7 -->
            <AssemblyAttributes Include="AssemblyVersion">
                <_Parameter1>$(MyAssemblyVersionDotted)</_Parameter1>
            </AssemblyAttributes>
        </ItemGroup>
        <WriteCodeFragment
            Language="C#"
            OutputFile="MyVersion.cs"
            AssemblyAttributes="@(AssemblyAttributes)"
            />
    </Target>

</Project>
```

This is shown with an inline task because presumably you may need to
have some more sophistication in your version numbering scheme, but
note that the specific MakeDate (1) task behavior above can be performed
with property functions alone, replacing the task invocation (5) with the
following, which first calculates the (Year % 100) value and then
formats the YYDDD property directly:

```
<PropertyGroup>
    <_CurrentYy>$(
        [System.Math]::IEEERemainder(
            $(_CurrentYear),
            100))</_CurrentYy>
    <MyBuildDate>$(
        [System.String]::Format(
            '{0:00}{1:000}',
```

```
        $(_CurrentYy),
        $([System.Convert]::ToInt32(
            $(_DayOfYear)))))</MyBuildDate>
</PropertyGroup>
```

With either approach, the resulting $(MyBuildDate) property would receive a unique number for each day until the year 2066, when the dates roll over the 64K limit for version fields. For example, this property would have a value of 12001 for Jan 1, 2012, and 20365 for December 32, 2020.

In the GenerateVersionNumber target, the first section of code (2) declares properties including the major and minor version numbers and a $(_MajorDotMinor) calculated from these. The declarations of these major and minor properties should exist in a single project wide configuration properties import, or the continuous build system could feed them into the build on the command line. The next two properties (3) use property functions to extract the current year and day of year using property functions of System.DateTime. In this listing, the build revision (4) is hard-coded to 100—per-build incrementing of this property number is covered separately in the next *trick #101, How to auto-increment the daily build revision,* which shows how each subsequent build in the day receives a unique number, making the full version number unique for every build.

Next the MakeDate inline task is called which defines the $(MyBuildDate) property in the YYDDD form described earlier. When combined with the Major.Minor version number, and a trailing asterisk, these numbers become paramters (6) for the FormatVersion MSBuild task, which is called here twice; once with FormatType set to "Path" and a second time with "Version," creating two new properties $(MyAssemblyVersionPath) and $(MyAssemblyVersionDotted). All the relevant properties created up to this point are then printed out with messages, producing the output shown below.

Output

```
GenerateVersionNumber:
  CurrentYear: '2011'
  DayOfYear:   '57'
  Date:        '11057'
  as Path:     '1_2_11057_100'
  as Version:  '1.2.11057.100'
```

Finally, the dotted version property is wrapped up in an attribute item array (7) passed to the WriteCodeFragment task as demonstrated in the previous trick, generating the file below, which if you decipher the build date, was created on a Saturday in February.

Generated MyVersion.cs

```
//--------------------------------------------------------------
// <auto-generated>
//     This code was generated by a tool.
//     Runtime Version:4.0.30319.1
//
//     Changes to this file may cause incorrect behavior and will ⮠
be lost if
//     the code is regenerated.
// </auto-generated>
//--------------------------------------------------------------

using System;
using System.Reflection;

[assembly: MyVersion("1.2.11057.100")]

// Generated by the MSBuild WriteCodeFragment class on 2/26/2011 ⮠
12:41:03 PM.
```

101. How to auto-increment the daily build revision

Since the build version being created in the past couple tricks now identifies the day on which it was built, the final of the four numbers available in the version number should be used to guarantee uniqueness. Since in a good build there is little done on the official build machine that isn't being done on a developers machine, and since it is never a good idea to release into the wild something built on a developers machine, it is a good practice to "brand" assemblies in a unique way so that your automated build release process (you have one of those, right?) can detect where they were built. Also, since during the daily edit-compile-debug process there is typically little need for minor version increment detection, I like to fix the build increment on developer machines to a fixed number, something like "9999" that is easy to notice. Further, I'll usually "brand" the build, at least on developer machines—and using a similar technique even on production build machines—with the name of the machine on which it was built; particularly useful when you have multiple build machines whose configuration is beyond your immediate control.

```
<PropertyGroup>
  <BuildRevision
    Condition="'$(DevMachine)' == 'true'">9999</BuildRevision>
  <BuildDescription>Built on $(COMPUTERNAME) by          ⮠
    $(USERNAME)</BuildDescription>
```

```
    </PropertyGroup>
    ...
    <ItemGroup>
        ...
        <AssemblyAttributes Include="Description">
            <_Parameter1>$(BuildDesription)</_Parameter1>
        </AssemblyAttributes>
    </ItemGroup>
```

These properties can then be fed into the build version and assembly version attributes as shown in the previous trick.

For the continuous or production build machines, you need something better than "9999" though. Presuming that you have fewer than a hundred build machines that produce fewer than a hundred builds a day, we can once again compose a number, in this case a four-digit number of the form MMBB. The first two digits "MM" uniquely identify the build machine on which it was built, and the last two are reserved for the build increment, which should start at "1" at midnight on each day and increase by one for each subsequent build.

Configuring the build machine digit can be straightforward and will depend heavily on how your build servers and your continuous build system are configured. Several options are available:

- Passing in a property, as /p:BuildMachineNumber=42

- In a per-build machine configuration .props file (see *trick #75, How to customize developer builds with My.props*)

- If build machine names are known, in a shared .props file

This last technique is shown below.

```
<PropertyGroup>
    <BuildMachineNumber
        Condition="'$(MACHINENAME)' == 'BUILDER_R2D2'"
        >22</BuildMachineNumber>
    <BuildMachineNumber
        Condition="'$(MACHINENAME)' == 'BUILDER_C3PO'"
        >30</BuildMachineNumber>
    <BuildMachineNumber
        Condition="'$(MACHINENAME)' == 'BUILDER_T800'"
        >80</BuildMachineNumber>
</PropertyGroup>
```

If machine names are provisioned automatically, perhaps you can convince IT to put these numbers in the machine names and extract them with a property function.

Next, the "BB" daily increment portion of the BuildRevision needs to be addressed. The "Increment Daily Build Number" target below performs the following steps, outlined individually in detail in the descriptions that follow. First, it creates an XML format BuildNumber file to hold the daily version number increment. If the file doesn't exist, it creates a new one with the build number increment initialized to zero. If the file does exist, the file ModifiedDate is checked to see if it is up-to-date, and the results of this test are stored in an MSBuild property named $(OutOfDate). Out-of-date files are deleted; when recreated the increment is reset to zero. Next, the build increment is read, incremented, then written back to the file, using the standard XmlPeek and XmlPoke tasks.

Now for a quick aside, since this technique involves modifying a file that is specific to a single build machine, there are a few decisions to be made about where this file is stored. While possible to have the build check the file in, since each build machine would need its own copy, and checking the file into source control would cause another build to be fired off in a continuous integration system. In addition, since automated builds often delete the whole source tree and check it out fresh, this technique requires that the file be located outside of the build tree under version control, or that it is otherwise left alone when the build refreshes sources. Simply keeping this file in the parent folder of the source tree and discovering it with a relative path is likely to work. Also keep in mind that many build systems already keep track of build increments, so it may be possible to rely on the number maintained by the continuous integration system and not have to calculate it as part of the build.

This first part shows the EnsureBuildConfigFileIsToday target, which will become a dependent target of the main IncrementDailyBuildNumber target:

Increment Daily Build Number.trkproj, Part 1

```
<!-- 1 -->
<UsingTask
    TaskName="CheckOutOfDate"
    TaskFactory="CodeTaskFactory"
    AssemblyFile=
      "$(MSBuildToolsPath)\Microsoft.Build.Tasks.v4.0.dll">
    <ParameterGroup>
      <File
          ParameterType="Microsoft.Build.Framework.ITaskItem"
          Required="true"
          />
      <OutOfDate
          ParameterType="System.Boolean"
          Output="true"
```

```
                      />                                          <!-- 4a -->
            </ParameterGroup>
            <Task>
                <Using Namespace="System" />
                <Code Type="Fragment" Language="cs">
                    <![CDATA[
                        var midnight = new DateTime(
                            DateTime.Now.Year,
                            DateTime.Now.Month,
                            DateTime.Now.Day);
                        OutOfDate =                               // 4b
                            DateTime.Parse(
                                File.GetMetadata("ModifiedTime"))
                                < midnight;                       // 3
                    ]]>
                </Code>
            </Task>
        </UsingTask>

        <Target Name="EnsureBuildConfigFileIsToday"
            Condition="Exists('BuildConfig.xml')">                <!-- 5 -->
            <ItemGroup>
                <_CheckForToday Include="BuildConfig.xml" />      <!-- 2 -->
            </ItemGroup>
            <CheckOutOfDate
                File="@(_CheckForToday)">
                <Output
                    TaskParameter="OutOfDate"
                    PropertyName="OutOfdate"
                    />
            </CheckOutOfDate>
            <Message Text="OutOfDate=$(OutOfDate)" />
            <Delete
                Condition="'$(OutOfDate)' == 'true'"
                Files="BuildConfig.xml"
                />                                                <!-- 6 -->
        </Target>
```

In this target, a custom inline task (1) is used to check the %(ModifiedTime) well-known metadata of a file that is passed in, in this case the BuildConfig.xml (2) file containing the previous build revision number. This is put into an inline task so that the last modification date of the file can be compared to midnight (3) of the current day, to see if the file was last updated today. The result of this test returned (4) in the output property $(OutOfDate). Note that the target has a condition (5) which prevents it from being run if the BuildConfig.xml file doesn't yet exist. Finally, if the file is determined to be out of date, it is deleted (6) in anticipation of being recreated with a new seed value.

The next target, also to be made a dependent of the main target, detects the case where the file does not exist and creates it.

Increment Daily Build Number.trkproj, Part 2

```
  <Target Name="EnsureBuildConfigFileExists"
    Condition="!Exists('BuildConfig.xml')">            <!-- 7 -->
    <PropertyGroup>
      <!-- 8 -->
      <EmptyBuildConfigFile>
        <![CDATA[
<?xml version="1.0" encoding="utf-8"?>
<Properties xmlns="http://schemas.k7ranch.net/msbuild/2011">
  <Property Name="DailyVersion" Value="0" />
  <Property Name="TimeStamp" Value="" />
</Properties>
        ]]>
      </EmptyBuildConfigFile>
    </PropertyGroup>
    <WriteLinesToFile
      File="BuildConfig.xml"
      Lines="$(EmptyBuildConfigFile)"
      />                                               <!-- 9 -->
  </Target>
```

Even though the file may have been just deleted by the prior dependent target, the condition on this target (7) will still evaluate properly. A property named $(EmptyBuildConfigFile) is declared in a CDATA section (8) and then written out to the file (9), simple enough. Notice that an "xmlns" is provided, which is required for the next steps:

Increment Daily Build Number.trkproj, Part 3

```
  <Target Name="IncrementDailyBuildNumber"
    DependsOnTargets="
      EnsureBuildConfigFileIsToday;
      EnsureBuildConfigFileExists">                    <!-- 10 -->
    <!-- 11 -->
    <XmlPeek
      XmlInputPath="./BuildConfig.xml"
      Namespaces="&lt;Namespace Prefix='x'
        Uri='http://schemas.k7ranch.net/msbuild/2011'/&gt;"
      Query="//x:Properties/x:Property[
        @Name='DailyVersion']/@Value">
      <Output
        TaskParameter="Result"
        PropertyName="BuildRevision"
        />
    </XmlPeek>

    <!-- 11 -->
    <Message Text="Reading BuildRevision: $(BuildRevision)" />
    <PropertyGroup>
                                                       <!-- 12 -->
      <BuildRevision>$([MSBuild]::Add(
        $(BuildRevision),
        1))</BuildRevision>
```

```
                                                          <!-- 13 -->
    <BuildRevisionOverrun>$([System.Math]::Floor(
        $([MSBuild]::Divide($([MSBuild]::Add(
            $(BuildRevision),
            .5)),
            100))))</BuildRevisionOverrun>
    <_BuildRevision00>$(BuildRevision.PadLeft(
        2, '0'))</_BuildRevision00>                       <!-- 15 -->
</PropertyGroup>
                                                          <!-- 14 -->

<Warning
    Condition="'$(BuildRevisionOverrun)' != '0'"
    Text="The build revision just rolled over 99!"
    />

<!-- 16 -->
<Message Text="Writing BuildRevision: $(BuildRevision)" />
<!-- 17 -->
<XmlPoke
    XmlInputPath="./BuildConfig.xml"
    Namespaces="&lt;Namespace Prefix='x'
        Uri='http://schemas.k7ranch.net/msbuild/2011'/&gt;"
    Query="//x:Properties/x:Property[
        @Name='DailyVersion']/@Value"
    Value="$(BuildRevision)"
    />
<XmlPoke
    XmlInputPath="./BuildConfig.xml"
    Namespaces="&lt;Namespace Prefix='x'
        Uri='http://schemas.k7ranch.net/msbuild/2011'/&gt;"
    Query="//x:Properties/x:Property[
        @Name='TimeStamp']/@Value"
    Value="$([System.DateTime]::Now)"
    />
</Target>
```

The listing above shows the main target. The two targets already discussed are executed as dependents (10). Since a file is now guaranteed to exist, the XmlPeek task is used to read the current value of the DailyVersion. The XmlPeek task requires a namespace qualification, which is why the namespace was added in the previously executed target that created the file. The Query attribute is an XPath expression that finds a child of the Properties element that is a Property element containing a Name attribute with the value "DailyVersion." The value of this property is extracted using @Value, and placed into an MSBuild property named $(BuildRevision), which is assigned from the output parameter named Result on the XmlPeek task. This property is then printed out (11).

Next, a series of property functions is used to (12) increment the value of the $(BuildRevision) property by one, and then (13) detect the condition where this incremented number has rolled over 99, which for this particular build number scheme will issue a warning (14) since any number over "99" can't be contained with the two characters available for it in the "BB" portion of the version number increment field we've been putting together.

The $(BuildNumber) property is derived from an integer, but since it will be appended to the build machine identifier, it needs it to be padded with zeros. Be careful about this, you may think that calling ToString("{0:00}") would work, but that would only work for an integer. Remember that MSBuild properties are strings, so you could either coerce the string to an integer and then format it as such, or else use the String.Pad function as is shown (15). The newly incremented $(BuildNumber) is again printed out (16).

Finally, XmlPoke is used (17) to replace the previous value with the incremented value. XmlPoke is nearly identical to XmlPeek, except that the value is an input rather than an output parameter. For grins, a second attribute containing the current timestamp is also updated in the file. Back in a previous listing (8) this attribute was seeded in the file as an empty string.

Typical output

```
EnsureBuildConfigFileIsToday:
  OutOfDate=False
IncrementDailyBuildNumber:
  Found "41".
  Reading BuildRevision: 41
  Writing BuildRevision: 42
  Made 1 replacement(s).
  Made 1 replacement(s).
```

Resulting BuildConfig.xml file

```
<?xml version="1.0" encoding="utf-8"?>
<Properties xmlns="http://schemas.k7ranch.net/msbuild/2011">
  <Property Name="DailyVersion" Value="42" />
  <Property Name="TimeStamp" Value="2/26/2011 4:06:47 PM" />
</Properties>
```

Output when rolling over 99

```
EnsureBuildConfigFileIsToday:
  OutOfDate=False
IncrementDailyBuildNumber:
  Found "99".
  Reading BuildRevision: 99
  ...\Increment Daily Build Number.trkproj(105,7): warning : The
  build revision just rolled over
  99!
```

```
Writing BuildRevision: 100
Made 1 replacement(s).
Made 1 replacement(s).
```

The output in a typical execution is shown above, along with the resulting file. The XmlPoke task, executed twice, emits "Made 1 replacement(s)" when the XPath resolves successfully to one or more values. When rolling over 99, a warning is emitted, but the build continues. In some cases, for instance if this scheme were being added to an assembly version number, an error would likely result when the assembly was compiled and the version field was determined to be over the 65,535 limit.

TestBuildNumberIncrement target

```xml
<Target Name="TestBuildNumberIncrement"
    DependsOnTargets="IncrementDailyBuildNumber">
    <PropertyGroup>
        <MajorRev>1</MajorRev>
        <MinorRev>0</MinorRev>
        <DailyRev>11057</DailyRev>
        <BuildMachineNumber>99</BuildMachineNumber>
        <BuildRev>$(BuildMachineNumber)$(_BuildRevision00)</BuildRev>
    </PropertyGroup>

    <Message
        Text="Complete Build Number is: $(_BuildRevision00)
            $(MajorRev).$(MinorRev).$(DailyRev).$(BuildRev)"
        />
</Target>
```

Output

```
EnsureBuildConfigFileIsToday:
  OutOfDate=False
IncrementDailyBuildNumber:
  Found "1".
  Reading BuildRevision: 1
  Writing BuildRevision: 2
  Made 1 replacement(s).
  Made 1 replacement(s).
TestBuildNumber:
  Complete Build Number is:
              1.0.11057.9901
```

The $(_BuildRevision00) property, containing the build increment number padded to two digits, was calculated and set previously by the IncrementDailyBuildNumber target. The remaining properties are proxy values from the discussions in the previous tricks. This final test target simply puts them all together into the common four-part version number format.

102. How to define self-documenting build files

The following trick is a bit more involved, but really just combines several techniques into one really useful convention.

Over time the number of 'Skip' or other configuration properties can grow to the point where you can't really keep track of them all. I can't count how many times I've had to pull open one of the build files and search on some known string just to find the exact name of the property to turn on or off some behavior, and I'm the guy who wrote the build. Imagine how tough it is for everyone else to even know these fine-grain control properties even exist.

This trick allows you to identify certain properties and other items as part of a list of self-documenting artifacts. A series of targets are described, culminating in a final "Help" target that can provide end-user help for your build customiazations.

Self-documenting properties

For a self-documenting property, create an item for the "Setting" item array that has the same item spec as the name of the property. These can be declared either together or, as shown below, separately. The first one is describing the SkipInstaller setting. The "Setting" item is given three pieces of item metadata named *Usage*, *For* and *Help*. These are described below, first one for the SkipInstaller property,

Self Documenting Help.trkproj

```
<PropertyGroup>
   <SkipInstaller
      Condition="'$(SkipInstaller)' == ''"
      >false</SkipInstaller>
</PropertyGroup>
<ItemGroup>
   <Setting Include="SkipInstaller">                    <!-- 1 -->
      <Usage>Optional</Usage>
      <Help>Controls if the lengthy installer compilation    ⤷
occurs.</Help>
   </Setting>
</ItemGroup>
```

And here is a second one, for SkipDocs,

```
<PropertyGroup>
    <SkipDocs Condition="'$(SkipDocs)' == ''">false</SkipDocs>
</PropertyGroup>
<ItemGroup>
    <Setting Include="SkipDocs">
        <Usage>Optional</Usage>
        <Help>Controls the lengthy docs copy.</Help>
    </Setting>
</ItemGroup>
```

Putting it all together is a target that is used to print out the self-describing documentation for these two settings. Take a look at the HelpSettings target below:

```
<Target Name="HelpSettings"
    Condition="'@(Setting)' != ''"
    Outputs="%(Setting.Identity)">                      <!-- 2 -->
    <Message
        Text="%(Setting.Identity)" />                   <!-- 3 -->
    <Message
        Text="    current value is '$(%(Setting.Identity))'" />
                                                         <!-- 4 -->
    <Message
        Text="    [%(Setting.Usage)] %(Setting.Help)"/> <!-- 5 -->
    <Message
        Text="" />
</Target>
```

The HelpSettings target is "target batched." This means that there is no Inputs attribute defined on the target, and that the Output attribute (2), which causes the target to be run once for each member of the item array. As an aside, I've always thought that this seemed like an odd overloading of the Outputs attribute. It seems like it would have made more sense if the implementers had defined a special attribute named "BatchingExpression" or something similar.

While inside the body of the target when this type of target batching is being used, the value of the item referenced in the Outputs attribute becomes a scalar list. Even though the @(Setting) item array contains two items, since %(Setting.Identity) was used as the target batching item, while inside the body of this target, @(Setting) will only contain a single value for each independently executed target instance in the batch. Since @(Setting) is now a scalar, the metadata for each definition can be retrieved individually (3, 4, 5).

Looking closely at (4), the value of %(Setting.Identity), which is the string "SkipInstaller" on the first instance (1) and "SkipDocs" on the second, is fed into an enclosing $(...) to dynamically reference the individual property. The first time, when %(Setting.Identity) has the value "SkipInstaller" the value of the $(SkipInstaller) property is evaluated. The Text for the message, which is defined as:

```
Text="   current value is '$(%(Setting.Identity))'"/>
```

...is evaluated first to this...

```
Text="   current value is '$(SkipInstaller)'"/>
```

...and then resolved to this:

```
Text="   current value is 'false'"/>
```

The Usage and Help metadata are formatted into a single line of output (5).

Self-documenting targets

Similarly, for documenting which targets are available, is the following scheme, which builds upon the example so far, adding the two targets named CompileInstaller and DeployDocs to the list of self-describing targets, using an item array with items named Targets. Note that the advice to use singular names for items can't be followed with the use of the singular name "Target," since that is a known XML element and is invalid as the child of an item array element. The item name TargetName is used instead.

```
<ItemGroup>
  <TargetName Include="CompileInstaller">
    <Help>Compile generated WiX file to.msi or .msm.</Help>
    <Settings>SkipInstaller;WixVersion</Settings>   <!-- 1 -->
  </TargetName>
  <TargetName Include="DeployDocs">
    <Help>Copy docs to application Help folder.</Help>
    <Settings>SkipDocs</Settings>
  </TargetName>
</ItemGroup>
```

In the above item array the item specification takes the name of the target to be documented, in this case "CompileInstaller" and "DeployDocs," and each defines two pieces of metadata, Help and Settings.

This next target uses target batching (2) in the same manner as the HelpSettings target previously described:

```
<Target Name="HelpTargets"
   Outputs="%(TargetName.Identity)">                      <!-- 2 -->
   <Message
      Text="/t:%(TargetName.Identity)" />
   <Message
      Condition="'%(TargetName.Settings)' != ''"
      Text="    Valid options: %(TargetName.Settings)"
      />                                                   <!-- 3 -->
   <Message
      Text="    %(TargetName.Help)" />                     <!-- 4 -->
   <Message
      Text="" />
</Target>
```

The only significant difference, other than being controlled by a different item array, is that since a target may not have any settings that control it, or at least none that you want documented, the Settings metadata (1), which is used to describe which settings control the target (3) is optional, as shown by the condition applied to the message that would print them out (4) in the target.

The Help target

Tying all of these targets together into a single Help target is now trivial:

```
<Target Name="Help">
   <Message
      Condition="'@(TargetName)' != ''"
      Text="========================= Available Targets" />
   <CallTarget
      Targets="HelpTargets" />
   <Message
      Condition="'@(Setting)' != ''"
      Text="========================= Setting Options" />
   <CallTarget
      Targets="HelpSettings" />
</Target>
```

Running this target will produce the following output:

Output

```
> msbuild My.proj /t:Help

Help:
   ========================= Available Targets
HelpTargets:
 /t:CompileInstaller
    Valid options: SkipInstaller;WixVersion
```

```
      Compile generated WiX file to.msi or .msm.
HelpTargets:
 /t:DeployDocs
     Valid options: SkipDocs
     Copy docs to application Help folder.
Help:
   ======================= Setting Options
HelpSettings:
  SkipInstaller
     current value is 'false'
     [Optional] Controls if the lengthy installer compilation
occurs.
HelpSettings:
  SkipDocs
     current value is 'false'
     [Optional] Controls the lengthy docs copy.
```

Examining the output you can see that the Help target is executed once, outputting lines that assist with readability, but the HelpTargets and HelpSettings target are executed once for each item in the item arrays that control them, as a result of the target batching.

103. How to safely connect to remote machines

To perform operations on a remote machine, the PsExec tool[17] from Microsoft is extremely useful. It allows you to remotely execute programs on another machine. For build operations, the scenario may involve the sequence:

- Connect to a remote share

- Copy executables and other support files to the remote share

- Run PsExec to execute the programs and files just copied

In order to run PsExec, you need to have the Windows remote management service running on your local machine. The following script demonstrates how to set up and tear down both the remote connection to a share and the local remote management service, and since operations involving remote connections are subject to an increased likely hood of failure, it also discusses some techniques for making the script fault tolerant.

Before getting to the example, it shows the direct execution of some Windows commands such as "net start" and "net use." For these specific commands, if you'd prefer to see them bundled in tasks, I'm going to recommend you look at the MSBuild Extension Pack, available on

---

[17] Find this on MSDN, or at http://bit.ly/psexec

CodePlex. It is maintained by Mike Fourie, who happens to work at Microsoft, though the project is not officially supported by Microsoft. Though some of it is a bit obsolete considering the power of MSBuild 4.0 property functions, if you're using SQLServer, TFS, or IIS, you'll likely find some nice surprises. I've elected not to use them here to keep the scripts clean and simple.

Connect to Remote Share.trkproj

```xml
<PropertyGroup>                                          <!-- 1 -->
    <RemoteDrive>Z:</RemoteDrive>
    <RemoteShare>\\ALDERAAN\OrganasDrop</RemoteShare>
    <RemoteUserName>Leia</RemoteUserName>
    <Password>H3lpMeOB1</Password>
</PropertyGroup>
                                                         <!-- 2 -->
<Target Name="Connect"
    DependsOnTargets="
        CleanRemoteConnection;
        ConnectToRemoteShare;
        StartWinRm;
        DoSomething;
        StopWinRm;
        DisconnectFromRemoteShare"
    />

<Target Name="ConnectToRemoteShare">
    <Exec
        Command="net use $(RemoteDrive) $(RemoteShare)
/USER:$(RemoteUserName) $(Password)"
        />                                               <!-- 3 -->
</Target>

<Target Name="DisconnectFromRemoteShare">
    <Exec
        Command="net use $(RemoteDrive) /delete"
        />                                               <!-- 4 -->
</Target>

<Target Name="StartWinRm">
    <Exec Command="net start winrm" />                   <!-- 5 -->
</Target>

<Target Name="StopWinRm">
    <Exec Command="net stop winrm" />                    <!-- 6 -->
</Target>
```

Some properties are declared (1) that represent the data needed to establish a remote connection. In this example they are hardcoded, but many approaches are possible, including the data picking technique one discussed in *trick #73, Picking from multiple data sets to drive build functionality*. I'm not a fan of putting passwords into build scripts like is shown here, so in most instances I'll just put in a verification target, something like this,

```
<Target "ValidateParameters">
  <Error
    Condition="'$(Password)' == ''"
    Text="You forgot a /p:Password=..."
    />
</Target>
```

and require that one is supplied on the command line. The main target named Connect (2) sets up a set of dependent targets. The first one, CleanRemoteConnection will be discussed shortly, so that we can focus here on the main operations. The ConnectToRemoteShare and DisconnectFromRemoteShare are trivial Exec tasks for the "net use" command (3, 4). Just type "net use /?" on a command line if you are unfamiliar. Likewise the remote management service is started and stopped with "net start" and "net stop" (5, 6). The problem is that these things often fail, due to network connectivity issues, security configurations, or in the case that the connection succeeds, the build may have produced something that won't execute properly on the remote machine. Any of these will cause a failure, which in typical usage will cause the build to terminate. When the build terminates, the cleanup targets, DisconnectFromRemoteShare and StopWinRm won't get a chance to execute, leaving the remoting portion of the build in a dangling state. Any user would then need to know they need to go to a command line and execute the commands manually in order to get back to a functional state. Despite the simplicity of the commands, this is actually too much to expect of a developer hot on the heels of some bug, one who doesn't have the time to be bothered diagnosing a build error. This next listing adds in some error recovery to help alleviate this condition.

Connect to Remote Share.trkproj, error recovery

```
<Target Name="DoSomething">                        <!-- 7 -->
  <Error
    Condition="'$(ForceError)' == 'true'"
    Text="Interrupted, won't disconnect"
    />                                             <!-- 8 -->
</Target>

<Target Name="CleanRemoteConnection">
  <Exec
    ContinueOnError="true"
    IgnoreExitCode="true"
    Command="net use $(RemoteDrive) /delete">      <!-- 9 -->
    <Output
      TaskParameter="ExitCode"
      PropertyName="_NetUseDeleteExitCode"
```

```
        />                                                      <!-- 10 -->
    </Exec>
    <Warning
        Condition="
            ! (('$(_NetUseDeleteExitCode)' != '0')
            OR ('$(_NetStopWinRmExitCode)' != '2'))"
        Text="Unexpected exit code '$(_NetUseDeleteExitCode)'
            returned while removing binding to $(RemoteDrive)"
        />

    <Exec
        ContinueOnError="true"
        IgnoreExitCode="true"
        Command="net stop winrm">
        <Output
            TaskParameter="ExitCode"
            PropertyName="_NetStopWinRmExitCode"
            />
    </Exec>
    <Warning
        Condition="
            ! ('$(_NetStopWinRmExitCode)' != '0'
            OR '$(_NetStopWinRmExitCode)' != '2')"
        Text="Unexpected exit code '$(_NetStopWinRmExitCode)'
            returned while stopping winrm service"
        />
</Target>
```

The DoSomething target (1) is where you would place any operations that need to be performed using the remote share or executing programs using a remote management tool enabled by the service. These tasks can either be coded directly in this target, or in a series of dependent targets. For this example any such code is excluded. Instead, an error task exists to allow a "forced error" to occur. Running with this command line,

```
> msbuild "Connect to Remote Share.trkproj" /p:ForceError=true
```

Will trigger the Error task (8) within the body of this target. This will leave the connection and the remote management service connected, which is a somewhat tenuous state to be in. Subsequent attempts to connect to the share or start the service will give errors. This is where the first target in the dependency list, CleanRemoteConnections, comes into play. It is executed first to get the machine into a clean state, so that any operations that follow don't need to worry about failures part of the way through. This target first attempts to remove the file share mapping (9), ignoring the exit code, but capturing it in a property in the enclosed Output (10) element, in a property named $(_NetUseDeleteExitCode). The warning task that immediately follows tests the exit code for the two possible values that indicate success; a value of zero which means the cleanup of a previously failed execution that left a dangling remote share connection was successful, or a value of two, which means that the connection was not found, and no cleanup was needed. Any other exit code is unknown and emits a warning. The same sequence is followed for the cleanup of the *winrm* command, which just happens to use the same two exit code values for the same results.

The output for a successful complete run is shown below. Following that, the output of the CleanRemoteConnection when run after an intentionally failed execution is shown:

Output, no errors

```
CleanRemoteConnection:
  The network connection could not be found.

  net stop winrm
  The Windows Remote Management (WS-Management) service is not
started.

  More help is available by typing NET HELPMSG 3521.

  The command "net stop winrm" exited with code 2.
ConnectToRemoteShare:
  net use Z: \\ALDERAAN\OrganasDrop /USER:Leia H3lpMeOB1
  The command completed successfully.

StartWinRm:
  net start winrm
  The Windows Remote Management (WS-Management) service is starting.
  The Windows Remote Management (WS-Management) service was started
successfully.

StopWinRm:
  net stop winrm
  The Windows Remote Management (WS-Management) service is stopping.
  The Windows Remote Management (WS-Management) service was stopped
successfully.
```

Output of CleanRemoteConnection, after forced error

```
CleanRemoteConnection:
  net use Z: /delete
  Z: was deleted successfully.

  net stop winrm
  The Windows Remote Management (WS-Management) service is stopping.
  The Windows Remote Management (WS-Management) service was stopped
successfully.
```

By placing the error recovery target as the first in the list, you can still leave your machine in an undesirable state between MSBuild executions, with dangling connections and a potentially dangerous service running, perhaps unknown to the user. To alleviate this, you can use the OnError task in each of the sensitive targets, to attempt cleanup if any failure occurs,

```
<Target Name="DoSomething">
   ...
   <OnError ExecuteTargets="CleanRemoteConnection" />
</Target>
```

Or provide coverage for all of the dependent targets by adding this to the original main target,

```
<Target Name="Connect"
   DependsOnTargets="
      CleanRemoteConnection;
      ConnectToRemoteShare;
      StartWinRm;
      DoSomething;
      StopWinRm;
      DisconnectFromRemoteShare">
   <OnError ExecuteTargets="CleanRemoteConnectionCopy" />
</Target>
```

Since it is possible that the dangling connections and services may exist outside of an MSBuild failure, it is best to have both an initial dependent target and the OnError handler in place. The problem is that MSBuild will allow the target to execute only a single time, so in order to have full coverage, you may need to duplicate the error recovery target in a second target, so that one can be listed in the dependency list, and the other specified in the OnError handler, which is hinted at above with the OnError task referencing a new target named CleanRemoteConnectionCopy, which would need to be a complete cut-and-paste copy of the original.

C++ Project Type Tricks

If you need to build both C# and C++ projects in the same build, or need to support the legacy .vcproj project file format, you're going to hit a few snags. Although both of these project types use the MSBuild engine, and eventually share some of the same targets files to unify their builds, there are some differences you need to understand. Here are a few tricks you may want to keep handy.

104. How to unify Platforms for multiple project types

If I had to pick one thing that the C# and C++ project teams did to make life difficult, it would have to be the way they chose the default platform names for building 64-bit projects.

In second place would be the subtle distinction between the use of "AnyCPU" without a space in C# projects, and "Any CPU" with a space in solutions.

As was mentioned in *trick #79, Know what should make you feel queasy,* the solution has some features that can cause problems even when using a homogenous collection of project types. When your collection starts to include multiple project types it can get downright nasty. This trick attempts to show some of the techniques you can use to unify a heterogeneous build. We'll start with a property import that can be used in C# projects.

Default.C#.props

```xml
<!-- defaults -->
<PropertyGroup>                                          <!-- 1 -->
  <Configuration
    Condition="'$(Configuration)' == ''">Debug</Configuration>
  <Platform
    Condition="'$(Platform)' == ''">AnyCPU</Platform>
</PropertyGroup>

<!-- for IDE builds -->
<PropertyGroup>                                          <!-- 2 -->
  <__Platform
    Condition="'$(Platform)' == 'Win32'">Win32</__Platform>
  <__Platform
    Condition="'$(Platform)' == 'Win64'">Win64</__Platform>
  <__Platform
    Condition="'$(Platform)' == 'x86'">Win32</__Platform>
  <__Platform
    Condition="'$(Platform)' == 'x64'">Win64</__Platform>
</PropertyGroup>

<PropertyGroup
  Condition="'$(Platform)' == 'AnyCPU'">                  <!-- 3 -->
  <__Platform
    Condition="'$(PROCESSOR_ARCHITECTURE)' == 'x86'"
    >Win32</__Platform>
  <__Platform
    Condition="'$(PROCESSOR_ARCHITECTURE)' == 'AMD64'"
    >Win64</__Platform>
  <__Platform
    Condition="'$(PROCESSOR_ARCHITECTUREW6432)' == 'AMD64'"
    >Win64</__Platform>
</PropertyGroup>
```

```
<PropertyGroup>                                          <!-- 4 -->
    <!-- non standard, possible error -->
    <__Platform
        Condition="'$(__Platform)' == ''"
        >$(Platform)</__Platform>

    <!-- for command line builds -->
    <__Platform
        Condition="'$(PlatformName)' != ''"
        >$(PlatformName)</__Platform>                    <!-- 5 -->
</PropertyGroup>

<PropertyGroup>                                          <!-- 6 -->
    <OutputPart>$(__Platform).$(Configuration)</OutputPart>
    <OutputPath>bin\$(OutputPart)\</OutputPath>
    <IntermediateOutputPath
        >obj\$(OutputPart)\</IntermediateOutputPath>
</PropertyGroup>
```

When imported into a C# project, the property import project above will first set default values (1) for the two main configuration selection properties, $(Configuration) and $(Platform). While your defaults may not be the same, if for instance the bitness of the build is important for your program and you can't make use of AnyCPU, the pattern shown here would remain the same.

When being built from the IDE, a value for $(Platform) will always be set to something. The next properties (2) provide a mechanism for converting the IDE's notion of a $(Platform) to a customized internal property representing a "normalized" platform in the property named $(__Platform). Because I make heavy use of a single leading underscore for property names, I tend to use a double underscore for these sorts of things that are very global and very much a workaround, so that there is no possible conflict. Note that both "Win32" and "x86" are normalized to "Win32." The normalized value to use is a matter of preference, it could have just as easily been "x86" or even "32Bit" provided that all of the projects were defined to support the platform name specified. I've chosen "Win32" and "Win64" as the normalized names because they are consistent with each other. Also important is to realize that I couldn't have just redeclared $(Platform) to be some arbitrary value, as the values of $(Platform) are special in many build files, particularly in C++ projects where they become part of a path to pick up the proper imports when the project file is processed during the build.

The next property group chooses a value for $(__Platform) of a specific bitness when the $(Platform) is specified as AnyCPU. You may also need a variation that supports "Any CPU" with a space if the IDE is involved in executing the build of this project. The code above shows selection of this bit-specific value based on the environment in which it is being built, assuming that you want it to match the settings in the command line environment. You can follow the advice in *trick #59, Know even more property functions, 32 and 64 Bitness*, for alternate approaches.

Finally, if nothing has been specified, a last ditch effort is made to collect a value (5). This may not work for your build and you may be better served with an error message if this condition is detected, perhaps setting an error sentry value that can be detected in an early target. With the IDE support now worked out, the final value is pulled from a property named $(PlatformName). This is the property you would specify if when building from the command line you wanted to build a platform other than the default, and don't want to rely on automatic selection based on some ambient value such as the environment variables used in (3).

In the next property group (6) we arrive back at familiar properties usually declared in the project file, $(OutDir), $(OutPath) and $(IntermediateOutputPath), all of which are now derived from the temporary property $(__Platform) and the current $(Configuration), which is a well behaved property that doesn't need any special handling.

For C++ projects, there is less work to do:

Default.C++.props

```
<!-- Win64 -->
<PropertyGroup Condition="'$(Platform)' == 'x64'">
    <__Platform>Win64</__Platform>
    <OutDir>bin\$(__Platform).$(Configuration)\</OutDir>
    <IntDir>obj\$(__Platform).$(Configuration)\</IntDir>
</PropertyGroup>
<!-- Win32 -->
<PropertyGroup Condition="'$(Platform)' == 'Win32'">
    <__Platform>Win32</__Platform>
    <OutDir>bin\$(__Platform).$(Configuration)\</OutDir>
    <IntDir>obj\$(__Platform).$(Configuration)\</IntDir>
</PropertyGroup>
```

To unify the 64-bit output folder names, simply name $(OutDir) and $(IntDir) accordingly. C++ projects have to be built with $(Platform) specified according to how the targets and props files shipped with the compiler are laid out in the file system. The whole exercise above was really about coercing a C# project build to use the properties required by the C++ build. In both cases, for further shared customization, you can code your customizations to work from the normalized value of

$(__Platform) and not have to worry about which of the many possible permutations of the value of $(Platform) is actually being used.

105. How to supply dynamic properties to .vcproj files

If you still have to use the Visual Studio 2008 version 9.0 format for some of your C++ project files, those with the old .vcproj extension, you may think that you're out of luck when it comes to most MSBuild customizations. There is a simple trick that might be useful though—a way to provide MSBuild properties to these projects that aren't in MSBuild format.

It turns out that the only real extension point for parameterizing 9.0 project files is the use of user "macros" in a property file. These aren't the Visual Studio for Applications style executable macros, but rather properties of the form,

```
<UserMacro
    Name="MSBUILD_PATH"
    Value="$(ProgramFiles)\MSBuild"
    PerformEnvironmentSet="true"
    />
```

When declared in a Visual Studio property file, these can be referenced from a 2008 C++ project using the InheritedPropertySheets value in the project.

MyProject.90.vcproj, C++ project partial listing

```
<?xml version="1.0" encoding="Windows-1252"?>
<VisualStudioProject
    ProjectType="Visual C++"
    Version="9.00"
    Name="MyProject.90"
    ProjectGUID="{SOME-GUID-HERE}"
    RootNamespace="trickery"
    Keyword="Win32Proj"
    TargetFrameworkVersion="196613"
    >
    <Platforms>
        <Platform
            Name="Win32"
            />
        <Platform
            Name="x64"
            />
    </Platforms>
    <ToolFiles>
    </ToolFiles>
    <Configurations>
        <Configuration
```

```
            Name="Debug|Win32"
            ConfigurationType="2"
            InheritedPropertySheets=".\MyProperties.vsprops"
            CharacterSet="1"
            >
    ...repeat for Release configuration...
```

In the partial listing above, the Configurations | Configuration | Inherit-edPropertySheets value is set to the path of a .vsprops file. This file is shown below, in which is declared a single user macro,

MyProperties.vsprops

```
<?xml version="1.0" encoding="Windows-1252"?>
  <VisualStudioPropertySheet
    ProjectType="Visual C++"
    Version="8.00"
    Name="My Property Sheet 1.0"
    >
  <UserMacro
    Name="MY_CUSTOM_PATH"
    Value=".\SomePath\"
    PerformEnvironmentSet="true"
    />
</VisualStudioPropertySheet>
```

Oddly, the version number for property sheets is 8.0, which is different from the version number for the project that imports them, which is 9.00, it isn't a typo. In the property sheet, the user macro named "MY_CUSTOM_PATH" is similar in usage to an MSBuild property that would be named $(MY_CUSTOM_PATH). In fact, in the project file, it is referenced with the same syntax, and the value, currently ".\SomePath\" can be manipulated in the IDE project properties editor UI.

So how does MSBuild come into the picture? How about something like this, for which you may need to hold your nose,

Build 9.0 Project.trkproj

```
<PropertyGroup>                                            <!-- 2 -->
  <PropertySheetContents
><![CDATA[<?xml version="1.0" encoding="Windows-1252"?>
  <VisualStudioPropertySheet
    ProjectType="Visual C++"
    Version="8.00"
    Name="My Property Sheet 1.0"
    >
  <UserMacro
    Name="MY_CUSTOM_PATH"
    Value="$(MY_CUSTOM_PATH)"
    PerformEnvironmentSet="true"
```

```
      />
</VisualStudioPropertySheet>]]></PropertySheetContents>
</PropertyGroup>

<ItemGroup>
    <Lines Include="$(PropertySheetContents)" />          <!-- 3 -->
</ItemGroup>

<Target Name="Build90">
    <WriteLinesToFile
      Lines="@(Lines)"
      File="MyProperties.vsprops"
      Overwrite="true"
      />                                                   <!-- 1 -->
    <Exec
      Command="vcbuild MyProject.90.vcproj"
      />                                                   <!-- 4 -->
</Target>
```

Running the target above from the command line with a value for the MY_CUSTOM_PATH property,

```
> msbuild "Build 9.0 Project.trkproj" /p:MY_CUSTOM_PATH=.\PathTo\
```

will cause the creation of the desired property sheet (1), which will substitute the passed in property within the CDATA contained $(PropertySheetContents) property defined above (2), which you'll notice makes use of the $(MY_CUSTOM_PATH) MSBuild property you just passed. The resulting file will be identical to the listing shown previously, with the user macro containing the dynamically specified value,

```
<UserMacro
    Name="MY_CUSTOM_PATH"
    Value=".\PathTo\"
    PerformEnvironmentSet="true"
    />
```

This property is fed into a transitory item array (3) which is used to write out the property sheet file. With everything properly set up, the *vcbuild* command line tool can be executed to build the project, which is unaware it is being controlled by a more intelligent MSBuild 4.0 script! I did say to hold your nose, right? If nothing else, it is yet another reason to upgrade.

Inside the C++ project file, whether in the regular properties or in custom build steps, you can now reference this property that originated in your MSBuild driven build file.

Part III

Afterword

Concluding remarks

My hope is that by examining and understanding all of the tricks that I've just presented, you'll gain a deeper appreciation for just how much you can easily do in your MSBuild files. That you will add this rich functionality to the project files and build scripts you use every day, and that your team becomes more productive as your build becomes more feature rich.

In the end, I hope you've learned enough to discover your own tricks, and that if you've ever had the thought "I wish the build could take care of this," that you'll now be better suited to pull it off.

If you have comments or ideas for additional tricks and would like to share them, feel free to email me at trickery@k7ranch.net.

About the Author

I live in the beautiful Texas Hill Country with my equally beautiful wife and our four children. We're all hoping to finish that barn on the cover just as soon as the temperature ducks below 100. Now that this book is complete, and the companion book well under way, maybe I'll finally have the time to get the roof on it.

Summer 2011

Bing Index

This index associates short, successful Bing searches I use all the time with the General Index and the page numbers of the first mention.

MSBuild Reserved, 12, *Reserved properties, those that start with $(MSBuild...)*
MSBuild Factory, 53, *various task factories, Xaml, PowerShell, IronPython*
MSBuild Functions, 78, *for a listing of MSBuild Property Functions*
MSBuild Item Functions, 84, *ditto but for Item Functions*
Debugging MSBuild, 84 *Dan Moseley's three part blog*
MSBuild Special, 208, *Special character escape values*
Rule Properties SwitchPrefix, *select "Rule Properties" for comprehensive list*
XamlDataDrivenToolTask, *more documentation for Xaml Task Factories*

General Index